THE IMPLEME
OF FUNCTION
PROGRAMMING LANGUAGES

Prentice-Hall International
Series in Computer Science

C.A.R. Hoare, Series Editor

BACKHOUSE, R.C., *Program Construction and Verification*
BACKHOUSE, R.C., *Syntax of Programming Languages, Theory and Practice*
de BAKKER, J.W., *Mathematical Theory of Program Correctness*
BJÖRNER, C., and JONES, C.B., *Formal Specification and Software Development*
BORNAT, R., *Programming from First Principles*
CLARK, K.L., and McCABE, F.G., *micro-PROLOG: Programming in Logic*
DROMEY, R.G., *How to Solve it by Computer*
DUNCAN, F., *Microprocessor Programming and Software Development*
ELDER, J., *Construction of Data Processing Software*
GOLDSCHLAGER, L., and LISTER, A., *Computer Science: A Modern Introduction*
HAYES, L., (Editor), *Specification Case Studies*
HEHNER, E.C.R., *The Logic of Programming*
HENDERSON, P., *Functional Programming: Application and Implementation*
HOARE, C.A.R., and SHEPHERDSON, J.C., (Editors), *Mathematical Logic and Programming Languages*
INMOS LTD, *Occam Programming Manual*
JACKSON, M.A., *System Development*
JOHNSTON, H., *Learning to Program*
JONES, C.B., *Systematic Software Development Using VDM*
JONES, G., *Programming in Occam*
JOSEPH, M., PRASAD, V.R., and NATARAJAN, N., *Multiprocessor Operating System*
LEW, A., *Computer Science: A Mathematical Introduction*
MacCALLUM, I., *Pascal for the Apple*
MacCALLUM, I., *UCSD Pascal for the IBM PC*
MARTIN, J.J., *Data Types and Data Structures*
PEYTON JONES, S.L., *The Implementation of Functional Programming Languages*
POMBERGER, G., *Software Engineering and Modula-2*
REYNOLDS, J.C., *The Craft of Programming*
SLOMAN, M., and KRAMER, J., *Distributed Systems and Computer Networks*
TENNENT, R.D., *Principles of Programming Languages*
WELSH, J., and ELDER, J., *Introduction to Pascal, 2nd Edition*
WELSH, J., ELDER, J., and BUSTARD, D., *Sequential Program Structures*
WELSH, J., and HAY, A., *A Model Implementation of Standard Pascal*
WELSH, J., and McKEAG, M., *Structured System Programming*

THE IMPLEMENTATION OF FUNCTIONAL PROGRAMMING LANGUAGES

Simon L. Peyton Jones

Department of Computer Science,
University College London

with chapters by

Philip Wadler, Programming Research Group, Oxford
Peter Hancock, Metier Management Systems Ltd
David Turner, University of Kent, Canterbury

Prentice/Hall International

Englewood Cliffs, NJ London Mexico New Delhi
Rio de Janeiro Singapore Sydney Tokyo Toronto

To Dorothy

Library of Congress Cataloging-in-Publication Data

Peyton Jones, Simon L., 1958–
The implementation of functional programming languages.

'7th May 1986.'
Bibliography: p.
Includes index.
1. Functional programming languages. I. Title.
QA76.7.P495 1987 005.13'3 86-20535
ISBN 0-13-453333-X

British Library Cataloguing in Publication Data

Peyton Jones, Simon L.
The implementation of functional programming languages –
(Prentice-Hall International series in computer science)
1. Electronic digital computers – Programming
I. Title II. Wadler, Philip III. Hancock, Peter
005.1 QA76.6

ISBN 0-13-453333-X
ISBN 0-13-453325-9 Pbk

Prentice-Hall Inc., *Englewood Cliffs, New Jersey*
Prentice-Hall International (UK) Ltd, *London*
Prentice-Hall of Australia Pty Ltd, *Sydney*
Prentice-Hall Canada Inc., *Toronto*
Prentice-Hall Hispanoamericana S.A., *Mexico*
Prentice-Hall of India Private Ltd, *New Delhi*
Prentice-Hall of Japan Inc., *Tokyo*
Prentice-Hall of Southeast Asia Pte Ltd, *Singapore*
Editora Prentice-Hall do Brasil Ltda, *Rio de Janeiro*

Printed and bound in Great Britain for
Prentice-Hall International (UK) Ltd,
66 Wood Lane End, Hemel Hempstead, Hertfordshire, HP2 4RG
by A. Wheaton & Co. Ltd, Exeter

1 2 3 4 5 91 90 89 88 87

ISBN 0-13-453333-X
ISBN 0-13-453325-9 PBK

CONTENTS

Preface xvii

1 INTRODUCTION 1

1.1 Assumptions 1
1.2 Part I: compiling high-level functional languages 2
1.3 Part II: graph reduction 4
1.4 Part III: advanced graph reduction 5
References 6

PART I COMPILING HIGH-LEVEL FUNCTIONAL LANGUAGES

2 THE LAMBDA CALCULUS 9

2.1 The syntax of the lambda calculus 9
2.1.1 Function application and currying 10
2.1.2 Use of brackets 11
2.1.3 Built-in functions and constants 11
2.1.4 Lambda abstractions 12
2.1.5 Summary 13
2.2 The operational semantics of the lambda calculus 14
2.2.1 Bound and free variables 14
2.2.2 Beta-conversion 15
2.2.3 Alpha-conversion 18
2.2.4 Eta-conversion 19
2.2.5 Proving interconvertibility 19
2.2.6 The name-capture problem 20
2.2.7 Summary of conversion rules 21
2.3 Reduction order 23
2.3.1 Normal order reduction 24
2.3.2 Optimal reduction orders 25
2.4 Recursive functions 25
2.4.1 Recursive functions and Y 26
2.4.2 Y can be defined as a lambda abstraction 27

2.5 The denotational semantics of the lambda calculus 28
2.5.1 The Eval function 29
2.5.2 The symbol ⊥ 31
2.5.3 Defining the semantics of built-in functions and constants 31
2.5.4 Strictness and laziness 33
2.5.5 The correctness of the conversion rules 34
2.5.6 Equality and convertibility 34
2.6 Summary 35
References 35

3 TRANSLATING A HIGH-LEVEL FUNCTIONAL LANGUAGE INTO THE LAMBDA CALCULUS 37

3.1 The overall structure of the translation process 38
3.2 The enriched lambda calculus 39
3.2.1 Simple let-expressions 40
3.2.2 Simple letrec-expressions 42
3.2.3 Pattern-matching let- and letrec-expressions 43
3.2.4 Let(rec)s versus lambda abstractions 43
3.3 Translating Miranda into the enriched lambda calculus 44
3.4 The **TE** translation scheme 45
3.4.1 Translating constants 46
3.4.2 Translating variables 46
3.4.3 Translating function applications 46
3.4.4 Translating other forms of expressions 47
3.5 The **TD** translation scheme 47
3.5.1 Variable definitions 47
3.5.2 Simple function definitions 47
3.6 An example 48
3.7 The organization of Chapters 4–9 49
References 50

4 STRUCTURED TYPES AND THE SEMANTICS OF PATTERN-MATCHING Simon L. Peyton Jones and Philip Wadler 51

4.1 Introduction to structured types 52
4.1.1 Type variables 53
4.1.2 Special cases 53
4.1.3 General structured types 55
4.1.4 History 56
4.2 Translating Miranda into the enriched lambda calculus 57
4.2.1 Introduction to pattern-matching 57
4.2.2 Patterns 59
4.2.3 Introducing pattern-matching lambda abstractions 60
4.2.4 Multiple equations and failure 61
4.2.5 Multiple arguments 62

4.2.6 Conditional equations 63
4.2.7 Repeated variables 65
4.2.8 Where-clauses 66
4.2.9 Patterns on the left-hand side of definitions 67
4.2.10 Summary 67
4.3 The semantics of pattern-matching lambda abstractions 67
4.3.1 The semantics of variable patterns 68
4.3.2 The semantics of constant patterns 69
4.3.3 The semantics of sum-constructor patterns 69
4.3.4 The semantics of product-constructor patterns 70
4.3.5 A defence of lazy product-matching 72
4.3.6 Summary 74
4.4 Introducing case-expressions 74
4.5 Summary 76
References 77

5 EFFICIENT COMPILATION OF PATTERN-MATCHING
Philip Wadler **78**

5.1 Introduction and examples 78
5.2 The pattern-matching compiler algorithm 81
5.2.1 The function match 81
5.2.2 The variable rule 83
5.2.3 The constructor rule 84
5.2.4 The empty rule 87
5.2.5 An example 88
5.2.6 The mixture rule 88
5.2.7 Completeness 90
5.3 The pattern-matching compiler in Miranda 90
5.3.1 Patterns 90
5.3.2 Expressions 91
5.3.3 Equations 92
5.3.4 Variable names 92
5.3.5 The functions partition and foldr 92
5.3.6 The function match 93
5.4 Optimizations 94
5.4.1 Case-expressions with default clauses 94
5.4.2 Optimizing expressions containing [] and FAIL 96
5.5 Uniform definitions 98
References 103

6 TRANSFORMING THE ENRICHED LAMBDA CALCULUS **104**

6.1 Transforming pattern-matching lambda abstractions 104
6.1.1 Constant patterns 104
6.1.2 Product-constructor patterns 105
6.1.3 Sum-constructor patterns 106

6.1.4 Reducing the number of built-in functions 107
6.1.5 Summary 109
6.2 Transforming let and letrec 109
6.2.1 Conformality checking and irrefutable patterns 110
6.2.2 Overview of let and letrec transformations 110
6.2.3 Transforming simple lets into the ordinary lambda calculus 112
6.2.4 Transforming irrefutable lets into simple lets 112
6.2.5 Transforming irrefutable letrecs into simple letrecs 113
6.2.6 Transforming irrefutable letrecs into irrefutable lets 114
6.2.7 Transforming general let(rec)s into irrefutable let(rec)s 115
6.2.8 Dependency analysis 118
6.3 Transforming case-expressions 121
6.3.1 Case-expressions involving a product type 122
6.3.2 Case-expressions involving a sum type 122
6.3.3 Using a let-expression instead of UNPACK 123
6.3.4 Reducing the number of built-in functions 124
6.4 The [] operator and FAIL 125
6.5 Summary 126
References 126

7 LIST COMPREHENSIONS Philip Wadler **127**

7.1 Introduction to list comprehensions 127
7.2 Reduction rules for list comprehensions 129
7.3 Translating list comprehensions 132
7.4 Using transformations to improve efficiency 133
7.5 Pattern-matching in comprehensions 136
Reference 138

8 POLYMORPHIC TYPE-CHECKING Peter Hancock **139**

8.1 Informal notation for types 140
8.1.1 Tuples 140
8.1.2 Lists 141
8.1.3 Structured types 141
8.1.4 Functions 142
8.2 Polymorphism 143
8.2.1 The identity function 143
8.2.2 The length function 144
8.2.3 The composition function 145
8.2.4 The function foldr 146
8.2.5 What polymorphism means 147
8.3 Type inference 148
8.4 The intermediate language 150
8.5 How to find types 151
8.5.1 Simple cases, and lambda abstractions 151
8.5.2 A mistyping 154
8.5.3 Top-level lets 155

8.5.4 Top-level letrecs 157
8.5.5 Local definitions 159
8.6 Summary of rules for correct typing 160
8.6.1 Rule for applications 160
8.6.2 Rule for lambda abstractions 160
8.6.3 Rule for let-expressions 161
8.6.4 Rule for letrec-expressions 161
8.7 Some cautionary remarks 161
References 162

9 A TYPE-CHECKER Peter Hancock **163**

9.1 Representation of programs 163
9.2 Representation of type expressions 164
9.3 Success and failure 165
9.4 Solving equations 166
9.4.1 Substitutions 166
9.4.2 Unification 168
9.5 Keeping track of types 171
9.5.1 Method 1: look to the occurrences 171
9.5.2 Method 2: look to the variables 171
9.5.3 Association lists 173
9.6 New variables 175
9.7 The type-checker 176
9.7.1 Type-checking lists of expressions 177
9.7.2 Type-checking variables 177
9.7.3 Type-checking application 178
9.7.4 Type-checking lambda abstractions 179
9.7.5 Type-checking let-expressions 179
9.7.6 Type-checking letrec-expressions 180
References 182

PART II GRAPH REDUCTION

10 PROGRAM REPRESENTATION 185

10.1 Abstract syntax trees 185
10.2 The graph 186
10.3 Concrete representations of the graph 187
10.3.1 Representing structured data 187
10.3.2 Other uses for variable-sized cells 189
10.4 Tags and type-checking 189
10.5 Compile-time versus run-time typing 190
10.6 Boxed and unboxed objects 190
10.7 Tagged pointers 191
10.8 Storage management and the need for garbage collection 192
References 192

11 SELECTING THE NEXT REDEX 193

11.1 Lazy evaluation 193
- 11.1.1 The case for lazy evaluation 194
- 11.1.2 The case against lazy evaluation 194
- 11.1.3 Normal order reduction 194
- 11.1.4 Summary 195

11.2 Data constructors, input and output 195
- 11.2.1 The printing mechanism 196
- 11.2.2 The input mechanism 197

11.3 Normal forms 197
- 11.3.1 Weak head normal form 198
- 11.3.2 Top-level reduction is easier 199
- 11.3.3 Head normal form 199

11.4 Evaluating arguments of built-in functions 200

11.5 How to find the next top-level redex 201

11.6 The spine stack 202
- 11.6.1 Pointer-reversal 203
- 11.6.2 Argument evaluation using pointer-reversal 204
- 11.6.3 Stacks versus pointer-reversal 205

References 206

12 GRAPH REDUCTION OF LAMBDA EXPRESSIONS 207

12.1 Reducing a lambda application 207
- 12.1.1 Substituting pointers to the argument 208
- 12.1.2 Overwriting the root of the redex 209
- 12.1.3 Constructing a new instance of the lambda body 209
- 12.1.4 Summary 210

12.2 Reducing a built-in function application 212

12.3 The reduction algorithm so far 213

12.4 Indirection nodes 213
- 12.4.1 Updating with unboxed objects 214
- 12.4.2 Updating where the body is a single variable 215
- 12.4.3 Evaluating the result before updating 216
- 12.4.4 Summary: indirection nodes versus copying 217

12.5 Implementing Y 218

References 219

13 SUPERCOMBINATORS AND LAMBDA-LIFTING 220

13.1 The idea of compilation 220

13.2 Solving the problem of free variables 222
- 13.2.1 Supercombinators 223
- 13.2.2 A supercombinator-based compilation strategy 224

13.3 Transforming lambda abstractions into supercombinators 226
- 13.3.1 Eliminating redundant parameters 228
- 13.3.2 Parameter ordering 229

13.4 Implementing a supercombinator program 230
References 231

14 RECURSIVE SUPERCOMBINATORS 232

14.1 Notation 233
14.2 Lets and letrecs in supercombinator bodies 233
14.3 Lambda-lifting in the presence of letrecs 235
14.4 Generating supercombinators with graphical bodies 236
14.5 An example 236
14.6 Alternative approaches 238
14.7 Compile-time simplifications 240
14.7.1 Compile-time reductions 240
14.7.2 Common subexpression elimination 241
14.7.3 Eliminating redundant lets 241
References 242

15 FULLY-LAZY LAMBDA-LIFTING 243

15.1 Full laziness 243
15.2 Maximal free expressions 245
15.3 Lambda-lifting using maximal free expressions 247
15.3.1 Modifying the lambda-lifting algorithm 247
15.3.2 Fully lazy lambda-lifting in the presence of letrecs 249
15.4 A larger example 250
15.5 Implementing fully lazy lambda-lifting 252
15.5.1 Identifying the maximal free expressions 252
15.5.2 Lifting CAFs 253
15.5.3 Ordering the parameters 253
15.5.4 Floating out the lets and letrecs 254
15.6 Eliminating redundant full laziness 256
15.6.1 Functions applied to too few arguments 257
15.6.2 Unshared lambda abstractions 258
References 259

16 SK COMBINATORS 260

16.1 The SK compilation scheme 260
16.1.1 Introducing S, K and I 261
16.1.2 Compilation and implementation 263
16.1.3 Implementations 265
16.1.4 SK combinators perform lazy instantiation 265
16.1.5 I is not necessary 266
16.1.6 History 266
16.2 Optimizations to the SK scheme 267

16.2.1 K optimization 267
16.2.2 The B combinator 268
16.2.3 The C combinator 269
16.2.4 The S′ combinator 270
16.2.5 The B′ and C′ combinators 272
16.2.6 An example 273
16.3 Director strings 274
16.3.1 The basic idea 275
16.3.2 Minor refinements 277
16.3.3 Director strings as combinators 277
16.4 The size of SK combinator translations 278
16.5 Comparison with supercombinators 279
16.5.1 In favor of SK combinators 279
16.5.2 Against SK combinators 279
References 280

17 STORAGE MANAGEMENT AND GARBAGE COLLECTION 281

17.1 Criteria for assessing a storage manager 281
17.2 A sketch of the standard techniques 282
17.3 Developments in reference-counting 285
17.3.1 Reference-counting garbage collection of cyclic structures 285
17.3.2 One-bit reference-counts 286
17.3.3 Hardware support for reference-counting 286
17.4 Shorting out indirection nodes 287
17.5 Exploiting cell lifetimes 287
17.6 Avoiding garbage collection 288
17.7 Garbage collection in distributed systems 288
References 289

PART III ADVANCED GRAPH REDUCTION

18 THE G-MACHINE 293

18.1 Using an intermediate code 294
18.1.1 G-code and the G-machine compiler 294
18.1.2 Other fast sequential implementations of lazy languages 295
18.2 An example of G-machine execution 296
18.3 The source language for the G-compiler 299
18.4 Compilation to G-code 300
18.5 Compiling a supercombinator definition 301
18.5.1 Stacks and contexts 302
18.5.2 The **R** compilation scheme 304
18.5.3 The **C** compilation scheme 306
18.6 Supercombinators with zero arguments 311
18.6.1 Compiling CAFs 311
18.6.2 Garbage collection of CAFs 312

18.7 Getting it all together 312
18.8 The built-in functions 313
18.8.1 $NEG, $+, and the EVAL instruction 314
18.8.2 $CONS 316
18.8.3 $HEAD 316
18.8.4 $IF, and the JUMP instruction 317
18.9 Summary 318
References 318

19 G-CODE – DEFINITION AND IMPLEMENTATION 319

19.1 What the G-code instructions do 319
19.1.1 Notation 320
19.1.2 State transitions for the G-machine 320
19.1.3 The printing mechanism 322
19.1.4 Remarks about G-code 324
19.2 Implementation 324
19.2.1 VAX Unix assembler syntax 324
19.2.2 The stack representation 325
19.2.3 The graph representation 325
19.2.4 The code representation 326
19.2.5 The dump representation 326
19.3 Target code generation 326
19.3.1 Generating target code from G-code instructions 327
19.3.2 Optimization using a stack model 328
19.3.3 Handling EVALs and JUMPs 329
19.4 More on the graph representation 330
19.4.1 Implementing tag case analysis 330
19.4.2 Implementing EVAL 331
19.4.3 Implementing UNWIND 332
19.4.4 Indirection nodes 334
19.4.5 Boxed versus unboxed representations 335
19.4.6 Summary 336
19.5 Getting it all together 336
19.6 Summary 336
References 337

20 OPTIMIZATIONS TO THE G-MACHINE 338

20.1 On not building graphs 338
20.2 Preserving laziness 339
20.3 Direct execution of built-in functions 340
20.3.1 Optimizations to the **R** scheme 340
20.3.2 The **E** scheme 341
20.3.3 The **RS** and **ES** schemes 343
20.3.4 η-reduction and lambda-lifting 346

20.4 Compiling FATBAR and FAIL 347
20.5 Evaluating arguments 349
20.5.1 Optimizing partial applications 349
20.5.2 Using global strictness information 350
20.6 Avoiding EVALs 352
20.6.1 Avoiding re-evaluation in a function body 352
20.6.2 Using global strictness information 352
20.7 Avoiding repeated unwinding 354
20.8 Performing some eager evaluation 355
20.9 Manipulating basic values 356
20.10 Peephole optimizations to G-code 360
20.10.1 Combining multiple SLIDEs and MKAPs 360
20.10.2 Avoiding redundant EVALs 361
20.10.3 Avoiding allocating the root of the result 361
20.10.4 Unpacking structured objects 362
20.11 Pattern-matching revisited 363
20.12 Summary 363
Reference 366

21 OPTIMIZING GENERALIZED TAIL CALLS Simon L. Peyton Jones and Thomas Johnsson **367**

21.1 Tail calls 368
21.2 Generalizing tail calls 371
21.2.1 W is an application node 372
21.2.2 W is a supercombinator of zero arguments 373
21.2.3 W is a function of three arguments 373
21.2.4 W is a function of less than three arguments 373
21.2.5 W is a function of more than three arguments 374
21.3 Compilation using DISPATCH 376
21.3.1 Compilation schemes for DISPATCH 376
21.3.2 Compile-time optimization of DISPATCH 376
21.4 Optimizing the E scheme 377
21.5 Comparison with environment-based implementations 378
References 379

22 STRICTNESS ANALYSIS **380**

22.1 Abstract interpretation 380
22.1.1 An archetypical example – the rule of signs 380
22.1.2 History and references 383
22.2 Using abstract interpretation to do strictness analysis 383
22.2.1 Formulating the question 383
22.2.2 Choosing an appropriate abstract interpretation 384
22.2.3 Developing f# from f 386
22.2.4 Fitting strictness analysis into the compiler 387

22.3 Coping with recursion 387
22.3.1 The first wrong way 388
22.3.2 The second wrong way 388
22.3.3 The right way 389
22.3.4 Order of analysis and mutual recursion 390
22.4 Extensions to Mycroft's work, and other work 390
22.4.1 Higher-order functions 390
22.4.2 Non-flat domains 391
22.4.3 Other related work 391
22.5 Annotating the program 391
22.5.1 Annotating function definitions 392
22.5.2 Annotating application nodes 393
22.5.3 Why both annotations are needed 394
22.5.4 Summary 394
References 394

23 THE PRAGMATICS OF GRAPH REDUCTION 396

23.1 The time behavior of functional programs 397
23.2 The delicacy of full laziness 398
23.2.1 Ordering of parameters 398
23.2.2 Full laziness and recursion 399
23.2.3 Summary 400
23.3 The space behavior of lazy functional programs 400
23.3.1 Space leaks 400
23.3.2 Unevaluated components of data structures 402
23.3.3 Summary 403
23.4 Transient store usage 403
23.4.1 Recursion 403
23.4.2 Excessive sharing 405
23.4.3 Transient lists 406
23.4.4 Summary 407
23.5 Conclusions 407
References 408

24 PARALLEL GRAPH REDUCTION 409

24.1 The challenge of parallelism 409
24.2 Parallel functional programming 410
24.2.1 The opportunity for parallelism 410
24.2.2 Writing parallel functional programs 411
24.2.3 Writing parallel programs is easier in a functional language 412
24.3 Parallel graph reduction 413
24.3.1 A model for parallel reduction 413
24.4 Sparking tasks 415
24.4.1 Conservative parallelism 415

24.4.2 Speculative parallelism 417
24.4.3 Too little parallelism 418
24.4.4 Too much parallelism 419
24.4.5 Granularity, and the problem of tiny tasks 419
24.4.6 Scheduling 420
24.5 Blocking tasks 421
24.5.1 The need for blocking 421
24.5.2 The blocking mechanism 421
24.5.3 Reducing mutual exclusion 422
24.6 What is a task? 424
24.6.1 Pointer-reversal 424
24.6.2 Using a stack 425
24.6.3 Reawakening blocked tasks 425
24.7 Locality 426
24.7.1 What is locality? 426
24.7.2 Shared memory and distributed memory 427
24.7.3 Locality versus concurrency 428
24.8 Parallel reduction machine projects 428
24.9 Summary 429
References 429

Appendix An Introduction to Miranda™ David Turner **431**

Index 439

PREFACE

This book is about implementing functional programming languages using graph reduction.

Functional languages have become the focus of much active research in recent years [Backus, 1978] [Peyton Jones, 1984], but their acceptance has been delayed by the inefficiency of their available implementations when compared with more conventional languages.

This situation has changed recently, with the advent of rather fast implementations of functional languages such as Cardelli's ML [Cardelli, 1983], Fairbairn's Ponder [Fairbairn, 1982], and the Chalmers Lazy ML compiler [Johnsson, 1984]. These implementations rival the speed of compilers for more conventional languages.

There appear to be two main approaches to the efficient implementation of functional languages. The first is an *environment-based* scheme, exemplified by Cardelli's ML implementation, which derives from the experience of the Lisp community. The other is *graph reduction*, a much newer technique first invented by Wadsworth [Wadsworth, 1971], and on which the Ponder and Lazy ML implementations are founded. Despite the radical differences in beginnings, the most sophisticated examples of each approach show remarkable similarities.

The techniques of graph reduction are to be found scattered amongst the proceedings of various conferences and workshops, and it is one purpose of this book to collect some of this work together. The book is intended to have two main applications:

(i) As a course text for part of an undergraduate or postgraduate course on the implementation of functional languages.
(ii) As a handbook for those attempting to write a functional language implementation based on graph reduction.

The material is presented in a fairly informal tutorial fashion, the idea being to convey the framework and some of the intuitions that will render the original sources more accessible.

Chapters 5 and 7 were written by Philip Wadler, of the Programming Research Group, Oxford, and Chapter 4 was written in collaboration with him. Chapters 8 and 9 were written by Peter Hancock, of Metier Management Systems Ltd, and currently at the Programming Research Group, Oxford. I gratefully acknowledge their patience in writing and rewriting their drafts.

I am extremely grateful to a number of other people who have made significant technical contributions to the book. David Turner's help was invaluable, in offering comments on the parts of the book that relate to Miranda. The Appendix which gives an introduction to Miranda, was written by him. (Miranda is a trademark of Research Software Limited.)

Much of the information about Miranda in the first part of the book is based on a prerelease version of the Miranda system, and I am grateful to Research Software Limited for the permission to include this material.

Simon Finn, of the University of Stirling, made a number of penetrating observations about the treatment of pattern-matching, which resulted in significant improvements in Chapters 4 and 6.

Several long discussions with Thomas Johnsson, of Chalmers University, Göteborg, radically changed the shape of the G-machine chapters, and Chapter 21 was written in collaboration with him. John Fairbairn and Stuart Wray, of Cambridge, also made important contributions in this area.

Paul Hudak and Robert Keller helped me in writing the last section of Chapter 24.

Many other people have given me welcome help and encouragement, and have helped enormously by reading the text and making constructive suggestions. These include Lennart Augustsson, Philip Boswell, Geoff Burn, Nigel Chapman, Chris Clack, Pierre-Louis Curien, Dan Friedman, Kevin Hammond, Peter Hancock, Chris Hankin, John Hughes, Thomas Johnsson, Dick Kieburtz, Phil Molyneux, Benedict Nixon, Martin Packer, Ellen Poon, Jon Salkild, William Stoye, David Turner, Phil Wadler, John Washbrook and Russel Winder. I am particularly grateful to John Washbrook for his unfailing support.

Simon L. Peyton Jones
University College London
London WC1E 6BT
simonpj @uk.ac.ucl.cs

References

Backus, J. 1978. Can programming be liberated from the von Neumann style? A functional style and its algebra of programs. *Communications of the ACM*. Vol. 21, no. 8, pp. 613–41.

Cardelli, L. 1983. The functional abstract machine. *Polymorphism*. Vol. 1, no. 1.

Fairbairn, J. 1982. Ponder and its type system. *Technical Report 31*. Computer Lab., Cambridge. November.

Johnsson, T. 1984. Efficient compilation of lazy evaluation. In *Proceedings of the ACM Conference on Compiler Construction, Montreal*, pp. 58–69. June.

Peyton Jones, S.L. 1984. Directions in functional programming research. In *SERC Distributed Computing Systems*, pp. 220–49. Duce (editor). Peter Peregrinus.

Wadsworth, C.P. 1971. Semantics and pragmatics of the lambda calculus, Chapter 4. PhD thesis, Oxford.

One

INTRODUCTION

This book is about implementing functional programming languages using *lazy graph reduction*, and it divides into three parts.

The first part describes how to translate a high-level functional language into an intermediate language, called the lambda calculus, including detailed coverage of pattern-matching and type-checking. The second part begins with a simple implementation of the lambda calculus, based on graph reduction, and then develops a number of refinements and alternatives, such as supercombinators, full laziness and SK combinators. Finally, the third part describes the G-machine, a sophisticated implementation of graph reduction, which provides a dramatic increase in performance over the implementations described earlier.

One of the agreed advantages of functional languages is their semantic simplicity. This simplicity has considerable payoffs in the book. Over and over again we are able to make semi-formal arguments for the correctness of the compilation algorithms, and the whole book has a distinctly mathematical flavor – an unusual feature in a book about implementations.

Most of the material to be presented has appeared in the published literature in some form (though some has not), but mainly in the form of conference proceedings and isolated papers. References to this work appear at the end of each chapter.

1.1 Assumptions

This book is about implementations, not languages, so we shall make no attempt to extol the virtues of functional languages or the functional programming style. Instead we shall assume that the reader is familiar with functional programming; those without this familiarity may find it heavy going. A brief introduction to functional programming may be found in Darlington [1984], while Henderson [1980] and Glaser *et al.* [1984] give more substantial treatments. Another useful text is Abelson and Sussman [1985] which describes Scheme, an almost-functional dialect of Lisp.

An encouraging consensus seems to be emerging in the basic features of high-level functional programming languages, exemplified by languages such as SASL [Turner, 1976], ML [Gordon *et al.*, 1979], KRC [Turner, 1982], Hope [Burstall *et al.*, 1980], Ponder [Fairbairn, 1985], LML [Augustsson, 1984], Miranda [Turner, 1985] and Orwell [Wadler, 1985]. However, for the sake of definiteness, we use the language Miranda as a concrete example throughout the book (When used as the name of a programming language, 'Miranda' is a trademark of Research Software Limited.) A brief introduction to Miranda may be found in the appendix, but no serious attempt is made to give a tutorial about functional programming in general, or Miranda in particular. For those familiar with functional programming, however, no difficulties should arise.

Generally speaking, all the material of the book should apply to the other functional languages mentioned, with only syntactic changes. The only exception to this is that we concern ourselves almost exclusively with the implementation of languages with *non-strict semantics* (such as SASL, KRC, Ponder, LML, Miranda and Orwell). The advantages and disadvantages of this are discussed in Chapter 11, but it seems that graph reduction is probably less attractive than the environment-based approach for the implementation of languages with strict semantics; hence the focus on non-strict languages. However, some functional languages are strict (ML and Hope, for example), and while much of the book is still relevant to strict languages, some of the material would need to be interpreted with care.

The emphasis throughout is on an informal approach, aimed at developing understanding rather than at formal rigor. It would be an interesting task to rewrite the book in a formal way, giving watertight proofs of correctness at each stage.

1.2 Part I: Compiling High-level Functional Languages

It has been widely observed that most functional languages are quite similar to each other, and differ more in their syntax than their semantics. In order to simplify our thinking about implementations, the first part of this book shows how to translate a high-level functional program into an *intermediate language* which has a very simple syntax and semantics. Then, in the second and third parts of the book, we will show how to implement this intermediate language using graph reduction. Proceeding in this way allows us to describe graph reduction in considerable detail, but in a way that is not specific to any particular high-level language.

The intermediate language into which we will translate the high-level functional program is the notation of the *lambda calculus* (Figure 1.1). The lambda calculus is an extremely well-studied language, and we give an introduction to it in Chapter 2.

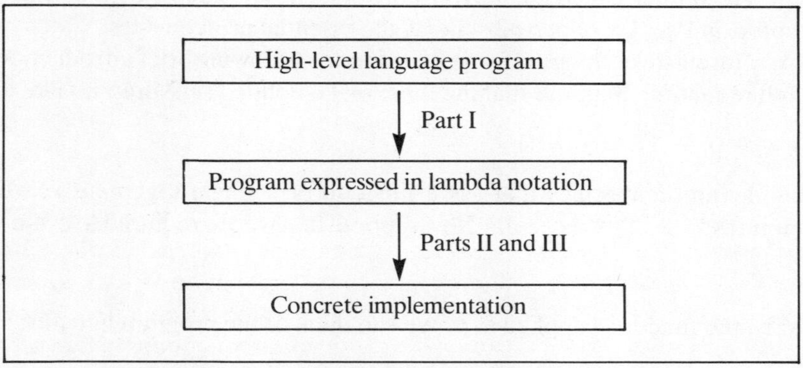

Figure 1.1 Implementing a functional program

The lambda calculus is not only simple, it is also sufficiently expressive to allow us to translate any high-level functional language into it. However, translating some high-level language constructs into the lambda notation is less straightforward than it at first appears, and the rest of Part I is concerned with this translation.

Part I is organized as follows. First of all, in Chapter 3, we define a language which is a superset of the lambda calculus, which we call the *enriched lambda calculus*. The extra constructs provided by the enriched lambda calculus are specifically designed to allow a straightforward translation of a Miranda program into an expression in the enriched lambda calculus, and Chapter 3 shows how to perform this translation for simple Miranda programs.

After a brief introduction to pattern-matching, Chapter 4 then extends the translation algorithm to cover more complex Miranda programs, and gives a formal semantics for pattern-matching. Subsequently, Chapter 7 rounds out the picture, by showing how Miranda's ZF expressions can also be translated in the same way. (Various advanced features of Miranda are not covered, such as algebraic types with laws, abstract data types, and modules.)

Much of the rest of Part I concerns the transformation of enriched lambda calculus expressions into the ordinary lambda calculus subset, a process which is quite independent of Miranda. This language-independence was one of the reasons for defining the enriched lambda calculus language in the first place. Chapter 5 shows how expressions involving pattern-matching constructs may be transformed to use case-expressions, with a considerable gain in efficiency. Then Chapter 6 shows how all the constructs of the enriched lambda calculus, including case-expressions, may be transformed into the ordinary lambda calculus.

Part I concludes with Chapter 8 which discusses type-checking in general, and Chapter 9 in which a type-checker is constructed in Miranda.

1.3 Part II: Graph Reduction

The rest of the book describes how the lambda calculus may be implemented using a technique called *graph reduction*. It is largely independent of the later chapters in Part I, Chapters 2–4 being the essential prerequisites.

As a foretaste of things to come, we offer the following brief introduction to graph reduction. Suppose that the function f is defined (in Miranda) like this:

```
f x = (x + 1) * (x - 1)
```

This definition specifies that f is a function of a single argument x, which computes '(x + 1) * (x − 1)'. Now suppose that we are required to evaluate

```
f 4
```

that is, the function f applied to 4. We can think of the program like this:

where the @ stands for function application. Applying f to 4 gives

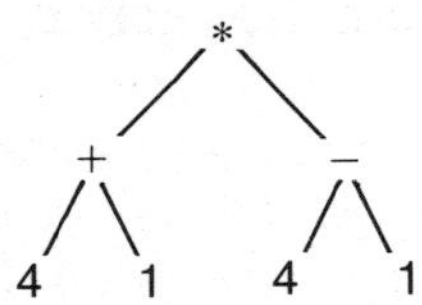

(Note: in the main text we will use a slightly different representation for applications of $*$, $+$ and $-$, but this fact is not significant here.) We may now execute the addition and the subtraction (in either order), giving

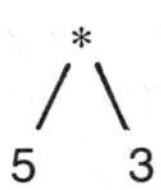

Finally we can execute the multiplication, to give the result

15

From this simple example we can see that:

(i) *Executing* a functional program consists of *evaluating* an expression.
(ii) A functional program has a natural representation as a *tree* (or, more generally, a *graph*).
(iii) Evaluation proceeds by means of a sequence of simple steps, called *reductions*. Each reduction performs a local transformation of the graph (hence the term *graph reduction*).
(iv) Reductions may safely take place in a variety of orders, or indeed in parallel, since they cannot interfere with each other.

(v) Evaluation is complete when there are no further reducible expressions.

Graph reduction gives an appealingly simple and elegant model for the execution of a functional program, and one that is radically different from the execution model of a conventional imperative language.

We begin in Chapter 10 by discussing the representation of a functional program as a graph. The next two chapters form a pair which discusses first the question of deciding which reduction to perform next (Chapter 11), and then the act of performing the reduction (Chapter 12).

Chapters 13 and 14 introduce the powerful technique of *supercombinators*, which is the key to the remainder of the book. This is followed in Chapter 15 with a discussion of *full laziness*, an aspect of lazy evaluation; this chapter can be omitted on first reading since later material does not depend on it.

Chapter 16 then presents *SK combinators*, an alternative implementation technique to supercombinators. Hence, this chapter can be understood independently of Chapters 13–15. Thereafter, however, we concentrate on supercombinator-based implementations.

Part II concludes with a chapter on *garbage collection*.

1.4 Part III: Advanced Graph Reduction

It may seem at first that graph reduction is inherently less efficient than more conventional execution models, at least for conventional von Neumann machines. The bulk of Part III is devoted to an extended discussion of the G-machine, which shows how graph reduction can be compiled to a form that is suitable for *direct execution* by ordinary sequential computers.

In view of the radical difference between graph reduction on the one hand, and the linear sequence of instructions executed by conventional machines on the other, this may seem a somewhat surprising achievement. This (fairly recent) development is responsible for a dramatic improvement in the speed of functional language implementations.

Chapters 18 and 19 introduce the main concepts of the G-machine, while Chapters 20 and 21 are devoted entirely to optimizations of the approach.

The book concludes with three chapters that fill in some gaps, and offer some pointers to the future.

Chapter 22 introduces *strictness analysis*, a compile-time program analysis method which has been the subject of much recent work, and which is crucial to many of the optimizations of the G-machine.

Perhaps the major shortcoming of functional programming languages, from the point of view of the programmer, is the difficulty of estimating the space and time complexity of the program. This question is intimately bound up with the implementation, and we discuss the matter in Chapter 23.

Finally, the book concludes with a chapter on parallel implementations of graph reduction.

References

Abelson, H., and Sussman, G.J. 1985. *Structure and Interpretation of Computer Programs*. MIT Press.

Augustsson, L. 1984. A compiler for lazy ML. *Proceedings of the ACM Symposium on Lisp and Functional Programming, Austin*. August, pp. 218–27.

Burstall, R.M., MacQueen, D.B., and Sanella, D.T. 1980. *Hope: an experimental applicative language*. CSR-62-80. Department of Computer Science, University of Edinburgh. May.

Darlington, J. 1984. Functional programming. In *Distributed Computing*. Duce (Editor). Academic Press.

Fairbairn, J. 1985. Design and implementation of a simple typed language based on the lambda calculus. PhD thesis, *Technical Report 75*. University of Cambridge. May.

Glaser, H., Hankin, C., and Till, D. 1984. *Principles of Functional Programming*. Prentice-Hall.

Gordon, M.J., Milner, A.J., and Wadsworth, C.P. 1979. *Edinburgh LCF*. LNCS 78. Springer Verlag.

Henderson, P. 1980. *Functional Programming*. Prentice-Hall.

Turner, D.A. 1976. *The SASL language manual*. University of St Andrews. December.

Turner, D.A. 1982. Recursion equations as a programming language. In *Functional Programming and Its Applications*, Darlington *et al.* (editors), pp. 1–28. Cambridge University Press.

Turner, D.A. 1985. Miranda – a non-strict functional language with polymorphic types. In *Conference on Functional Programming Languages and Computer Architecture, Nancy*, pp. 1–16. Jouannaud (editor), LNCS 201. Springer Verlag.

Wadler, P. 1985. *Introduction to Orwell*. Programming Research Group, University of Oxford.

Part I

COMPILING HIGH-LEVEL FUNCTIONAL LANGUAGES

Two

THE LAMBDA CALCULUS

This chapter introduces the lambda calculus, a simple language which will be used throughout the rest of the book as a bridge between high-level functional languages and their low-level implementations. The reasons for introducing the lambda calculus as an intermediate language are:

(i) It is a *simple* language, with only a few syntactic constructs, and simple semantics. These properties make it a good basis for a discussion of implementations, because an implementation of the lambda calculus only has to support a few constructs, and the simple semantics allows us to reason about the correctness of the implementation.

(ii) It is an *expressive* language, which is sufficiently powerful to express all functional programs (and indeed, all computable functions). This means that if we have an implementation of the lambda calculus, we can implement any other functional language by translating it into the lambda calculus.

In this chapter we focus on the syntax and semantics of the lambda calculus itself, before turning our attention to high-level functional languages in the next chapter.

2.1 The Syntax of the Lambda Calculus

Here is a simple expression in the lambda calculus:

```
(+ 4 5)
```

All function applications in the lambda calculus are written in *prefix* form, so, for example, the function + precedes its arguments 4 and 5. A slightly more complex example, showing the (quite conventional) use of brackets, is

```
(+ (* 5 6) (* 8 3))
```

In both examples, the outermost brackets are redundant, but have been added for clarity (see Section 2.1.2).

From the implementation viewpoint, a functional program should be thought of as an *expression*, which is 'executed' by *evaluating* it. Evaluation proceeds by repeatedly selecting a *reducible expression* (or *redex*) and reducing it. In our last example there are two redexes: (* 5 6) and (* 8 3). The whole expression (+ (* 5 6) (* 8 3)) is not a redex, since a + needs to be applied to two *numbers* before it is reducible. Arbitrarily choosing the first redex for reduction, we write

```
(+ (* 5 6) (* 8 3))  →  (+ 30 (* 8 3))
```

where the → is pronounced 'reduces to'. Now there is only one redex, (* 8 3), which gives

```
(+ 30 (* 8 3))  →  (+ 30 24)
```

This reduction creates a new redex, which we now reduce

```
(+ 30 24)  →  54
```

When there are several redexes we have a choice of which one to reduce first. This issue will be addressed later in this chapter.

2.1.1 Function Application and Currying

In the lambda calculus, function application is so important that it is denoted by simple juxtaposition; thus we write

```
f x
```

to denote 'the function f applied to the argument x'. How should we express the application of a function to several arguments? We could use a new notation, like (f (x,y)), but instead we use a simple and rather ingenious alternative. To express 'the sum of 3 and 4' we write

```
((+ 3) 4)
```

The expression (+ 3) denotes the function that adds 3 to its argument. Thus the whole expression means 'the function + applied to the argument 3, the result of which is a function applied to 4'. (In common with all functional programming languages, the lambda calculus allows a function to return a function as its result.)

This device allows us to think of *all functions* as having a *single argument only*. It was introduced by Schonfinkel [1924] and extensively used by Curry [Curry and Feys, 1958]; as a result it is known as *currying*.

2.1.2 Use of Brackets

In mathematics it is conventional to omit redundant brackets to avoid cluttering up expressions. For example, we might omit brackets from the expression

$$(ab) + ((2c)/d)$$

to give

$$ab + 2c/d$$

The second expression is easier to read than the first, but there is a danger that it may be ambiguous. It is rendered unambiguous by establishing conventions about the precedence of the various functions (for example, multiplication binds more tightly than addition)..

Sometimes brackets cannot be omitted, as in the expression:

$$(b + c)/a$$

Similar conventions are useful when writing down expressions in the lambda calculus. Consider the expression:

```
((+ 3) 2)
```

By establishing the convention that *function application associates to the left*, we can write the expression more simply as:

```
(+ 3 2)
```

or even

```
+ 3 2
```

We performed some such abbreviations in the examples given earlier. As a more complicated example, the expression:

```
((f ((+ 4) 3)) (g x))
```

is fully bracketed and unambiguous. Following our convention, we may omit redundant brackets to make the expression easier to read, giving:

```
f (+ 4 3) (g x)
```

No further brackets can be omitted. Extra brackets may, of course, be inserted freely without changing the meaning of the expression; for example

```
(f (+ 4 3) (g x))
```

is the same expression again.

2.1.3 Built-in Functions and Constants

In its purest form the lambda calculus does not have built-in functions such as +, but our intentions are practical and so we extend the pure lambda calculus with a suitable collection of such built-in functions.

These include arithmetic functions (such as +, −, ∗, /) and constants (0, 1, . . .), logical functions (such as AND, OR, NOT) and constants (TRUE, FALSE), and character constants ('a', 'b', . . .). For example

```
          - 5 4  →  1
AND TRUE FALSE  →  FALSE
```

We also include a conditional function, IF, whose behavior is described by the reduction rules:

$$\text{IF TRUE } E_t\ E_f \rightarrow E_t$$
$$\text{IF FALSE } E_t\ E_f \rightarrow E_f$$

We will initially introduce data constructors into the lambda calculus by using the built-in functions CONS (short for CONSTRUCT), HEAD and TAIL (which behave exactly like the Lisp functions CONS, CAR and CDR). The constructor CONS builds a compound object which can be taken apart with HEAD and TAIL. We may describe their operation by the following rules:

```
HEAD (CONS a b)  →  a
 TAIL (CONS a b)  →  b
```

We also include NIL, the empty list, as a constant. The data constructors will be discussed at greater length in Chapter 4.

The exact choice of built-in functions is, of course, somewhat arbitrary, and further ones will be added as the need arises.

2.1.4 Lambda Abstractions

The only functions introduced so far have been the built-in functions (such as + and CONS). However, the lambda calculus provides a construct, called a *lambda abstraction*, to denote new (non-built-in) functions. A lambda abstraction is a particular sort of expression which denotes a function. Here is an example of a lambda abstraction:

```
(λx . + x 1)
```

The λ says 'here comes a function', and is immediately followed by a variable, x in this case; then comes a . followed by the *body* of the function, (+ x 1) in this case. The variable is called the *formal parameter*, and we say that the λ *binds* it. You can think of it like this:

```
(λ                   x    .    +    x     1)
↑                    ↑    ↑    ↑    ↑     ↑
That function of x which adds x to 1
```

A lambda abstraction *always* consists of all the four parts mentioned: the λ, the formal parameter, the . and the body.

A lambda abstraction is rather similar to a function definition in a conventional language, such as C:

```
Inc( x )
int x;
{ return( x + 1 ); }
```

The formal parameter of the lambda abstraction corresponds to the formal parameter of the function, and the body of the abstraction is an expression rather than a sequence of commands. However, functions in conventional languages must have a name (such as Inc), whereas lambda abstractions are 'anonymous' functions.

The body of a lambda abstraction extends *as far to the right as possible*, so that in the expression

```
(λx.+ x 1) 4
```

the body of the λx abstraction is (+ x 1), not just +. As usual, we may add extra brackets to clarify, thus

```
(λx.(+ x 1)) 4
```

When a lambda abstraction appears in isolation we may write it without any brackets:

```
λx.+ x 1
```

2.1.5 Summary

We define a *lambda expression* to be an expression in the lambda calculus, and Figure 2.1 summarizes the forms which a lambda expression may take. Notice that a lambda *abstraction* is not the same as a lambda *expression*; in fact the former is a particular instance of the latter.

```
<exp> :: = <constant>                Built-in constants
        |   <variable>                Variable names
        |   <exp> <exp>               Applications
        |   λ <variable>.<exp>        Lambda abstractions
```

This is the *abstract* syntax of lambda expressions. In order to write down such an expression in *concrete* form we use brackets to disambiguate its structure (see Section 2.1.2).

We will use lower-case letters for variables (e.g. x, f), and upper-case letters to stand for whole lambda expressions (e.g. M, E).

The choice of constants is rather arbitrary; we assume integers and booleans (e.g. 4, TRUE), together with built-in functions to manipulate them (e.g. AND, IF, +). We also assume built-in list-processing functions (e.g. CONS, HEAD).

Figure 2.1 Syntax of a lambda expression (in BNF)

In what follows we will use lower-case names for variables, and single upper-case letters to stand for whole lambda expressions. For example we might say 'for any lambda expression E, . . .,'. We will also write the names of built-in functions in upper case, but no confusion should arise.

2.2 The Operational Semantics of the Lambda Calculus

So far we have described only the *syntax* of the lambda calculus, but to dignify it with the title of a 'calculus' we must say how to 'calculate' with it. We will do this by giving three *conversion rules* which describe how to convert one lambda expression into another.

First, however, we introduce an important piece of terminology.

2.2.1 Bound and Free Variables

Consider the lambda expression

```
(λx.+ x y) 4
```

In order to evaluate this expression completely, we need to know the 'global' value of y. In contrast, we do not need to know a 'global' value for x, since it is just the formal parameter of the function, so we see that x and y have a rather different status.

The reason is that x occurs *bound* by the λx; it is just a 'hole' into which the argument 4 is placed when applying the lambda abstraction to its argument.

An occurrence of a variable must be either free or bound.

Definition of 'occurs free'

x occurs free in x (but not in any other variable or constant)

x occurs free in (E F)	⇔		x occurs free in E
		or	x occurs free in F
x occurs free in λy.E	⇔		x and y are different variables
		and	x occurs free in E

Definition of 'occurs bound'

x occurs bound in (E F)	⇔		x occurs bound in E
		or	x occurs bound in F
x occurs bound in λy.E	⇔		(x and y are the same variable *and* x occurs free in E)
		or	x occurs bound in E

(No variable occurs bound in an expression consisting of a single constant or variable.)

Note: '⇔' means 'if and only if'

Figure 2.2 Definitions of bound and free

On the other hand, y is not bound by any λ, and so occurs *free* in the expression. In general, the value of an expression depends only on the values of its free variables.

An occurrence of a variable is bound if there is an enclosing lambda abstraction which binds it, and is free otherwise. For example, x and y occur bound, but z occurs free in this example:

```
λx.+ ((λy.+ y z) 7) x
```

Notice that the terms 'bound' and 'free' refer to *specific occurrences* of the variable in an expression. This is because a variable may have both a bound occurrence and a free occurrence in an expression; consider for example

```
+ x ((λx.+ x 1) 4)
```

in which x occurs free (the first time) and bound (the second time). Each individual occurrence of a variable must be either free or bound.

Figure 2.2 gives formal definitions for 'free' and 'bound', which cover the forms of lambda expression given in Figure 2.1 case by case.

2.2.2 Beta-conversion

A lambda abstraction denotes a function, so we must describe how to apply it to an argument. For example, the expression

```
(λx.+ x 1) 4
```

is the juxtaposition of the lambda abstraction (λx.+ x 1) and the argument 4, and hence denotes the application of a certain function, denoted by the lambda abstraction, to the argument 4. The rule for such function application is very simple:

> The result of applying a lambda abstraction to an argument is an instance of the body of the lambda abstraction in which (free) occurrences of the formal parameter in the body are replaced with (copies of) the argument.

Thus the result of applying the lambda abstraction (λx.+ x 1) to the argument 4 is

```
+ 4 1
```

The (+ 4 1) is an instance of the body (+ x 1) in which occurrences of the formal parameter, x, are replaced with the argument, 4. We write the reduction using the arrow '→' as before:

```
(λx.+ x 1) 4  →  + 4 1
```

This operation is called *β-reduction*, and much of this book is concerned with its efficient implementation. We will use a series of examples to show in detail how β-reduction works.

2.2.2.1 Simple examples of beta-reduction

The formal parameter may occur several times in the body:

```
(λx.+ x x) 5  →  + 5 5
              →  10
```

Equally, there may be no occurrences of the formal parameter in the body:

```
(λx.3) 5  →  3
```

In this case there are no occurrences of the formal parameter (x) for which the argument (5) should be substituted, so the argument is discarded unused.

The body of a lambda abstraction may consist of another lambda abstraction:

```
(λx.(λy.- y x)) 4 5  →  (λy.- y 4) 5
                     →  - 5 4
                     →  1
```

Notice that, when constructing an instance of the body of the λx abstraction, we copy the entire body including the embedded λy abstraction (while substituting for x, of course). Here we see currying in action: the application of the λx abstraction returned a function (the λy abstraction) as its result, which when applied yielded the result (- 5 4).

We often abbreviate

```
(λx.(λy.E))
```

to

```
(λx.λy.E)
```

Functions can be arguments too:

```
(λf.f 3) (λx.+ x 1)  →  (λx.+ x 1) 3
                     →  + 3 1
                     →  4
```

An instance of the λx abstraction is substituted for f wherever f appears in the body of the λf abstraction.

2.2.2.2 Naming

Some slight care is needed when formal parameter names are not unique. For example

```
     (λx.(λx.+ (- x 1)) x 3) 9
  →  (λx.+ (- x 1)) 9 3
  →  + (- 9 1) 3
  →  11
```

Notice that we did *not* substitute for the inner x in the first reduction, because it was shielded by the enclosing λx; that is, the inner occurrence of x is not free in the body of the outer λx abstraction.

Given a lambda abstraction (λx.E), how can we identify exactly those occurrences of x which should be substituted for? It is easy: we should substitute for *those occurrences of* x *which are free* in E, because, if they are free in E, then they will be bound by the λx abstraction (λx.E). So, when applying the outer λx abstraction in the above example, we examine its body

```
(λx.+ (− x 1)) x 3
```

and see that only the second occurrence of x is free, and hence qualifies for substitution.

This is why the rule given above specified that only the *free* occurrences of the formal parameter in the body are to be substituted for. The nesting of the scope of variables in a block-structured language is closely analogous to this rule.

Here is another example of the same kind

```
(λx.λy.+ x ((λx.− x 3) y)) 5 6
→   (λy.+ 5 ((λx.− x 3) y)) 6
→   + 5 ((λx.− x 3) 6)
→   + 5 (− 6 3)
→   8
```

Again, the inner x is not substituted for in the first reduction, since it is not free in the body of the outer λx abstraction.

2.2.2.3 A larger example

As a larger example, we will demonstrate the somewhat surprising fact that data constructors can actually be modelled as pure lambda abstractions. We define CONS, HEAD and TAIL in the following way:

```
CONS  = (λa.λb.λf.f a b)
HEAD  = (λc.c (λa.λb.a))
TAIL  = (λc.c (λa.λb.b))
```

These obey the rules for CONS, HEAD and TAIL given in Section 2.1.3. For example,

```
    HEAD (CONS p q)
=   (λc.c (λa.λb.a)) (CONS p q)
→   CONS p q (λa.λb.a)
=   (λa.λb.λf. f a b) p q (λa.λb.a)
→   (λb.λf. f p b) q (λa.λb.a)
→   (λf. f p q) (λa.λb.a)
→   (λa.λb.a) p q
→   (λb.p) q
→   p
```

This means, incidentally, that there is no essential need for the built-in functions CONS, HEAD and TAIL, and it turns out that all the other built-in functions can also be modelled as lambda abstractions. This is rather satisfying from a theoretical viewpoint, but all practical implementations support built-in functions for efficiency reasons.

2.2.2.4 Conversion, reduction and abstraction

We can use the β-rule backwards, to introduce new lambda abstractions, thus

$$+ \ 4 \ 1 \ \leftarrow \ (\lambda x.+ \ x \ 1) \ 4$$

This operation is called *β-abstraction*, which we denote with a backwards reduction arrow '$\leftarrow$'. *β-conversion* means β-reduction or β-abstraction, and we denote it with a double-ended arrow '$\underset{\beta}{\leftrightarrow}$'. Thus we write

$$+ \ 4 \ 1 \ \underset{\beta}{\leftrightarrow} \ (\lambda x.+ \ x \ 1) \ 4$$

The arrow is decorated with β to distinguish β-conversion from the other forms of conversion we will meet shortly. An undecorated reduction arrow '$\rightarrow$' will stand for one or more β-reductions, or reductions of the built-in functions. An undecorated conversion arrow '$\leftrightarrow$' will stand for zero or more conversions, of any kind.

Rather than regarding β-reduction and β-abstraction as *operations*, we can regard β-conversion as expressing the *equivalence* of two expressions which 'look different' but 'ought to mean the same'. It turns out that we need two more rules to satisfy our intuitions about the equivalence of expressions, and we turn to these rules in the next two sections.

2.2.3 Alpha-conversion

Consider the two lambda abstractions

$$(\lambda x.+ \ x \ 1)$$

and

$$(\lambda y.+ \ y \ 1)$$

Clearly they 'ought' to be equivalent, and *α-conversion* allows us to change the name of the formal parameter of any lambda abstraction, so long as we do so consistently. So

$$(\lambda x.+ \ x \ 1) \ \underset{\alpha}{\leftrightarrow} \ (\lambda y.+ \ y \ 1)$$

where the arrow is decorated with an α to specify an α-conversion. The newly introduced name must not, of course, occur free in the body of the original lambda abstraction. α-conversion is used solely to eliminate the sort of name clashes exhibited in the example in the previous section.

Sometimes α-conversion is essential (see Section 2.2.6).

2.2.4 Eta-conversion

One more conversion rule is necessary to express our intuitions about what lambda abstractions 'ought' to be equivalent. Consider the two expressions

(λx. + 1 x)

and

(+ 1)

These expressions behave in exactly the same way when applied to an argument: they add 1 to it. η-*conversion* is a rule expressing their equivalence:

$$(\lambda x.+\ 1\ x) \underset{\eta}{\leftrightarrow} (+\ 1)$$

More generally, we can express the η-conversion rule like this:

$$(\lambda x.F\ x) \underset{\eta}{\leftrightarrow} F$$

provided x does not occur free in F, and F denotes a function.

The condition that x does not occur free in F prevents false conversions. For example,

(λx. + x x)

is not η-convertible to

(+ x)

because x occurs free in (+ x). The condition that F denotes a function prevents other false conversions involving built-in constants; for example:

TRUE

is not η-convertible to

(λx. TRUE x)

When the η-conversion rule is used from left to right it is called η-*reduction*.

2.2.5 Proving Interconvertibility

We will quite frequently want to prove the interconvertibility of two lambda expressions. When the two expressions denote a function such proofs can become rather tedious, and in this section we will demonstrate a convenient method that abbreviates the proof without sacrificing rigor.

As an example, consider the two lambda expressions:

IF TRUE ((λp. p) 3)

and

(λx. 3)

Both denote the same function, namely the function which always delivers the result 3 regardless of the value of its argument, and we might hope that they were interconvertible. This hope is justified, as the following sequence of conversions shows:

$$\begin{aligned}\text{IF TRUE } ((\lambda p.p)\ 3) &\underset{\beta}{\leftrightarrow} \text{IF TRUE } 3\\ &\underset{\eta}{\leftrightarrow} (\lambda x.\text{IF TRUE } 3\ x)\\ &\leftrightarrow (\lambda x.3)\end{aligned}$$

The final step is the reduction rule for IF.

An alternative method of proving convertibility of expressions denoting functions, which is often more convenient, is to apply both expressions to an arbitrary argument, w, say:

$$\begin{array}{ll}\text{IF TRUE } ((\lambda p.p)\ 3)\ w & (\lambda x.3)\ w\\ \rightarrow (\lambda p.p)\ 3 & \rightarrow 3\\ \rightarrow 3 & \end{array}$$

Hence

$$(\text{IF TRUE } ((\lambda p.p)\ 3)) \leftrightarrow (\lambda x.\ 3)$$

This proof has the advantage that it only uses reduction, and it avoids the explicit use of η-conversion. If it is not immediately clear why the final step is justified, consider the general case, in which we are given two lambda expressions F_1 and F_2. If we can show that

$$F_1\ w \rightarrow E$$

and

$$F_2\ w \rightarrow E$$

where w is a variable which does not occur free in F_1 or F_2, and E is some expression, then we can reason as follows:

$$\begin{aligned}F_1 &\underset{\eta}{\leftrightarrow} (\lambda w.F_1\ w)\\ &\leftrightarrow (\lambda w.E)\\ &\leftrightarrow (\lambda w.F_2\ w)\\ &\underset{\eta}{\leftrightarrow} F_2\end{aligned}$$

and hence $F_1 \leftrightarrow F_2$.

It is not always the case that lambda expressions which 'ought' to mean the same thing are interconvertible, and we will have more to say about this point in Section 2.5.

2.2.6 The Name-capture Problem

As a warning to the unwary we now give an example to show why the lambda calculus is trickier than meets the eye. Fortunately, it turns out that none of our implementations will come across this problem, so this section can safely be omitted on first reading.

Suppose we define a lambda abstraction TWICE thus:

```
TWICE = (λf.λx.f (f x))
```

Now consider reducing the expression (TWICE TWICE) using β-reductions:

```
    TWICE TWICE
=   (λf.λx.f (f x)) TWICE
→   (λx.TWICE (TWICE x))
```

Now there are two β-redexes, (TWICE x) and (TWICE (TWICE x)), so let us (arbitrarily) choose the inner one for reduction, first expanding the TWICE to its lambda abstraction:

```
=   (λx.TWICE ((λf.λx.f (f x)) x))
```

Now we see the problem. To apply TWICE to x, we must make a new instance of the body of TWICE (underlined) replacing occurrences of the formal parameter, f, with the argument, x. But x is *already used as a formal parameter* inside the body. It is clearly wrong to reduce to

```
    (λx.TWICE ((λf.λx.f (f x)) x))
→   (λx.TWICE (λx.x (x x)))              wrong!
```

because then the x substituted for f would be 'captured' by the inner λx abstraction. This is called the *name-capture* problem. One solution is to use α-conversion to change the name of one of the λx's; for instance:

```
    (λx.TWICE ((λf.λx.f (f x)) x))
↔α  (λx.TWICE ((λf.λy.f (f y)) x))
→   (λx.TWICE (λy.x (x y)))              right!
```

We conclude:

(i) β-reduction is only valid provided the free variables of the argument do not clash with any formal parameters in the body of the lambda abstraction.

(ii) α-conversion is sometimes necessary to avoid (i).

2.2.7 Summary of Conversion Rules

We have now developed three conversion rules which allow us to interconvert expressions involving lambda abstractions. They are

(i) *Name changing.* α-conversion allows us to change the name of the formal parameter of a lambda abstraction, so long as we do so consistently.

(ii) *Function application.* β-reduction allows us to apply a lambda abstraction to an argument, by making a new instance of the body of the abstraction, substituting the argument for free occurrences of the formal parameter. Special care needs to be taken when the argument contains free variables.

(iii) *Eliminating redundant lambda abstractions.* η-reduction can sometimes eliminate a lambda abstraction.

Within this framework we may also regard the built-in functions as one more form of conversion, δ-conversion. For this reason the reduction rules for built-in functions are sometimes called *delta rules.*

As we have seen, the application of the conversion rules is not always straightforward, so it behoves us to give a formal definition of exactly what the conversion rules are. This requires us to introduce one new piece of notation.

The notation

E[M/x]

means the expression E with M substituted for free occurrences of x.

As a mnemonic, imagine 'multiplying' E by M/x, giving M where the x's cancel out, so that x[M/x] = M. This notation allows us to express β-conversion very simply:

$$(\lambda x.E)\ M \underset{\beta}{\leftrightarrow} E[M/x]$$

and it is useful for α-conversion too.

Figures 2.3 and 2.4 give the formal definitions of substitution and conversion. They are rather forbidding, but all the complexity arises because of the name-capture problem described in Section 2.2.6 which will not arise at all in our implementations. Hence α-conversion will not be necessary, β-reduction can proceed by simple substitution, and η-reduction will prove to be a compile-time technique only.

To summarize our progress so far, we now have:

(i) a set of formal rules for constructing expressions (Figure 2.1);
(ii) a set of formal rules for converting one expression into an equivalent one (Figures 2.2–2.4).

```
x [M/x]       = M
c [M/x]       where c is any variable or constant other than x
              = c
(E F)[M/x]    = E[M/x] F[M/x]
(λx.E)[M/x]   = λx.E
(λy.E)[M/x]   where y is any variable other than x
              = λy.E[M/x]    if  x does not occur free in E
                                 or y does not occur free in M
              = λz.(E[z/y])[M/x] otherwise
                where z is a new variable name which does not
                 occur free in E or M
```

Figure 2.3 Definition of E[M/x]

It turns out that this small formal base is sufficient to build a large and complex theory of interconvertibility; the standard work is Barendregt [1984]. While this book is very well written, it is not intended for the casual reader, and Stoy [1981] gives a less comprehensive but more readable treatment. Curry and Feys also give a clear account of the historical origins and basic properties of the lambda calculus [Curry and Feys, 1958]. The lambda calculus was originally invented by Church [1941].

We will not take the lambda calculus any further as an end in itself; rather we will simply appropriate the fruits of the theory as and when we need them.

α-conversion:	if y is not free in E then $(\lambda x.E) \underset{\alpha}{\leftrightarrow} (\lambda y.E[y/x])$
β-conversion:	$(\lambda x.E)\ M \underset{\beta}{\leftrightarrow} E[M/x]$
η-conversion:	if x is not free in E and E denotes a function then $(\lambda x.E\ x) \underset{\eta}{\leftrightarrow} E$

When used left to right, the β and η rules are called reductions, and may be written with a '$\rightarrow$' arrow.

Figure 2.4 Definitions of α-, β- and η-conversions

2.3 Reduction Order

If an expression contains no redexes then evaluation is complete, and the expression is said to be in *normal form*. So the evaluation of an expression consists of successively reducing redexes until the expression is in normal form.

However, an expression may contain more than one redex, so *reduction can proceed by alternative routes*. For example, the expression (+ (* 3 4) (* 7 8)) can be reduced to normal form with the sequence

```
   (+ (* 3 4) (* 7 8))
→  (+ 12 (* 7 8))
→  (+ 12 56)
→  68
```

or the sequence

```
   (+ (* 3 4) (* 7 8))
→  (+ (* 3 4) 56)
→  (+ 12 56)
→  68
```

Not every expression has a normal form; consider for example

(D D)

where D is (λx.x x). The evaluation of this expression would not terminate since (D D) reduces to (D D):

```
(λx.x x) (λx.x x)  →  (λx.x x) (λx.x x)
                   →  (λx.x x) (λx.x x)
```

This situation corresponds directly to an imperative program going into an infinite loop.

Furthermore, *some* reduction sequences may reach a normal form while *others do not*. For example, consider

(λx.3) (D D)

If we first reduce the application of (λx.3) to (D D) (without evaluating (D D)) we get the result 3; but if we first reduce the application of D to D, we just get (D D) again, and if we keep choosing the (D D) the evaluation will fail to terminate.

2.3.1 Normal Order Reduction

These complications raise an embarrassing question: can two different reduction sequences lead to different normal forms? Fortunately the answer is 'no'. This is a consequence of a profound and powerful pair of theorems, the *Church-Rosser Theorems I and II*, which save the day.

> THEOREM
>
> *Church-Rosser Theorem I* (CRT I)
>
> If $E_1 \leftrightarrow E_2$, then there exists an expression E, such that
>
> $E_1 \rightarrow E$ and $E_2 \rightarrow E$

The following corollary is an easy consequence:

Corollary. No expression can be converted to two distinct normal forms (that is, normal forms that are not α-convertible).

Proof. Suppose that $E \leftrightarrow E_1$ and $E \leftrightarrow E_2$, where E_1 and E_2 are in normal form. Then, $E_1 \leftrightarrow E_2$ and, by CRT I, there must exist an expression F, such that $E_1 \rightarrow F$ and $E_2 \rightarrow F$. But E_1 and E_2 have no redexes, so $E_1 = F = E_2$.

Informally, the corollary says that all reduction sequences which terminate will reach the same result. The second Church-Rosser Theorem concerns a particular reduction order, called *normal order*:

THEOREM

Church-Rosser Theorem II (CRT II)

If $E_1 \rightarrow E_2$, and E_2 is in normal form, then there exists a *normal order* reduction sequence from E_1 to E_2.

This is as much as we can hope for; there is at most one possible result, and normal order reduction will find it if it exists. Notice that no reduction sequence can give the 'wrong' answer – the worst that can happen is non-termination.

Normal order reduction specifies that the *leftmost outermost redex* should be reduced first.

Thus, in our example above ((λx.3) (D D)), we would choose the λx-redex first, not the (D D). This rule embodies the intuition that *arguments to functions may be discarded*, so we should apply the function (λx.3) first, rather than first evaluating the argument (D D).

The shortest proofs of the Church-Rosser Theorem I (which is the harder one) are in Welch [1975] and Rosser [1982].

2.3.2 Optimal Reduction Orders

While normal order reduction guarantees to find a normal form (if one exists), it does *not* guarantee to do so in the fewest possible number of reductions. In fact, for tree reduction (see Section 12.1.1) it is provably least favorable, but fortunately for graph reduction (see Section 12.1.1) it seems that normal order is 'almost optimal', and that it probably takes more time to find the optimal redex than to pursue normal order. Some work has been done on finding more nearly optimal reduction orders that preserve the desirable properties of normal order [Levy, 1980].

For SK-combinator reduction (see Chapter 16), normal order graph reduction has been shown to be optimal. This result, among many others on graph reduction, is shown in Staples' series of papers [Staples, 1980a, 1980b, 1980c]. A more accessible treatment of this work is given by Kennaway [1984].

2.4 Recursive Functions

We began by saying that we propose to translate all functional programs into the lambda calculus. One pervasive feature of all functional programs is recursion, and this throws the viability of the whole venture into doubt, because the lambda calculus appears to lack anything corresponding to recursion.

In the remainder of this section, therefore, we will show that the lambda calculus is capable of expressing recursive functions without further extension. This is quite a remarkable feat, as the reader may verify by trying it before reading the following sections.

2.4.1 Recursive Functions and Y

Consider the following recursive definition of the factorial function:

```
FAC = (λn.IF (= n 0) 1 (* n (FAC (- n 1))))
```

The definition relies on the ability to name a lambda abstraction, and then to refer to this name inside the lambda abstraction itself. No such construct is provided by the lambda calculus. The problem is that lambda abstractions are *anonymous* functions, so they cannot name (and hence refer to) themselves.

We proceed by simplifying the problem to one in which recursion is expressed in its purest form. We begin with a recursive definition:

```
FAC = λn. (... FAC ...)
```

(We have written parts of the body of the lambda abstraction as '...' to focus attention on the recursive features alone.)

By performing a β-abstraction on FAC, we can transform its definition to:

```
FAC = (λfac. (λn. (... fac ...))) FAC
```

We may write this definition in the form:

```
FAC = H FAC                                   (2.1)
```

where

```
H = (λfac. (λn. (... fac ...)))
```

The definition of H is quite straightforward. It is an ordinary lambda abstraction and does not use recursion. The recursion is expressed solely by definition (2.1).

The definition (2.1) is rather like a mathematical equation. For example, to solve the mathematical equation

$$x^2 - 2 = x$$

we seek values of x which satisfy the equation (namely $x = -1$ and $x = 2$). Similarly, to solve (2.1) we seek a lambda expression for FAC which satisfies (2.1). As with mathematical equations, there may be more than one solution.

The equation (2.1)

```
FAC = H FAC
```

states that when the function H is applied to FAC, the result is FAC. We say that FAC is a *fixed point* (or *fixpoint*) of H. A function may have more than one fixed point. For example, both 0 and 1 are fixed points of the function

```
λx.* x x
```

which squares its argument.

To summarize our progress, we now seek a fixed point of H. It is clear that this can depend on H only, so let us invent (for now) a function Y which takes a function and delivers a fixed point of the function as its result. Thus Y has the behavior that

```
Y H = H (Y H)
```

and as a result Y is called a *fixpoint combinator*. Now, if we can produce such a Y, our problems are over. For we can now give a solution to (2.1), namely

```
FAC = Y H
```

which is a non-recursive definition of FAC. To convince ourselves that this definition of FAC does what is intended, let us compute (FAC 1). We recall the definitions for FAC and H:

```
FAC = Y H
H   = λfac.λn.IF (= n 0) 1 (* n (fac (- n 1)))
```

So

```
     FAC 1
=    Y H 1
=    H (Y H) 1
=    (λfac.λn.IF (= n 0) 1 (* n (fac (- n 1)))) (Y H) 1
→    (λn.IF (= n 0) 1 (* n (Y H (- n 1)))) 1
→    IF (= 1 0) 1 (* 1 (Y H (- 1 1)))
→    * 1 (Y H 0)
=    * 1 (H (Y H) 0)
=    * 1 ((λfac.λn.IF (= n 0) 1 (* n (fac (- n 1)))) (Y H) 0)
→    * 1 ((λn.IF (= n 0) 1 (* n (Y H (- n 1)))) 0)
→    * 1 (IF (= 0 0) 1 (* 0 (Y H (- 0 1))))
→    * 1 1
→    1
```

2.4.2 Y Can Be Defined as a Lambda Abstraction

We have shown how to transform a recursive definition of FAC into a non-recursive one, but we have made use of a mysterious new function Y. The property that Y must possess is

```
Y H = H (Y H)
```

and this seems to express recursion in its purest form, since we can use it to express all other recursive functions. Now here comes the magic: Y can be defined as a lambda abstraction, without using recursion!

```
Y = (λh. (λx.h (x x)) (λx.h (x x)))
```

To see that Y has the required property, let us evaluate

```
    Y H
=   (λh. (λx.h (x x)) (λx.h (x x))) H
↔   (λx.H (x x)) (λx.H (x x))
↔   H ((λx.H (x x)) (λx.H (x x)))
↔   H (Y H)
```

and we are home and dry.

For those interested in *polymorphic typing* (see Chapter 8), the only respect in which Y might be considered an 'improper' lambda abstraction is that the subexpression (λx.h (x x)) does not have a finite type.

The fact that Y can be defined as a lambda abstraction is truly remarkable from a mathematical point of view. From an implementation point of view, however, it is rather inefficient to implement Y using its lambda abstraction, and most implementations provide Y as a built-in function with the reduction rule

```
Y H → H (Y H)
```

We mentioned above that a function may have more than one fixed point, so the question arises of which fixed point Y produces. It seems to be the 'right' one, in the sense that the reduction sequence of (FAC 1) given above does mirror our intuitive understanding of recursion, but this is hardly satisfactory from a mathematical point of view. The answer is to be found in *domain theory*, and the solution produced by (Y H) turns out to be the unique *least fixpoint* of H [Stoy, 1981], where 'least' is used in a technical domain-theoretic sense.

2.5 The Denotational Semantics of the Lambda Calculus

There are two ways of looking at a function: as an algorithm which will produce a value given an argument, or as a set of ordered argument–value pairs.

The first view is 'dynamic' or *operational*, in that it sees a function as a sequence of operations in time. The second view is 'static' or *denotational*: the function is regarded as a fixed set of associations between arguments and the corresponding values.

In the previous three sections we have seen how an expression may be evaluated by the repeated application of reduction rules. These rules prescribe purely *syntactic* transformations on permitted expressions, without reference to what the expressions 'mean'; and indeed the lambda calculus can be regarded as a formal system for manipulating syntactic symbols. Nevertheless, the development of the conversion rules was based on our intuitions about abstract functions, and this has, in effect, provided us with an *operational semantics* for the lambda calculus. But what reason have we to suppose that the lambda calculus is an accurate expression of the idea of an abstract function?

To answer this question requires us to give a *denotational semantics* for the lambda calculus. The framework of denotational semantics will be useful in the rest of the book, so we offer a brief sketch of it in the remainder of this section.

2.5.1 The **Eval** Function

The purpose of the denotational semantics of a language is to assign a *value* to every *expression* in that language. An expression is a *syntactic* object, formed according to the syntax rules of the language. A value, by contrast, is an *abstract* mathematical object, such as 'the number 5', or 'the function which squares its argument'.

We can therefore express the semantics of a language as a (mathematical) function, **Eval**, from expressions to values:

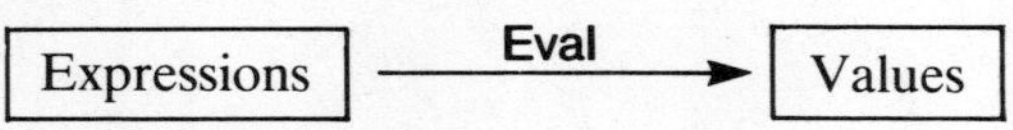

We can now write equations such as

Eval⟦ + 3 4 ⟧ = 7

This says 'the meaning (i.e. value) of the expression (+ 3 4) is the abstract numerical value 7'. We use bold double square brackets to enclose the argument to **Eval**, to emphasize that it is a syntactic object. This convention is widely used in denotational semantics. We may regard the expression (+ 3 4) as a *representation* or *denotation* of the value 7 (hence the term *denotational semantics*).

We will now give a very informal development of the **Eval** function for the lambda calculus. The task is to give a value for **Eval**⟦ E ⟧, for every lambda expression E, and we can proceed by direct reference to the syntax of lambda expressions (Figure 2.1), which gives the possible forms which E might take.

For the moment we will omit the question of constants and built-in functions, returning to it in Section 2.5.3. Suppose, then, that E is a variable, x. What should be the value of

Eval⟦ x ⟧

where x is a variable? Unfortunately, the value of a variable is given by its surrounding context, so we cannot tell its value in isolation. We can solve this problem by giving **Eval** an extra parameter, ρ, which gives this contextual information. The argument ρ is called an *environment*, and it is a function which maps variable names on to their values. Thus

Eval⟦ x ⟧ $\rho = \rho$ x

The notation $(\rho\ x)$, on the right-hand side, means 'the function ρ applied to the argument x'.

Next we treat applications. It seems reasonable that the value of $(E_1\ E_2)$ should be the value of E_1 applied to the value of E_2:

$$\mathbf{Eval}[\![\ E_1\ E_2\ ]\!]\ \rho = (\mathbf{Eval}[\![\ E_1\ ]\!]\ \rho)\ (\mathbf{Eval}[\![\ E_2\ ]\!]\ \rho)$$

The final case is that of a lambda abstraction. What should be the value of $(\mathbf{Eval}[\![\ \lambda x.E\ ]\!]\ \rho)$? It is certainly a function, and so we can fully define it by giving its value when applied to an arbitrary argument, a:

$$(\mathbf{Eval}[\![\ \lambda x.E\ ]\!]\ \rho)\ a$$

(Following our usual conventions about currying, we will omit the brackets in future.) The following statement sums up our intuitions about lambda abstractions:

> The value of a lambda abstraction, applied to an argument, is the value of the body of the lambda abstraction, in a context where the formal parameter is bound to the argument.

Formally, we write

$$\mathbf{Eval}[\![\ \lambda x.E\ ]\!]\ \rho\ a = \mathbf{Eval}[\![\ E\ ]\!]\ \rho[x{=}a]$$

where the notation $\rho[x{=}a]$ means 'the function ρ extended with the information that the variable x is bound to the value a'. More precisely:

$$\rho[x{=}a]\ x = a$$
$$\rho[x{=}a]\ y = \rho\ y$$

if y is a different variable from x.

That's it! Apart from constants and built-in functions, each of which require individual treatment, we have now provided a simple denotational semantics for the lambda calculus. Figure 2.5 summarizes our progress.

Needless to say, this account is greatly simplified (though hopefully not misleading). The main component that is missing is a description of the collection of all possible values which **Eval** can produce. This collection is called a *domain*, and it is quite a complicated structure, since it includes all the

$$\mathbf{Eval}[\![\ k\ ]\!]\ \rho = \text{<see Section 2.5.3>}$$
$$\mathbf{Eval}[\![\ x\ ]\!]\ \rho = \rho\ x$$
$$\mathbf{Eval}[\![\ E_1\ E_2\ ]\!]\ \rho = (\mathbf{Eval}[\![\ E_1\ ]\!]\ \rho)\quad(\mathbf{Eval}[\![\ E_2\ ]\!]\ \rho)$$
$$\mathbf{Eval}[\![\ \lambda x.E\ ]\!]\ \rho\ a = \mathbf{Eval}[\![\ E\ ]\!]\ \rho[x{=}a]$$

where	k	is a constant or built-in function
	x	is a variable
	E, E_1, E_2	are expressions

Figure 2.5 Denotational semantics of the lambda calculus

functions and data values that can be denoted by a lambda expression. The really serious complication is that, in view of the self-application required in the lambda abstraction for Y, the domain must include its own function space. Giving a sound theory to such domains is the purpose of *domain theory* [Scott, 1981].

We will take the existence and soundness of domain theory and denotational semantics for granted, and the framework they provide will prove to be quite useful. They are rich and beautiful areas of computer science, and Stoy [1981] is a good starting-point for further reading.

A note on notation: as we have seen, the environment ρ is an essential argument to **Eval**. Nevertheless, in all the situations where we use **Eval** in the rest of this book, ρ plays no significant role. For the sake of simplicity, we will therefore omit the argument ρ from now on – it could be restored by adding ρ to every call of **Eval**. For example, we will write

Eval⟦ E_1 ⟧ = **Eval**⟦ E_2 ⟧

where we should more correctly write

Eval⟦ E_1 ⟧ ρ = **Eval**⟦ E_2 ⟧ ρ

2.5.2 The Symbol ⊥

One of the most useful features of the theory we have described in this section is that it gives us a way to reason about the termination (or otherwise) of programs.

As remarked in Section 2.3, the reduction of an expression may not reach a normal form. What value should the semantics assign to such programs? All that we have to do is to include an element ⊥, pronounced 'bottom', in the value domain, which is the value assigned to an expression without a normal form:

Eval⟦ <expression with no normal form> ⟧ = ⊥

⊥ has a perfectly respectable mathematical meaning in domain theory, and, like the symbol 0 (which also stands for 'nothing'), its use often allows us to write down succinct equations instead of rambling words. For example, instead of saying 'the evaluation of the expression E fails to terminate', we can write

Eval⟦ E ⟧ = ⊥

2.5.3 Defining the Semantics of Built-in Functions and Constants

In this section we will see how to define the value of **Eval**⟦ k ⟧, where k is a constant or built-in function.

For example, what is the value of **Eval**⟦ * ⟧? It is certainly a function of two arguments, and we can define it by giving the value of this function applied to arbitrary arguments:

Eval⟦ $*$ ⟧ a b = a × b

This gives the meaning of the lambda calculus $*$ in terms of the mathematical operation of multiplication ×. The distinction between the $*$ and × is crucial: the $*$ is a syntactic expression in the lambda calculus, while × is the abstract mathematical operation. In the case of multiplication, the mathematical notation × differs from the program notation $*$, but in the case of addition (for example) the symbol + is used by both. This is a ready source of confusion, and we must keep a clear head!

We will use lower-case letters, such as a and b, to stand for values in semantic equations.

The equation given above is, however, an incomplete specification for $*$. We must define what $*$ does to each possible argument, *including* ⊥. The full set of equations should therefore be:

Eval⟦ $*$ ⟧ a b = a × b   if a≠⊥ and b≠⊥
Eval⟦ $*$ ⟧ ⊥ b = ⊥
Eval⟦ $*$ ⟧ a ⊥ = ⊥

The two new equations complete the definition of $*$, by specifying that if either argument of $*$ fails to terminate, then so does the application of $*$.

They are not the only possible set of equations for a multiplication operator. For example, here are the equations for a more 'intelligent' multiplication operator, #:

Eval⟦ # ⟧ a b = a × b   if a≠⊥ and a≠0 and b≠⊥
Eval⟦ # ⟧ 0 b = 0
Eval⟦ # ⟧ a ⊥ = ⊥   if a≠0
Eval⟦ # ⟧ ⊥ b = ⊥

These equations imply that # should evaluate its first argument and, if it is zero, return the result zero without examining the second argument at all; otherwise it behaves just like $*$. Using # instead of $*$ would cause the evaluation of some expressions to terminate when they would not have done so before.

The point of the example is that the semantic equations for a built-in function enable us to express subtle variations in its behavior, with a precision that is hard to achieve by giving reduction rules. The semantic equations for a function both specify the meaning of the function and imply its operational behavior (reduction rules).

Strictly speaking we should also provide equations such as

Eval⟦ 6 ⟧ = 6

where the '6' on the left-hand side is a lambda expression, and the '6' on the right-hand side is the abstract mathematical object. Ideally, we should distinguish the two kinds of '6' typographically, but common practice is to write them in the same way and distinguish them only by context. This applies to all constants and built-in functions. Thus we write

```
Eval[[ TRUE ]] = TRUE
Eval[[ IF ]]   = IF
Eval[[ + ]]    = +
```

and so on.

This is sloppy, but it saves clutter. For example, using this more relaxed notation, we could write the following semantic equations for the built-in function IF:

```
IF TRUE  a b = a
IF FALSE a b = b
IF ⊥     a b = ⊥
```

The use of = and the occurrence of ⊥ continue to remind us that we are looking at semantic equations rather than reduction rules.

2.5.4 Strictness and Laziness

We say that a function is *strict* if it is sure to need the value of its argument. This is a concept that will arise repeatedly in the book. Can we give a denotational definition of strictness?

If a function, f, is sure to need the value of its argument, and the evaluation of the argument will not terminate, then the application of f to the argument will certainly fail to terminate. This verbose, operational argument suggests the following concise, denotational, definition of strictness:

> DEFINITION
>
> A function f is *strict* if and only if
>
> f ⊥ = ⊥

The definition generalizes easily to functions of several arguments. For example, if g is a function of three arguments, then g is strict in its second argument if and only if

```
g a ⊥ c = ⊥
```

for all values of a and c.

If a function is non-strict, we say that it is *lazy*. Technically, this is an abuse of terminology, since lazy evaluation is an implementation technique which implements non-strict semantics. However, 'lazy' is such an evocative term that it is often used where 'non-strict' would be more correct.

2.5.5 The Correctness of the Conversion Rules

The conversion rules given earlier in this chapter express equivalences between lambda expressions. It is vital that these equivalences are mirrored in the denotational world. For example, using α-conversion we may write

$$(\lambda x.+\ x\ 1) \underset{\alpha}{\leftrightarrow} (\lambda y.+\ y\ 1)$$

Our hope is that both of these expressions mean the same thing or, more precisely, denote the same function, so that

$$\textbf{Eval}[\![\ \lambda x.+\ x\ 1\ ]\!] = \textbf{Eval}[\![\ \lambda y.+\ y\ 1\ ]\!]$$

In general, we hope that *conversion preserves meaning*, which we may state as follows:

$$E_1 \leftrightarrow E_2$$

implies

$$\textbf{Eval}[\![\ E_1\ ]\!] = \textbf{Eval}[\![\ E_2\ ]\!]$$

In other words, if E_1 is convertible to E_2 then the meaning of E_1 is certainly the same as the meaning of E_2. (As we will see in the next section, however, the reverse is not always true.) There is a burden of proof here, to show that the above statement always holds, given the conversion rules and the semantic function **Eval**. We will content ourselves with observing that proof is required, leaving the hard work to Stoy [1981].

Since the *reduction* rules (β-reduction and η-reduction) are a subset of the conversion rules, we certainly know that

$$E_1 \rightarrow E_2$$

implies

$$E_1 \leftrightarrow E_2$$

and hence

$$E_1 \rightarrow E_2$$

implies

$$\textbf{Eval}[\![\ E_1\ ]\!] = \textbf{Eval}[\![\ E_2\ ]\!]$$

2.5.6 Equality and Convertibility

In the previous section we saw that conversion preserves equality. But is the reverse true? In particular, does the equality of two expressions imply their interconvertibility? The answer is 'no', as the following example shows. Consider the two lambda abstractions, which we will call F_1 and F_2:

$$F_1 = (\lambda x.+\ x\ x)$$
$$F_2 = (\lambda x.*\ x\ 2)$$

It is clear that F_1 cannot be converted into F_2 using the conversion rules of the lambda calculus. To a mathematician, however, a function is a 'black box', and two functions are the same if (and only if) they give the same result for each possible argument. This sort of equality of functions is called *extensional equality*. The function denoted by F_1 and that denoted by F_2 are certainly (extensionally) equal, so we may write

$$\textbf{Eval}[\![F_1]\!] = \textbf{Eval}[\![F_2]\!]$$

So F_1 and F_2 are not interconvertible, but they do denote the same function.

To summarize the main conclusion:

If $\quad E_1 \leftrightarrow E_2$

then $\quad \textbf{Eval}[\![E_1]\!] = \textbf{Eval}[\![E_2]\!]$

but not necessarily the other way around.

We can therefore regard conversion as a weak form of reasoning about the equality of expressions. It can never cause us to believe that two expressions are equal when they are not, but it may not allow us to prove the equality of two expressions which are in fact equal. From this point of view, reduction is a still weaker form of inference.

2.6 Summary

A working understanding of the lambda calculus will prove extremely useful for the rest of the book, and in this chapter we have tried to give a compact summary of the material we will require. The treatment has necessarily been rather superficial, and the reader is again referred to Stoy [1981] or Barendregt [1984] for fuller treatments.

References

Barendregt, H.P. 1984. *The Lambda Calculus – Its Syntax and Semantics*, 2nd edition. North-Holland.

Church, A. 1941. *The Calculi of Lambda Conversion*. Princeton University Press.

Curry, H.B., and Feys, R. 1958. *Combinatory Logic*, Vol. 1. North-Holland.

Kennaway, J.R. 1984. *An Outline of Some Results of Staples on Optimal Reduction Orders in Replacement Systems*. CSA/19/1984. School of Information Systems, University of East Anglia. March.

Levy, J.J. 1980. Optimal reductions in the lambda calculus. In *Essays on Combinatory Logic*, pp. 159–92. Hindley and Seldin (editors). Academic Press.

Rosser, J.B. 1982. Highlights of the history of the lambda calculus. *Proceedings of the ACM Symposium on Lisp and Functional Programming, Pittsburgh*, pp. 216–25. August.

Schonfinkel, M. 1924. Uber die Bausteine der mathematischen Logik. *Mathematische Annalen*. Vol. 92, pp. 305–16.

Scott, D. 1981. *Lectures on a Mathematical Theory of Computation*. PRG-19. Programming Research Group, Oxford. May.

Staples, J. 1980a. Computation on graph-like expressions. *Theoretical Computer Science*. Vol. 10, pp. 171–85.

Staples, J. 1980b. Optimal evaluations of graph-like expressions. *Theoretical Computer Science*. Vol. 10, pp. 297–316.

Staples, J. 1980c. Speeding up subtree replacement systems. *Theoretical Computer Science*. Vol. 11, pp. 39–47.

Stoy, J.E. 1981. *Denotational Semantics*. MIT Press.

Welch, P. 1975. *Some Notes on the Martin–Lof Proof of the Church Rosser Theorem as Rediscovered by Park*. Computer Lab., University of Kent. October.

Three

TRANSLATING A HIGH-LEVEL FUNCTIONAL LANGUAGE INTO THE LAMBDA CALCULUS

In the next few chapters we will describe how to translate a high-level functional language into the lambda calculus.

We can regard this translation in two ways:

(i) As a description of the semantics of the language, giving the meaning of each of its constructs in terms of lambda expressions, whose meaning is well understood. This is precisely the approach taken by *denotational semantics* [Gordon, 1979].

(ii) As a step in the implementation of the high-level language, by expressing all its constructs in terms of the lambda notation.

For the sake of definiteness we use a subset of the language Miranda [Turner, 1985], but the techniques apply to any functional language. An introduction to Miranda can be found in the Appendix.

> **Disclaimer**
>
> In this book Miranda is used as an example of a modern functional programming language, to illustrate various points about the implementation of functional programming languages in general. This book is not intended to be a source of reference for the definition of Miranda. Note that:
>
> (i) Miranda has a number of features, both major and minor, which are not discussed here at all.
>
> (ii) The material about Miranda in this book was based on a prerelease version of the Miranda system and may therefore be inaccurate by the time it is published.
>
> The Miranda functional programming system is a product of Research Software Limited, and a full description of the language and its programming environment is in preparation by them.

3.1 The Overall Structure of the Translation Process

Miranda is a powerful, high-level functional language, providing a rich set of programming constructs. The purpose of the next few chapters is to demonstrate how some of these constructs can be translated into the lambda calculus. Specifically, we will discuss structured data types, pattern-matching, conditional equations and ZF expressions. Miranda includes a number of other constructs, such as abstract data types and structured data types with laws, which we will not study in this book.

Even so, the translation we describe is a substantial task, and we begin by outlining the structure of the translation process.

It might be possible to translate a program directly from Miranda into the lambda calculus, but this would be an extremely complicated translation, so we will take a more step-by-step approach. In order to do this, it is convenient to regard much of the translation as a process of successively *transforming* one program into another, until finally the result is a program in the lambda notation. (We are here using 'translation' to suggest a process which takes a program in one language and produces a program in another, while a 'transformation' produces a program in the *same* language.)

Two ways of organizing the translation then suggest themselves:

(i) We could perform most of the translation by successive transformations of one Miranda program into another, each transformation performing a simplification step. We would complete the process by translating the resulting (simple) Miranda program into the lambda calculus. The idea is that the earlier transformations would have done all the hard work, so the final step should consist of little more than a change of syntax.

(ii) Alternatively, we could begin the translation by performing a simple syntactic translation of the Miranda program into an enriched version of the lambda calculus. This enriched lambda calculus would include the ordinary lambda calculus as a subset, but would also include extra constructs, chosen so that the first step consists of little more than a change of syntax. Then we could do most of the hard work by successively transforming the expression into simpler and simpler forms, until it becomes an ordinary lambda expression, free from any of the extra constructs.

Initially, the first method looks more attractive than the second, because it does not require us to define a new language (the enriched lambda calculus). However, we choose to follow the second course of action for the following reasons:

(i) Miranda is designed to be a language for programmers, not compilers, and it lacks certain features that are desirable for a transformation-based compiler. (The particular features lacking are lambda abstractions and the ability to qualify any expression with local definitions. This is not a criticism of Miranda – it just has a different purpose.)

(ii) To a much greater extent than is the case for imperative languages, functional languages are largely syntactic variations of one another, with relatively few semantic differences. Using the second method allows the transformations we present to be applied easily to other languages, by altering only the translation of the high-level language into the enriched lambda calculus.

Figure 3.1 depicts the overall plan of action. We will use the term *ordinary lambda calculus* to refer to the language described in Chapter 2, and *enriched lambda calculus* to refer to the language introduced here.

The enriched lambda calculus is simply the ordinary lambda calculus augmented with extra constructs, chosen to allow an easy translation from Miranda. For each construct we will

(i) say what it looks like (give its syntax);
(ii) say what it means (give its semantics).

The semantics for each construct can be given by providing a simple transformation which shows how to express that construct in terms of the ordinary lambda calculus. Then we could, in principle, translate from Miranda into the ordinary lambda calculus by first translating into the enriched lambda calculus, and then using the semantics of each construct repeatedly to transform the expression into an ordinary lambda expression.

While this method generates correct results, far greater efficiency is attainable by using more complicated transformations, but we can always confirm their correctness by reference to the inefficient version.

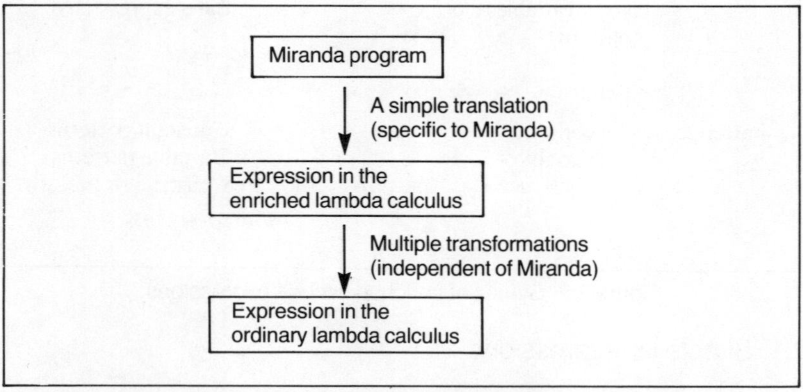

Figure 3.1 Translation of Miranda into the lambda calculus

3.2 The Enriched Lambda Calculus

The enriched lambda calculus is a superset of the ordinary lambda calculus, so that any expression in the ordinary lambda calculus is also an expression in the enriched lambda calculus. The syntax for function application, lambda abstractions, constants and built-in functions therefore remains exactly as described in Chapter 2. Likewise, all functions are written in prefix form, and the same conventions hold concerning brackets.

The only difference from the ordinary lambda calculus is the provision of four extra constructs. They are:

(i) let-expressions and letrec-expressions;
(ii) pattern-matching lambda abstractions;
(iii) the infix operator ▯;
(iv) case-expressions.

Of these, we will only describe the first here. The other three all concern pattern-matching, and cannot be defined before the discussion of pattern-matching itself. This is given in Chapter 4, and the remaining three constructs are defined there.

Figure 3.2 summarizes the syntax of the enriched lambda calculus for future reference.

```
<exp> ::= <constant>                                 Constants
       |  <variable>                                 Variables
       |  <exp> <exp>                                Applications
       |  λ <pattern> . <exp>                        Lambda abstractions
       |  let    <pattern> = <exp> in <exp>          Let-expressions
       |  letrec <pattern> = <exp>                   Letrec-expressions
                 ...
                 <pattern> = <exp>
          in <exp>
       |  <exp> ▯ <exp>                              Fat bar
       |  case <variable> of                         Case-expressions
          <pattern>  ⇒  <exp>
          ...
          <pattern>  ⇒ <exp>

<pattern> ::= <constant>                             Constant patterns
           |  <variable>                             Variable patterns
           |  <constructor> <pattern>                Constructor patterns
                            ...
                            <pattern>
```

Figure 3.2 Syntax of enriched lambda expressions

3.2.1 Simple let-expressions

One of the main constructs in any functional language is the *definition*, whereby a name is bound to a value. This mechanism is provided in the enriched lambda calculus, using let-expressions and letrec-expressions.

We begin by defining *simple* let-expressions. They are called 'simple' by contrast with *pattern-matching* let-expressions, which we deal with later. A simple let-expression has the following syntax:

```
let v = B in E
```

where the v is a variable, and B and E are expressions in the (enriched) lambda notation.

It introduces a definition for a variable v, which binds v to B in E. The definition is in scope with E but not B. We say that the 'v = B' is the *definition of the* let, the v is the variable *bound by the* let, and the B is the *definition body*.

For example, consider the following let-expression:

```
let x = 3 in (* x x)
```

Intuitively, the value of this expression is found by substituting 3 for x in the body (* x x), and then evaluating the body, giving the result 9:

```
   let x = 3 in (* x x)
→  * 3 3
→  9
```

A let-expression is an expression like any other, and can be used in the same way as any other expression. For example,

```
   + 1 (let x = 3 in (* x x))
→  + 1 (* 3 3)
→  + 1 9
→  10
```

For the same reason, let-expressions can be nested:

```
   let x = 3 in (let y = 4 in (* x y))
→  let y = 4 in (* 3 y)
→  * 3 4
→  12
```

As a matter of convenience, we also allow ourselves to write multiple definitions in the same let; thus:

```
let x = 3
    y = 4
in * x y
```

This expression means precisely the same as the previous one. We define a let-expression with several definitions to mean the same as the nested set of let-expressions which defines the same variables in the same order, one per let-expression. (Syntactically, it would have been possible to specify that multiple definitions are separated with semicolons, but layout will suffice for our purposes.)

Earlier in this section we developed an informal reduction rule for let-expressions. This involved *substitution* and is very reminiscent of the β-reduction rule, which also uses substitution. For example, to evaluate

```
(λx.* x x) 3
```

we substitute 3 for x in the body (* x x), and then evaluate the body.

Generalizing this idea, we can now define the semantics of a simple let-expression as follows:

```
(let v = B in E)  ≡  ((λv.E) B)
```

(We use the symbol ≡ to denote the equivalence of two expressions.) That is all that is needed to define its semantics! By repeated application of this equivalence, we could eliminate all simple let-expressions from an expression, in favor of lambda abstractions.

3.2.2 Simple letrec-expressions

The syntax of a *simple* letrec-expression is similar to that of a simple let-expression:

```
letrec v1 = E1
       v2 = E2
       ...
       vn = En
in
       E
```

where the v_i are variables, and E, E_1, . . ., E_n are expressions in the (enriched) lambda notation. We will sometimes abbreviate 'letrec-expression' to 'letrec' (and 'let-expression' to 'let'), where no ambiguity arises.

The term 'letrec' is short for 'let recursively', and it introduces possibly recursive bindings for a number of variables v_i. The difference between lets and letrecs is that the v_i are in scope in the E_i (as well as E) of a letrec. To take an example, the expression

```
letrec factorial = λn.IF (= n 0) 1 (* n (factorial (- n 1)))
in     factorial 4
```

defines a recursive function factorial, and applies it to the argument 4. The value of the expression is thus 24.

Like let-expressions, letrec-expressions can appear embedded anywhere in an expression. Unlike let-expressions, however, it is essential to allow multiple definitions in a letrec-expression, so as to permit mutual recursion. This is demonstrated by the following example:

```
letrec f = ...f...g...
       g = ...f...
in ...
```

Here, f refers to itself and g, and g refers to f. This cannot be transformed into a nested pair of letrecs, because then either g would not be in scope in the body of f, or vice versa.

It is easy to provide a semantics for a letrec with only a single definition, using the Y operator developed in Section 2.4. In particular,

```
(letrec v = B in E)  ≡  (let v = Y (λv.B) in E)
```

The use of Y renders the definition non-recursive, so we can then use a let-expression, whose semantics has already been defined.

The case of multiple definitions requires the use of pattern-matching, and so is postponed until Chapter 6.

3.2.3 Pattern-matching let- and letrec-expressions

We will also allow *patterns*, as well as variables, to appear on the left-hand side of definitions in lets and letrecs. We have not yet defined what a pattern is, so we postpone the topic until Chapter 6. However, a variable is just a simple form of pattern, so simple let(rec)-expressions are just simple forms of pattern-matching let(rec)-expressions.

3.2.4 Let(rec)s versus Lambda Abstractions

So far we have regarded the ordinary lambda calculus as the target language, into which we will transform the program, and let(rec)-expressions as intermediate embellishments. However, there are strong efficiency reasons for including *simple* let(rec)-expressions in the target language, rather than transforming them into the ordinary lambda calculus.

Specifically, the transformation of a let-expression

```
let v = B in E
```

into the application of a lambda abstraction

```
(λv.E) B
```

is using a sledgehammer (lambda abstraction) to crack a nut (let-expressions). The lambda abstration (λv.E) could be applied to many arguments, but it is in fact only ever applied to one, namely B. The generality of lambda abstraction is not required, and the special case (that of application to a unique argument) can be exploited by the more sophisticated compilers described later in this book.

This issue manifests itself in a number of ways:

(i) Miranda is a polymorphically typed language, and in Chapter 8 we give an algorithm for type-checking programs. Unfortunately, it is not possible to type-check the program once it has been transformed into the ordinary lambda calculus, but the addition of simple let(rec)-expressions is sufficient to solve the problem.

(ii) In all implementations except the very simplest, let-expressions can be evaluated very much more efficiently than the corresponding application of a lambda abstraction. This applies to all the implementations described from Chapter 14 onwards.

(iii) A related problem is that the transformation of letrec-expressions into the ordinary lambda calculus compels us to use Y to express recursion.

The resulting expression is not an efficient implementation, and a more sophisticated compiler may wish to handle recursion in a different way (see Chapter 14). Keeping the recursion explicit using letrec allows scope for these optimizations.

To summarize, all our implementations, except the very simplest, will require the program to be transformed into the ordinary lambda calculus augmented with simple let(rec)-expressions. This approach makes a dramatic contribution to the efficiency of the resulting implementations. On the other hand, little seems to be gained by augmenting the language still further.

3.3 Translating Miranda into the Enriched Lambda Calculus

A *program* consists of a set of definitions, together with an expression to be evaluated. To keep these two components of the program separate we will use a box, like this:

Set of definitions
Expression to be evaluated

For example, we could compute twice the square of 5 with the following Miranda program:

square n = n*n
2 * (square 5)

(Note: Miranda is an interactive language, and defines a 'program' to be a set of definitions, while the 'expression to be evaluated' is typed by the user. For the rest of this book, however, we will use 'program' to mean 'a set of definitions together with an expression to be evaluated'.) Proceeding informally, we can translate this Miranda program into the enriched lambda calculus quite easily, to produce the expression

```
let square = λn.* n n
in (* 2 (square 5))
```

We now introduce some notation to help describe the translation process. Consider the translation of the Miranda expression (2 * (square 5)) into the lambda expression (* 2 (square 5)). We may regard this translation process as a *function* **TE**, which takes the Miranda expression as its input, and produces the lambda expression as its output. We write the translation like this:

TE⟦ 2 * (square 5) ⟧ ≡ * 2 (square 5)

The double square brackets ⟦ ⟧ are used to enclose the Miranda expression, to emphasize that the argument to **TE** is a *syntactic* object. This convention was used in Chapter 2, but the difference on this occasion is that the result of the translation is a syntactic object also, and we use ≡ rather than = to remind us of this fact. We call **TE** a *translation scheme*.

We also need another translation scheme **TD**, which translates Miranda definitions into definitions suitable for a letrec. For example,

$$\mathbf{TD}[\![\ \mathsf{square\ n = n{*}n}\ ]\!] \equiv \mathsf{square} = \lambda \mathsf{n.{*}\ n\ n}$$

Here we see another reason for using ≡ when writing translation schemes: it avoids confusion with = symbols in the program being translated. We can now generalize the translation scheme as follows. Given the Miranda program

```
Definition₁
. . .
Definitionₙ
-----------
Expression
```

we generate the following (enriched) lambda expression:

```
letrec
  TD⟦ Definition₁ ⟧
  . . .
  TD⟦ Definitionₙ ⟧
in
  TE⟦ Expression ⟧
```

In the previous example we used a let instead of a letrec, but Miranda definitions are all potentially recursive, so we must use a letrec in general (later work will optimize this – Section 6.2.8).

What we have now done is to reduce the translation problem to one of defining the two translation schemes **TD** and **TE**. We will define them for simple cases in the succeeding two sections, and then lay out the plan of the next few chapters, which will extend them to cover more complicated cases.

For the moment, we completely avoid the question of declarations of new types and type-checking. The former will be introduced in Chapter 4 and the latter in Chapter 8.

3.4 The TE Translation Scheme

The translation scheme **TE** is a function, which takes a Miranda expression as its argument, and produces an equivalent lambda expression as its result, thus:

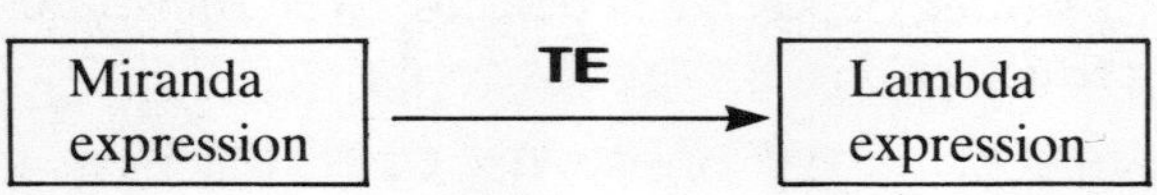

We will describe TE by case analysis, giving a rule for each possible form of a Miranda expression.

3.4.1 Translating Constants

To translate a constant or built-in function is straightforward, assuming that the lambda notation into which we are translating supports the same set of constants. The following rule is all that is required:

$$\mathsf{TE}[\![\ \mathsf{k}\ ]\!] \equiv \mathsf{k}$$

where k is a constant or built-in function name (we include all Miranda's operators, and literal constants in this category). Thus, for example

$$\mathsf{TE}[\![\ 5\ ]\!] \equiv 5$$
$$\mathsf{TE}[\![\ +\ ]\!] \equiv +$$

This translation assumes that all the constants and built-in functions have the same names in the lambda notation. It is straightforward to describe changes of name, however. For example, the following set of rules for TE translates the operators +, −, etc. in Miranda into PLUS, MINUS, etc.:

$$\mathsf{TE}[\![\ +\ ]\!] \equiv \mathsf{PLUS}$$
$$\mathsf{TE}[\![\ -\ ]\!] \equiv \mathsf{MINUS}$$

etc.

3.4.2 Translating Variables

An equally simple rule suffices to translate variables:

$$\mathsf{TE}[\![\ \mathsf{v}\ ]\!] \equiv \mathsf{v}$$

where v is a variable (including the names of user-defined functions and constructors).

3.4.3 Translating Function Applications

Function application in Miranda is denoted by juxtaposition, thus (f x). The same syntax is used in the lambda notation, so the rule for translation is simple:

$$\mathsf{TE}[\![\ \mathsf{E}_1\ \mathsf{E}_2\ ]\!] \equiv \mathsf{TE}[\![\ \mathsf{E}_1\ ]\!]\ \mathsf{TE}[\![\ \mathsf{E}_2\ ]\!]$$

where E_1 and E_2 are arbitrary Miranda expressions. In the case of certain common operators (such as +, etc.), Miranda provides infix syntax (that is, the operator is written between its operands). The translation rule to deal with these constructs is:

$$\mathsf{TE}[\![\ \mathsf{E}_1\ \mathsf{infix}\ \mathsf{E}_2\ ]\!] \equiv \mathsf{TE}[\![\ \mathsf{infix}\ ]\!]\ \mathsf{TE}[\![\ \mathsf{E}_1\ ]\!]\ \mathsf{TE}[\![\ \mathsf{E}_2\ ]\!]$$

where 'infix' is an infix operator, and E_1 and E_2 are arbitrary Miranda expressions. We must apply **TE** to 'infix' to accomplish any change of name (see above).

Furthermore, Miranda allows user-defined functions to be used as infix operators by prefixing their names with $. We can treat this case with the rule

```
TE[[ E1 $v E2 ]]  ≡  TE[[ v ]] TE[[ E1 ]] TE[[ E2 ]]
```

3.4.4 Translating Other Forms of Expressions

We shall consider two other forms of Miranda expression, namely

(i) list expressions such as [2,5,1];
(ii) ZF expressions.

We will deal with these in Chapters 4 and 7 respectively.

3.5 The TD Translation Scheme

The **TD** scheme takes a Miranda definition as its argument and produces a letrec definition as its result. We will only give a rather simplified **TD** scheme here, leaving a more powerful one for later chapters.

There are two cases that we can handle immediately, namely variable definitions and simple function definitions.

3.5.1 Variable Definitions

Consider the Miranda definition

```
v = 5*7
```

It can be translated very easily to

```
v = * 5 7
```

All that is required is to translate the body of the definition, using the **TE** scheme. In general:

```
TD[[ v = E ]]  ≡  v = TE[[ E ]]
```

where v is a variable and E is an expression.

3.5.2 Simple Function Definitions

We have already seen an example of translating a simple function definition, when we translated the Miranda definition

```
square n = n*n
```

TE⟦ Exp ⟧ transplates the expression Exp

```
TE[[ k ]]             ≡ k                    (assumes no name-changing)
TE[[ v ]]             ≡ v
TE[[ E1 E2 ]]         ≡ TE[[ E1 ]] TE[[ E2 ]]
TE[[ E1 infix E2 ]]   ≡ TE[[ infix ]] TE[[ E1 ]] TE[[ E2 ]]
TE[[ E1 $v E2 ]]      ≡ TE[[ v ]] TE[[ E1 ]] TE[[ E2 ]]

      where  k        is a literal constant or built-in operator
             v        is a variable
             E1       is an expression
             infix    is an infix operator
```

TD⟦ Def ⟧ translates the definition Def

```
TD[[ v = E ]]               ≡ v = TE[[ E ]]
TD[[ f v1 ... vn = E ]]     ≡ f = λv1...λvn.TE[[ E ]]

      where  v, v1, f   are variables
             E          is an expression
```

Figure 3.3 Translation schemes **TE** and **TD** (simple versions)

into the letrec definition

```
square = λn.* n n
```

The body of the definition is translated, and a lambda abstraction is generated around it. We can generalize this as follows:

```
TD[[ f v1 ... vn = E ]]   ≡   f = λv1 ... λvn.TE[[ E ]]
```

where f, v_1, ...,v_n are variables and E is an expression.

3.6 An Example

We have now shown how to translate a simple subset of Miranda into the enriched lambda notation. Our progress is summarized in Figure 3.3.

To illustrate the translation in action, consider the following Miranda program:

```
average a b = (a+b)/2
---------------------
average 2 (3*5)
```

This will be transformed to

```
letrec
  TD[[ average a b = (a+b)/2 ]]
in
  TE[[ average 2 (3+5) ]]
```

Application of the rules for **TE** gives

```
TE[[ average 2 (3+5) ]]
≡  TE[[ average ]] TE[[ 2 ]] TE[[ 3+5 ]]
≡  average 2 (TE[[ + ]] TE[[ 3 ]] TE[[ 5 ]])
≡  average 2 (+ 3 5)
```

Similarly, the rules for **TD** give

```
TD[[ average a b = (a+b)/2 ]]
≡  average = λa.λb.TE[[ (a+b)/2 ]]
≡  average = λa.λb.(TE[[ / ]] TE[[ a+b ]] TE[[ 2 ]])
≡  average = λa.λb.(/ (TE[[ + ]] TE[[ a ]] TE[[ b ]]) 2 )
≡  average = λa.λb.(/ (+ a b) 2)
```

Putting it all together gives the result of the translation:

```
letrec
  average = λa.λb.(/ (+ a b) 2)
in
  average 2 (+ 3 5)
```

To complete the example, let us transform the expression into the ordinary lambda calculus. Let us suppose that we spot that the letrec may be replaced with a let, because the definition is non-recursive (the method is described in Chapter 6). Then we can use the semantics of let-expressions to produce the ordinary lambda expression

```
(λaverage.(average 2 (+ 3 5))) (λa.λb.(/ (+ a b) 2))
```

You can see why we prefer to write programs in Miranda!

3.7 The Organization of Chapters 4–9

In the interests of simplicity, the equations for **TD** and **TE** given in Figure 3.3 are far from comprehensive. The rest of Part I of the book is devoted to filling in the details.

Chapter 4 introduces structured data objects, pattern-matching and conditional equations, and gives a simple translation into the enriched lambda calculus. This translation is rather inefficient, and Chapter 5 shows how pattern-matching can be compiled far more efficiently. Chapter 6 then shows how to transform all the constructs of the enriched lambda calculus into the ordinary lambda calculus.

Miranda contains constructs called ZF expressions (also known as list comprehensions). We discuss their translation in Chapter 7.

Finally, Miranda is a polymorphically typed language, and we have so far paid no attention to the question of type-checking. This is addressed in Chapters 8 and 9.

The organization of these chapters is depicted in Figure 3.4.

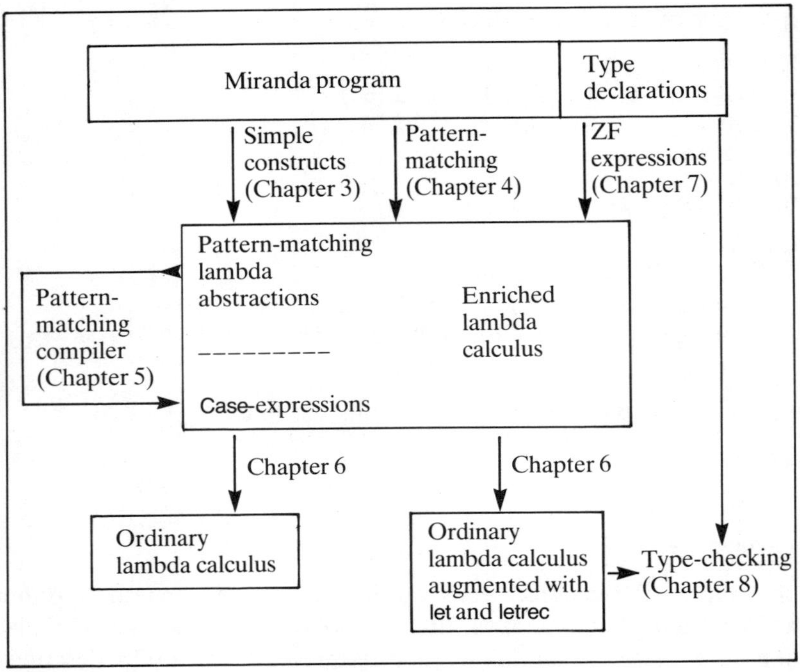

Figure 3.4 Organization of Chapters 4–8

References

Gordon, M.J.C. 1979. *The Denotational Description of Programming Languages*. Springer Verlag.

Turner, D.A. 1985. Miranda – a non-strict functional language with polymorphic types. In *Conference on Functional Programming Languages and Computer Architecture, Nancy*, pp. 1–16, Jouannaud (editor). LNCS 201. Springer Verlag.

Four

STRUCTURED TYPES AND THE SEMANTICS OF PATTERN-MATCHING

Simon L. Peyton Jones and Philip Wadler

This chapter concerns structured types, a powerful and general mechanism for defining data types, provided by several functional languages, including Miranda, ML and Hope. Intimately associated with structured types is a notational device known as pattern-matching, which is used by such languages for defining functions.

Section 4.1 gives a general introduction to structured types and pattern-matching. Section 4.2 begins with a more in-depth look at pattern-matching and conditional equations, and then introduces two new constructs in the enriched lambda calculus, ▯ and pattern-matching lambda abstractions. Using these constructs, we then show how to translate a general Miranda function definition into the enriched lambda calculus. Section 4.3 is devoted to providing a precise semantics for pattern-matching lambda abstractions.

We conclude in Section 4.4 by defining case-expressions, the last new construct of the enriched lambda calculus. This clears the way for Chapter 5, which will show how to transform pattern-matching lambda abstractions into case-expressions, thus giving a considerable gain in efficiency.

What in this chapter are called 'structured types' are called 'algebraic types' in Miranda, and 'free data types' by some others [Burstall and Goguen, 1982].

4.1 Introduction to Structured Types

Suppose that we wish to define binary trees with leaves that are numbers. In the notation of Miranda, this could be done by declaring a structured type tree as follows:

```
tree ::= LEAF num | BRANCH tree tree
```

(The symbol ::= identifies this as a type declaration.) This might be read as follows: 'a tree is either a LEAF, which contains a num, or a BRANCH, which contains a tree and a tree'. Here LEAF and BRANCH are called *constructors* of the type. Miranda requires that constructors (and only constructors) begin with an upper-case letter, but we will always write them entirely in upper case. LEAF has one *field*, of type num, and BRANCH has two, both of type tree. The number of fields associated with a constructor is called its *arity*; thus LEAF has arity 1 and BRANCH has arity 2.

Constructors can be used as functions, to create values of type tree. For example, the equation

```
tree1 = BRANCH (BRANCH (LEAF 1) (LEAF 2)) (LEAF 3)
```

defines tree1 to be a tree. Informally, this tree might be drawn as:

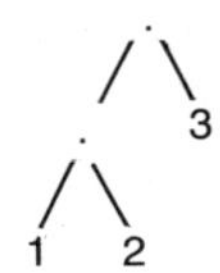

Constructors can also appear on the left-hand side of an equation, as in the following Miranda function definition:

```
reflect (LEAF n)          = LEAF n
reflect (BRANCH t1 t2) = BRANCH (reflect t2) (reflect t1)
```

For example, (reflect tree1) returns

```
BRANCH (LEAF 3) (BRANCH (LEAF 2) (LEAF 1))
```

A definition with patterns on the left-hand side, such as that of reflect, is said to use *pattern-matching* to perform *case analysis*. For example, in evaluating reflect t) there are two cases to choose from: t matches the pattern (LEAF n), or t matches the pattern (BRANCH t1 t2). If, say, t is (LEAF 1) then the first case is chosen, with n bound to 1. Much more will be said about pattern-matching later.

An important difference in the treatment of structured types in Miranda from that in ML or Hope, is that in Miranda constructor functions are lazy; that is, they do not evaluate their arguments. The components of a structured object are evaluated only when (and if) they are subsequently extracted and used, not when the object is built.

4.1.1 Type Variables

Type declarations may also contain type variables. For example, the definition of the type tree above may be rewritten to allow trees with leaves of any type:

```
tree * ::= LEAF * | BRANCH (tree *) (tree *)
```

Here * is called a *generic* (or *schematic*) *type variable*. The declaration could be read as follows: 'a tree of * is either a LEAF, which contains a *, or a BRANCH which contains a tree of * and a tree of *, for any type *'.

Leaves of any particular tree must all contain values of the same type, but different trees may have leaves of different types. Examples of trees and their types are

```
BRANCH (LEAF 1) (LEAF 2)          :: tree num
BRANCH (LEAF 'a') (LEAF 'b')      :: tree char
```

(The symbol :: is pronounced 'has type'.) Here, 'tree' is called a *type-forming operator*, since it takes a type (such as num or char) as an 'argument' and produces a type (respectively, (tree num) or (tree char)).

The repeated use of * on the right-hand side of the type declaration specifies that the two branches of a tree must be of uniform type. For example,

```
BRANCH (LEAF 1) (LEAF 'a')
```

is not legal, since it has leaves of mixed type. More will be said about types and type variables in Chapter 8.

4.1.2 Special Cases

This section shows how three 'built-in' types, namely lists, tuples and enumerated types, can be regarded as instances of general structured types.

4.1.2.1 Lists

Miranda has a special syntax to denote lists, but lists are just an instance of a general structured type. Lists could be defined as follows:

```
list * ::= NIL | CONS * (list *)
```

This type declaration defines the two new constructors NIL and CONS. Miranda's built-in syntax for lists could then be translated to use NIL and CONS, as follows:

[ ] is translated to NIL

(x:xs) is translated to (CONS x xs).

[x,y,z] is a Miranda abbreviation for (x:y:z:[ ]) and hence is translated to (CONS x (CONS y (CONS z NIL)))

[*] is translated to (list *)

TE⟦ : ⟧	≡	CONS
TE⟦ [ ] ⟧	≡	NIL
TE⟦ [E_1, E_2, . . ., E_n] ⟧	≡	CONS **TE**⟦ E_1 ⟧ **TE**⟦ [E_2, . . ., E_n] ⟧
TE⟦ (E_1, E_2) ⟧	≡	PAIR **TE**⟦ E_1 ⟧ **TE**⟦ E_2 ⟧
TE⟦ (E_1, E_2, E_3) ⟧	≡	TRIPLE **TE**⟦ E_1 ⟧ **TE**⟦ E_2 ⟧ **TE**⟦ E_3 ⟧
and so on		
TE⟦ True ⟧	≡	TRUE
TE⟦ False ⟧	≡	FALSE

Figure 4.1 Modifications to the **TE** scheme for lists, tuples and booleans

(Note: the last example is different from the others, because it describes a type-expression rather than a value-expression.)

We can conveniently perform this translation when translating from Miranda into the enriched lambda calculus; Figure 4.1 gives the required equations.

Notice that the elements of a list of type (list ∗) must all be of type ∗, but the number of elements in a list is not determined by its type. Thus (CONS 2 NIL) and (CONS 3 (CONS 6 NIL)) are both of type (list num), though they are of different lengths.

4.1.2.2 Tuples

Miranda also provides special syntax to denote tuples, and these also can be defined using a structured type. Tuples could be defined as follows:

```
pair       *  **            ::= PAIR       *  **
triple     *  **  ***       ::= TRIPLE     *  **  ***
quadruple  *  **  ***  **** ::= QUADRUPLE  *  **  ***  ****
```

Notice the difference between 'pair' and 'PAIR': the former is a type-forming operator, used only in type-expressions, while the latter is the constructor function of the type, used only in value-expressions.

As with lists, Miranda's special syntax can be translated as follows:

(x,y) is translated to (PAIR x y)
(x,y,z) is translated to (TRIPLE x y z)

and so on.

(∗,∗∗) is translated to (pair ∗ ∗∗)
(∗,∗∗,∗∗∗) is translated to (triple ∗ ∗∗ ∗∗∗)

Figure 4.1 gives the required equations.

Notice that a tuple may contain elements of mixed type; for example

```
(3, TRUE)       :: PAIR num bool
('a', (3, 2))   :: PAIR char (PAIR num num)
```

However, the type of a tuple completely determines the number and the types of its fields. For example, a pair always contains exactly two fields, a triple contains exactly three fields, and so on.

4.1.2.3 Enumerated types

The type declaration

```
color ::= VERMILLION | PUCE | LAVENDER
```

in which each constructor has zero fields, is just like an enumerated type in Pascal. Thus, we can define the type of boolean values:

```
bool ::= TRUE | FALSE
```

The usual functions on booleans can then be defined using pattern-matching; for example:

```
if TRUE  e1 e2 = e1
if FALSE e1 e2 = e2
```

Miranda uses the names 'True' and 'False' for its built-in truth-values.

4.1.2.4 Summary

Since it is easy to translate 'built-in' types like lists and tuples into equivalent structured types, then any implementation of a functional language that handles structured types will also handle these 'built-in' types for free. This can greatly simplify an implementation. Instead of implementing several type mechanisms, one for lists, one for tuples, one for enumerated types, and so on, we need only implement a single mechanism for structured types, and translate other types into structured types. Figure 4.1 gives the required equations.

4.1.3 General Structured Types

In general, the form of a structured type definition is:

$$
\begin{aligned}
T ::= \; & c_1\ T_{1,1}\ \ldots\ T_{1,r_1} \\
| \; & \ldots \\
| \; & c_n\ T_{n,1}\ \ldots\ T_{n,r_n}
\end{aligned}
$$

where the $T_{i,j}$ are types and the c_i are constructors of arity r_i. In the 'tree' example above, T was (tree $*$), c_1 was LEAF, $T_{1,1}$ was num, c_2 was BRANCH, $T_{2,1}$ was (tree $*$), and $T_{2,2}$ was (tree $*$).

Readers familiar with the mathematical operations for constructing types will recognize that the general type above can be written as the sum (that is, discriminated union):

$$T = T_1 + \ldots + T_n$$

where each T_i, for i from 1 to n, can be written as a product:

$$T_i = T_{i,1} \times T_{i,2} \times \ldots \times T_{i,r_i}$$

In other words, a structured type is a *sum-of-products*.

When n=1 we say that the type is a *product type*; the types (pair * **), (triple * ** ***) . . . are all product types. When n>1 we say that the type is a *sum type*, since it is the sum of more than one domain; the types (tree *), (list *), color and bool are all sum types. Thus a product type has exactly one constructor, and a sum type has two or more constructors.

We will often wish to distinguish between the constructors of product types and sum types. Just as we use the names c_i to stand for constructors of all types, we will use the name t to stand for the constructor of a product type, and the names s and s_i to stand for the constructors of a sum type (t suggests 'tuple' and s suggests 'sum').

(Note: we use lower-case letters to *stand for* constructors, to avoid confusion with the constructors *themselves*, which are written in upper case. Similarly, we use upper-case letters to stand for types, which are themselves written in lower case – see Section 4.1.)

(*Important*: at the time when this chapter was first written the semantics of Miranda provisionally specified that a structured type with only one constructor was a product type, as above. However, an alternative view is that a structured type with only one constructor should behave as a sum type with one component in the sum, and that product types (tuples) be treated as an independent construct. It now seems likely that Research Software Limited will follow this latter course in their definition of Miranda. As a consequence some of the statements made in this chapter about the semantics of structured types in Miranda may be incorrect. We draw the reader's attention to the caveat on page 37.)

4.1.4 History

As mentioned, structured types are a combination of sum types and product types, which have a long history in mathematics.

Landin's Iswim, one of the earliest functional languages, was described using a stylized form of English for defining structured types [Landin, 1966]. Burstall introduced a more formal notation for defining such types in NPL [Burstall, 1977]. Hope and ML have type systems based on separate sum and product types, whereas Miranda and Orwell have type systems based on a sum-of-product types.

Iswim also contained a simple form of pattern-matching, where one could write definitions such as

```
addPair (x,y) = x + y
```

However, the important idea of using pattern-matching for case analysis appears to have been developed independently by Burstall and Turner. Pattern-matching appeared in NPL and SASL, and was used to good effect in proofs by structural induction [Burstall, 1969] and program transformation [Burstall and Darlington, 1977]. It was incorporated into many later languages such as Hope, KRC, ML, Miranda and Orwell.

4.2 Translating Miranda into the Enriched Lambda Calculus

We must now demonstrate how to translate Miranda function definitions involving pattern-matching into the enriched lambda calculus. In the process of doing so we will introduce *pattern-matching lambda abstractions* and the ▯ operator, two of the constructs in the enriched lambda calculus whose explanation was postponed.

4.2.1 Introduction to Pattern-matching

We begin this section by illustrating some further aspects of pattern-matching, which have to be handled by an implementation. (Not all the illustrations should be taken as examples of good programming style. Some are expressly chosen to demonstrate all the possible nasty things that can happen!)

Recall the definition of reflect:

```
reflect (LEAF n)          = LEAF n
reflect (BRANCH t1 t2) = BRANCH (reflect t2) (reflect t1)
```

The terms (LEAF n) and (BRANCH t1 t2) occurring on the left-hand side of these equations are called *patterns*. When reflect is applied to an argument, the argument is first evaluated to see whether it *matches* the pattern (LEAF n) or (BRANCH t1 t2). It will certainly match one or the other, because the type-checker ensures that reflect is only applied to objects of type (tree $*$), for some type $*$. For example, if reflect is applied to an expression which evaluates to (BRANCH E_1 E_2), the second equation is selected, with t1 bound to E_1 and t2 bound to E_2.

In the preceding example, the order in which the equations were written was immaterial, but this is not always the case. Consider the Miranda function definition

```
factorial 0 = 1
factorial n = n * factorial (n-1)
```

The order of the equations in this definition is significant. In the evaluation of (factorial x), there are two cases to choose from: either x matches 0 (that is, x evaluates to 0), so the first equation is chosen, or it does not, so the second case is chosen with n bound to x. The equations are tried out one at a time, from top to bottom. If they had been written in the other order then the first equation would always match. In this situation we say that the patterns *overlap*. (As we shall see in Chapter 5, there are good reasons to avoid writing overlapping patterns, but occasionally they prove useful.)

Another point, illustrated by the first factorial equation, is that a pattern may consist of a literal constant, such as a number or character.

As another example, consider the Miranda function definition

```
lastElt (x:[])  = x
lastElt (x:xs)  = lastElt xs
```

The function call (lastElt xs) returns the last element of the list xs. Again, the order of the equations is significant, since the patterns overlap. Furthermore, the first pattern is an example of a *nested* pattern, in which the pattern [] is nested inside the pattern (x:[]). Finally, the equations are not exhaustive, since neither pattern matches the argument []. If lastElt is applied to [] some sort of error should be reported.

Pattern-matching can apply to several arguments, as the following Miranda definition shows:

```
xor False y     = y
xor True  False = True
xor True  True  = False
```

Another feature of Miranda that is closely connected with pattern-matching is *conditional equations*, which control the selection of *alternatives* by the use of *guards*. We could, for example, rewrite the factorial function in the following way:

```
factorial n = 1,            n=0
            = n * factorial (n-1)
```

A single left-hand side governs several alternatives, which together constitute the right-hand side. In this case there is only one guard, namely the boolean-valued expression 'n=0', which appears following a comma. Guards are evaluated one at a time, beginning at the top, and when a guard evaluates to True, the corresponding alternative expression is selected. The guard may be omitted in the final right-hand side, giving an 'otherwise' case (equivalent to a guard of True).

The factorial example shows, incidentally, that a constant appearing in a pattern can easily be eliminated by replacing it with a variable and adding a guard to the equation instead.

Conditional equations interact with pattern-matching, as demonstrated in the next example. The function funnyLastElt returns the last element of its argument list, except that if a negative element is encountered then it is returned instead:

```
funnyLastElt (x:xs) = x,        x<0
funnyLastElt (x:[]) = x
funnyLastElt (x:xs) = funnyLastElt xs
```

Pattern-matching proceeds, as usual, from top to bottom; when a left-hand side matches the argument, the guarded alternative(s) are tried, from top to bottom. If none of the guards is True, then pattern-matching continues, starting with the next equation. Applying funnyLastElt to the list [1,2] would cause this behavior, since the first equation would match, but the guard fails, so the second and then third equations are tried.

Finally, variables may be repeated on the left-hand side of an equation. For example, the function noDups eliminates adjacent duplicate elements in a list:

```
noDups []        = []
noDups [x]       = [x]
noDups (x:x:xs)  = noDups (x:xs)
noDups (x:y:ys)  = x : noDups (y:ys)
```

The third equation matches only if the first two elements of the argument list are equal; the repeated use of x on the left-hand side implies the equality condition.

We may summarize the features that the implementation must support as follows:

(i) overlapping patterns;
(ii) constant patterns;
(iii) nested patterns;
(iv) multiple arguments;
(v) non-exhaustive sets of equations;
(vi) conditional equations;
(vii) repeated variables.

Given these complications it is unwise to rely on a purely intuitive understanding of what a function definition using pattern-matching means. The rest of this section and the next is therefore devoted to providing a formal semantics of pattern-matching.

4.2.2 Patterns

First of all, we will need a precise definition of patterns.

DEFINITION

A pattern p is:
either a variable v,
or a constant k, such as a number, a character, a boolean and so on.
or a constructor pattern, of the form (c p_1 ... p_r) where c is a constructor of arity r, and p_1, ..., p_r are themselves patterns.

All of the variables in a pattern should be distinct.

A pattern of the form (s p_1 ... p_r), where s is a sum constructor, is called a *sum-constructor pattern*, or *sum pattern*. A pattern of the form (t p_1 ... p_r), where t is a product constructor, is called a *product-constructor pattern*, or *product pattern*.

Note: according to this definition, patterns may not contain repeated variables, although Miranda allows them to do so. This point is discussed in Section 4.2.7.

Here are some examples of patterns:

```
x
3
LEAF n
BRANCH (LEAF n) t
CONS x xs                written (x:xs) in Miranda
CONS x (CONS 3 NIL)      written [x,3] in Miranda
PAIR x 4                 written (x,4) in Miranda
```

The term (PAIR z z) is not a pattern, because it contains a repeated variable. The term (CONS x) is not a pattern, because the CONS does not have enough arguments.

Miranda allows patterns with repeated variables, like (PAIR z z) but the patterns defined here do not. This is discussed in Section 4.2.7.

A constructor pattern is *simple* if it has the form (c $v_1 \ldots v_r$), where $v_1, \ldots, v_r$ are distinct variables. If a constructor pattern is not simple it is *nested*.

4.2.3 Introducing Pattern-matching Lambda Abstractions

Up to now we have translated function definitions into the lambda calculus using the following rule:

$$\textbf{TD}[\![\ f\ v_1 \ldots v_n = E\ ]\!] \equiv f = \lambda v_1 \ldots \lambda v_n.\textbf{TE}[\![\ E\ ]\!]$$

where $v_1, \ldots, v_n$ are variables. Temporarily restricting our attention to functions of a single variable, we could derive the less general rule

$$\textbf{TD}[\![\ f\ v = E\ ]\!] \equiv f = \lambda v.\textbf{TE}[\![\ E\ ]\!]$$

By analogy, given the function definition

$$f\ p = E$$

(where p is a pattern), it seems plausible to translate it using the rule

$$\textbf{TD}[\![\ f\ p = E\ ]\!] \equiv f = \lambda p.\textbf{TE}[\![\ E\ ]\!]$$

This is not quite right yet, because we must remember to translate the pattern, so that Miranda's list notation is translated into uses of CONS and NIL (and likewise for tuples and booleans). Fortunately, the syntax of patterns is a subset of that of expressions, so we can use the **TE** scheme.

$$\textbf{TD}[\![\ f\ p = E\ ]\!] \equiv f = \lambda\textbf{TE}[\![\ p\ ]\!].\textbf{TE}[\![\ E\ ]\!]$$

For example, consider the Miranda function definition for fst:

```
fst (x,y) = x
```

Using the rule above gives:

$$\textbf{TD}[\![\ fst\ (x,y) = x]\!] \equiv f = \lambda(\text{PAIR}\ x\ y).x$$

This introduces a new sort of lambda abstraction, a *pattern-matching lambda abstraction*, which has the form (λp . E) where p is a pattern. This leaves us with two questions:

(i) How can we translate a general Miranda function definition into pattern-matching lambda abstractions?
(ii) What, exactly, does (λp . E) mean?

We discuss the first in the remainder of this section, leaving the second for the next section.

4.2.4 Multiple Equations and Failure

Consider first a Miranda function definition of the form

```
f p₁ = E₁
f p₂ = E₂
...
f pₙ = Eₙ
```

Intuitively, we expect the semantics to be 'try the first equation, and if that fails try the second, and so on'. This introduces the idea that a pattern-match might *fail*. Such failure does not necessarily indicate an error, since there might be a subsequent equation which would match. Hence, we introduce a new built-in value FAIL, which is returned when a pattern-match fails.

With the aid of this idea, we can translate the definition of f into the following enriched lambda calculus expression:

```
f = λx.( ((λp₁'.E₁') x)
         ▯ ((λp₂'.E₂') x)
         ...
         ▯ ((λpₙ'.Eₙ') x)
         ▯ ERROR)
```

where x is a new variable name that does not occur free in any E_i, the expressions E_i' are the result of translating the E_i, and the patterns p_i' are the result of translating the p_i. The new definition of f can be read 'try to apply ($\lambda p_1' . E_1'$) to x, and if that succeeds return its result; otherwise try ($\lambda p_2' . E_2'$), and so on; if they all fail, return ERROR'.

Here ERROR is meant to be a special value whose evaluation indicates an error, an event which should never occur.

The function ▯ is an infix function, whose behavior is described by the semantic equations:

```
a    ▯ b = a        if a≠⊥ and a≠FAIL
FAIL ▯ b = b
⊥    ▯ b = ⊥
```

Operationally, ▯ evaluates its left argument; if the evaluation terminates and yields something other than FAIL, then ▯ returns that value (first rule); if it evaluates to FAIL, ▯ returns its right argument (second rule); if the evaluation of the left argument fails to terminate, then so does the application of ▯ (third rule).

It is easy to verify that ▯ is an *associative* operator, and has *identity* FAIL. Its associativity means that we may write expressions such as (E_1 ▯ E_2 ▯ E_3) without ambiguity. It is extremely convenient to write ▯ *between* its operands (that is, infix) but, since all functions are written prefix in the lambda calculus, we are forced to dignify ▯ by making it one of the new constructs of the enriched lambda calculus. The sole reason for doing so is notational.

As an example of the suggested translation in action, recall the definition of the reflect function:

```
reflect (LEAF n)          = LEAF n
reflect (BRANCH t1 t2) = BRANCH (reflect t2) (reflect t1)
```

This would be translated to:

```
reflect = λt.( ((λ(LEAF n).LEAF n) t)
               ▯ ((λ(BRANCH t1 t2).BRANCH (reflect t2) (reflect t1)) t)
               ▯ ERROR)
```

In this case, of course, ERROR can never be returned, since one of the previous pattern-matches will succeed. This is not always the case, as the following example shows. Consider the Miranda definition of hd, which extracts the first element of a list:

```
hd (x:xs) = x
```

It would be translated to

```
hd = λxs'.(((λ(CONS x xs).x) xs') ▯ ERROR)
```

If hd is applied to NIL, then ERROR will be the result. (We have used xs′ as the formal parameter of the lambda abstraction, to avoid confusion with the xs in the pattern. Technically, however, there would be no problem with using xs, or any other variable, since hd has no free variables.)

4.2.5 Multiple Arguments

Functions with multiple arguments are easily handled. As we recalled earlier, the basic approach is to translate a function of several arguments using the rule

$$\mathbf{TD}[\![\ f\ v_1\ \ldots\ v_n = E\ ]\!] \ \equiv\ f = \lambda v_1 \ldots \lambda v_n.\mathbf{TE}[\![\ E\ ]\!]$$

Combining this with the approach of the previous section suggests that we should translate the definition

$$f\ p_1\ p_2\ \ldots\ p_m = E$$

where p_1, . . ., p_m are patterns, into

$$f = \lambda v_1 \ldots \lambda v_m . (((\lambda p_1' \ldots \lambda p_m' . E')\ v_1\ \ldots\ v_m)\ \text{[]}\ \text{ERROR})$$

where v_1, . . ., v_m are new variables that do not occur free in E, the p_i' are the results of translating the p_i, and E′ is the result of translating E. The only new complication is that we must specify that happens in case of failure. Suppose f is applied to m arguments, and the first pattern-match fails:

$$(\lambda p_1' \ldots \lambda p_m' . E')\ E_1\ E_2 \ldots E_m \;\rightarrow\; \text{FAIL}\ E_2 \ldots E_m$$

Then we want the whole expression to fail, so we need to add a reduction rule for FAIL:

$$\text{FAIL}\ E \;\rightarrow\; \text{FAIL}$$

Now we can continue reduction:

$$\text{FAIL}\ E_2\ E_3 \ldots E_m \;\rightarrow\; \text{FAIL}\ E_3 \ldots E_m \;\rightarrow\; \ldots \;\rightarrow\; \text{FAIL}$$

The translation is readily extended for the case when f is defined by several equations. To see an example of this in action, consider the definition of xor given above:

```
xor False y     = y
xor True  False = True
xor True  True  = False
```

Combining the rules of this section and the last allows us to transform this to

(Notice that the arguments are matched from left to right)

```
xor = λx.λy.( ((λFALSE.λy.y) x y)
              [] ((λTRUE.λFALSE.TRUE) x y)
              [] ((λTRUE.λTRUE.FALSE) x y)
              [] ERROR)
```

4.2.6 Conditional Equations

Next, we describe how to translate conditional equations into the enriched lambda calculus. Consider the following Miranda definition:

```
gcd a b = gcd (a-b) b, a>b
        = gcd a (b-a), a<b
        = a,           a=b
```

It is easy to see that the right-hand side of this definition could be translated to

```
(IF (> a b) (gcd (- a b) b)
(IF (< a b) (gcd a (- b a))
(IF (= a b) a FAIL)))
```

Notice that if all the guards fail, then FAIL is returned by the nested IF expression. (In the case of gcd this can never occur, and a very clever compiler might be able to discover this fact and optimize the last IF.) In a more complicated definition, the failure of all the guards would cause the next equation to be tried (see example below).

Regarding all of an equation after the first = sign as a 'right-hand side', we can now give a new translation scheme, **TR**, which translates right-hand sides:

> **TR**[[rhs]] translates the right-hand side of a definition
>
> $$\textbf{TR}\left[\!\left[\begin{array}{l} \quad A_1,\ G_1 \\ = A_2,\ G_2 \\ \quad \ldots \\ = A_n,\ G_n \end{array}\right]\!\right] \equiv \begin{array}{l} (\text{IF } \textbf{TE}[\![\ G_1\ ]\!]\ \textbf{TE}[\![\ A_1\ ]\!] \\ (\text{IF } \textbf{TE}[\![\ G_2\ ]\!]\ \textbf{TE}[\![\ A_2\ ]\!] \\ \ldots \\ (\text{IF } \textbf{TE}[\![\ G_n\ ]\!]\ \textbf{TE}[\![\ A_n\ ]\!]\ \text{FAIL})\ \ldots)) \end{array}$$
>
> where A_i is an expression and G_i is a boolean-valued expression.

Now we can use **TR** instead of **TE** to translate the right-hand sides of function definitions. As an example, recall the definition of funnyLastElt:

```
funnyLastElt (x:xs)  = x,        x<0
funnyLastElt (x:[])  = x
funnyLastElt (x:xs)  = funnyLastElt xs
```

We can now translate it to

```
funnyLastElt = λv.( ((λ(CONS x xs).IF (< x 0) x FAIL) v)
                  [] ((λ(CONS x NIL).x) v)
                  [] ((λ (CONS x xs).funnyLastElt xs) v)
                  [] ERROR)
```

If the first equation matches, but the guard fails, then the IF returns FAIL, and the next equation is tried.

In Miranda, the final guard G_n may be omitted, which is equivalent to giving a final guard of True. In this case, the innermost IF is of the form

```
IF TRUE E1 FAIL
```

which can be optimized to

```
E1
```

For example, the definition of factorial

```
factorial n = 1,                    n=0
            = n * factorial (n-1)
```

would be translated to

```
factorial = λv.( ((λn.IF (= n 0) 1 (* n (factorial (- n 1)))) v)
               [] ERROR)
```

This can be simplified further, since the pattern-match cannot fail, and this special case will be spotted by the transformations of Chapter 5.

4.2.7 Repeated Variables

It appears at first that it is easy to use a conditional equation to eliminate repeated variables, by introducing a new variable name to replace one of the occurrences of the repeated variable, and adding an appropriate equality condition. For example, we could rewrite the definition of noDups (given in Section 4.2.1) thus:

```
noDups []         = []
noDups [x]        = [x]
noDups (x:y:ys) = noDups (y:ys), x=y
noDups (x:y:ys) = x : noDups (y:ys)
```

(The last two equations could now be combined into a conditional equation with two alternatives.) Unfortunately, this approach occasionally conflicts with the left-to-right rule originally given for pattern-matching. For example, given the following definition:

```
nasty x x True = 1
nasty x y z    = 2
```

consider the evaluation of

```
nasty bottom 3 False
```

where the evaluation of bottom fails to terminate (for example, bottom could be defined by the degenerate equation: bottom = bottom). We might expect that the evaluation (nasty bottom 3 False) would not terminate, since we will try to evaluate bottom in order to compare it with 3. However, suppose we transformed the definition of nasty to use a conditional equation:

```
nasty' x y True = 1,    x = y
nasty' x y z    = 2
```

Now, if we evaluate (nasty' bottom 3 False), bottom will match x and 3 will match y, but the match of True against False will fail, so the second equation will be tried, and deliver the answer 2. Hence, nasty and nasty' behave differently, and the transformation is invalid. (Note: nasty and nasty' also behave differently for expressions such as (nasty 1 2 bottom).)

There is a further complication raised by repeated variables. Consider the function multi:

```
multi p q q p = 1
multi p q r s = 2
```

Should we compare the first and fourth arguments, and then compare the second and third arguments, or the other way around? The order of comparison is important, because it affects termination; consider (multi bottom 2 3 4).

This section has shown that repeated variables in a pattern are not as straightforward as at first appeared (the examples were suggested by Simon

Finn of the University of Stirling). To simplify the rest of this chapter we will therefore side-step these complications, by restricting our attention to a subset of Miranda which does not allow repeated variables in a pattern. We lose no expressive power thereby, though we do lose some notational convenience.

4.2.8 Where-clauses

Miranda allows the right-hand side of a definition to be qualified with a where-clause. For example,

```
sumsq x y = xsq + ysq
            where
               xsq = x*x
               ysq = y*y
```

It is intuitively clear that this could be translated to

```
sumsq = λx.λy.(let xsq = * x x
                   ysq = * y y
               in
                   (+ xsq ysq))
```

where we use a let-expression instead of a where-clause. In general, the definitions in a where-clause may be mutually recursive, so we have to use a letrec-expression instead. This will be optimized in Section 6.2.8.

Finally, the scope of a where-clause may include a set of alternatives and guards in a conditional equation:

```
gcd a b = gcd diff b,       a>b
        = gcd a (-diff),    a<b
        = a,                a=b
          where
            diff = a-b
```

TR⟦ rhs ⟧ translates the right-hand side of a definition

```
TR ⟦    A1, G1  ⟧  ≡  letrec TD⟦ D1 ⟧
   ⟦ =  ...     ⟧            ...
   ⟦ =  An, Gn  ⟧            TD⟦ Dm ⟧
   ⟦ where      ⟧     in
   ⟦    D1      ⟧            (IF TE⟦ G1 ⟧ TE⟦ A1 ⟧
   ⟦    ...     ⟧            ...
   ⟦    Dm      ⟧            (IF TE⟦ Gn ⟧ TE⟦ An ⟧ FAIL) ...)
```

If G_n is absent, or True, then the final IF-expression should be replaced by **TE**⟦ A_n ⟧

where A_i is an expression
G_i is a boolean-valued expression
D_i is a definition

Figure 4.2 The final **TR** translation scheme

The scope of the definition of diff includes all the alternatives and guards.

Figure 4.2 gives the final **TR** translation scheme, which translates right-hand sides, using a letrec to translate a where-clause.

4.2.9 Patterns on the Left-hand Side of Definitions

So far we have only described how to translate *function* definitions, but Miranda also allows a *pattern* to appear on the left-hand side of a definition. For example, consider the following Miranda definition:

```
addPair w = x + y
            where (x,y) = w
```

The product pattern (x,y) appears on the left-hand side of the definition in the where-clause. It implies that w evaluates to a pair, and it binds the names x and y to the components of w.

As mentioned in Section 3.2.3, we also allow general patterns to appear on the left-hand side of definitions in a let(rec). This extension allows us to make a simple translation of addPair to

```
addPair = λw.(letrec (PAIR x y) = w in (+ x y))
```

The hard work of dealing with patterns on the left-hand side of definitions is now carried out by transforming this letrec into the ordinary lambda calculus, which is described in Section 6.2. The modification required to **TD** is very simple:

TD⟦ p = R ⟧ ≡ **TE**⟦ p ⟧ = **TR**⟦ R ⟧

where p is a pattern and R is a right-hand side.

4.2.10 Summary

We have now completed the development of the translation of a significant subset of Miranda into the enriched lambda calculus. The final translation schemes, summarized in Figures 4.2, 4.3 and 4.4, look rather forbidding, but this is because of their generality rather than their complexity.

4.3 The Semantics of Pattern-matching Lambda Abstractions

Having described how to translate from Miranda into a language involving pattern-matching lambda abstractions, we now give the semantics of pattern-matching lambda abstractions of the form (λp.E).

We will do so by devoting a subsection to each form of the pattern, p: variable, constant, sum-constructor and product-constructor.

TE⟦ Exp ⟧ translates the expression Exp

TE⟦ : ⟧	≡	CONS
TE⟦ [ ] ⟧	≡	NIL
TE⟦ [E_1, E_2, ..., E_n] ⟧	≡	CONS **TE**⟦ E_1 ⟧ **TE**⟦ [E_2, ..., E_n] ⟧
TE⟦ (E_1, E_2) ⟧	≡	PAIR **TE**⟦ E_1 ⟧ **TE**⟦ E_2 ⟧
TE⟦ (E_1, E_2, E_3) ⟧	≡	TRIPLE **TE**⟦ E_1 ⟧ **TE**⟦ E_2 ⟧ **TE**⟦ E_3 ⟧
and so on		
TE⟦ True ⟧	≡	TRUE
TE⟦ False ⟧	≡	FALSE
TE⟦ k ⟧	≡	k
TE⟦ v ⟧	≡	v
TE⟦ E_1 E_2 ⟧	≡	**TE**⟦ E_1 ⟧ **TE**⟦ E_2 ⟧
TE⟦ E_1 infix E_2 ⟧	≡	**TE**⟦ infix ⟧ **TE**⟦ E_1 ⟧ **TE**⟦ E_2 ⟧
TE⟦ E_1 \$v E_2 ⟧	≡	**TE**⟦ v ⟧ **TE**⟦ E_1 ⟧ **TE**⟦ E_2 ⟧

where k is a literal constant or built-in operator
v, v_i are variables
E, E_i are expressions
infix is an infix operator

Figure 4.3 The final **TE** translation scheme

TD⟦ Def ⟧ translates the definition Def

TD⟦ p = R ⟧ ≡ **TE**⟦ p ⟧ = **TR**⟦ R ⟧

TD⟦ f $p_{1,1}$ ... $p_{1,m}$ = R_1
. . . .
f $p_{n,1}$ ... $p_{n,m}$ = R_n ⟧

≡ f = ($\lambda v_1 \ldots \lambda v_m$.((($\lambda$**TE**⟦ $p_{1,1}$ ⟧...λ**TE**⟦ $p_{1,m}$ ⟧. **TR**⟦ R_1 ⟧) v_1 ... v_m)
▯ ...
▯ ((λ**TE**⟦ $p_{n,1}$ ⟧...λ**TE**⟦ $p_{n,m}$ ⟧. **TR**⟦ R_n ⟧) v_1 ... v_m)
▯ ERROR))

where f is a variable
v_i is a variable not free in any R_j
$p_{i,j}$ is a pattern
R is a right-hand side
R_i is a right-hand side

Figure 4.4 The final **TD** translation scheme

4.3.1 The Semantics of Variable Patterns

If the pattern p is a variable v, then the pattern-matching lambda abstraction (λp.E) is just an ordinary lambda abstraction (λv.E), whose semantics have already been discussed in Section 2.5.

4.3.2 The Semantics of Constant Patterns

To describe the semantics of constant patterns we must specify the value of

Eval⟦ λk.E ⟧

where k is a constant. Its value is certainly a function, so we can specify it by giving the value of

Eval⟦ λk.E ⟧ a

for any argument a. There are three possibilities: either a is the same as k, or it is ⊥, or it is something else. This leads to the following semantic equations:

Eval⟦ λk.E ⟧ a = **Eval**⟦ E ⟧ if a = **Eval**⟦ k ⟧
Eval⟦ λk.E ⟧ a = FAIL if a ≠ **Eval**⟦ k ⟧ and a ≠ ⊥
Eval⟦ λk.E ⟧ ⊥ = ⊥

The first equation says that if (λk.E) is applied to something that evaluates to k, then the result comes from evaluating E. The second equation says that the result is FAIL if the argument evaluates to anything else, and the third equation specifies that, if the evaluation of the argument fails to terminate, then so does the whole application. As usual, these semantic equations specify reduction rules by implication. Thus, for example

(λ1.+ 3 4) 1 → + 3 4
(λ1.+ 3 4) 2 → FAIL

It is also possible to regard constants as sum-constructors of arity zero, as outlined in Section 4.1.2.3, in which case the rules of this section become a special case of those of the next.

4.3.3 The Semantics of Sum-constructor Patterns

Next, we consider the case of constructor patterns, of the form (s p_1 ... p_r). Initially we will only consider sum patterns, since product patterns turn out to require special treatment. Here are the semantic rules for such patterns:

Eval⟦ λ(s $p_1 \ldots p_r$).E ⟧ (s $a_1 \ldots a_r$) = **Eval**⟦ λ$p_1 \ldots$λp_r.E ⟧ $a_1 \ldots a_r$
Eval⟦ λ(s $p_1 \ldots p_r$).E ⟧ (s′ $a_1 \ldots a_{r'}$) = FAIL if s ≠ s′
Eval⟦ λ(s $p_1 \ldots p_r$).E ⟧ ⊥ = ⊥

Operationally, the rules work as follows. To apply (λ(s p_1 ... p_r).E) to an argument A we first evaluate A to find out what sort of object it is. This implies that if the evaluation of A does not terminate then neither does the application in question (third rule). (Note: to 'evaluate A' we only evaluate it to constructor form; we do not evaluate its components. They will be evaluated only if they are extracted and used. This is what it means for constructors to be lazy.)

If A evaluates to an object built with a constructor other than s, then the pattern-match fails (second rule). To see how this rule works, consider an application of the lambda abstraction (λ(BRANCH t1 t2).BRANCH t2 t1) to (LEAF 0):

```
(λ(BRANCH t1 t2).BRANCH t2 t1) (LEAF 0)  →  FAIL
```

The application returns FAIL because the constructor in the pattern is different from that of the argument.

Finally, if A was built with the same constructor as the pattern, then the first rule applies. To see how this rule works, consider an application of the same abstraction to a BRANCH:

```
(λ(BRANCH t1 t2).BRANCH t2 t1) (BRANCH (LEAF 0) (LEAF 1))
  →  (λt1.λt2.BRANCH t2 t1) (LEAF 0) (LEAF 1)
  →  (λt2.BRANCH t2 (LEAF 0)) (LEAF 1)
  →  BRANCH (LEAF 1) (LEAF 0)
```

In this case the match succeeds, and t1 and t2 are bound to the components of the branch with the ordinary β-reduction rule.

Notice that for constructors of arity zero (r=0) the three rules correspond exactly to those of the previous section. For example, using the first case of the xor function gives:

```
(λFALSE.λy.y) FALSE TRUE  →  (λy.y) TRUE
                          →  TRUE
```

Finally, notice that the rules deal correctly with nested patterns. Consider, for example, the following application of the first case of the function lastElt to (CONS 4 (CONS 3 NIL)):

```
(λ(CONS x NIL).x) (CONS 4 (CONS 3 NIL))
  →  (λx.λNIL.x) 4 (CONS 3 NIL)      (first rule)
  →  (λNIL.4) (CONS 3 NIL)           (normal β-rule)
  →  FAIL                            (second rule)
```

Here, the outer pattern matches but the inner one does not, so the whole expression returns FAIL.

4.3.4 The Semantics of Product-constructor Patterns

Finally we consider the semantics of matching product patterns. This is an area in which a rather subtle issue surfaces.

Consider the Miranda functions

```
zeroAny x     = 0
zeroList []   = 0
zeroPair (x,y) = 0
```

The function zeroAny takes a single argument and returns 0. Miranda's lazy semantics clearly means that the argument is not evaluated, so that 0 is returned even if the evaluation of the argument is very expensive or non-terminating:

Eval⟦ zeroAny ⟧ $\perp$ = 0

We say that zeroAny is *lazy* since it does not evaluate its argument.

The semantics of the function zeroList has already been described by the preceding sections. It specifies that zeroList evaluates its argument, and checks whether it is [ ]. If it is, then zeroList returns 0, otherwise it returns ERROR. We say that zeroList is *strict* since it does evaluate its argument:

Eval⟦ zeroList ⟧ $\perp = \perp$

Should the zeroPair function be lazy or strict? Since the argument is a tuple there is no point in evaluating it to check that it really is a tuple, as was required in the case of zeroList, because the check would always succeed (assuming that the program is type-checked). It would be more in the spirit of a lazy language to specify that

Eval⟦ zeroPair ⟧ $\perp$ = 0

and the Miranda language specifies this choice. We call this *lazy product-matching*. On the other hand, an alternative choice would be to specify that

Eval⟦ zeroPair ⟧ $\perp = \perp$

and we call this *strict product-matching*.

Notice that there is no 'right' or 'wrong' answer; it is simply a question of making a clear choice of semantics for product-matching. The only 'wrong' approach is not to notice that there is a choice to be made (and hence to risk making different choices in different parts of the implementation, with unpredictable results).

Nevertheless, we contend that there are persuasive arguments in favor of the lazy approach. We discuss this issue in the next section, while in the rest of this section we concentrate on the semantics of lazy product-matching.

We may describe lazy product-matching by the following semantic rule:

Eval⟦ λ(t p_1 ... p_r).E ⟧ a = **Eval**⟦ $\lambda p_1 \ldots \lambda p_r$.E ⟧ (SEL-t-1 a)
...
(SEL-t-r a)

Here SEL-t-i is a built-in function which selects the ith field from a structured object built with constructor t. It may be described by the following semantic equations:

SEL-t-i (t a_1 ... a_i ... a_r) = a_i
SEL-t-i $\perp$ = $\perp$

Suppose that (λp . E), where p is a product pattern, is applied to an expression A. The rule for lazy product-matching postpones the evaluation of the argument A by binding the names for the components to applications of SEL-t-i to A, rather than evaluating A and extracting its components directly. If none of the components of A is evaluated, then A will not be evaluated either, which is the effect we wanted to achieve.

Let us see how this works on zeroPair:

```
zeroPair = λ(PAIR x y).0
```

Hence,

$$
\begin{aligned}
& \textbf{Eval}[\![\ \text{zeroPair}\ ]\!]\ \bot \\
= {} & \textbf{Eval}[\![\ \lambda(\text{PAIR x y}).0\ ]\!]\ \bot \\
= {} & \textbf{Eval}[\![\ \lambda x.\lambda y.0\ ]\!]\ (\text{SEL-PAIR-1}\ \bot)\ (\text{SEL-PAIR-2}\ \bot) \\
= {} & \textbf{Eval}[\![\ \lambda y.0\ ]\!]\ (\text{SEL-PAIR-2}\ \bot) \\
= {} & 0
\end{aligned}
$$

as required.

4.3.5 A Defence of Lazy Product-matching

Consider the Miranda function firsts, which takes a list of numbers, and returns a pair consisting of the first odd and first even elements of the list:

```
firsts []     = (0,0)
firsts (x:xs) = combine x (firsts xs)

combine x (od,ev) = (x,ev),        odd x
                  = (od,x),        even x
```

Suppose that we were to use strict product-matching, so that when evaluating an application (combine A_1 A_2) we would first evaluate A_2. Now consider evaluating (firsts [1..]), where [1..] is the infinite list of integers starting at 1:

```
firsts [1..]  →  combine 1 (firsts [2..])
              →  combine 1 (combine 2 (firsts [3..]))
```

and so on.

The evaluation of (firsts [1..]) will never terminate. This is hardly satisfactory, because it is clear that the value of (firsts [1..]) should be (1,2).

As is well, however, if we use lazy product-matching. Then, in effect, the evaluation goes like this:

```
firsts [1..]  →  combine 1 (firsts [2..])
              →  (1, SEL-PAIR-2 (firsts [2..]))
              →  (1, SEL-PAIR-2 (combine 2 (firsts [3..])))
              →  (1, SEL-PAIR-2 (SEL-PAIR-1 (firsts [3..]), 2))
              →  (1, 2)
```

Under lazy product-matching, combine does not evaluate its second argument. Instead it binds od to (SEL-PAIR-1 A) and ev to (SEL-PAIR-2 A), where A is the argument.

We conclude that lazy product-matching gives significant benefits to the programmer. The effect is quite subtle: strict product-matching caused the entire argument list to be scanned even though all the operations on lists are lazy. One purpose of this section is to point out that it is easy for a subtle difference in evaluation strategy (strict versus lazy product-matching) to cause a gross difference in the operational behavior of the program (scanning the whole of an infinite list versus looking at the first element only). The example is derived from a paper by Wadler [1985].

A further reason for advocating lazy product-matching is that it allows us to describe mutual recursion correctly. For an explanation of this point, see Section 6.2.6.

There is another interesting mathematical way of looking at the differences between strict and lazy product-matching. In domain theory there is more than one way of forming the product of two domains A and B, that vary in their treatment of $\bot$. The *ordinary product*, $A \times B$, is defined like this:

$$A \times B = \{(a,b) \mid a \in A \text{ and } b \in B\}$$

All the elements of this domain are pairs, and the bottom element of $A \times B$ is $(\bot,\bot)$.

The *lifted product*, $(A \times B)_\bot$ is defined like this:

$$(A \times B)_\bot = (A \times B) \ \cup \{\bot\}$$

In this product the element $\bot$ is distinct from $(\bot,\bot)$. This corresponds closely to our operational ideas of how tuples (or any other data structure) are formed: $\bot$ stands for a non-terminating computation, while $(\bot,\bot)$ is a pair, both of whose elements are non-terminating computations.

The key insight is that lazy product-matching corresponds to ordinary product, and strict product-matching corresponds to lifted product. To implement the ordinary product domain $(A \times B)$ we have to make $(\bot,\bot)$ indistinguishable from non-termination. Since they clearly differ operationally, the only way to conceal their differences is to *use* values in an ordinary product domain in a way that makes them indistinguishable. This is precisely what the lazy product-matching rule does:

$$\begin{aligned} & \textbf{Eval}[\![\ \lambda(\text{PAIR } p_1\ p_2).\text{E}\ ]\!]\ \bot \\ = & \ \textbf{Eval}[\![\ \lambda p_1.\lambda p_2.\text{E}\ ]\!]\ (\text{SEL-PAIR-1}\ \bot)\ (\text{SEL-PAIR-2}\ \bot) \\ = & \ \textbf{Eval}[\![\ \lambda p_1.\lambda p_2.\text{E}\ ]\!]\ \bot\ \bot \end{aligned}$$

$$\begin{aligned} & \textbf{Eval}[\![\ \lambda(\text{PAIR } p_1\ p_2).\text{E}\ ]\!]\ (\text{PAIR}\ \bot\ \bot) \\ = & \ \textbf{Eval}[\![\ \lambda p_1.\lambda p_2.\text{E}\ ]\!]\ (\text{SEL-PAIR-1}\ (\text{PAIR}\ \bot\ \bot))\ (\text{SEL-PAIR-2}\ (\text{PAIR}\ \bot\ \bot)) \\ = & \ \textbf{Eval}[\![\ \lambda p_1.\lambda p_2.\text{E}\ ]\!]\ \bot\ \bot \end{aligned}$$

In other words, the abstraction (λ(PAIR p1 p2).E) is indifferent to whether its argument is $\bot$ or $(\bot,\bot)$; it returns the same result in either case. So lazy product-matching can be regarded as a way of implementing ordinary product domains $(A \times B)$ by using the values in the lifted product domain $(A \times B)_\bot$ in such a way that $(\bot,\bot)$ is indistinguishable from $\bot$.

Finally, it is worth noting that the use of lazy product-matching carries an implementation cost. Consider a function addPair, which adds together the elements of a pair:

```
addPair = λ(PAIR x y).+ x y
```

Now, using lazy product-matching, the reduction of (addPair (PAIR 3 4)) goes as follows:

```
addPair (PAIR 3 4)
=  (λ(PAIR x y).+ x y) (PAIR 3 4)
→  (λx.λy.+ x y) (SEL-PAIR-1 (PAIR 3 4)) (SEL-PAIR-2 (PAIR 3 4))
→  (λy.+ (SEL-PAIR-1 (PAIR 3 4)) y) (SEL-PAIR-2 (PAIR 3 4))
→  + (SEL-PAIR-1 (PAIR 3 4)) (SEL-PAIR-2 (PAIR 3 4))
→  + 3 (SEL-PAIR-2 (PAIR 3 4))
→  + 3 4
→  7
```

This takes one reduction to apply the addPair lambda abstraction, and then two further reductions (subsequently) to reduce the two applications of SEL-PAIR. Contrast this with the effect of using strict product-matching:

```
addPair (PAIR 3 4)
= (λ(PAIR x y).+ x y) (PAIR 3 4)
→  (λx.λy.+ x y) 3 4
→  (λy.+ 3 y) 4
→  + 3 4
→  7
```

This uses fewer reductions, since the application of the addPair lambda abstraction also takes the argument apart. Furthermore, it uses less store to hold the temporary applications of SEL-PAIR. This suggests that we should use strict product-matching instead of lazy product-matching wherever this does not affect the semantics.

In the case of addPair, it is clear that the argument will certainly be evaluated in the end, so it would do no harm to evaluate it at the time of function application (that is, to use strict product-matching). In general, whenever a function is strict in an argument (see Section 2.5.4) it is safe to use strict product-matching for that argument. The process of working out which functions are strict is called *strictness analysis*, and is discussed in Chapter 22.

4.3.6 Summary

This section has examined the semantics of pattern-matching in some detail, because much confusion has surrounded this area in the past. Figure 4.5 summarizes the results of the section. The distinction between strict and lazy product-matching, and the use of [] and FAIL, are both first described in Turner's thesis [Turner, 1981], but the present formulation based on structured types is due to the authors.

4.4 Introducing case-expressions

The transformations in the last section produce remarkably inefficient programs! The main reason for this is that pattern-matches are attempted, testing for FAIL each time, as each equation in the function definition is tried in turn.

Frequently, however, a single test would suffice to select the appropriate equation. For example, recall again the reflect function:

```
reflect (LEAF n)          = LEAF n
reflect (BRANCH t1 t2) = BRANCH (reflect t2) (reflect t1)
```

To apply reflect, it would suffice to test the argument, and select the first or second right-hand side according to whether it was a LEAF or a BRANCH.

In this section, therefore, we introduce case-expressions, a convenient construct for describing a particularly simple form of pattern-matching which has this single-test property. Chapter 5 will then demonstrate how to translate Miranda function definitions into case-expressions, and Chapter 6 will show how case-expressions can be transformed into the ordinary lambda calculus. The net effect will be a significant improvement in the efficiency of the resulting program.

Case-expressions are a notation for describing a simple form of pattern-matching. To begin with an example, we may translate the definition of reflect, using a case-expression, in the following way:

```
reflect = λt.case t of
                    LEAF n            => LEAF n
                    BRANCH t1 t2 => BRANCH (reflect t2) (reflect t1)
```

The important points about a case-expression are that the patterns are *simple* (that is, not nested) and *exhaustive* (that is, they cover all constructors of the type). This makes them particularly simple to implement.

The general form of a case-expression is

$$
\begin{array}{l}
\text{case } v \text{ of} \\
\quad c_1\ v_{1,1}\ \ldots\ v_{1,r_1}\ \Rightarrow\ E_1 \\
\quad \ldots \\
\quad c_n\ v_{n,1}\ \ldots\ v_{n,r_n}\ \Rightarrow\ E_n
\end{array}
$$

where v is a variable, $E_1 \ldots E_n$ are expressions, the $v_{i,j}$ are distinct variables, and the $c_1 \ldots c_n$ are a *complete family* of constructors from a structured type declaration. The syntax of case-expressions was defined in Figure 3.2.

Operationally, to evaluate this case-expression, v is first evaluated. Then, according to what constructor v was built with, the appropriate E_i is selected and evaluated, with the $v_{i,j}$ bound to the components of v.

Formally, the construct is defined to be equivalent to

$$
\begin{array}{l}
\quad ((\lambda(c_1\ v_{1,1}\ \ldots\ v_{1,r_1}).E_1)\ v) \\
▯\ \ldots \\
▯\ ((\lambda(c_n\ v_{n,1}\ \ldots\ v_{n,r_n}).E_n)\ v)
\end{array}
$$

but a case-expression is far more readable!

Intuitively, case-expressions correspond to a multiway jump, whereas the equivalent expression using ▯ corresponds to a sequential 'if. . . then. . . elseif. . .'

The semantic equations of $(\lambda p . E)$ are:

$$\begin{array}{lll}
\textbf{Eval}[\![\ \lambda k.E\ ]\!]\ a = \textbf{Eval}[\![\ E\ ]\!] & \text{if } a = \textbf{Eval}[\![\ k\ ]\!] \\
\textbf{Eval}[\![\ \lambda k.E\ ]\!]\ a = \text{FAIL} & \text{if } a \neq \textbf{Eval}[\![\ k\ ]\!] \text{ and } a \neq \bot \\
\textbf{Eval}[\![\ \lambda k.E\ ]\!]\ \bot = \bot &
\end{array}$$

$$\begin{array}{ll}
\textbf{Eval}[\![\ \lambda(s\ p_1 \ldots p_{r_s}).E\ ]\!]\ (s\ a_1 \ldots a_{r_s}) & = \textbf{Eval}[\![\ \lambda p_1 \ldots \lambda p_{r_s}.E\ ]\!]\ a_1 \ldots a_{r_s} \\
\textbf{Eval}[\![\ \lambda(s\ p_1 \ldots p_{r_s}).E\ ]\!]\ (s'\ a_1 \ldots a_{r_{s'}}) & = \text{FAIL} \quad \text{if } s \neq s' \\
\textbf{Eval}[\![\ \lambda(s\ p_1 \ldots p_{r_s}).E\ ]\!]\ \bot & = \bot
\end{array}$$

$$\begin{array}{lll}
\textbf{Eval}[\![\ \lambda(t\ p_1 \ldots p_{r_t}).E\ ]\!]\ a = & \textbf{Eval}[\![\ \lambda p_1 \ldots \lambda p_{r_t}.E\ ]\!] & (\text{SEL-t-1}\ a) \\
 & & \ldots \\
 & & (\text{SEL-t-}r_t\ a)
\end{array}$$

where k is a constant
s is a sum constructor of arity r_s
t is a product constructor of arity r_t
p_i is a pattern
E is an expression
a_i, a are values

The SEL-t-i functions are defined as follows:

$$\begin{array}{ll}
\text{SEL-t-i}\ (t\ a_1 \ldots a_i \ldots a_r) & = a_i \\
\text{SEL-t-i}\ \ \bot & = \bot
\end{array}$$

where t is a product constructor of arity r.

The $\|$ operator is defined as follows:

$$\begin{array}{ll}
a\ \ \|\ b = a & \text{if } a \neq \bot \text{ and } a \neq \text{FAIL} \\
\text{FAIL}\ \|\ b = b & \\
\bot\ \ \|\ b = \bot &
\end{array}$$

Figure 4.5 Semantics of pattern-matching lambda abstractions and $\|$

structure. Indeed, the implementation described in Chapters 18–20 will compile case-expressions and $\|$ respectively to precisely such machine code!

4.5 Summary

Structured data types have proved more complicated than at first appeared! We have discussed the background and semantics of pattern-matching, showing how to translate a Miranda function definition involving pattern-matching into the enriched lambda calculus. This required us to define two new constructs, pattern-matching lambda abstractions and the $\|$ operator, whose semantics we then defined. To clear the way for a more efficient translation, we then introduced case-expressions, describing their semantics in terms of a transformation into the constructs previously described.

The next two chapters complete the pattern-matching story. Chapter 5 gives a more efficient translation of Miranda function definitions into case-expressions, and Chapter 6 shows how to transform the new constructs into the ordinary lambda calculus.

References

Burstall, R.M. 1969. Proving properties of programs by structural induction. *The Computer Journal*. Vol. 12, No. 1, pp. 41–8.

Burstall, R.M. 1977. Design considerations for a functional programming language. In *Proceedings Infotech State of the Art Conference, Copenhagen*, pp. 54–7.

Burstall, R.M., and Darlington, J. 1977. A transformation system for developing recursive programs. *Journal of the ACM*. Vol. 24, No. 1, pp. 44–67.

Burstall, R.M., and Goguen, J.A. 1982. *Algebras, Theories, and Freeness: An Introduction for Computer Scientists*. Report CSR-101-82, Dept of Computer Science, University of Edinburgh. February.

Landin, P.J. 1966. The next 700 programming languages. *Communications of the ACM*. Vol. 9, No. 3, pp. 157–64.

Turner, D.A., 1981. Aspects of the implementation of programming languages. D.Phil. thesis, University of Oxford. February.

Wadler, P. 1985. *A Splitting Headache – and Its Cure*. Programming Research Group, Oxford. January.

Five

EFFICIENT COMPILATION OF PATTERN-MATCHING

Philip Wadler

This chapter shows how to compile function definitions with pattern-matching into case-expressions that can be efficiently evaluated. Previously, pattern-matching has been formally defined, and we have seen some examples of function definitions with pattern-matching.

5.1 Introduction and Examples

We begin by reviewing two examples.

The first example shows pattern-matching on more than one pattern. The function call (mappairs f xs ys) applies the function f to corresponding pairs from the lists xs and ys.

```
mappairs f [] ys          = []
mappairs f (x:xs) []      = []
mappairs f (x:xs) (y:ys) = f x y : mappairs f xs ys
```

For example, (mappairs (+) [1,2] [3,4]) returns [4,6]. The definition given here specifies that if the argument lists are not the same length, then the result will be as long as the shorter of the two lists. For example, (mappairs (+) [1,2] [3,4,5]) also returns [4,6].

The simplest way to think of pattern-matching is as trying to match each equation in turn. Within each equation, patterns are matched from left to right. For example, evaluating (mappairs (+) [1,2] [3,4] first matches (+) against f in the first equation, which succeeds, and then matches [1,2] against

[ ], which fails. Then the second equation is tried. Matching (+) against f and [1,2] against (x:xs) both succeed, but matching [3,4] against [ ] fails. Finally, matching in the third equation succeeds, binding f to (+), x to 1, xs to [2], y to 3, and ys to [4]. This corresponds exactly to the way pattern-matching was defined in Chapter 4.

Performing pattern-matching in this way can require a lot of work. The example above had to examine the list [1,2] three times and the list [3,4] twice. It seems clear that it should be possible to evaluate this function application in a more efficient manner that examines each list only once, but still gives the result prescribed by the semantics. This can be done by transforming the above definition into an equivalent one using case-expressions:

```
mappairs
= λf.λxs'.λys'.
    case xs' of
    NIL          ⇒  NIL
    CONS x xs    ⇒  case ys' of
                    NIL          ⇒ NIL
                    CONS y ys    ⇒ CONS (f x y) (mappairs f xs ys)
```

(Case-expressions were introduced in Section 4.4.) This chapter describes an algorithm that can automatically translate the first definition into the second. This algorithm is called the pattern-matching compiler.

The second example shows pattern-matching on a nested pattern. The function call (nodups xs) removes adjacent duplicate elements from a list xs. It can be defined as follows:

```
nodups [ ]        = [ ]
nodups [x]        = [x]
nodups (y:x:xs)   = nodups (x:xs),       y = x
                  = y : nodups (x:xs),   otherwise
```

(As you would expect, the guard 'otherwise' applies if no other guard does. See Appendix.) For example, (NODUPS [3,3,1,2,2,2,3]) returns [3,1,2,3]. Note that the naming need not be consistent: x stands for the first element of the list in the second equation, and for the second element of the list in the third equation.

Again, one can apply this definition by matching each equation in turn. For example, evaluation of (nodups [1,2,3]) will first try to match [1,2,3] against [ ], which fails. Next, it will try to match [1,2,3] against [x], which also fails. Finally, it will succeed in matching [1,2,3] against (y:x:xs), binding y to 1, x to 2 and xs to [3]. Again, this corresponds exactly to the semantics in Chapter 4.

As before, this is not very efficient. The list [1,2,3] is examined three times, and the sublist [2,3] is examined twice (once in the second equation, where it fails to match [ ], and once in the third equation, where it succeeds in matching (x:xs)). The pattern-matching compiler can transform this into a form that examines the list and the sublist only once:

```
nodups
= λxs''. case xs'' of
         NIL         ⇒ NIL
         CONS x' xs' ⇒
                 case xs' of
                 NIL         ⇒ CONS x' NIL
                 CONS x xs   ⇒ IF (= x' x)
                                  (nodups (CONS x xs))
                                  (CONS x' (nodups (CONS x xs)))
```

(Here x′ is the variable that was called x in the second equation and y in the third.)

The two kinds of pattern-matching, nested patterns and multiple patterns, are closely related to one another. The pattern-matching compiler discussed below works uniformly for both.

In the examples above, the patterns on the left-hand sides of the equations do not overlap. Many people would rewrite the first definition in the form:

```
mappairs' f [] ys        = []
mappairs' f xs []        = []
mappairs' f (x:xs) (y:ys) = f x y : mappairs' f xs ys
```

In this case, the patterns overlap because both the first and the second equation match against (mappairs′ f [] []).

One reason for preferring mappairs′ to mappairs is that it is considered to be more efficient. Indeed, if the simplest implementation of pattern-matching is used, matching each equation in turn, then it is slightly less work to match against xs than to match against (x:xs). However, as we shall see, this definition may actually be *less* efficient when the pattern-matching compiler is used. Some other problems with definitions like mappairs′ will be discussed in Section 5.5.

The remainder of this chapter is organized as follows. Section 5.2 explains the pattern-matching compiler algorithm. Section 5.3 presents a Miranda program that implements the algorithm. Section 5.4 describes some optimizations to the pattern-matching compiler. Section 5.5 discusses a restricted class of definitions, called uniform definitions, which have useful properties.

Credit for the first published description of a pattern-matching compiler goes to Augustsson, who used it in the LML compiler [Augustsson, 1985]. Techniques similar to Augustsson's have been discovered independently by several researchers, including the authors of the Hope compiler [Burstall *et al.*, 1980]. The material presented here is derived partly from Augustsson's paper and partly from original work by the author (Wadler).

It is also possible to derive the pattern-matching compiler from its specification using program transformation techniques; see Barrett and Wadler [1986].

5.2 The Pattern-matching Compiler Algorithm

A Miranda function definition of the form

```
f p1,1 ... p1,n = E1
...
f pm,1 ... pm,n = Em
```

can be translated into the enriched lambda calculus definition

```
f = λu1...λun. ((λp1,1'. ... λp1,n'.E1') u1 ... un)
               [] ...
               [] ((λpm,1'. ... λpm,n'.Em') u1 ... un)
               [] ERROR
```

where the u_i are new variables which do not occur free in any E_i, and the E_i' and $p_{i,j}'$ are the result of translating the E_i and $p_{i,j}$ respectively. It was shown how to do this translation in Chapter 4, using the **TD** translation scheme.

This section shows how to transform the definition of f into a form which uses case-expressions, removing all use of pattern-matching lambda abstractions. The transformation applies to the entire body of the $\lambda u_1 \ldots \lambda u_n$ abstraction, except that we generalize slightly to allow an arbitrary expression instead of ERROR.

For the sake of simplicity, we assume that constant patterns have been replaced by conditional equations, as described in Section 4.2.1.

5.2.1 The Function **match**

Our goal, then, is to transform an expression of the form

```
   ((λp1,1...λp1,n.E1) u1 ... un)
[] ...
[] ((λpm,1. ... λpm,n.Em) u1 ... un)          (5.1)
[] E
```

into an equivalent expression which uses case-expressions rather than pattern-matching lambda abstractions.

The transformation is a bit complicated, and so we will use some new notation to describe it. Specifically, we will use a function **match**, which takes as its arguments the various parts of the input expression, namely the $p_{i,j}$, E_i and u_j, and produces as its output the transformed expression. The function **match** is similar to the **TD** and **TE** translation schemes introduced in Chapter 3, except that both its input and its result are enriched lambda calculus expressions. Furthermore, the double square bracket syntax becomes somewhat cumbersome, so we use a syntax like Miranda instead.

Here, then, is the call to **match** which we will use to compile the expression

(5.1) given above:

```
match [u1, ..., un]
      [( [p1,1, ..., p1,n], E1 ),
       ...
       ( [pm,1, ..., pm,n], Em )]
      E
```

This call should return an expression equivalent to the expression (5.1), and we take (5.1) as the *definition* of **match** from a semantic point of view. A call of **match** takes three arguments: a list of variables, a list of equations and a default expression. Each equation is a pair, consisting of a list of patterns (representing the left-hand side of the equation) and an expression (representing the right-hand side). Notice that the list of variables and each list of patterns have the same length.

We will also sometimes write calls of **match** in the form

```
match us qs E
```

Here us is the list of argument variables (of length n), and qs is a list of equations (of length m). Each equation q_i in qs has the form (ps_i, E_i), where ps_i is the list of patterns on the left-hand side (of length n) and E_i is the expression on the right-hand side.

As a running example, we will use the following Miranda function:

```
demo f [] ys          = A f ys
demo f (x:xs) []      = B f x xs
demo f (x:xs) (y:ys)  = C f x xs y ys
```

This function is similar in structure to mappairs, but it has been changed slightly in order to simplify and clarify the following examples. The right-hand sides use three unspecified expressions A, B and C.

Translating this into the enriched lambda calculus using **TD** gives:

```
demo
= λu1.λu2.λu3. ((λf.λNIL.λys.A f ys) u1 u2 u3)
               [] ((λf.λ(CONS x xs).λNIL.B f x xs) u1 u2 u3)
               [] ((λf.λ(CONS x xs).λ(CONS y ys).C f x xs y ys) u1 u2 u3)
               [] ERROR
```

where u_1, u_2, u_3 are new variable names which do not occur free in A, B or C. Now, we transform the definition of demo, by replacing its body with a call of **match**:

```
demo
= λu1.λu2.λu3. match [u1, u2, u3]
                     [ ( [f, NIL,        ys       ], (A f ys)        ),
                       ( [f, CONS x xs, NIL       ], (B f x xs)      ),
                       ( [f, CONS x xs, CONS y ys], (C f x xs y ys)) ]
                     ERROR
```

The following sections give rules to transform any call of **match** to an equivalent case-expression. We begin with rules for simple cases and proceed to more general cases.

5.2.2 The Variable Rule

In the example above, we have the following call on **match**:

```
match [u1, u2, u3]
      [ ( [f, NIL,          ys          ], (A f ys)         ),
        ( [f, CONS x xs, NIL            ], (B f x xs)       ),
        ( [f, CONS x xs, CONS y ys], (C f x xs y ys) ) ]
        ERROR
```

In this case, the list of patterns in every equation begins with a variable. This may be reduced to the equivalent call:

```
match [u2, u3]
      [ ( [NIL,          ys          ], (A u1 ys)         ),
        ( [CONS x xs, NIL            ], (B u1 x xs)       ),
        ( [CONS x xs, CONS y ys], (C u1 x xs y ys) ) ]
      ERROR
```

This is derived by removing the first variable, u_1, and in each equation removing the corresponding formal variable, f, and replacing f by u_1 in the right-hand side of each equation.

The same method works whenever each equation begins with a variable, even if each equation begins with a different variable. For example,

```
match [u2, u3]
      [ ( [x, NIL],          (B x) ),
        ( [y, CONS x xs], (C y x xs) ) ]
      ERROR
```

reduces to the call,

```
match [u3]
      [ ( [NIL],          (B u2) ),
        ( [CONS x xs],  (C u2 x xs) ) ]
      ERROR
```

(This particular example arises when compiling the definition of nodups.)

In general, if every equation begins with a variable pattern, then the call of **match** will have the form:

```
match (u:us)
      [ ( (v1:ps1), E1 ),
        . . .
        ( (vm:psm), Em ) ]
      E
```

This can be reduced to the equivalent call:

```
match us
      [ ( ps₁, E₁[u/v₁] ),
        . . .
        ( psₘ, Eₘ[u/vₘ] )]
      E
```

where, as usual, E[M/x] means 'E with M substituted for x'. In order to avoid too many subscripts, a Miranda-like notation has been used here; for example, we write (u:us) instead of $[u_1, \ldots, u_n]$. The general case corresponds to the first example above, where u is u_1, us is $[u_2, u_3]$, v_1 is f, ps_1 is [NIL, ys], and so on.

It is not hard to show that the rule is correct, that is, that the two **match** expressions are equivalent. This follows from the definition of **match** and the semantics of pattern-matching.

5.2.3 The Constructor Rule

The above step has left us with the following call of **match**:

```
match [u₂, u₃]
      [ ( [NIL,          ys          ], (A u₁ ys)            ),
        ( [CONS x xs, NIL         ], (B u₁ x xs)          ),
        ( [CONS x xs, CONS y ys], (C u₁ x xs y ys) ) ]
      ERROR
```

In this case, the list of patterns in every equation begins with a constructor. This call is equivalent to the following case-expression:

```
case u₂ of
     NIL          ⇒  match [u₃]
                         [ ( [ys],                  (A u₁ ys)            ) ]
                         ERROR
     CONS u₄ u₅   ⇒  match [u₄, u₅, u₃]
                         [ ( [x, xs, NIL],          (B u₁ x xs)          ),
                           ( [x, xs, CONS y ys], (C u₁ x xs y ys) ) ]
                         ERROR
```

This call is derived by grouping together all equations that begin with the same constructor. Within each group, new variables are introduced corresponding to each field of the constructor. Thus NIL, which has no fields, requires no new variables, while CONS, which has two fields, introduces the variables u_4 and u_5. These new variables are matched against the corresponding subpatterns of the original patterns.

It may be useful here to look at a second example. In compiling the definition of a function like nodups, one would encounter the following call of

match:

```
match [u₁]
  [ ( [NIL],                       A            ),
    ( [CONS x NIL],                (B x)        ),
    ( [CONS y (CONS x xs)],        (C y x xs) ) ]
  ERROR
```

This can be reduced to the equivalent expression:

```
case u₁ of
   NIL         => match []
                    [ ( [],                  A          ) ]
                    ERROR
   CONS u₂ u₃  => match [u₂, u₃]
                    [ ( [x, NIL],            (B x)       ),
                      ( [y, CONS x xs],      (C y x xs) ) ]
                    ERROR
```

Again, NIL introduces no new variables (leaving a call of **match** with an empty list of variables), and CONS introduces two new variables, u_2 and u_3.

More generally, it may be the case that not all equations beginning with the same constructor appear next to each other. For example, one might have a call of **match** such as:

```
match [u₁]
  [ ( [CONS x NIL],                (B x)        ),
    ( [NIL],                       A            ),
    ( [CONS y (CONS x xs)],        (C y x xs)  ) ]
  ERROR
```

It is always safe to exchange two equations that begin with a different constructor, so we may rearrange the above to the equivalent call:

```
match [u₁]
  [ ( [NIL],                       A            ),
    ( [CONS x NIL],                (B x)        ),
    ( [CONS y (CONS x xs)],        (C y x xs) ) ]
  ERROR
```

which may be transformed as before.

It may also be the case that not all constructors appear in the original list of equations. For example, a function definition such as:

```
last [x]          = x
last (y:(x:xs))   = last (x:xs)
```

will result in the following call of **match**:

```
match [u₁]
  [ ( [CONS x NIL],                x                         ),
    ( [CONS y (CONS x xs)],        (last (CONS x xs)) ) ]
  ERROR
```

This can be reduced to the equivalent expression:

```
case u1 of
    NIL           ⇒  match [] [] ERROR
    CONS u2 u3    ⇒  match [u2, u3]
                        [( [x, NIL],              x                   ),
                         ( [y, CONS x xs], (last (CONS x xs)) ) ]
                        ERROR
```

The case-expression must still contain a clause for the missing constructor, and the call of **match** in this clause will have an empty list of equations. (From the definition of **match**, we know that (**match** [] [] ERROR) is equivalent to ERROR.)

We now discuss the general rule for reducing a call of **match** where every equation begins with a constructor pattern. Say that the constructors are from a type which has constructors $c_1, \ldots, c_k$. Then the equations can be rearranged into groups of equations $qs_1, \ldots, qs_k$, such that every equation in group qs_i begins with constructor c_i. (If there is some constructor c_i that begins no equation, like NIL in the last example above, then the corresponding group qs_i will be empty.) The call of **match** will then have the form:

```
match (u:us) (qs1 ++ ... ++ qsk) E
```

where each qs_i has the form:

```
[ ( ((ci ps'i,1):psi,1), Ei,1 )
  ...
  ( ((ci ps'i,mi):psi,mi), Ei,mi ) ]
```

(++ is list append.) In this expression we have abbreviated the constructor pattern (c $p_1 \ldots p_r$) to the form (c ps), where ps stands for the list of patterns [$p_1, p_2, \ldots, p_r$]. This call to **match** is reduced to the case-expression:

```
case u of
    c1 us'1  ⇒  match (us'1 ++ us) qs'1 E
    ...
    ck us'k  ⇒  match (us'k ++ us) qs'k E
```

where each qs'_i has the form:

```
[ ( (ps'i,1 ++ psi,1), Ei,1 ),
  ...
  ( (ps'i,mi ++ psi,mi), Ei,mi ) ]
```

Here each us'_i is a list of new variables, containing one variable for each field in c_i.

For instance, in the example at the beginning of this section, qs_2 is

```
[ ( [CONS x xs, NIL       ], (B u1 x xs)       ),
  ( [CONS x xs, CONS y ys], (C u1 x xs y ys) ) ]
```

and c_2 is CONS, $ps'_{2,1}$ is [x, xs], $ps_{2,1}$ is [NIL], $E_{2,1}$ is (B u_1 x xs), $ps'_{2,2}$ is [x, xs], $ps_{2,2}$ is [CONS y ys], and $E_{2,2}$ is (C u_1 x xs y ys). The corresponding qs'_2 is

```
[ ( [x, xs, NIL        ], (B u1 x xs)        ),
  ( [x, xs, CONS y ys], (C u1 x xs y ys) ) ]
```

The corresponding list of new variables, us_2', is [u_4,u_5].

This notation is, of necessity, rather clumsy. The reader will be pleased to discover, in Section 5.3, that this transformation can be written as a functional program which is more concise and (with experience) easier to read.

Again, the correctness of this rule can be proved using the definition of **match** and the semantics of pattern-matching.

5.2.4 The Empty Rule

After repeated application of the rules above, one eventually arrives at a call of **match** where the variable list is empty, such as the following:

```
match []
      [ ( [], (A u1 u3) ) ]
      ERROR
```

This reduces to:

```
(A u1 u3)
```

The correctness of this follows immediately from the definition of **match**, since A cannot return FAIL.

In general, the call of **match** may involve zero, one or more equations. Zero equations may result if the constructor rule is applied and some constructor of the type appears in no equations, as in last above. More than one equation can result if some of the original equations overlap.

Thus, the general form of a call of **match** with an empty variable list is:

```
match []
      [ ( [], E1 ),
         ...
        ( [], Em ) ]
      E
```

where $m \geq 0$. From the definition of **match**, this reduces to

```
E1 [] ... [] Em [] E
```

Further, we can often guarantee that none of E_1, ..., E_m can be equal to FAIL. In this case, the above **match** expression reduces to E_1 if $m > 0$ and to E if $m = 0$. Section 5.4.2 discusses this optimization further.

5.2.5 An Example

The rules given so far are sufficient to translate the definitions of mappairs and nodups to the corresponding case-expressions given in the introduction. Notice that the variable names used in the introduction were chosen for readability. In practice, the translation algorithm will usually pick new names.

The reader may wish to verify that the rules given above are indeed sufficient to translate the definition

```
mappairs f [] ys        = []
mappairs f (x:xs) []    = []
mappairs f (x:xs) (y:ys) = f x y : mappairs f xs ys
```

to the equivalent:

```
mappairs
= λu1.λu2.λu3.
   case u2 of
   NIL        ⇒ NIL
   CONS u4 u5 ⇒ case u3 of
                NIL        ⇒ NIL
                CONS u6 u7 ⇒ CONS (u1 u4 u6)
                                   (mappairs u1 u5 u7)
```

The reader may also wish to check that the function nodups transforms to the case-expression given in the introduction.

5.2.6 The Mixture Rule

The above rules are sufficient for compiling most function definitions into case-expressions. However, there is still one case which has not been covered. This arises when not all equations begin with a variable, and not all equations begin with a constructor; that is, when there is a mixture of both kinds of equation. For example, here is an alternative definition of demo (similar in structure to the alternative definition of mappairs):

```
demo' f [] ys        = A f ys
demo' f xs []        = B f xs
demo' f (x:xs) (y:ys) = C f x xs y ys
```

Converting this to a **match** expression and applying the variable rule to eliminate f results in the following:

```
match [u2,u3]
      [ ( [NIL,        ys         ], (A u1 ys)          ),
        ( [xs,         NIL        ], (B u1 xs)          ),
        ( [CONS x xs,  CONS y ys], (C u1 x y xs ys) ) ]
      ERROR
```

Neither the variable rule nor the constructor rule applies to this expression, because some equations begin with constructors and others with variables.

This is where the third argument to the **match** function is useful. The above expression is equivalent to:

```
match [u2, u3]
      [([NIL, ys], (A u1 ys))]
      ( match [u2, u3]
              [([xs, NIL], (B u1 xs))]
              ( match [u2, u3]
                      [([CONS x xs, CONS y ys], (C u1 x y xs ys))]
                      ERROR ))
```

That is, the equations are broken into groups; first an equation beginning with a constructor, then one beginning with a variable, and then one beginning with a constructor again. If the equation in the first call of **match** fails to match the arguments then the value of the second call of **match** is returned. Similarly, if the equation in the second call does not match then the third call is returned, and if the equation in the third call does not match then ERROR is returned.

The reader may verify that reducing the three calls of **match** using the variable, constructor and base case rules results in the following definition of demo′:

```
demo'
= λu1.λu2.λu3.
      case u2 of
      NIL          => (A u1 u3)
      CONS u4 u5   =>
            case u3 of
            NIL          => (B u1 u2)
            CONS u6 u7   =>
                  case u2 of
                  NIL          => ERROR
                  CONS u4 u5   =>
                        case u3 of
                        NIL          => ERROR
                        CONS u6 u7   => (C u1 u4 u5 u6 u7)
```

This involves four case-expressions. When the second and third arguments are both non-empty lists then each list is examined twice, as compared with once for the definition of demo. This confirms the claim made in the introduction that 'optimizing' the definition of mappairs by transforming it into mappairs′ can actually result in worse code.

It may be possible to devise a compilation algorithm that would produce better code for this case. This could be done by simplifying a case-expression that appears inside another case-expression for the same variable. This sort of optimization is straightforward, although it requires considerably more book-keeping. In this case, mappairs′ would compile to the same case-expression as mappairs, although the compilation process would be rather more complicated.

In general, a call of **match** where some equations begin with variables and some with constructors may be transformed as follows. Say we are given a call of **match** of the form

```
match us qs E
```

The equation list qs may be partitioned into k lists qs_1, ..., qs_k such that

```
qs = qs₁ ++ ... ++ qsₖ
```

The partition should be chosen so that each qs_i either has every equation beginning with a variable or every equation beginning with a constructor. (In the example above, each qs_i had length 1, but in general this need not be the case.) Then the call of **match** can be reduced to:

```
match us qs₁ (match us qs₂ ( ... (match us qsₖ E)...))
```

It is easy to use the definition of **match** to show that this rule is correct.

5.2.7 Completeness

With the addition of the mixture rule, it is now possible to reduce any possible call of **match** to a case-expression. This can be seen by a simple analysis. Given a call (**match** us qs E) then us will be either empty, so the empty rule applies, or non-empty. If us is non-empty then each equation must have a non-empty pattern list, which must begin with either a variable or a constructor. If all equations begin with a variable then the variable rule applies; if all begin with a constructor then the constructor rule applies; and if some begin with variables and some with constructors then the mixture rule applies.

Further, define the 'size' of an equation list as the sum of the sizes of all the patterns in the equation list. It can be seen that all four of the rules result in calls of **match** with smaller equation lists. This guarantees that the algorithm must eventually terminate.

5.3 The Pattern-matching Compiler in Miranda

This section presents the transformation algorithm as a functional program in Miranda.

5.3.1 Patterns

First, it is necessary to give a data type for representing patterns.

```
pattern     ::= VAR variable
              |   CON constructor [pattern]

variable    == [char]
constructor == [char]
```

For example, (x:xs) is represented by (CONS "CONS" [VAR "x", VAR "xs"]).

We need two functions on constructor names. The function arity given a constructor returns its arity, and the function constructors given a constructor returns a list of all constructors of its type:

```
arity        :: constructor -> num
constructors :: constructor -> [constructor]
```

For example (arity "NIL") returns 0, and (arity "CONS") returns 2. Both (constructors "NIL") and (constructors "CONS") return the list ["NIL", "CONS"].

5.3.2 Expressions

Next, we need a data type for representing expressions:

```
expression ::= CASE variable [clause]
               | FATBAR expression expression
               | ...

clause     ::= CLAUSE constructor [variable] expression
```

For example, the case-expression:

```
case xs of
     NIL       => E1
     CONS y ys => E2
```

would be represented by

```
CASE "xs"
       [CLAUSE "NIL" [] E1',
        CLAUSE "CONS" ["y", "ys"] E2']
```

where E_1', E_2' are the representations of the expressions E_1, E_2. Similarly, the expression

E_1 [] E_2

would be represented by

FATBAR E_1' E_2'

The '. . .' in the definition of the type expression stands for other constructors used to represent other expressions, such as variables, applications and lambda abstractions. We do not need to know anything about these other expressions, except that there is a substitution function defined for them.

```
subst :: expression -> variable -> variable -> expression
```

For example, if E represents the expression (f x y), then (subst E "_u1" "x") represents the expression (f _ul y).

5.3.3 Equations

An equation is a list of patterns paired with an expression:

```
equation == ([pattern], expression)
```

We will use the letter q to denote equations, or else write (ps,e).

We need functions to determine if an equation begins with a variable or a constructor. If it begins with a constructor, we also need a function to return that constructor.

```
isVar                           :: equation -> bool
isVar (VAR v       : ps, e)     = True
isVar (CON c ps'   : ps, e)     = False

isCon                           :: equation -> bool
isCon q                         = ~ (isVar q)
getCon                          :: equation -> constructor
getCon (CON c ps' : ps, e)= c
```

5.3.4 Variable Names

We need some way of generating the new variable names, u1, u2, and so on. To do this we introduce a function makeVar that, given a number, returns a variable name.

```
makeVar    :: num -> variable
makeVar k  = "_u" ++ show k
```

For example, (makeVar 3) returns '_u3'. Here we preface each new variable name with '_' to avoid it being confused with any variable already in the program.

5.3.5 The Functions partition and foldr

The implementation of the mixture rule uses a function called partition. The call (partition f xs) returns a list $[xs_1, \ldots, xs_n]$ such that $xs = xs_1$ ++ ... ++ xs_n, and such that f x = f x′ for any elements x and x′ in xs_i, i from 1 to n, and such that f x ≠ f x′ for any elements x in xs_i and x′ in xs_{i+1}, i from 1 to n−1. For example,

```
partition odd [1,3,2,4,1] = [ [1,3], [2,4], [1] ]
```

The function partition is defined as follows:

```
partition              :: (* -> **) -> [*] -> [ [*] ]
partition f []         = []
partition f [x]        = [ [x] ]
partition f (x:x':xs)  = tack x (partition f (x':xs)),   f x = f x'
                       = [x] : partition f (x':xs),       otherwise

tack x xss             = (x : hd xss) : tl xss
```

Incidentally, the following definition of tack is *not* equivalent to the above definition:

```
tack x (xs:xss) = (x : xs) : xss
```

The difference between the two is closely related to the question of strict and lazy pattern-matching, mentioned in Section 4.3.5 in connection with the function firsts.

The pattern-matching compiler also uses the standard function foldr. The function foldr is defined so that

```
foldr f a [x1, x2, ..., xn] = f x1 (f x2 ( ... (f xn a)...))
```

For example, (foldr (+) 0 xs) returns the sum of the list of numbers xs. The function foldr is defined by:

```
foldr            :: (* -> ** -> **) -> ** -> [*] -> **
foldr f a []     = a
foldr f a (x:xs) = f x (foldr f a xs)
```

5.3.6 The Function match

We are now ready to define the function match. Calls of match have the form (match k us qs def). Here, as in Section 5.2, us represents a list of variables, qs represents a list of equations and def is a default expression. The argument k is added to help in generating new variable names; it should be chosen so that for every i>k, (makeVar i) is a new variable not in us, qs or def.

For example, the initial call to match to compile the definitions of mappairs would be:

```
match 3
      ["_u1", "_u2", "_u3"]
      [ ( [VAR "f", CONS "NIL" [],
                    VAR "ys"       ], E1 ),
        ( [VAR "f", CON "CONS" [VAR "x", VAR "xs"],
                    CON "NIL" [] ], E2 ),
        ( [VAR "f", CON "CONS" [VAR "x", VAR "xs"],
                    CON "CONS" [VAR "y", VAR "ys"] ], E3 ) ]
      error
```

where E_1, E_2 and E_3 represent the three expressions on the right-hand sides of the equation, and error represents the expression ERROR.

The definition of match can now be derived in a fairly straightforward way from the description given in Section 5.2. The type of match is:

```
match :: num -> [variable] -> [equation] -> expression -> expression
```

The equations for the top-level of match come from the empty rule and the mixture rule.

```
match k []     qs def = foldr FATBAR def [e | ([],e) <- qs ]
match k (u:us) qs def
  = foldr (matchVarCon k (u:us)) def (partition isVar qs)
```

The function matchVarCon is given a list of equations that either all begin with a variable or all begin with a constructor. It calls matchVar or matchCon, as appropriate.

```
matchVarCon k us qs def
 = matchVar k us qs def,        isVar (hd qs)
 = matchCon k us qs def,        isCon (hd qs)
```

The function matchVar implements the variable rule.

```
matchVar k (u:us) qs def
 = match k us [(ps, subst e u v) | (VAR v : ps, e) <- qs] def
```

The functions matchCon and matchClause implement the constructor rule. The call (choose c qs) returns all equations that begin with constructor c.

```
matchCon k (u:us) qs def
 = CASE u [matchClause c k (u:us) (choose c qs) def | c <- cs]
   where
   cs = constructors (getCon (hd qs))

matchClause c k (u:us) qs def
 = CLAUSE c us' (match (k'+k)
                       (us'++us)
                       [(ps'++ps, e) | (CON c ps' : ps, e) <- qs]
                       def )
   where
   k'  = arity c
   us' = [makeVar (i+k) | i <- [1..k'] ]

choose c qs = [q | q <- qs; getCon q = c]
```

This completes the Miranda program for the pattern-matching compiler.

5.4 Optimizations

This section discusses some optimizations to the pattern-matching compiler. Section 5.4.1 describes an optimization which gives greater efficiency when compiling overlapping equations. This involves further uses of [] and FAIL, and Section 5.4.2 describes how these may often be eliminated.

5.4.1 Case-expressions with Default Clauses

If overlapping equations are allowed, then sometimes the pattern-matching compiler described above may transform a small set of equations into a case-expression that is much larger. For example, consider the function defined by:

```
unwieldy [] []  = A
unwieldy xs ys = B xs ys
```

The pattern-matching compiler transforms this into:

```
unwieldy = λxs.λys. case xs of
                      NIL          ⇒ case ys of
                                         NIL          ⇒ A
                                         CONS y' ys'  ⇒ B xs ys
                      CONS x' xs'  ⇒ B xs ys
```

Here the expression (B xs ys) appears twice. If (B xs ys) were replaced by a very large expression, the increase in size caused by the compilation process could be very significant.

The problem can be avoided by modifying the rules given in Section 5.2 so that right-hand sides are never duplicated during the compilation process. In fact, only one rule can cause right-hand sides to be duplicated, the constructor rule. This rule is modified as follows.

Recall that the constructor rule transforms a call of **match** of the form:

match (u:us) (qs_1 ++ ... ++ qs_k) E

to a case-expression of the form:

case u of
    c_1 us_1' ⇒ **match** (us_1' ++ us) qs_1' E
    ...
    c_k us_k' ⇒ **match** (us_k' ++ us) qs_k' E

where qs_1, ..., qs_k and qs_1', ..., qs_k' are as described in Section 5.2.3.

Normally E will be ERROR, but if the mixture rule is used then E may itself be a **match** expression containing right-hand sides; it is in this case that duplication may occur. The modified rule prevents this by using ▯ and FAIL to avoid duplicating E.

This is done by replacing the case-expression above with the equivalent expression:

(case u of
    c_1 us_1' ⇒ **match** (us_1' ++ us) qs_1' FAIL
    ...
    c_k us_k' ⇒ **match** (us_k' ++ us) qs_k' FAIL)
▯ E

If we call the old case-expression C, then the new expression is (C′ ▯ E), where C′ is formed by replacing each E in C by FAIL. It is clear that the new expression is equivalent to the old expression and, as desired, E is not duplicated by the new rule.

For example, using the new rule, the definition of unwieldy will now transform to:

```
unwieldy = λxs.λys.
             (case xs of
                  NIL          ⇒ (case ys of
                                        NIL         ⇒ A
                                        CONS y' ys' ⇒ FAIL) (a)
                                  [] FAIL                   (b)
                  CONS x' xs'  ⇒ FAIL)
             [] B xs ys                                     (c)
```

This expression is a little larger than the previous version of unwieldy, but now (B xs ys) appears only once. If (B xs ys) stands for a large expression, then this new expression may be much smaller than the previous one.

As an example of how this sort of expression is evaluated, consider the call

```
(unwieldy NIL (CONS 1 NIL))
```

This is evaluated as follows. First, the outer case-expression is evaluated. Since xs is NIL, this causes the inner case to be evaluated. Since ys is (CONS 1 NIL), the inner case-expression returns FAIL; see line (a). So the expression after the inner [] is returned, which is also FAIL; see line (b). Thus, the outer case-expression returns FAIL. So the expression after the outer [] is returned; see line (c). This is (B NIL (CONS 1 NIL)), which is the value returned by the call of unwieldy.

5.4.2 Optimizing Expressions Containing [] and FAIL

It is often the case that all occurrences of FAIL, and its companion, [], can be eliminated. Most of these optimizations depend on reasoning that FAIL can never be returned by an expression, because in this case an occurrence of [] can be eliminated.

Suppose that FAIL is returned by an expression E. Then it is necessary (though not sufficient) that one of the following conditions must hold:

(i) FAIL is mentioned explicitly in E;
(ii) E contains a pattern-matching lambda abstraction, whose application may fail;
(iii) FAIL is the value of one of the free variables of E.

If the pattern-matching compiler described in this chapter is applied throughout, then no pattern-matching lambda abstractions will remain in the transformed program, and hence (ii) cannot occur. Since the programmer presumably cannot write FAIL explicitly in his program, it is not hard (although perhaps tedious) to verify that (iii) cannot occur either.

These observations focus our attention on all the places where FAIL can be introduced explicitly by the compiler. There are only two such places:

(i) In the translation of conditional equations (Section 4.2.6). Fortunately, we can easily transform conditional equations to avoid the use of [] and FAIL, and we show how to do so below.

(ii) In the variant of the pattern-matching compiler described in the last section, where the introduction of [] and FAIL seems unavoidable. This problem motivates the discussion in Section 5.5, in which we describe a restricted class of function definitions that can always be compiled without using [] and FAIL.

5.4.2.1 Rules for transforming [] and FAIL

We now give some rules for transforming expressions involving [] and FAIL to a simpler form. In all cases their correctness follows directly from the semantics of [].

First, we may eliminate [] if FAIL cannot occur on the left:

$$E_1 \; [] \; E_2 \;\equiv\; E_1$$

provided that E_1 cannot return FAIL.

For example, this rule is used to derive the optimized version of the empty rule in Section 5.2.4.

Second, we may eliminate [] if FAIL definitely occurs on the right:

$$E \; [] \; \text{FAIL} \;\equiv\; E$$

For example, this rule can be used to simplify the final definition of unwieldy in Section 5.4.1.

Third, there is the following useful transformation involving IF:

$$(\text{IF } E_1 \; E_2 \; E_3) \; [] \; E \;\equiv\; \text{IF } E_1 \; E_2 \; (E_3 \; [] \; E)$$

provided that neither E_1 nor E_2 can return FAIL.

This rule will be useful in simplifying conditional equations, which we now attend to.

5.4.2.2 Eliminating [] and FAIL from conditional equations

The empty rule for **match**, which was described in Section 5.2.4, resulted in an expression of the form

$$E_1 \; [] \; \ldots \; [] \; E_m \; [] \; E$$

Now, the E_i are just the right-hand sides of the original equations. If a right-hand side consisted of a set of guarded alternatives without a final 'otherwise' case, then it will have been translated to the form:

$$\text{IF } G_1 \; A_1 \; (\text{IF } \ldots \; (\text{IF } G_g \; A_g \; \text{FAIL}) \; \ldots \;)$$

where g is the number of alternatives (see Section 4.2.6). If there was a final 'otherwise' case (that is, a final alternative with no guard, so that the right-hand side never fails), then it would have been translated to the form:

$$\text{IF } G_1 \; A_1 \; (\text{IF } \ldots \; (\text{IF } G_{g-1} \; A_{g-1} \; A_g) \; \ldots \;)$$

Notice that G_i and A_i cannot be equal to FAIL, because they are only the transformed versions of expressions written by the programmer.

If the right-hand side is of the first form, we can use the third rule of the previous section repeatedly, followed by the second, to give:

$$\text{(IF } G_1 \; A_1 \text{ (IF } \ldots \text{ (IF } G_g \; A_g \text{ FAIL) } \ldots \text{)) } [] \text{ E}$$
$$\equiv$$
$$\text{IF } G_1 \; A_1 \text{ (IF } \ldots \text{ (IF } G_g \; A_g \text{ E) } \ldots \text{)}$$

If the right-hand side is of the second form, it cannot return FAIL, and so we can use the first rule of the previous section.

Application of these three rules will eliminate all occurrences of [] and FAIL in the expression generated by the empty rule, and incidentally thereby give a worthwhile improvement in efficiency.

5.4.2.3 Clever compilation

Using these rules, many of the instances of [] and FAIL remaining in a function definition can be eliminated. Later we will consider compiling an expression into low-level machine code. When we do this, we will see that it is possible to compile the remaining expressions involving [] and FAIL in a surprisingly efficient way, so that [] requires no code at all, and the FAIL simply compiles to a jump instruction. This is discussed in Section 20.4.

5.5 Uniform Definitions

This section introduces a restricted class of function definitions, called *uniform definitions*. There are two motivations for studying this class. First, uniform definitions avoid certain problems with reasoning about function definitions that involve pattern-matching. Second, uniform definitions are easier to compile, and are guaranteed to avoid certain kinds of inefficient code.

We begin by discussing some problems with reasoning about function definitions containing pattern-matching. Consider again the alternate definition of mappairs:

```
mappairs' f [] ys          = []
mappairs' f xs []          = []
mappairs' f (x:xs) (y:ys) = f x y : mappairs' f xs ys
```

Now, consider evaluation of the expression:

```
mappairs' (+) bottom []
```

where the evaluation of bottom would fail to terminate (for example, bottom could be defined by the degenerate equation bottom = bottom). Matching against the first equation binds f to (+) and then attempts to match [] against bottom. In order to perform this match it is necessary to evaluate bottom, and this of course causes the entire expression to fail to terminate.

On the other hand, consider evaluation of:

```
mappairs' (+) [] bottom
```

Now matching against the first equation binds f to (+), matching [] against [] succeeds, and then ys is bound to bottom (without evaluating bottom). So the expression returns [] instead of failing to terminate. This means that the definition of mappairs' is not as symmetric as it appears.

Further, if the first two equations of mappairs' were written in the opposite order, the two expressions above would change their meaning: now the first would return [] and the second would fail to terminate. So even though the first and second equations have the same right-hand side, the order in which they are written is important.

The original definition of mappairs has none of these problems:

```
mappairs f [] ys          = []
mappairs f (x:xs) []      = []
mappairs f (x:xs) (y:ys)  = f x y : mappairs f xs ys
```

Now the asymmetry between (mappairs (+) [] bottom) and (mappairs (+) bottom []) is apparent from the equations. Further, changing the order of the equations does not change the meaning of the function.

In general, one might expect that whenever the equations do not overlap, the order in which they are written does not matter. In fact, this is not true. Consider the definition:

```
diagonal x     True  False = 1
diagonal False y     True  = 2
diagonal True  False z     = 3
```

The three equations of this definition are non-overlapping, that is, at most one equation can apply. However, by this definition, the evaluation of:

```
diagonal bottom True False
```

would return 1. On the other hand, if the order of equations in the definition were reversed, so the third equation came first, then the above expression would fail to terminate. So even though the equations do not overlap, the order in which they are written is important.

Clearly, it would be useful to have a test that guarantees that the order of the equations does not matter. We now define the class of *uniform* definitions, which have this property. The definition of 'uniformity' is designed so that it is easy to test whether a definition is uniform while applying the pattern-matching compiler to it.

DEFINITION

A set of equations is *uniform* if one of the following three conditions holds:

(i) either, all equations begin with a variable pattern, and applying the variable rule (of Section 5.2.2) yields a new set of equations that is also uniform;
(ii) or, all equations begin with a constructor pattern, and applying the constructor rule (of Section 5.2.3) yields new sets of equations that are all also uniform;
(iii) or, all equations have an empty list of patterns, so the empty rule (of Section 5.2.4) applies, and there is at most one equation in the set.

That is, a set of equations is uniform if it can be compiled without using the mixture rule (of Section 5.2.6), and if the empty rule is only applied to sets containing zero or one equations. (It is easy for the reader to check that when the empty rule is applied to more than one equation, the order is relevant.)

Such equation sets are called 'uniform' because all equations must begin the same way, either with a variable pattern or a constructor pattern, whereas the mixture rule applies when some equations begin with variable patterns and some with constructor patterns.

It is not difficult to prove the following:

THEOREM

If a definition is uniform, changing the order of the equations does not change the meaning of the definition.

The proof is a straightforward induction, and is similar in structure to the proof of correctness of the pattern-matching compiler that was outlined (along with its definition) in Section 5.2.

This shows that being uniform is a sufficient condition for the order of the equations not to matter. It is not a necessary condition, as is shown by the function dummy:

```
dummy []  = 1
dummy xs  = 1, xs = []
```

Clearly, dummy is not uniform, but the order of the equations does not matter. However, the following result shows that being uniform is indeed necessary if one considers only the left-hand sides:

THEOREM

If the left-hand sides of a definition are such that the order of the equations does not matter (regardless of the right-hand sides or condition parts of the equations), the definition is uniform.

For example, the order of the equations would matter in dummy if the 1 in the second equation were changed to a 2. Again, the proof of the theorem is a straightforward induction. These two theorems give us a simpler way of characterizing uniform equations, without referring to the pattern-matching compiler. Namely, a definition is uniform if and only if its left-hand sides are such that the order of the equations does not matter.

It is also possible to show that every uniform definition is non-overlapping. The converse is not true: the function diagonal is non-overlapping but is not uniform. Researchers have often referred to 'lack of overlapping' as an important property, but perhaps they should refer to 'uniformity' instead, since this is the property that guarantees that the order of equations does not matter.

Uniform equations are related to *strongly left-sequential equations* as defined by Hoffman and O'Donnell [1983], which are in turn related to *sequential equations* as defined by Huet and Levy [1979].

Notice that although uniform equations are independent of 'top-to-bottom' order, they still have a 'left-to-right' bias. For example, although the following definition is uniform:

```
xor False x     = x
xor True  False = True
xor True  True  = False
```

the same definition with the arguments interchanged is not:

```
xor' x     False = x
xor' False True  = True
xor' True  True  = False
```

Of course, we can always get around this bias by using extra definitions to rearrange the arguments. For example, we can define

```
xor'' x y = xor y x
```

and then xor'' is equivalent to xor', and both xor'' and xor have uniform definitions.

The existence of left-to-right bias is due to the semantics of pattern-matching that we have chosen. A different definition of pattern-matching that avoids left-to-right bias is possible; see Huet and Levy [1979].

There is a second reason why uniform equations are important: they are easier to implement. The problems with implementing non-uniform definitions have been referred to implicitly in previous sections. In summary, they are as follows:

(i) The resulting case-expressions may examine some variables more than once (see Section 5.2.6).

(ii) The compiler must use a modified constructor rule to avoid duplicating the right-hand side of equations (see Section 5.4.1).

(iii) The resulting expressions may contain [] and FAIL. Implementing such expressions efficiently requires additional simplification rules and/or a special way of implementing FAIL using jump instructions (see Section 5.4.2).

The result is that the pattern-matching compiler must be significantly more complicated if it is to deal with non-uniform expressions. Further, the first point above means that it may be difficult to know how efficient the code compiled for a non-uniform definition will be.

An issue related to uniformity is the way conditionals are handled. In languages such as SASL, conditional expressions and where expressions may appear anywhere in an expression, and the semantics of each is defined independently. In Miranda, conditions and where clauses are not separate expressions, but rather must be associated with the right-hand side of definitions. This increases the power of Miranda, in some ways, but only when non-uniform definitions are used. Hence, a restriction to uniform equations would also allow this part of the language to be simplified.

On the other hand, it should be pointed out that non-uniform definitions are sometimes very convenient. For example, the following definition reverses lists of length two, and leaves all other lists the same:

```
reverseTwo [x,y] = [y,x]
reverseTwo xs    = xs
```

The most straightforward way of rewriting this as a uniform definition is much more long-winded:

```
reverseTwo []           = []
reverseTwo [x]          = [x]
reverseTwo [x,y]        = [y,x]
reverseTwo (x:y:z:ws)   = x:y:z:ws
```

In this case, it is easy to see another way of rewriting reverseTwo, but, in general, rewriting may not be so easy.

Functional language designers have long debated whether or not definitions with overlapping equations should be allowed in functional languages. As has been shown, it may be more appropriate to debate the merits of uniform – as opposed to non-overlapping – equations. Several arguments in favor of restricting definitions to uniform equations have been raised here; but it is also true that non-uniform definitions are on occasion quite convenient. No doubt the debate will continue to be a lively one.

* * *

Acknowledgements: For help with my work on chapters 4, 5 and 7 I would like to thank the following. Simon Finn made valuable comments, both detailed and deep. Simon Peyton Jones and I are listed as co-authors only on Chapter 4, but he has provided as much thoughtful help as a co-author on the other chapters as well. For help of a very different nature, I thank Catherine Lyons.

This work was performed while on a research fellowship supported by ICL.

References

Augustsson, L. 1985. Compiling pattern matching. In *Conference on Functional Programming Languages and Computer Architecture, Nancy*, pp. 368–81. Jouannaud (editor), LNCS 201. Springer Verlag.

Barrett, G., and Wadler, P. 1986. *Derivation of a Pattern-matching Compiler*. Programming Research Group, Oxford.

Burstall, R.M., MacQueen, D.B., and Sanella, D.T. 1980. HOPE: an experimental applicative language. In *Proceedings of the ACM Lisp Conference*. August.

Hoffmann, C.M., and O'Donnell, M.J. 1983. Implementation of an interpreter for abstract equations. In *10th ACM Symposium on Principles of Programming Languages*, pp. 111–21. ACM.

Huet, G., and Levy, J.J. 1979. *Computations in Non-ambiguous Linear Term Rewriting Systems*. INRIA technical report 359.

Six

TRANSFORMING THE ENRICHED LAMBDA CALCULUS

Having now defined the semantics of pattern-matching, we are in a position to show how to transform all the constructs of the enriched lambda calculus into the ordinary lambda calculus.

Section 6.1 shows how to transform pattern-matching lambda abstractions into the ordinary lambda calculus, while Section 6.2 deals with let- and letrec-expressions; Sections 6.3 and 6.4 deal with case-expressions and the ▯ operator.

6.1 Transforming Pattern-matching Lambda Abstractions

In order to translate Miranda function definitions involving pattern-matching into the enriched lambda calculus, we had to introduce pattern-matching lambda abstractions as a new construct. In this section we will show how they can be transformed into the ordinary lambda calculus. For each form of (λp . E) we will give an equivalent form that does not use pattern-matching lambda abstractions.

In the case when the pattern p is a variable there is nothing to do, because no pattern-matching is involved. The remaining cases are when the pattern is a constant, a product-constructor pattern or a sum-constructor pattern. These are dealt with in the following three subsections.

6.1.1 Constant Patterns

This section shows how to transform a pattern-matching lambda abstraction (λk . E), with a constant pattern k, into the ordinary lambda calculus. First of all, we recall the semantics of (λk.E) from Section 4.3.2:

```
Eval[[ λk.E ]] a = Eval[[ E ]]        if a = Eval[[ k ]]
Eval[[ λk.E ]] a = FAIL               if a ≠ Eval[[ k ]] and a ≠ ⊥
Eval[[ λk.E ]] ⊥ = ⊥
```

Operationally, (λk.E) tests whether its argument is equal to k; if so, it returns E, if not it returns FAIL. This simple test can be carried out by the built-in IF function, using the following transformation:

```
(λk.E)  ≡  (λv.IF (= k v) E FAIL)
```

where v is a new variable which does not occur free in E. It should be clear (and can be proved, using the semantics of (λk.E) and the semantics of IF and =) that these two lambda abstractions have the same meaning, and hence are equivalent. Notice the way in which we introduce a new λv abstraction, so that we can name the argument directly in its body.

As an example, consider the Miranda definition

```
flip 0 = 1
flip 1 = 0
```

This will be translated to

```
flip = λx.( ((λ0.1) x)
          [] ((λ1.0) x)
          [] ERROR)
```

Now, transforming out the pattern-matching lambda abstractions gives

```
flip = λx.( ((λv.IF (= 0 v) 1 FAIL) x)
          [] ((λv.IF (= 1 v) 0 FAIL) x)
          [] ERROR)
```

It is now easy to verify that

```
flip 0  →  ...  →  1
flip 1  →  ...  →  0
flip 2  →  ...  →  ERROR
```

6.1.2 Product-constructor Patterns

Next we consider the case of (λp.E), where p is the product pattern (t p_1 ... p_r), and t is a product constructor of arity r. As before, we recall its semantics (Section 4.3.4):

```
Eval[[ λ(t p1 ... pr).E ]] a = Eval[[ λp1...λpr.E ]] (SEL-t-1 a)
                                                     ...
                                                     (SEL-t-r a)
```

To implement this semantics, we invent a new function

UNPACK-PRODUCT-t for each product constructor t, and use it in this transformation:

$$(\lambda(\text{t } p_1 \ \dots \ p_r).\text{E}) \ \equiv \ \text{UNPACK-PRODUCT-t } (\lambda p_1 \dots \lambda p_r.\text{E})$$

The idea is that UNPACK-PRODUCT-t takes two arguments, a function and a structured object, and applies the function to the lazily selected components of the object. It is defined by the following semantic equation:

$$\text{UNPACK-PRODUCT-t f a} = \text{f (SEL-t-1 a)} \ \dots \ \text{(SEL-t-r a)}$$

It can easily be shown that the transformation is valid, by comparing the semantics of the expression before and after the transformation.

The right-hand side of the transformation still has pattern-matching lambda abstractions in it, but they are smaller than the one we began with, and repeated use of the rules for transforming pattern-matching lambda abstractions will eliminate them.

As an example, consider the function addPair, which adds together the elements of a pair:

```
addPair = λ(PAIR x y).+ x y
```

This will be transformed to

```
addPair = UNPACK-PRODUCT-PAIR (λx.λy.+ x y)
```

We can check that it gives the right results by reducing (addPair (PAIR 3 4)):

```
addPair (PAIR 3 4)
=  UNPACK-PRODUCT-PAIR (λx.λy.+ x y) (PAIR 3 4)
→  (λx.λy.+ x y) (SEL-PAIR-1 (PAIR 3 4)) (SEL-PAIR-2 (PAIR 3 4))
→  (λy.+ (SEL-PAIR-1 (PAIR 3 4)) y) (SEL-PAIR-2 (PAIR 3 4))
→  + (SEL-PAIR-1 (PAIR 3 4)) (SEL-PAIR-2 (PAIR 3 4))
→  + 3 (SEL-PAIR-2 (PAIR 3 4))
→  + 3 4
→  7
```

6.1.3 Sum-constructor Patterns

Finally, consider the case of $(\lambda \text{p}.\text{E})$, where p is a sum pattern $(\text{s } p_1 \ \dots \ p_r)$, and s is a sum constructor of arity r. The semantics of such lambda abstractions was derived in Section 4.3.3:

$$\begin{array}{ll}
\textbf{Eval}[\![\ \lambda(\text{s } p_1 \dots p_r).\text{E} \ ]\!] \ (\text{s } a_1 \dots a_r) & = \textbf{Eval}[\![\ \lambda p_1 \dots \lambda p_r.\text{E} \ ]\!] \ a_1 \dots a_r \\
\textbf{Eval}[\![\ \lambda(\text{s } p_1 \dots p_r).\text{E} \ ]\!] \ (\text{s}' \ a_1 \dots a_{r'}) & = \text{FAIL} \quad \text{if s} \neq \text{s}' \\
\textbf{Eval}[\![\ \lambda(\text{s } p_1 \dots p_r).\text{E} \ ]\!] \ \bot & = \bot
\end{array}$$

We can make a very similar transformation to the product-constructor case, leaving all the hard work to a new function UNPACK-SUM-s:

$$(\lambda(\text{s } p_1 \dots p_r).\text{E}) \ \equiv \ \text{UNPACK-SUM-s } (\lambda p_1 \dots \lambda p_r.\text{E})$$

The function UNPACK-SUM-s takes two arguments, a function (in this case $(\lambda p_1 \ldots \lambda p_r . E)$), and a structured object. It checks whether the object is built with constructor s: if not, FAIL is returned; if so, UNPACK-SUM-s takes the object apart and applies the function (its first argument) to its components. UNPACK-SUM-s is specified by the following semantic equations:

```
UNPACK-SUM-s f (s a₁ ... aᵣ)   = f a₁ ... aᵣ
UNPACK-SUM-s f (s' a₁ ... aᵣ') = FAIL        if s ≠ s'
UNPACK-SUM-s f ⊥               = ⊥
```

As an example, recall the Miranda definition of reflect:

```
reflect (LEAF n)         = LEAF n
reflect (BRANCH t1 t2) = BRANCH (reflect t2) (reflect t1)
```

This is translated to:

```
reflect = λt.( ((λ(LEAF n).LEAF n) t)
              ▯ ((λ(BRANCH t1 t2).BRANCH (reflect t2) (reflect t1)) t)
              ▯ ERROR)
```

Now, applying the transformation gives:

```
reflect
= λt.( (UNPACK-SUM-LEAF (λn.LEAF n) t)
      ▯ (UNPACK-SUM-BRANCH (λt1.λt2.BRANCH (reflect t2) (reflect t1)) t)
      ▯ ERROR)
```

6.1.4 Reducing the Number of Built-in Functions

The trouble with the transformations of the previous section is that they introduce several functions associated with each constructor. In this section we discuss the implementation of these functions.

A structured object will be represented by the implementation as an aggregate, consisting of the component fields together with a *structure tag*, which distinguishes objects built by different constructors from each other (see Section 10.3.1). It is this tag which can be used by UNPACK-SUM-s to identify the constructor used.

In a type-checked system it is only necessary to distinguish objects from other objects of the same type, so the structure tag can be a small integer in the range $1 \ldots n$ (where n is the number of constructors in the type). This means that, instead of requiring an UNPACK-SUM-s function for each constructor s, it is only necessary to have a single family of functions UNPACK-SUM-d-r_s, where d is the integer structure tag which is recognized by UNPACK-SUM-d-r_s, and r_s is the arity of s. In a similar way, the sum constructor functions can be replaced with a family of functions PACK-SUM-d-r_s, which take r_s arguments and construct an aggregate with r_s fields and structure tag d.

We can perform an analogous set of replacements for the functions associated with product types. UNPACK-PRODUCT-t can be replaced with

UNPACK-PRODUCT-r_t, where r_t is the arity of t (there is no need for a structure tag here, since UNPACK-PRODUCT does not examine it). Similarly, the product-constructor functions can be replaced with PACK-PRODUCT-r_t, and the selector functions SEL-t-i can be replaced with SEL-r_t-i. It is sensible to keep PACK-SUM and PACK-PRODUCT distinct because, having no structure tag, objects of product type may have a different representation from objects of sum type.

To summarize:

s (a sum-constructor function)	is replaced by PACK-SUM-d-r_s
UNPACK-SUM-s	is replaced by UNPACK-SUM-d-r_s
t (a product-constructor function)	is replaced by PACK-PRODUCT-r_t
UNPACK-PRODUCT-t	is replaced by UNPACK-PRODUCT-r_t
SEL-t-i	is replaced by SEL-r_t-i

where r_s = arity of s,
d = structure tag of s,
r_t = arity of t.

For example, assuming that we implement lists with structure tag 1 for NIL and 2 for CONS, then the following replacements would take place:

NIL	is replaced by	PACK-SUM-1-0
CONS	is replaced by	PACK-SUM-2-2
UNPACK-SUM-NIL	is replaced by	UNPACK-SUM-1-0
UNPACK-SUM-CONS	is replaced by	UNPACK-SUM-2-2

Likewise, if the type tree is declared as before:

```
tree ::= LEAF num | BRANCH tree tree
```

and LEAF and BRANCH are assigned structure tags 1 and 2 respectively, the following replacements would take place:

LEAF	is replaced by	PACK-SUM-1-1
BRANCH	is replaced by	PACK-SUM-2-2
UNPACK-SUM-LEAF	is replaced by	UNPACK-SUM-1-1
UNPACK-SUM-BRANCH	is replaced by	UNPACK-SUM-2-2

Finally, if the type pair is declared as before:

```
pair * ** ::= PAIR * **
```

the following replacements would take place:

PAIR	is replaced by	PACK-PRODUCT-2
UNPACK-PRODUCT-PAIR	is replaced by	UNPACK-PRODUCT-2
SEL-PAIR-1	is replaced by	SEL-2-1
SEL-PAIR-2	is replaced by	SEL-2-2

Since functions with different types may be replaced by the same function (for example, CONS and BRANCH are both replaced by PACK-SUM-2-2), these replacements should not be performed until after type-checking. For the same reason, none of these replacements is possible for a system that performs run-time type-checking (see Section 10.5).

6.1.5 Summary

Figure 6.1 summarizes the transformations developed in this section, and Figure 6.2 gives the semantics for the two new families of functions we introduced in order to perform the transformations.

$$(\lambda k\,.\,E) \equiv (\lambda v\,.\,IF\ (=\ k\ v)\ E\ FAIL)$$

where v is a new variable that does not occur free in E

$$(\lambda(t\ p_1\ \ldots\ p_{r_t})\,.\,E) \equiv (UNPACK\text{-}PRODUCT\text{-}t\ (\lambda p_1 \ldots \lambda p_{r_t}\,.\,E))$$
$$(\lambda(s\ p_1\ \ldots\ p_{r_s})\,.\,E) \equiv (UNPACK\text{-}SUM\text{-}s\ (\lambda p_1 \ldots \lambda p_{r_s}\,.\,E))$$

where k is a constant
t is a product constructor of arity r_t
s is a sum constructor of arity r_s

Figure 6.1 Transforming out pattern-matching lambda abstractions

$$UNPACK\text{-}PRODUCT\text{-}t\ f\ a = f\ (SEL\text{-}t\text{-}1\ a)\ \ldots\ (SEL\text{-}t\text{-}r_t\ a)$$

$$UNPACK\text{-}SUM\text{-}s\ f\ (s\ a_1\ \ldots\ a_{r_s}) = f\ a_1\ \ldots\ a_{r_s}$$
$$UNPACK\text{-}SUM\text{-}s\ f\ (s'\ a_1\ \ldots\ a_{r_{s'}}) = FAIL \qquad \text{if } s \neq s'$$
$$UNPACK\text{-}SUM\text{-}s\ f\ \bot = \bot$$

where t is a product constructor of arity r_t
s is a product constructor of arity r_s

Figure 6.2 Semantics of UNPACK-PRODUCT and UNPACK-SUM

6.2 Transforming let and letrec

In Section 4.2.9 we introduced a new complication to let(rec)-expressions, by allowing the left-hand side of definitions to be an arbitrary pattern rather than a simple variable. In this section we show how to transform these generalized lets and letrecs into successively simpler forms, arriving eventually at the ordinary lambda calculus.

Rather than defining the semantics of let and letrec directly, as we did for pattern-matching lambda abstractions, we will regard the transformations described in this section as a definition of their semantics. To define their meaning in a more direct way would require more mathematical machinery than we have available in this book.

We begin by sketching a new problem which is introduced by allowing arbitrary patterns on the left-hand side of definitions. This leads us to define a class of patterns, the *irrefutable* patterns, which do not suffer from the problem. Then, before embarking on the transformations themselves, we give a 'map' to explain their structure.

6.2.1 Conformality Checking and Irrefutable Patterns

Allowing arbitrary patterns on the left-hand side of a definition introduces a new and somewhat subtle complication. Consider the expression

```
let (CONS x xs) = B in E
```

Here, the pattern (CONS x xs) appears on the left-hand side of the definition. This raises the nasty possibility that B might evaluate to NIL instead of (CONS B_1 B_2), in which case the pattern would not match, and some sort of error should, presumably, be reported. This requires that a *conformality check* be made, to ensure that B conforms with the specified pattern.

Conformality checking will carry some implementation cost, so we would like to avoid it whenever possible. It can be avoided in precisely those cases when the pattern match cannot fail; for example, simple product patterns. However, there are some nested patterns which cannot fail also, which motivates the following definition:

> DEFINITION
>
> A pattern p is *irrefutable* if it is
>
> (i) either a variable v
>
> (ii) or a product pattern of form (t p_1 ... p_r) where p_1, ..., p_r are irrefutable patterns.
>
> Otherwise the pattern is *refutable.*

In other words, the irrefutable patterns consist of arbitrarily nested product constructors with variables at the leaves. These patterns cannot fail to match in a type-checked implementation. Variables and simple product patterns are just two examples of irrefutable patterns.

However, even a single constant or sum constructor (even if nested inside a product pattern) makes the pattern refutable, since there is a possibility that it may not match. We need to perform conformality checking for refutable definitions only.

6.2.2 Overview of let and letrec Transformations

We are now ready to describe the various transformations to simplify let(rec)-expressions. While few are complicated, they are quite numerous, so we begin by offering a 'map' to aid in navigation through the rest of the section.

For a start, we establish the following terminology:

(i) The left-hand side of each definition of a *simple* let(rec)-expression must be a variable.
(ii) The left-hand side of each definition of an *irrefutable* let(rec)-expression must be an irrefutable pattern.
(iii) The left-hand side of each definition of a *general* let(rec)-expression may be any arbitrary pattern.

With the aid of this terminology, Figure 6.3 depicts the transformations which will be described below, giving the appropriate section number in brackets.

For the reasons discussed in Section 3.2.4, there are two possible forms into which we may wish to transform the program, which differ only in their treatment of let and letrec:

(i) We may transform the program into the ordinary lambda calculus; this gives the simplest resulting program. In this case, general lets are transformed into the ordinary calculus via irrefutable lets and simple lets. General letrecs, on the other hand, are first transformed into irrefutable lets via irrefutable letrecs, and then use the let transformations.
(ii) We may transform the program into the ordinary lambda calculus augmented with simple let(rec)-expressions; the resulting program is slightly more complicated, but can be implemented more efficiently (Section 3.2.4). In this case, general lets are transformed only into simple lets, and general letrecs are transformed into simple letrecs, via irrefutable letrecs.

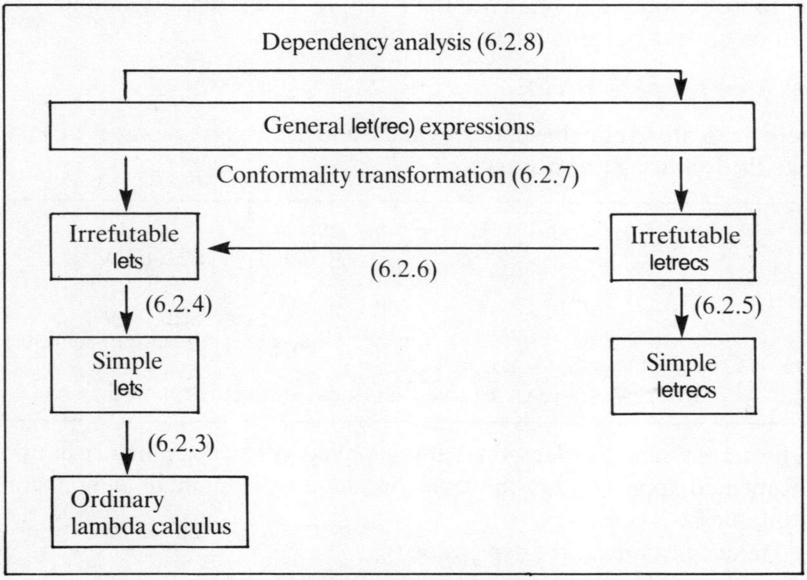

Figure 6.3 Map of let(rec) transformations

Both possibilities are catered for by the transformations shown in Figure 6.3.

In what follows, when considering let-expressions we assume that they contain only one definition. This gives no loss of generality, since a let-expression with multiple definitions is trivially equivalent to a nested set of single-definition let-expressions.

The following sections deal with the transformations depicted in Figure 6.3.

6.2.3 Transforming Simple lets into the Ordinary Lambda Calculus

Once we have arrived at an expression in which all let-expressions are simple, it is easy to remove them altogether, using the transformation given in Section 3.2.1:

```
let v = B in E   ≡   (λv.E) B
```

For example,

```
let x = 4 in (+ x 6)   ≡   (λx.+ x 6) 4
```

6.2.4 Transforming Irrefutable lets into Simple lets

Consider the case of an irrefutable let-expression, of the form

```
let p = B in E
```

where p is irrefutable. Since the pattern on the left-hand side of the definition is irrefutable, it must either be a variable or a product pattern. In the former case there is nothing to do, since the let-expression is already simple. In the latter case, the let-expression takes the form

```
let (t p1 ... pr) = B in E
```

where the p_i are irrefutable patterns, and B and E are expressions. We can now make the following transformation:

```
let (t p1 ... pr) = B in E   ≡   let v = B
                                 in (let p1 = SEL-t-1 v
                                         ...
                                         pr = SEL-t-r v
                                     in E)
```

where v is a new variable that does not occur free in E.

The p_i are bound to selector functions applied to v, which is in turn bound to B. Repeated application of this transformation will eliminate all non-simple irrefutable let-expressions.

To take an example, the expression

```
let (PAIR x y) = B in E
```

would be transformed to

```
let v = B in (let x = SEL-PAIR-1 v
                  y = SEL-PAIR-2 v
              in E)
```

Notice that if neither x nor y is evaluated in E, then B will not be evaluated either, so the transformation implements lazy product-matching. Lazy product-matching is just as much of an advantage here as it was in function definitions. For example, we could recode the function 'firsts' from Section 4.3.5 in the following way:

```
firsts []     = (0, 0)
firsts (x:xs) = (x, ev),        odd x
              = (od, x),        even x
                where
                (od, ev) = firsts xs
```

We would expect this definition to behave just like that of Chapter 4, so that if lazy product-matching is used for function definitions then it should also be used for let(rec)-expressions.

(Note: an alternative transformation would have been possible in this section, namely:

```
let p = B in E  ≡  (λp.E) B
```

where p is an irrefutable pattern. From a semantic point of view, this is entirely equivalent to the transformation used above. However, for the efficiency reasons outlined in Section 3.2.4, we prefer to stay in the world of let-expressions as long as possible; hence our choice.)

6.2.5 Transforming Irrefutable letrecs into Simple letrecs

The transformation from a letrec involving only irrefutable definitions into a simple letrec is very similar to that for let-expressions:

```
letrec (t p1 ... pr) = B  ≡  letrec v = B
       <other definitions>          p1 = SEL-t-1 v
in E                                ...
                                    pr = SEL-t-r v
                                    <other definitions>
                             in E
```

where v is a new variable that does not occur free in E or B.

All the transformed definitions must be in a single letrec, to ensure that variables in the patterns p_i are in scope in B. The '<other definitions>' simply takes into account the fact that the letrec may contain multiple definitions, and this transformation should be applied to each of them separately.

Repeated application of the transformation will simplify the p_i successively, until the letrec is simple.

6.2.6 Transforming Irrefutable letrecs into Irrefutable lets

In showing how to eliminate letrec-expressions altogether, we could take as our starting-point the simple letrec-expressions produced by the transformation described in the preceding section. However, it is slightly more efficient to start from an earlier stage, the irrefutable letrec-expressions.

First of all, we recall from Section 3.2.2 how to transform a simple letrec containing only a single definition:

```
(letrec v = B in E)   ≡   (let v = Y (λv.B) in E)
```

We simply use the built-in function Y, which was introduced in Section 2.4, to make the definition non-recursive. Now that the definition is non-recursive, we can use let instead of letrec, and the job is done.

When there is more than one definition, we apply the following sequence of two transformations. First of all, we apply the transformation

```
letrec p1 = B1   ≡   letrec (t p1 ... pn) = (t B1 ... Bn) in E
       ...
       pn = Bn
in E
```

where t is a product constructor of arity n.

In other words, we simply package up the right-hand sides into a tuple and match it against a product pattern on the left-hand side. Furthermore, since the p_i are irrefutable, the pattern (t p_1 ... p_n) is also irrefutable.

Now the letrec contains only a single definition with an irrefutable pattern on its left-hand side, and we can proceed by analogy with the simple case described above, using Y. This analogy yields the following transformation:

```
letrec p = B in E   ≡   let p = Y (λp.B) in E
```

where p is an irrefutable pattern.

Y is used exactly as before, to make the definition non-recursive. The new feature is the use of a pattern-matching lambda abstraction, where we used only a simple lambda abstraction before. The result is a let-expression with an irrefutable pattern on its left-hand side, which is therefore amenable to the transformations of Section 6.2.4.

To see this transformation in action, consider the following letrec-expression:

```
letrec x = CONS 1 y
       y = CONS 2 x
in x
```

It defines the infinite list [1,2,1,2,. . .,]. Applying the first transformation, we package up the definitions into one:

```
letrec (PAIR x y) = PAIR (CONS 1 y) (CONS 2 x) in x
```

Now, applying the second transformation gives:

```
let (PAIR x y) = Y (λ(PAIR x y).PAIR (CONS 1 y) (CONS 2 x)) in x
```

It is vital that the pattern-matching lambda abstraction should use lazy product-matching. If it were to use strict product-matching instead, the expression would yield ⊥ rather than [1,2,1,2, . . .,]. In fact, mutual recursion cannot be implemented using Y without some form of lazy product-matching.

Using the transformations for let-expressions and pattern-matching lambda abstractions, we could complete the transformation of the current example as follows:

```
(λv.(λx.λy.x) (SEL-PAIR-1 v) (SEL-PAIR-2 v))
(Y (UNPACK-PRODUCT-PAIR (λx.λy.PAIR (CONS 1 y) (CONS 2 x))))
```

This expression is not a pretty sight, but it gives the correct answer (that is, the infinite list [1,2,1,2,1,2,. . .,]).

It should be clear from this example that implementing letrec using tuples carries a run-time cost, both to build the tuple and to take it apart. This is one of the reasons why more sophisticated implementations implement simple let(rec)s directly (see Section 3.2.4 and Chapter 14).

6.2.7 Transforming General let(rec)s into Irrefutable let(rec)s

In Miranda, arbitrary patterns may appear on the left-hand side of a definition. For example, consider the following Miranda definition of the function head, which extracts the first element of a list:

```
head xs = y
          where (y:ys) = xs
```

The pattern (y:ys) appears on the left-hand side of the definition in the where-clause. But this raises an awkward question: what would happen if the pattern (y:ys) did not match the result of evaluating xs? In particular, what would happen if we evaluated (head [])?

It is clearly unacceptable for the system to proceed in ignorance that anything is wrong, so it is necessary to check that xs matches the pattern, rather than assume that it always will. This is called the *conformality check*, since it checks that xs conforms to the pattern.

Notice that the possibility of a mismatch only arises in the case of refutable patterns, involving sum-constructor patterns or constants. The irrefutable patterns, involving variables and product-constructor patterns only, cannot fail to match (in a type-checked implementation).

The translation into the enriched lambda calculus does not affect the problem of conformality checking. For example, the definition of head translates to:

```
head = λxs.(letrec (CONS y ys) = xs in y)
```

The pattern (CONS y ys) is refutable, and may fail to match. The problem applies equally to lets and letrecs.

Having decided that conformality checking is essential, the next question is: when is the conformality check performed? There are two possible answers:

(i) When the evaluation of the entire let(rec)-expression begins.
(ii) On the first occasion when either y or ys is used.

To illustrate the consequences of this choice, consider the (rather contrived) expression

```
let (CONS y ys) = NIL in 6
```

The first answer specifies that the evaluation of this expression should cause an error, while the second specifies that it should return 6.

In keeping with its lazy approach, the semantics of Miranda specifies the second of the two answers, and so this property should be inherited by let(rec)-expressions. How is this to be achieved? The simplest way seems to be to transform the expression

```
let (CONS y ys) = B in E
```

into

```
let (PAIR y ys) = (((λ(CONS y ys).PAIR y ys) B) ▯ ERROR) in E
```

and reply on the transformation of the previous section to cope with the simple product pattern (PAIR y ys). The expression on the right-hand side will evaluate B, check that it is an object constructed with CONS, take it apart, and construct a pair containing its two components. These components are then bound to y and ys using a simple product pattern on the left-hand side.

If it is not an object constructed with CONS, then the application of the pattern-matching lambda abstraction to B will return FAIL, and ▯ will return its second argument, namely ERROR.

There are two points to notice about this transformation:

(i) No conformality check will be made if neither y nor ys is used in E, because the lazy product-matching ensures that the right-hand side of the definition is not evaluated unless at least one of the components of the tuple is used.
(ii) The conformality check is made at most once. The evaluation of y or ys will cause the evaluation of the right-hand side of the definition, at which point the conformality check will be made, and the tuple built. Now, further use of y or ys will simply access the components of this tuple.

It seems hard to improve on these two properties, so we now generalize the method to handle any let(rec)-expression. Given a definition of the form

p = B

where p is a refutable pattern, we use the following transformation:

$$\text{p} = \text{B} \equiv (\text{t } v_1 \ldots v_n) = ((\lambda\text{p}.(\text{t } v_1 \ldots v_n))\ \text{B}) \mathbin{[]} \text{ERROR}$$

where t is a product constructor of arity n. The resulting definition now has an irrefutable pattern on the left-hand side. We call this the *conformality transformation*, and it applies separately to any definition in a let or letrec which has a refutable pattern on the left-hand side.

The variables $v_1 \ldots v_n$ are simply the variables that appear anywhere in the pattern p. This suggests a new definition.

> DEFINITION
>
> For any pattern p, the set of variables of p, abbreviated Var(p), is defined thus:
>
> if p is a variable v, then Var(p) = {v}
> if p is a constant k, then Var(p) = { }
> if p is a structured pattern $(\text{c } p_1 \ldots p_r)$,
> then $\text{Var(p)} = \text{Var}(p_1) \cup \ldots \cup \text{Var}(p_r)$

Now we see that the variables $v_1 \ldots v_n$ in the conformality transformation are simply the variables of p, namely Var(p). Hence, we can express the conformality transformation as follows:

> $$\text{p} = \text{B} \equiv (\text{t } v_1 \ldots v_n) = ((\lambda\text{p}.(\text{t } v_1 \ldots v_n))\ \text{B}) \mathbin{[]} \text{ERROR}$$
>
> where $\{v_1, \ldots, v_n\} = \text{Var(p)}$,
> t is a product constructor of arity n.

We would like to use the pattern-matching compiler of Chapter 5 to transform the new right-hand side of the definition to an efficient form, and a small modification to the conformality transformation will make its result directly amenable to such transformation:

> $$\text{p} = \text{B} \equiv (\text{t } v_1 \ldots v_n) = \text{let v} = \text{B}$$
> $$\text{in } ((\lambda\text{p}.(\text{t } v_1 \ldots v_n))\ \text{v}) \mathbin{[]} \text{ERROR}$$
>
> where $\{v_1, \ldots, v_n\} = \text{Var(p)}$,
> t is a product constructor of arity n,
> v is a new variable which is distinct from all the v_i.

The pattern-matching compiler relies on the fact that the pattern-matching lambda abstractions are applied to variables only, which we achieve by binding B to a new variable v using a let-expression. Now the expression

```
((λp.(t v1 ... vn)) v) [] ERROR
```

can be transformed by the pattern-matching compiler.

There are some unexpected consequences of the rule that the complete conformality check is performed whenever any variable from the pattern is used. For example, consider the following Miranda function definitions:

```
f1 x = y where y      = x
               (h:t)  = []
f2 x = y where (y,(h:t)) = (x,[])
f3 x = y where (y,z)  = (x,[])
               (h:t)  = z
```

Given the rules of this section, f1 will behave as the identity function, ignoring the mismatch between (h:t) and []. The function f3 will behave in the same way; it binds z to [], but ignores the mismatch between (h:t) and z. However, f2 will always return ERROR, because when extracting y from the pair it will perform a conformality check on the whole pattern, and discover that (h:t) does not match []. Nevertheless, the programmer might be forgiven for thinking that f1, f2 and f3 should all behave in the same way.

In this section we have given a complete and consistent semantics for refutable patterns in let(rec)s, which we believe accurately describes the (current) semantics of this part of Miranda. As we have seen, however, the semantics gives results which may occasionally be unexpected, which is only to say that it is not the only possible choice. The examples of unexpected behavior were suggested by Simon Finn, of the University of Stirling.

6.2.8 Dependency Analysis

The transformation of where-clauses given in Section 4.2.8 does not introduce any let-expressions. The reason for this is that all definitions in a where-clause may potentially be mutually recursive, so we assume the worst and generate a single letrec-expression. Similar remarks apply to the overall scheme described in Section 3.3.

This is often unnecessarily pessimistic, and in this section we show how to replace letrecs with lets wherever possible, and how to sort mutually recursive definitions into minimal groups. For example, consider the following letrec-expression:

```
letrec x   = fac z
       fac = λn.IF (= n 0) 1 (* n (fac (- n 1)))
       z   = 4
       sum = λx.λy.IF (= x 0) y (sum (- x 1) (+ y 1))
in sum x z
```

An equivalent expression, which exposes more information, would be

```
let
     z = 4
in letrec
     sum = λx.λy.IF (= x 0) y (sum (- x 1) (+ y 1))
in letrec
     fac = λn.IF (= n 0) 1 (* n (fac (- n 1)))
in let
     x = fac z
in
     sum x z
```

In this latter form, the structure of the expression exposes clearly which definitions depend on each other, and the use of letrec is restricted to the occasion where it is actually necessary. Even when recursion is being used, separate groups of recursive definitions are in separate letrecs (so that sum and fac are in separate letrecs).

This transformation is called *dependency analysis*, since it sorts definitions into groups according to the dependency relationships which hold between them. It is closely related to *data flow analysis* techniques used in conventional compilers.

It is highly desirable to perform dependency analysis, for two reasons:

(i) Let-expressions can be implemented considerably more efficiently than letrec-expressions, so the use of the latter should be avoided unless recursion is actually present.
(ii) Type-checking may be impossible if dependency analysis is not performed (see Chapter 8). Furthermore, other steps such as strictness analysis (see Chapter 22) become considerably more efficient if dependency analysis is performed first.

We will now describe the dependency analysis algorithm in more detail, using the following example as an illustration:

```
letrec
       a = ...
       b = ...a...
       c = ...h...b...d...
       d = ...c...
       f = ...g...h...a...
       g = ...f...
       h = ...g...
in
        ...
```

The example is a simple letrec, but the algorithm requires only minor modification to deal with general let(rec)s.

The algorithm divides into four steps, which are performed separately on each letrec.

(1) For each letrec construct a (directed) graph in which the nodes are the variables bound by the letrec. There is an arc from one variable, f, to another variable, g, if g occurs free in the definition of f (i.e. the definition of f depends *directly* on g). We call this graph the *dependency graph*. Figure 6.4 shows the dependency graph for our example.

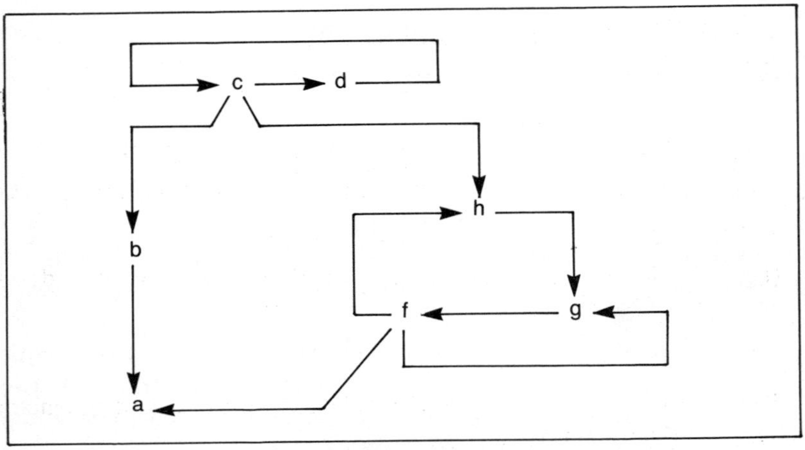

Figure 6.4 Example dependency graph

(2) Now, two variables x and y are mutually recursive if there is a path (direct or otherwise) in the dependency graph from x to y and from y to x. But this is precisely the definition of a *strongly connected component* of a graph, so the next phase is to discover the strongly connected components of the dependency graph. There are a number of standard algorithms for doing this (see, for example, Aho *et al.* [1974, 1983a] and Dijkstra [1976]).

In our example, the strongly connected components are

{c,d} {f,g,h} {b} {a}

(We put non-recursive variables, such as a and b, in a singleton component.) Each of the variables in each group depends on the others, and these are the largest such groups.

(3) Next we need to sort the strongly connected components into dependency order. In our example above this is to ensure that the let-expression for a will enclose the let-expression for b. First of all we coalesce each strongly connected component to a single node, forming a new graph (the coalesced graph) which is guaranteed to be acyclic. Figure 6.5 shows the effect of this operation. Now we can perform a *topological sort* to put them in dependency order (this is again a standard algorithm [Aho *et al.*, 1983b]). A topological sort puts the nodes of an acyclic graph into a linear order such that no node has an arc to an earlier node. Alternatively, a suitable strongly connected component algorithm (such as those given above) will produce the components in topologically sorted order, so that a separate topological sort would not be necessary.

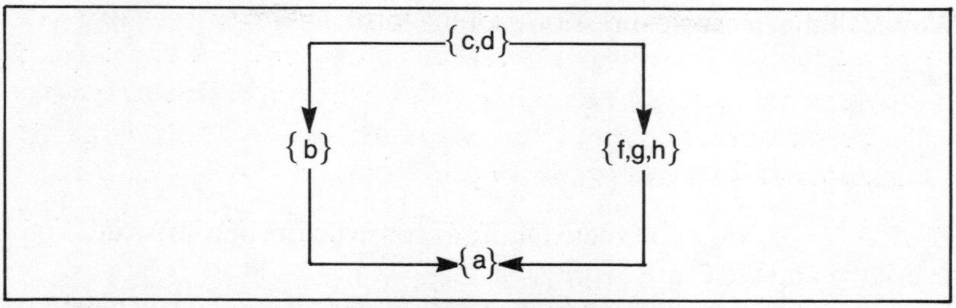

Figure 6.5 Example coalesced graph

A possible result of the topological sort in our example is

{c,d}, {b}, {f,g,h}, {a}

This tells us that it is acceptable for the definition of {a} to enclose that of {f,g,h}, which encloses that of {b}, which encloses that of {c,d}. An alternative result is

{c,d}, {f,g,h}, {b}, {a}

The fact that more than one result is valid reflects the lack of dependency between {f,g,h} and {b}.

Non-recursive definitions will be singleton components which do not point to themselves in the dependency graph; we will produce let-expressions for these.

(4) Finally we generate a let- or letrec-expression for each definition group in the topologically sorted order. For our example this would generate the following expression:

```
let
            a  = ...
in let
            b  = ...a...
in letrec
            f  = ...g...h...a...
            g  = ...f...
            h  = ...g...
in letrec
            c  = ...h...b...d...
            d  = ...c...
in
            ...
```

6.3 Transforming case-expressions

The translation scheme of Chapter 5 made use of the case-expression construct, and we now demonstrate how case-expressions may be transformed into an expression in the ordinary lambda calculus.

We recall that a case-expression is of the form

```
case v of
      c1 v1,1 ... v1,r1  ⇒  E1
      ...
      cn vn,1 ... vn,rn  ⇒  En
```

where c_1, ..., c_n are a complete family of constructors of a structured type, v is a variable and the E_i are expressions.

As usual, there are two possibilities to consider, depending on whether the constructors in the case-expression are those of a sum type or a product type.

6.3.1 Case-expressions Involving a Product Type

The general case-expression for product types is of the form:

```
case v of
      t v1 ... vr  ⇒  E1
```

where t is the constructor of a product type. This case-expression is degenerate, since there is no need to test v to determine which case to pick, so we should perform lazy product-matching. We can therefore use the following transformation:

```
case v of                    ≡ UNPACK-PRODUCT-t (λv1...λvr.E1) v
      t v1 ... vr  ⇒  E1
```

remembering that UNPACK-PRODUCT works lazily. For example, consider the following Miranda definition of addPair:

```
addPair (x,y) = x + y
```

Translated into the enriched lambda calculus, and transformed into case-expressions, this becomes

```
addPair = λw.(case w of (PAIR x y)  ⇒  (+ x y))
```

Now transforming the case-expression gives

```
addPair = λw.(UNPACK-PRODUCT-PAIR (λx.λy.+ x y) w)
```

and a final η-reduction is now available, giving finally

```
addPair = UNPACK-PRODUCT-PAIR (λx.λy.+ x y)
```

6.3.2 Case-expressions Involving a Sum Type

Now suppose that the constructors are those of a sum type. Then the case-expression is of the form:

```
case v of
      s1 v1,1 ... v1,r1  ⇒  E1
      ...
      sn vn,1 ... vn,rn  ⇒  En
```

where s_1, . . ., s_n are the constructors of a sum type T. We can transform this case-expression using the following transformation:

```
case v of
      s1 v1,1 ... v1,r1  => E1
      ...
      sn vn,1 ... vn,rn  => En

≡     CASE-T v (UNPACK-SUM-s1 (λv1,1...λv1,r1.E1) v)
                ...
               (UNPACK-SUM-sn (λvn,1...λvn,rn.En) v)
```

The function CASE-T, of which there is one for each sum type T, selects one of its n arguments depending on the constructor used to build its first argument:

```
CASE-T (si a1 ... ari) b1 ... bi ... bn = bi
CASE-T ⊥               b1 ... bi ... bn = ⊥
```

where T is a sum type. Operationally speaking, CASE-T evaluates its first argument and returns the argument corresponding to the constructor.

We could use CASE-T to translate the definition of reflect, for which we have the following case-expression (see Section 4.4):

```
reflect = λt.case t of
                 LEAF n         => LEAF n
                 BRANCH t1 t2   => BRANCH (reflect t2) (reflect t1)
```

Applying the transformation gives:

```
reflect
= λt.CASE-tree
        t
        (UNPACK-SUM-LEAF (λn.LEAF n) t)
        (UNPACK-SUM-BRANCH
                (λt1.λt2.BRANCH (reflect t2) (reflect t1)) t)
```

This is a more satisfactory definition than the one we produced in Section 6.1.3, because it will execute in fewer reductions, and because no check for FAIL need be made by CASE-tree. Furthermore, UNPACK-SUM-LEAF is guaranteed only to be applied to leaves, so it need not check the constructor of its argument, thus giving a further gain in efficiency. Similar remarks apply to UNPACK-SUM-BRANCH.

6.3.3 Using a let-expression Instead of UNPACK

The transformations given in the previous sections both introduced a new lambda abstraction. For all but the simplest implementations, simple let-expressions can be implemented much more efficiently than lambda abstractions (Section 3.2.4), so in this section we will see how to transform case-expressions into simple let-expressions instead.

In the case of a product type, we use the following transformation:

```
case v of                      ≡  let v1 = SEL-t-1 v
     t v1 ... vr  =>  E1                ...
                                      vr = SEL-t-r v
                                  in E1
```

This transformation is precisely equivalent to the one given before, as can be confirmed by transforming the let-expression into lambda abstractions using the transformation that defines simple let-expressions (Section 3.2.1). The addPair example would then become

```
addPair = λw.(let x = SEL-PAIR-1 w
                  y = SEL-PAIR-2 w
              in (+ x y))
```

This looks more complicated than the previous version, but it is more efficient, because addPair can now be applied in fewer reductions.

This idea can be applied to the sum-constructor case as well, by applying the transformation

```
case v of
     s1 v1,1 ... v1,r1  =>  E1
     ...
     sn vn,1 ... vn,rn  =>  En
≡  CASE-T v (let v1,1  = SEL-SUM-s1-1 v
                 ...
                 v1,r1 = SEL-SUM-s1-r1 v
             in E1)
            ...
            (let vn,1  = SEL-SUM-sn-1 v
                 ...
                 vn,rn = SEL-SUM-sn-rn v
             in En)
```

The selector function SEL-SUM-s-i selects the ith component of an object built with the sum constructor s. (Remember that the selector functions SEL-t-i apply only to objects of product type.) Again, the correctness of this transformation can easily be shown using the equations for CASE-T and the definition of simple let-expressions.

As before, the transformation seems to increase the complexity of the expression, but it achieves the important objective of eliminating a lambda abstraction. The result may run less efficiently on simple implementations, but it will run much more efficiently on sophisticated implementations (see Sections 20.10.4 and 20.11).

6.3.4 Reducing the Number of Built-in Functions

The ideas of Section 6.1.4 can be applied to case functions also, to reduce the number of built-in functions required.

Specifically, CASE-T can be replaced by CASE-n, where n is the number of constructors for the type T. The integer structure tag of the first argument can be used directly to select the appropriate one of the other arguments. Similarly, SEL-SUM-s-i can be replaced with SEL-SUM-r-i, where r is the arity of s. As before, these replacements should only take place after type-checking.

As a bonus, the use of let-expressions instead of lambda abstractions has also avoided the introduction of UNPACK-SUM and UNPACK-PRODUCT. If all pattern-matching is compiled to case-expressions, then UNPACK-SUM and UNPACK-PRODUCT do not need to be implemented at all!

The CASE-T function has deliberately been defined to *select* one of its arguments (based on the constructor of its first argument), rather than *apply* one of its arguments to the components of its first argument. This latter approach might at first seem more efficient, but there are two reasons for not taking it:

(i) When performing the replacements described in this section, CASE-T would have to be replaced by CASE-n-r_1-r_2. . .-r_n, where r_i is the arity of the ith constructor of type T. This seems rather excessive!

(ii) More importantly, it allows us to use let-expressions rather than lambda abstractions, when transforming case-expressions to the ordinary lambda calculus.

6.4 The ▯ Operator and FAIL

Finally, we must transform the ▯ construct into the ordinary lambda calculus. This is not difficult, because the ▯ construct was only syntactic sugar which allowed us to write ▯ as an infix operator. We therefore use the transformation:

$$E_1 \;[]\; E_2 \;\equiv\; \text{FATBAR } E_1\ E_2$$

where FATBAR is a built-in function, with the same semantic equations as ▯:

```
FATBAR a    b = a        if a ≠ FAIL and a ≠ ⊥
FATBAR FAIL b = b
FATBAR ⊥    b = ⊥
```

It would be better still to eliminate ▯ and FAIL from the program altogether, and optimizations which often succeed in doing this are described in Section 5.4.2. Any remaining occurrences of ▯ and FAIL can still be compiled surprisingly efficiently by a sophisticated implementation (Section 20.4).

6.5 Summary

In this chapter we have seen how to transform all the constructs of the enriched lambda calculus into the ordinary lambda calculus, using Y to express recursion. This is the method we will assume for the early implementations of Part II.

In addition, we have seen that it is also possible to transform the program into the ordinary lambda calculus augmented with simple lets and letrecs. This is essential for type-checking, though it can be transformed into the ordinary lambda calculus after that, but the use of let and letrec makes it easier for later parts of the compiler to produce more efficient code. Subsequent implementations, from Chapter 14 onwards, will therefore use the latter form exclusively.

References

Aho, A.V., Hopcroft, J.E., and Ullman, D. 1974. *The Design and Analysis of Computer Algorithms*, pp. 189–95. Addison Wesley.

Aho, A.V., Hopcroft, J.E., and Ullman, D. 1983a. *Data Structures and Algorithms*, pp. 222–6. Addison Wesley.

Aho, A.V., Hopcroft, J.E., and Ullman, D. 1983b. *Data Structures and Algorithms*, pp. 221–2. Addison Wesley.

Dijkstra, E.J.W. 1976. *A Discipline of Programming*, pp. 192–200. Prentice-Hall.

Seven

LIST COMPREHENSIONS

Philip Wadler

List comprehensions are a syntactic feature of several functional languages, which, like pattern-matching, can greatly increase the ease with which one can read and write functional programs. Like pattern-matching, they add no fundamental new power to the language, and it is easy to translate a program containing list comprehensions into an equivalent program that does not contain them.

This chapter is organized as follows. Section 7.1 explains the list comprehension notation. Section 7.2 gives a formal semantics of list comprehensions in terms of reduction rules. Section 7.3 presents a method of translating comprehensions into the enriched lambda calculus, and Section 7.4 uses program transformation techniques to improve this method. For simplicity, Sections 7.2–7.4 do not allow patterns in comprehensions, and the results of these sections are extended to include patterns in Section 7.5.

7.1 Introduction to List Comprehensions

Set comprehensions were introduced by Burstall in an early version of the language NPL (which later evolved into Hope, but without set comprehensions). List comprehensions were first used by Turner in KRC, where they were called ZF expressions [Turner, 1982]. List comprehensions have since been included into several other functional languages, including Miranda and SASL (in both of which they are called ZF expressions), and Orwell.

(List comprehensions have sometimes been called set abstractions. This name is unfortunate, since they operate on lists rather than sets, and since the word 'abstraction' already has too many other meanings.)

List comprehensions are analogous to set comprehensions in Zermelo-Frankel set theory. An example of a set comprehension in mathematics is

$$B = \{\text{square } x \mid x \in A \;\&\; \text{odd } x\}$$

that is, the squares of the odd elements of the set A. For example, if A is $\{1,2,3\}$ then B is $\{1,9\}$. The corresponding list comprehension in Miranda is

```
ys = [ square x | x <- xs; odd x ]
```

The only difference in notation is that the curly braces are changed to square brackets, the & is changed to a semi-colon, and the symbol $\in$ is changed to <−, which is pronounced 'drawn from'. A much more important difference is that the result is a list, not a set. Thus, if xs is [1,2,3] then ys is [1,9] and if xs is [3,2,1] then ys is [9,1].

In general, a list comprehension has the form,

```
[<expression> | <qualifier>; . . . ; <qualifier>]
```

where each <qualifier> is either a *generator* (such as 'x <− xs') or a *filter* (such as 'odd x').

Here are some more examples of list comprehensions. The function cp finds the Cartesian product of two lists:

```
cp xs ys = [ (x,y) | x <- xs; y <- ys ]
```

For example,

```
cp ['a','b'] [1,2,3] = [ ('a',1), ('a',2), ('a',3),
                         ('b',1), ('b',2), ('b',3) ]
```

Note that the last generator changes most rapidly.

The function pyth returns a list of all Pythagorean triangles with sides of total length less than n:

```
pyth n = [ (a,b,c) | a, b, c <- [1..n];
                     a + b + c <= n;
                     square a + square b = square c ]
```

(Here [1..n] returns the list of numbers from 1 to n, and a generator such as 'x,y <− zs' is shorthand for 'x <− zs; y <− zs'.) This function may be written a little more efficiently as

```
pyth n = [ (a,b,c) | a <- [1..n];
                     b <- [1..n-a];
                     c <- [1..n-a-b];
                     square a + square b = square c ]
```

A later qualifier may refer to a variable defined in an earlier one, but not vice versa.

The function sort sorts a list into ascending order. The method used is that of quicksort: the list is divided into those elements less than or not less than the first element, and the two sublists are sorted recursively:

```
sort []      = []
sort (x:xs)  = sort [y | y <- xs; y < x]
               ++ [x] ++
               sort [y | y <- xs; y >= x]
```

(Here, ++ is list append.)

Patterns may appear to the left of the <– arrow. For example, suppose that the function zip returns a list of pairs of corresponding elements of a pair of lists, so that

```
zip ([1,2,3], [4,5,6]) = [(1,4), (2,5), (3,6)]
```

Then we can define a function vecAdd for performing vector addition (adding corresponding elements of two lists) as follows:

```
vecAdd xs ys = [x+y | (x,y) <- zip (xs,ys)]
```

The pattern (x,y) appears to the left of a <– arrow. For example,

```
vecAdd [1,2,3] [4,5,6] = [5,7,9]
```

It is often convenient to use zip with list comprehensions in this way.

More generally, in a generator 'p <– L' the pattern p may be refutable. In this case, elements of the list L which do not match the pattern are simply filtered out. The function singletons takes a list of lists and returns the elements of each list of length one:

```
singletons xs = [x | [x] <- xs]
```

For example,

```
singletons [ [1,2], [5], [], [2] ] = [5, 2]
```

Here the '[x]' to the left of the arrow is the refutable pattern. The elements [1,2] and [] do not match the pattern, and so are filtered out.

For simplicity, in Sections 7.2–7.4 we will ignore the fact that a pattern may appear on the left of the <– arrow, and only deal with variables. The results of these sections will then be extended to patterns in Section 7.5.

(In Miranda there is a second form of ZF expression, written with curly braces, which indicates that duplicates should be removed from the result list and generators should be 'diagonalized'. This form will not be dealt with here. There is also another form of generator which we do not cover here.)

7.2 Reduction Rules for List Comprehensions

Just as reduction rules (such as the β-rule) can be given to define the behavior of lambda abstractions, so can reduction rules to define the behavior of list comprehensions be given.

To present these rules, we will write comprehensions in the form

```
[E | Q]
```

where E is an expression and Q is a sequence of zero or more qualifiers. The sequence Q will

(i) either begin with a generator, in which case the rule is of the form

```
[E | v <- L; Q']
```

where v is a variable and L is a list-valued expression;

(ii) or begin with a filter, in which case the rule is of the form

```
[E | B; Q']
```

where B is a boolean-valued expression;

(iii) or will be empty, in which case the rule is of the form

```
[E | ]
```

One does not normally see comprehensions with no qualifiers such as [E |], but they are useful for defining reduction rules in a uniform way.

Abbreviations should be expanded so that all comprehensions are in the above form. In particular, generators of the form

$$v_1, \ldots, v_n \texttt{ <- } L$$

should be expanded to

$$v_1 \texttt{ <- } L; \ldots ; v_n \texttt{ <- } L$$

where $v_1, \ldots, v_n$ are variables.

After abbreviations are expanded, the following five reduction rules suffice to define list comprehensions:

```
(1)  [E | v <- [] ; Q]      →  []
(2)  [E | v <- E':L' ; Q]   →  [E | Q][E'/v] ++ [E | v <- L'; Q]
(3)  [E | False ; Q]        →  []
(4)  [E | True  ; Q]        →  [E | Q]
(5)  [E | ]                 →  [E]
```

The first two rules define the behavior of generators, the second two define the behavior of filters, and the last 'cleans up' after all the generators and filters have been processed. The second rule uses the substitution notation of Chapter 2, so [E | Q][E'/v] means [E | Q] with all free occurrences of v replaced by E'.

From rules (1) and (2) we can see that

$$\text{(2b)}\quad [E \mid v \texttt{ <- } [E_1, \ldots, E_n];\ Q] \;\rightarrow\; [E \mid Q][E_1/v] \texttt{ ++ } \ldots \texttt{ ++ } [E \mid Q][E_n/v]$$

which may be an easier way to think of the rule for generators. For example,

```
[square x | x <- [1, 2, 3]; odd x]
   → [square 1 | odd 1] ++ [square 2 | odd 2] ++ [square 3 | odd 3]
                                                  (by rules (1) and (2))
   → [square 1 | True] ++ [square 2 | False] ++ [square 3 | True]
                                                        (reducing odd)
   → [square 1 | ] ++ [] ++ [square 3 | ]
                                                  (by rules (3) and (4))
   → [square 1] ++ [] ++ [square 3]
                                                         (by rule (5))
   → [1, 9]
```

These rules are based upon using append (++) to combine the result lists, rather than cons (:) as one might expect. This is necessary in order to make it easy for filters to remove elements (by reducing to the empty list, as with [square 2 | odd 2] in the example above). It is also necessary for multiple generators, as in the example below:

```
cp ['a','b'] [1,2,3]
   → [(x,y) | x <- ['a','b']; y <- [1,2,3] ]
                                                     (definition of cp)
   → [('a',y) | y <- [1,2,3] ] ++ [('b',y) | y <- [1,2,3] ]
                                                  (by rules (1) and (2))
   → [('a',1) | ] ++ [('a',2) | ] ++ [('a',3) | ] ++
     [('b',1) | ] ++ [('b',2) | ] ++ [('b',3) | ]
                                            (by rules (1) and (2) again)
   → [('a',1), ('a',2), ('a',3),
      ('b',1), ('b',2), ('b',3) ]
                                                         (by rule (5))
```

The careful reader will have noticed that the above examples have ignored lazy evaluation. A lazy evaluator would begin to reduce the first example as follows:

```
[square x | x <- [1, 2, 3]; odd x]
   → [square 1 | odd 1] ++ [square x | x <- [2, 3]; odd x]
                                                         (by rule (2))
   → [square 1 |]        ++ [square x | x <- [2, 3]; odd x]
                                                         (by rule (4))
   → [square 1]          ++ [square x | x <- [2, 3]; odd x]
                                                         (by rule (5))
   → 1 : [square x | x <- [2, 3]; odd x]
```

and so the first element of the result can be returned without examining the entire input list.

7.3 Translating List Comprehensions

The above rules provide a concise definition of list comprehensions. In this section we will see that a very similar set of rules can be used to translate Miranda list comprehensions into the enriched lambda calculus.

The translation requires one new function, flatMap. This is defined in Miranda as follows:

```
flatMap f []     = []
flatMap f (x:xs) = (f x) ++ (flatMap f xs)
```

That is, (flatMap f xs) applies a list-valued function f to each element of a list xs, and then appends all the resulting lists together.

The rules for translation can be expressed by giving some extra rules for the **TE** scheme, which was introduced in Chapter 3, and Figure 7.1 gives these extra rules.

```
(a)  TE⟦ [E | v <- L; Q] ⟧  ≡  flatMap (λv.TE⟦ [E | Q] ⟧) TE⟦ L ⟧
(b)  TE⟦ [E | B; Q] ⟧       ≡  IF TE⟦ B ⟧ TE⟦ [E | Q] ⟧ NIL
(c)  TE⟦ [E | ] ⟧           ≡  CONS TE⟦ E ⟧ NIL

where E is an expression
      B is a boolean-valued expression
      L is a list-valued expression
      Q is a sequence of zero or more qualifiers
      v is a variable
```

Figure 7.1 Translation scheme for list comprehensions

It is not hard to see that rule (a), together with the definition of flatMap, is equivalent to rules (1) and (2) of the preceding section. Similarly, rule (b) is equivalent to rules (3) and (4), and rule (c) is equivalent to rule (5).

Here are two examples, showing how to compile comprehensions like those used in the examples in the preceding section:

```
TE⟦ [square x | x <- xs; odd x] ⟧
≡  flatMap (λx.TE⟦ [square x | odd x] ⟧) xs                 (rule (a))
≡  flatMap (λx.IF (odd x) TE⟦ [square x | ] ⟧ NIL) xs       (rule (b))
≡  flatMap (λx.IF (odd x) (CONS (square x) NIL) NIL) xs     (rule (c))

TE⟦ [(x,y) | x <- xs; y <- ys] ⟧
≡  flatMap (λx.TE⟦ [(x,y) | y <- ys] ⟧) xs                   (rule (a))
≡  flatMap (λx.flatMap (λy.TE⟦ [(x,y) | ] ⟧) ys) xs          (rule (a))
≡  flatMap (λx.flatMap (λy.CONS TE⟦ (x,y) ⟧ NIL) ys) xs      (rule (c))
≡  flatMap (λx.flatMap (λy.CONS (PAIR x y) NIL) ys) xs
```

It is left as an exercise for the reader to evaluate the terms above (for some suitable values of xs and ys) and verify that they return the desired results.

7.4 Using Transformations to Improve Efficiency

The translation scheme described in the previous section is complete, but is not the most efficient translation method possible. This section uses well-known techniques of program transformation to derive a more efficient translation scheme.

The translation scheme will be improved in two steps. The first step improves efficiency using the well-known idea of expanding-out a program in place. Notice that an expression of the form

```
flatMap (λv.E) L
```

may be replaced by the equivalent enriched lambda calculus expression

```
letrec
   h = λus. case us of
                 NIL          ⇒  NIL
                 CONS v us′   ⇒  APPEND E (h us′)
in (h L)
```

where h, us and us′ are new variable names. It is straightforward to show that this expansion corresponds to the original definition of flatMap.

```
TE⟦ [E | v <- L; Q] ⟧
≡  letrec
      h = λus. case us of
                    NIL          ⇒  NIL
                    CONS v us′   ⇒  APPEND TE⟦ [E | Q] ⟧ (h us′)
   in (h TE⟦ L ⟧)
```

where h, us and us′ are new variables which do not occur free in E, L or Q

Figure 7.2 Improved rule (a) for translation scheme

If we apply this transformation to rule (a) then we get a new, equivalent rule, shown in Figure 7.2. Combining this rule with rules (b) and (c) gives a more long-winded, but more efficient, translation scheme. An example of the use of this scheme is shown in Figure 7.3.

```
TE⟦ [square x | x <- xs; odd x] ⟧
≡  letrec
      h = λus. case us of
                    NIL          ⇒  NIL
                    CONS x us′   ⇒  APPEND
                                       (IF (odd x) (CONS (square x) NIL) NIL)
                                       (h us′)
   in (h xs)
```

Figure 7.3 Example of a translation using the improved rule

This translation scheme is quite efficient, but there is room for further improvement. For instance, the example shown in Figure 7.3 contains the expression

```
APPEND (IF (odd x) (CONS (square x) NIL) NIL) (h us')
```

and it would have been more efficient to generate the equivalent expression

```
IF (odd x) (CONS (square x) (h us')) (h us')
```

instead.

In general, it would be desirable to eliminate all calls of APPEND. The reason for this is simple: rather than generating two lists and then appending them, it is better to generate the desired list directly. This will be significantly more efficient, since evaluating APPEND requires time and space proportional to the length of its first argument.

Surprisingly, it is indeed always possible to translate list comprehensions in such a way that APPEND does not appear in the final result. The second, and final, improvement in the translation scheme will be derived by applying program transformation methods to the first scheme to eliminate all appearances of APPEND.

Observe that the only place that APPEND appears in the current translation scheme is in the following phrase in the improved rule:

APPEND **TE**⟦ [E | Q] ⟧ (h us')

This suggests that we might define a new translation scheme that will translate the above expression directly. That is, we wish to define a new translation scheme **TQ**, such that

TQ⟦ [E | Q] ++ L ⟧ ≡ APPEND **TE**⟦ [E | Q] ⟧ **TE**⟦ L ⟧ (7.1)

for any expression E, list of qualifiers Q and list-valued expression L. Then we can replace the previous expression by:

TQ⟦ [E | Q] ++ (h us') ⟧

It is easy to prove this is equivalent to the previous expression using rule (7.1).

The rules defining **TQ** are given in Figure 7.4. Readers familiar with program transformation will see that it is easy to derive the new rules (A), (B) and (C) from the modified rule (a), and rules (b) and (c). For example, here is the derivation of rule (C):

TQ⟦ [E |] ++ L ⟧
≡ APPEND **TE**⟦ [E |] ⟧ **TE**⟦ L ⟧ (by (7.1))
≡ APPEND (CONS **TE**⟦ E ⟧ NIL) **TE**⟦ L ⟧ (by rule (c))
≡ CONS **TE**⟦ E ⟧ **TE**⟦ L ⟧ (by definition of APPEND)

The derivation of the other rules is not much harder, and is left as an exercise for the interested reader.

```
TE[[ [E | Q] ]]  ≡  TQ[[ [E | Q] ++ [] ]]
-------------------------------------------------------------------------
(A)  TQ[[ [E | v <- L1; Q] ++ L2 ]]
     ≡ letrec
            h = λus. case us of
                          NIL          => TE[[ L2 ]]
                          CONS v us'   => TQ[[ [E | Q] ++ (h us') ]]
         in (h TE[[ L1 ]])
(B)  TQ[[ [E | B; Q] ++ L ]]  ≡  IF TE[[ B ]] TQ[[ [E | Q] ++ L ]] TE[[ L ]]
(C)  TQ[[ [E | ] ++ L ]]      ≡  CONS TE[[ E ]] TE[[ L ]]
where h, us and us' are new variables which do not occur free in E, L1, L2 or Q
```

Figure 7.4 Optimal translation scheme for list comprehensions

```
TE[[ [square x | x <- xs; odd x] ]]
≡  letrec
      h = λus. case us of
                   NIL         => NIL
                   CONS x us'  => IF (odd x) (CONS (square x) (h us')) (h us')
   in (h xs)
TE[[ [(x,y) | x <- xs; y <- ys] ]]
≡  letrec
      g = λus. case us of
                   NIL          => NIL
                   CONS x us'   =>
                      letrec
                        h = λvs. case vs of
                                     NIL          => (g us')
                                     CONS y vs'   => CONS (PAIR x y) (h vs')
                        in (h ys)
   in (g xs)
```

Figure 7.5 Example translations using the optimal scheme

Figure 7.5 shows two examples of the translations produced by the new scheme. These should be compared with the examples at the end of the previous section. The reader will see that the new translations are considerably longer, but also considerably more efficient. Indeed, the translations produced by the new scheme are as good as the best translations one would make by hand.

More precisely, we can state that the new translation scheme is optimal in that it performs the minimum number of CONS operations. For a list comprehension, this means performing exactly one CONS operation for each element in the returned list. The old translation scheme performed rather more CONS operations than this, because of the extra CONS operations performed by APPEND. However, the new scheme is indeed optimal in this sense, as the reader may verify (informally or by a simple inductive proof).

Although the work here has been presented in an informal style, it is an excellent example of the power of formal methods. As has been pointed out, starting from the reduction rules of Section 7.2, one may derive the translation scheme of Section 7.3 and the improved translation scheme of this section. None of the transformation steps is particularly difficult. On the other hand, had formal methods not been used, the development would have been much more troublesome, and quite possibly the optimal translation scheme described here would not have been discovered.

7.5 Pattern-matching in Comprehensions

Sections 7.2–7.4 have ignored the fact that in general a pattern rather than a variable may appear to the left of the <- in a generator. This was done in order to make the presentation of the material a little simpler. This section updates the results of the previous sections to allow patterns in generators.

First, we consider the reduction rules that define the semantics of list comprehensions. Recall that the reduction rules for generators are:

```
(1)  [E | v <- []    ; Q]   →  []
(2)  [E | v <- E':L' ; Q]   →  [E | Q][E'/v] ++ [E | v <- L'; Q]
```

To allow for patterns in generators, these are replaced by:

```
(1')  [E | p <- []    ; Q]   →  []
(2')  [E | p <- E':L' ; Q]   →  ( ((λp.[E | Q]) E') ▯ [] )
                                 ++ [E | p <- L'; Q]
```

The only changes are that the variable v has been replaced by the pattern p, and that in the second rule the phrase

```
[E | Q][E'/v]
```

has been replaced by

```
((λp.[E | Q]) E') ▯ []
```

Thus, instead of substitution we use a pattern-matching lambda abstraction, as described in Chapter 4. If the pattern does not match then [] is returned; so, as desired, if an element does not match a pattern it is as if it had been filtered out of the list.

Notice that if the pattern p is replaced by a variable v then

((λv.[E | Q]) E′) ▯ [ ]
→ [E | Q][E′/v] ▯ [ ] (by β-reduction)
→ [E | Q][E′/v] (by definition of ▯)

so the rule for variables is just a special case of the rule for patterns.

Here is an example using the new reduction rules:

[x | [x] <− [[1,2], [5], [ ], [2]]
→ (((λ[x].[x |]) [1,2]) ▯ [ ]) ++
(((λ[x].[x |]) [5]) ▯ [ ]) ++
(((λ[x].[x |]) [ ]) ▯ [ ]) ++
(((λ[x].[x |]) [2]) ▯ [ ])
(by rules (1′) and (2′))
→ (FAIL ▯ [ ]) ++ ([5] ▯ [ ]) ++ (FAIL ▯ [ ]) ++ ([2] ▯ [ ])
(by the rules of pattern-matching and rule (5))
→ [ ] ++ [5] ++ [ ] ++ [2]
(by definition of ▯)
→ [5, 2]

which is the desired result, as described in Section 7.1.

The modification to the translation scheme is analogous to the modification to the reduction rules. The only rule which contains a generator is rule (a):

(a) **TE**⟦ [E | v <− L; Q] ⟧ ≡ flatMap (λv.**TE**⟦ [E | Q] ⟧) **TE**⟦ L ⟧

For patterns, this is modified to:

(a′) **TE**⟦ [E | p <− L; Q] ⟧
≡ flatMap (λu.(((λ**TE**⟦ p ⟧.**TE**⟦ [E | Q] ⟧) u) ▯ NIL)) **TE**⟦ L ⟧

where u is a new variable which does not occur free in p, E or Q.

Notice that the subexpression

((λ**TE**⟦ p ⟧.**TE**⟦ [E | Q] ⟧) u) ▯ NIL

is in exactly the right form to be further translated by the pattern-matching compiler described in Chapter 5. Moreover, in the case that the pattern p is just a variable v, applying the pattern-matching compiler to rule (a′) will yield the same result as rule (a), so again the rule for variables is just a special case of the rule for patterns. Further, just as one can show that rule (a) follows from rules (1) and (2), one may show that rule (a′) follows from rules (1′) and (2′).

Finally, the optimal translation scheme may be generalized in a similar way.

The translation rule (A) of Figure 7.4 should be replaced by the rule

```
(A')  TQ⟦ [E | p <- L1; Q] ++ L2 ⟧
        ≡ letrec
            h = λus. case us of
                         NIL          => TE⟦ L2 ⟧
                         CONS u us'   =>
                           ( ((λTE⟦ p ⟧.TQ⟦ [E | Q] ++ (h us') ⟧) u)
                             ▯ (h us') )
            in (h TE⟦ L1 ⟧)
```

where h, u, us and us′ are new variable names which do not occur free in E, L_1, L_2 or Q.

Again, the central phrase of this rule is in just the right form for further processing by the pattern-matching compiler, and the rule for variables emerges as a special case of the rule for patterns. And, again, just as rule (A) can be derived from rule (a), so rule (A′) can be derived from rule (a′). Furthermore, the new translation scheme is still optimal, in that it performs the minimum number of CONS operations.

In short, extending the results of the previous sections to allow patterns in generators is straightforward; the new rules have the old rules as a special case; the correctness of the new results may be shown in the same way; and the efficiency of the translations is unimpaired.

Reference

Turner, D.A. 1982. Recursion equations as a programming language. In *Functional Programming and Its Applications*. Darlington *et al.* (editors). Cambridge University Press.

Eight

POLYMORPHIC TYPE-CHECKING

Peter Hancock

In common with several other modern programming languages, Miranda has the property that a programmer need not specify the types of the objects defined in his program. The compiler can work out those types, if the program can be consistently typed at all. The part of the compiler that does this is usually called the 'type-checker'. It attempts to infer the types of expressions in the program from their contexts. This kind of type-checking was first implemented for the language ML, around 1976. The type discipline was first expounded by Milner [1978].

Whether or not a type-checker requires information from the programmer to check that a program is well typed, type-checking is of great value in drawing the programmer's attention to a variety of errors, from trivial slips in program entry, to gross logical blunders. It helps us to write robust programs.

Another advantage of type-checking is that it helps to build faster implementations of programming languages. If a program is passed by the type-checker, then no type error should occur at run-time, such as the use of an integer as if it were a function, a boolean as if it were an integer, or a function as if it were a tuple. In Milner's words, well-typed expressions do not 'go wrong': at run-time we will never misinterpret the representation of an expression. By omitting run-time checks for such errors, the implementation of a language can be made simpler and faster. Of course, any implementation should still provide for diagnosis of its own internal errors.

The purpose of this chapter is to explain in some detail how a type-checker works. Then, in Chapter 9, we put the ideas into practice by constructing a type-checker for a simple functional language. The type-checker is constructed in Miranda, in the hope that the development of such a functional program may itself be of some additional interest.

Given the informal spirit of this book, and its concentration on setting up intuitions rather than on attaining impregnable conceptual rigor, it is not appropriate to proceed 'from the ground up'. Instead, we shall assume that the reader already has some understanding of the notion of a type, and wishes to see how that notion can be applied in practice. Nevertheless, some cautionary remarks may be in order, and they are made at the end of the chapter.

This chapter is organized as follows. Section 8.1 reviews some basic concepts, and notations for types. Section 8.2 illustrates the concept of polymorphism, using several examples. Section 8.3 shows in an informal way how types may be inferred from the structure of a definition. Section 8.4 sets out the language for which we will build a type-checker. Section 8.5 considers the detailed type structure of expressions in the language, and attempts to clarify the rules of type inference, which are summarized in Section 8.6. Section 8.7 contains the cautionary remarks referred to before.

Important note: The type-checker described here is actually somewhat more liberal than that of the Miranda compiler itself, in that it will succeed in type-checking some programs which the Miranda compiler would reject. This difference is explained in Section 8.5.5. The Miranda type-checker is also considerably more sophisticated than the one we describe here, because it supports features, such as abstract data types and a module structure, which are beyond the scope of this book.

8.1 Informal Notation for Types

The types with which we are concerned in functional programming include ground types such as characters, numbers and booleans, types of tuples, lists and, of course, functions. To talk about these types, we will use the following notation. Capital letters will be used for type variables. A type variable A stands for a type in much the same way that a numerical variable *n* stands for a number in mathematics. Lower-case letters will be used for the elements of types. The notation

```
a :: A
```

means that a has type A. For example, 42::num, 'f'::char, where num is the type of numbers, and char is the type of characters. (Note: the notation used for types in this chapter differs from that of Miranda – in Miranda an upper case letter cannot stand for a type.)

8.1.1 Tuples

Given types A and B, (A,B) is the type of ordered pairs (a,b) where a::A, and b::B. Using Descartes' terminology, a is the first *coordinate* of (a,b), and b is the second. More generally, if $n \geq 2$ and $A_1, \ldots, A_n$ are types, then

$(A_1, \ldots, A_n)$

is the type whose values are of the form of tuples

$(a_1, \ldots, a_n)$

where $a_1::A_1, \ldots, a_n::A_n$. The important points about tuples, so far as typing is concerned, are:

(i) the coordinates of a tuple need not be of the same type;
(ii) the type of a tuple determines the number of its coordinates (that is, its dimension), and their types.

8.1.2 Lists

Given a type B, [B] is the type of lists whose entries are of type B. More specifically, an object of type [B] must be

(i) either the empty list, which is denoted by [ ];
(ii) or a non-empty list, formed by prefixing an object b::B to a list bs::[B], which is denoted by b:bs.

If all the successive entries $b_1, \ldots, b_k$ of a finite list are known, we may write it using the notation

$[b_1, \ldots, b_k]$

The important points about lists, so far as typing is concerned, are:

(i) In contrast with the coordinates of a tuple, all entries of a list must be of the same type. For example, it would make no sense to form a list in which the entries were alternately characters and truth values. (We could in fact define a type of such entities, but they would not be lists.)
(ii) In contrast with the dimension of a tuple, the length of a list is not determined by its type. Indeed, when programming in a lazy language, we may operate with infinite lists such as the list of positive integers. There is no requirement that a list must be built up from the empty list by a finite number of applications of the prefixing operation (b:bs), or that a principle of well-founded induction on the structure of lists should be valid.

8.1.3 Structured Types

Tuple types and list types are both examples of structured types, which were introduced in Chapter 4. As explained there, in Miranda the general form of a declaration of an operator for forming structured types is:

$$
\begin{aligned}
\text{name } v_1 \ldots v_k ::= \; & c_1 \; t_{1,1} \ldots t_{1,r_1} \\
| \; & \ldots \\
| \; & c_m \; t_{m,1} \ldots t_{m,r_m}
\end{aligned}
$$

where $m \geq 1$, $r_i \geq 0$ for $1 \leq i \leq m$, and $k \geq 0$. Here $v_1, \ldots, v_k$ stand for schematic type variables, which in Miranda have the special form $*$, $**$, $***$, etc. Also, $t_{1,1}, \ldots, t_{m,r_m}$ are type expressions, built up using variables from the list $v_1, \ldots, v_k$ and names for type-forming operations which are either built-in or declared elsewhere in the script.

For example, in the type declaration

```
tree * ::= LEAF * | BRANCH (tree *) (tree *)
```

v_1* is $*$, c_1 is LEAF, and $t_{1,1}$ is $*$; c_2 is BRANCH, and $t_{2,1}$, $t_{2,2}$ are both (tree $*$). 'tree' is a *type-forming operator* since, given a type as 'argument', it produces a type as its 'result'; for example, (tree char), (tree num), (tree (tree num)). In this sense, the built-in basic types (such as char, num, bool) are simply type-forming operators which take no arguments.

A declaration with the form above means that an object of a type

$$\text{name } t'_1 \ldots t'_k$$

must have one of the constructed forms

$$c_i \; x_1 \ldots x_{r_i}$$

where $x_j::t'_{i,j}$ for $1 \leq j \leq r_i$, and $t'_{i,j}$ denotes the result of simultaneously substituting the type expressions $t'_1, \ldots, t'_k$ for the type variables $v_1, \ldots, v_k$ in the type expression $t_{i,j}$.

For example here is an object of type (tree char):

```
BRANCH (LEAF 'a') (LEAF 'b')
```

In this case, t'_1 is char; the form of the object is a BRANCH, and x_1 is (LEAF 'a')::tree char, x_2 is (LEAF 'b')::tree char.

8.1.4 Functions

Given types A and B, we use the notation:

```
A -> B
```

to denote the type of functions f applicable to objects a::A, whose values (f a) are of type B.

For example, (char -> num) is the type of integer-valued functions of characters. The function 'code' which maps a character to its ASCII code is of this type.

(char -> bool) is the type of boolean-valued functions of characters. For example, the function

```
isdigit ch = (code '0' <= x) & (x <= code '9')
             where x = code ch
```

is a function of this type.

([char] -> [num]) is the type of functions whose arguments are lists of characters, and whose values are lists of integers. The function which returns the list of ASCII codes corresponding to a character list is of this type.

(Note: in functional programming, we consider a function to belong to a type (A -> B) even though it is not totally defined on the domain type A. For example, the partial function which assigns to every even number its successor has type (num -> num).)

The arrow in the function type notation (A -> B) is considered to be a right-associative binary operator. So

```
A -> B -> C
```

means the same as

```
A -> (B -> C)
```

and

```
     (A -> B -> C)
  -> (A -> B)
  -> A
  -> C
```

means the same as

```
(A -> (B -> C)) -> ((A -> B) -> (A -> C))
```

(We shall often lay out a large type expression over several lines, as above.)

The reason we choose -> to be right associative can be seen by considering a (curried) function f of two arguments a::A and b::B. Then we have:

```
f       :: A -> B -> C
(f a)   :: B -> C
(f a b) :: C
```

If -> were left associative, we would have to write

```
f :: A -> (B -> C)
```

which is less convenient, since it uses more brackets.

8.2 Polymorphism

Many of the functions we define in a functional program are to a greater or lesser degree indifferent to the types of their arguments. This can be illustrated with a few examples.

8.2.1 The Identity Function

The identity function id, defined by

```
id x = x
```

works equally well on arguments of any type. For example, in

```
id 3     = 3
id 'a'   = 'a'
```

```
id (3,'a') = (3,'a')
```

the function id is used with the types

```
num -> num
char -> char
(num,char) -> (num,char)
```

In this sense, id is *indifferent to the type of its arguments*. However, id always returns a result of the same type as its argument. We express this by saying that id is of type A -> A, for all types A.

Sometimes we omit the 'for all types A' (the jargon for which is *schematic generality*; A is said to be a *schematic* (or *generic*) *variable*). When the schematic variables are not given explicitly, every type variable is here to be understood as a schematic variable.

To say that id is of type (A -> A) for all types A means that the name id can occur in a larger expression in any context suitable for a function whose type is of that form. When we indicate a form by means of a type expression, we should say which parts of the expression may vary, by indicating the schematic variables. To say that a type T *is of the form*

```
...A...B...A...C...
```

where A and B are the schematic variables, is to say that T may be obtained by substituting certain types TA and TB for the schematic variables. In other words, T is a *substitution instance* of the indicated type. The types

```
num -> num
char -> char
(num,char) -> (num,char)
```

are all substitution instances of the form

```
A -> A
```

where it is understood that A is the schematic variable.

For a final example, consider the expression:

```
id (code (id 'a'))
```

The first occurrence of id must have type (num -> num), and the second must have type (char -> char). Since these are both substitution instances of the type of id, (A -> A), the expression is correctly typed.

Note: What we here call schematic type variables are called in Miranda generic type variables and written using the special symbols *, **, etc. to distinguish them from ordinary (non-generic) names for types.)

8.2.2 The length Function

The function which returns the length of a list may be defined by the equations

```
length []     = 0
length (x:xs) = (length xs) + 1
```

The function length works equally well on any list, regardless of the type of its entries. For example, in the equations:

```
length [7,1,4]              = 3
length ['7','1','4','z']    = 4
length [(3,'a'),(26,'z')]   = 2
length [id,id]              = 2
```

the function is used with the types:

```
[num]           -> num
[char]          -> num
[(num,char)]    -> num
[(A -> A)]      -> num
```

respectively. We express the type of length by

length :: [A] -> num, for all types A

which conveys that

(i) length is a function;
(ii) its arguments are lists;
(iii) its values are numbers;
(iv) the type of the entries in the argument lists does not matter.

8.2.3 The Composition Function

Let us represent the composition of two functions f and g with a right-associative infix dot, and define

```
(f . g) x = f (g x)
```

(We shall write the composition function 'compose' when we do not want to indicate its arguments.) Composition is well defined so long as both its left- and right-hand arguments are functions, and the type of arguments of its left-hand argument is the same as the type of values as its right-hand argument. For example, the following make perfect sense:

(i) decode . succ . code

where succ denotes the successor of an integer. The expression denotes a function which returns 'b' from 'a', 'c' from 'b', and so on. The composition function is used here with the type:

```
(num -> char) -> (char -> num) -> char -> char
```

at its first occurrence, and with the type:

```
(num -> num) -> (char -> num) -> char -> num
```

at its second.

(ii) code . id, and id . code

where I is the identity function discussed above. In these expressions, the composition function is used with the types:

```
(char -> num) -> (char -> char) -> char -> num
(num -> num) -> (char -> num) -> char -> num
```

respectively.

(iii) isdigit . decode

which is the predicate of an integer which is itself the ASCII code of a decimal digit. Here the composition function is used with type:

```
(char -> bool) -> (num -> char) -> num -> bool
```

We can express the constraint on the types of the arguments of compose by saying:

```
compose :: (B -> C) -> (A -> B) -> A -> C
```

where A, B and C are the schematic variables.

8.2.4 The Function foldr

The function foldr may be defined by the equation

```
foldr f b []     = b
foldr f b (a:as) = f a (foldr f b as)
```

Again, foldr is to a certain extent indifferent to the types of its arguments. For example, the following make perfect sense:

(i) foldr plus 0 [7,1,4]

where plus means binary addition. The function foldr is used here with the type:

```
      (num -> num -> num)
   -> num
   -> [num]
   -> num
```

(ii) foldr append [] ["str1","str2","str3"]

Here append is the function which concatenates two lists. The function foldr is being used here with type:

```
      (string -> string -> string)
   -> string
   -> [string]
   -> string
```

(iii) foldr cons [] [5,4,1,4,1]

Here cons x y = x:y. In this expression, foldr is used with the type:

```
        (num -> [num] -> [num])
    -> [num] -> [num] -> [num]
```

In general, foldr may be used in any context which requires a type of the form:

```
    (A -> B -> B)
 -> B
 -> [A]
 -> B
```

where A and B are the schematic variables.

8.2.5 What Polymorphism Means

Polymorphism is a style of type discipline which seems to have been first identified by Christopher Strachey [1967]. A programming language has a polymorphic type discipline if it permits us to define functions which work uniformly for arguments of different types. For example, in a polymorphic language, we can define a single function length of type:

```
[A] -> num
```

In contrast, a language with a monomorphic type discipline forces the programmer to define different functions to return the length of a list of integers, a list of floating point numbers, a list of binary numerical functions, and so on. Languages such as Pascal and Algol 68 are monomorphic.

Strachey distinguished between *ad hoc polymorphism*, and *parametric polymorphism*. A type discipline exhibits *ad hoc* polymorphism if it permits the use of the same expression to denote distinct operations at distinct types, such as the use of the addition symbol to denote addition of integers, rationals, real numbers, ordinals, complex numbers, and so on. This characteristic of a language is often now described as the ability to *overload* expressions. On the other hand, parametric polymorphism is just polymorphism as explained above.

The words *polymorphic* and *monomorphic* are also sometimes used to distinguish between objects whose types are described by expressions with schematic type variables, and those whose type expressions have none. For example, the empty list is polymorphic, the functions id, compose, length and foldr are polymorphic, while the function decode which returns from an integer the character with that ASCII code is monomorphic.

A polymorphic object may take on different types at different occurrences, where these different types are substitution instances of the schematic type of the function. For example, we do not need to have different versions of foldr for each pair of types that instantiate A and B in the type expression

```
(A -> B -> B) -> B -> [A] -> B
```

or to parameterize foldr with the type variables A and B. Precisely the same code is executed whatever the types A and B (at least in a naïve implementation of the compiler), and it would be artificial to duplicate that code, or name it differently for each pair of types.

The terminology is also sometimes (perhaps unfortunately) applied to types themselves. For example, it is said that foldr possesses a 'polymorphic' type, meaning that its type is expressed with schematic variables. (Going by etymology, 'polymorphic' should mean 'of many forms', and it is precisely in order to identify a single form that we use an expression with schematic variables.)

A polymorphic type discipline was first worked out for the language ML around 1976, and since then has been incorporated in a number of functional and imperative languages. In pragmatic terms at least, polymorphism represents a significant advance over the type disciplines of languages such as Pascal or Algol 68.

8.3 Type Inference

This type discipline is not only polymorphic; it has the property that the only places in a program where we have to mention types at all are in the type definitions themselves. The type-checker is able, as part of a single process,

(i) to determine whether the program is well typed; and
(ii) if the program *is* well typed, to determine the type of any expression in the program.

(Of course, to make a program easier to understand we should almost always accompany a definition with a specification of the type of the defined entity.)

Before delving into the details of type-checking, we should ask ourselves how we can informally deduce the types of functions given only their defining equations.

Consider the definition:

```
isdigit ch = (code '0' <= x) & (x <= code '9')
             where x = code ch
```

From the right-hand side of the definition we can see that, if the function is well defined at all, its value must be a truth-value, since the outermost operator & (conjunction) produces truth-values. Moreover, the infix operator <= which supplies its values as arguments to & also produces truth-values. (So we can see that & is used consistently with its type.) The arguments to <= must both have the type num, and this is clearly the case for the actual arguments, namely (code '0') and (code '9'). It follows that x must be a number, and for this to hold, ch must have type char. So the right-hand side of the definition is well typed, with type bool, provided that the argument ch has type char. Since the left-hand side of an equation must have the same type as the right-hand side, we deduce that:

```
isdigit :: char -> bool
```

Consider now the definition of length, repeated here:

```
length []     = 0
length (x:xs) = (length xs) + 1
```

From the first equation, it is clear that the type of length is of the form

```
[A] -> num
```

We must also look at the second equation to see whether it constrains the type A any further. For example, if the second equation were something like

```
length (x:xs) = (length xs) + 1,    x = 'a'
              = length xs
```

(using a conditional expression), we would have to conclude that the type A is not in fact completely general, but completely specific: it is the type char. But in the case of the function length, the second clause imposes no further constraint, so we can say that

```
length :: [A] -> num, for all types A
```

Consider now the function foldr, with definition

```
foldr f x = g where g []     = x
                    g (a:as) = f a (g as)
```

The local function g is evidently a function on lists, since it is defined by cases on the two constructors of list form. So suppose g has type ([A] -> B). Both x and (f a (g as)) must be of type B. Since (g as) has type B, f must have type (A -> B -> B). So, all in all,

```
foldr :: (A -> B -> B) -> B -> [A] -> B
```

In general, by examining the context of an expression, we may be able to deduce an expression for the form of the type of an object which can fit into that context. By examining the expression itself, we may be able to deduce the form of the types which that expression can take on. So we have two type expressions that will usually contain variables, the first giving the form of the type required by the context (deduced from the 'outside'), and the second giving the form of type which the object can take (deduced from the 'inside'). For the whole expression to be well typed, these two type expressions must match, in the sense that by substituting for the schematic variables of the type expressions, they can be brought to the same form.

8.4 The Intermediate Language

The language for which we will construct a type-checker is the language of the lambda calculus. We will use the form of that language in which recursion is expressed using the letrec construct rather than by using the Y combinator. Briefly, the forms of expression are these:

(i) Variables: x, y, etc.
(ii) Lambda abstractions: λx.E
(iii) Application: E_1 E_2
(iv) Simultaneous definitions (let-expressions):

```
let x1 = E1
    ...
    xk = Ek
in E
```

(v) Mutual recursion (letrec-expressions):

```
letrec x1 = E1
       ...
       xk = Ek
in E
```

The type-checker should be invoked when the source program has been brought into this form, and before lambda-lifting, or transformation to a supercombinator program (see Chapter 13). It is, however, important that the program is subjected to the dependency analysis referred to in Section 6.2.8 before type-checking. This is for the following reason. If we include in a letrec-expression a definition whose right-hand side does not 'really' depend on the other names defined in the letrec, we may not be able to type-check the program at all. (For an explanation of this, see Mycroft [1984].)

The most conspicuous absentee from this list of constructs is anything corresponding to function definitions by pattern-matching. But as is shown in Chapters 4–6, we can replace such definitions by using instead built-in case functions associated with the type-forming operations defined by the programmer or supplied by the system. The names of these case functions, and indeed of the associated discriminators and selectors, can be regarded as the names of variables with predeclared types. Hence they are of no special interest in the type-checker.

(In the same vein, we might have taken the easy way out in our treatment of recursion, and used the Y combinator, regarding this as having a priori the predeclared type

Y :: (A -> A) -> A, for all types A

However, the issues involved in the problem of how a type discipline should treat recursion are rather subtle. Although the solution we have adopted is in fact precisely equivalent to adoption of the Y combinator for the expression of recursion, we take the point of view that to do this would be to sweep the problem under the carpet.)

The type-checking algorithm can still be developed when pattern-matching is present in the language. Indeed for practical reasons it is better to type-check while the program is still close to the form in which it was entered, in order that error messages can refer to program text that the programmer can recognize.

8.5 How to Find Types

Presumably, when we construct an expression E in a program, we reason to ourselves that it is well typed. As a product of this reasoning, we are in a position to say what the type is of any subexpression E′ of E. We can, as it were, *label* each subexpression with the type which we think it has. When we enter that expression into the text of our program, that 'labelling' has been lost. It is the job of the type-checker to reason out the type structure of the expression once again, and to recover the labelling.

If we accept that type-checking is a species of inference, this raises the question as to what forms of inference we may validly employ in checking the type of an expression. We shall not go so far as to try to state those forms of inference explicitly (akin to an exercise in formal logic), but rather by considering a sufficient variety of examples (as it were, particular syllogisms), try to work up some confidence that we can tell the difference between right and wrong inference.

8.5.1 Simple Cases, and Lambda Abstractions

In order to make enough space to expose the type structure of an expression, let us lay it out as a tree, where at the top we have the variables and constants, and as we proceed down towards the root, we pass through nodes labelled with the constructors applied in the formation of the expression. For an example containing both application and abstraction nodes, take the expression

```
(λx.λy.λz. x z (y z))
```

Laid out as a tree this becomes

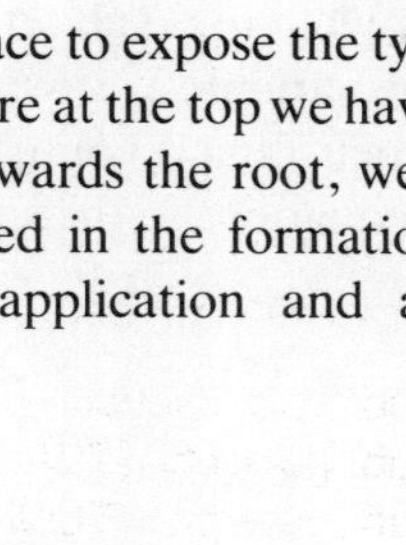

Each node in this tree corresponds to a subexpression of the original expression, and should therefore possess a type. Assign arbitrary type labels

T0, T1, ..., T7 to the nodes of the tree. Drawing the tree in a slightly different way to use less space, we get:

```
x:: T0  z:: T1        y:: T2  z:: T3
--------------@       --------------@
      T4                    T5
      ---------------------------@
                  T6
                 ----λx.λy.λz.
                  T7
```

In order to be sure than an expression (E_1 E_2) of application form is well typed, the function E_1 must have a functional type (A -> B), where E_2 is of type A, and (E_1 E_2) is of type B. So whatever else is clear, the types of the sub-expressions must be related by the following equations:

```
T0 = T1 -> T4
T2 = T3 -> T5
T4 = T5 -> T6
```

Substituting back in the tree, we get

```
x:: T1 -> T5 -> T6  z:: T1      y:: T3 -> T5  z:: T3
--------------------------@     --------------------@
         T5 -> T6                         T5
         ------------------------------------@
                          T6
                         ----λx.λy.λz.
                          T7
```

Now what should we say about the abstraction? Certainly T7 will have the form

```
(T1 -> T5 -> T6) -> (T3 -> T5) -> ...
```

but it is not immediately clear what to do about the two type labels T1 and T3 for the two occurrences of the variable z. It would be simple if we could see some reason to say that the labels T1 and T3 must stand for the same type. For then we could add two more equations to the set above, namely

```
T1 = T3
T7 = (T0 -> T2 -> T1 -> T6)
```

and then on substituting back in the tree we would get

```
x:: T1 -> T5 -> T6  z:: T1      y:: T1 -> T5  z:: T1
--------------------------@     --------------------@
         T5 -> T6                         T5
         ------------------------------------@
                          T6
   ----------------------------------------------λx.λy.λz.
   (T1 -> T5 -> T6) -> (T1 -> T5) -> T1 -> T6
```

On the other hand, we have already seen in Section 8.2.3 expressions such as

```
I . code . I
```

which make perfect sense, but in which the two occurrences of the composition function receive different types (to be sure, types sharing a common form, but nonetheless different).

So it is not obvious that we should require all occurrences of a variable bound by a lambda abstraction to have the same type. However, let us take this requirement as an assumption, and explore its consequences using the following example

```
F = λf.λa.λb.λc. c (f a) (f b)
```

and laid out as a tree, the expression is

```
                  f :: T0 a :: T1
                  ---------------@
        c :: T2          T3            f :: T4  b :: T5
        -------------------@           ----------------@
                  T6                        T7
                  ----------------------------@
                              T8
                              —λf.λa.λb.λc.
                              T9
```

from which we derive the equations

```
T0 = T1 -> T3
T2 = T3 -> T6
T4 = T5 -> T7
T6 = T7 -> T8
```

If we now require that the different occurrences of f have the same type, we can add the equation T0 = T4 to the list above. But then we must also have that T1 = T5 and T3 = T7, which gives the tree

```
                          f :: T1 -> T3  a :: T1
                          ----------------------@
   c :: T3 -> T3 -> T8               T3             f :: T1 -> T3  b :: T1
   -----------------------------------@             ----------------------@
             T3 -> T8                                          T3
             ---------------------------------------------------@
                                  T8
 ----------------------------------------------------- λf.λa.λb.λc.
 (T1 -> T3) -> T1 -> T1 -> (T3 -> T3 -> T8) -> T8
```

By demanding that both occurrences of f should have the same type, we have forced a and b to be of the same type. Renaming variables, the function F has type

```
(A -> B) -> A -> A -> (B -> B -> C) -> C
```

according to our assumption.

It is not hard to think of contexts (F f a b) which would make sense when a and b are of different types. For example

```
F I 0 'a'
```

seems to be the function which when applied to a function c of type (num -> char -> A) returns the value (c 0 'a'). On the other hand,

```
F code 0 'a' K
```

would certainly be an error, since it would result in the evaluation of (code 0), whereas the function code is applicable only to characters. At last we can see the point of the assumption. In order for an expression to be well typed, it is not enough that it cannot 'go wrong' when evaluated on its own, or in a particularly favorable context. We have to make sure that it cannot 'go wrong' when plugged into *any* well-typed context.

So we shall require that variables bound in a lambda abstraction receive the same type at all their occurrences. Without 'outside knowledge' of the arguments to which an abstraction will be applied, we must assume the worst: all occurrences of a variable bound by the same lambda abstraction must share the same type.

To sum up, so far we have adopted the following rules:

(i) The function part f of an application (f a) has a function type (A -> V), where A is the type of the argument part a and V is the type of the application (f a).
(ii) All occurrences of a λ-bound variable must have the same types.

Moreover, when solving a system of equations, we have used the following rule:

If (T1 -> T2) = (T1' -> T2'), then T1 = T1' and T2 = T2'

(This follows from a more general law which states that if two compound type expressions are equal, then they must be formed with the same construction, and their corresponding parts must be equal.)

8.5.2 A Mistyping

Consider the expression

```
λn.λa.λb. b n (n a b)
```

(This is sometimes used to define the successor function on natural numbers in the type-free lambda calculus.) Written as a tree, the expression is:

```
                                    n :: T0   a :: T1
                                    -----------------@
      b :: T2   n :: T3                    T4        b :: T5
      -----------------@                   -------------------@
             T6                                    T7
             -------------------------------------------------@
                                T8
                              --------λn.λa.λb.
                                T9
```

From which we get the equations:

```
T0 = T1 -> T4
T2 = T3 -> T6
T4 = T5 -> T7
T6 = T7 -> T8
T9 = T0 -> T1 -> T2 -> T8
T3 = T0
T5 = T2
```

Eliminating T4 and T6, these become

```
T0 = T1 -> T5 -> T7
T2 = T3 -> T7 -> T8
T9 = T0 -> T1 -> T2 -> T8
T3 = T0
T5 = T2
```

Now note that these equations contain a circularity. If we try to use the last two equations to eliminate T3 and T5, we get

```
T0 = T1 -> T2 -> T7                       (since T5 = T2)
   = T1 -> (T3 -> T7 -> T8) -> T7
   = T1 -> (T0 -> T7 -> T8) -> T7         (since T3 = T0)
```

So it is clear that the type T0 is not finite, and so neither is the type T9.

Nevertheless, T9 possesses an infinite type, which may be expressed informally:

```
T0 -> T1 -> T2-> T8
```

where

```
T0 = T1 -> (T0 -> T7 -> T8) -> T7
```

There are many difficulties in dealing with infinite types. We shall simply avoid them by imposing the rule:

> If T1 = ...T1..., where the type variable T1 occurs properly within the right-hand side of the equation, then the system of equations cannot be solved, and the expression from which the system was derived is ill-typed.

As a consequence of this, the definition in Section 2.4.2 of the fixed-point combinator Y is ill-typed.

8.5.3 Top-level lets

Consider the expression

```
let S = λx.λy.λz. x z (y z)
    K = λx.λy. x
in  S K K
```

It seems intuitively reasonable that we allow K to take on different types at its different occurrences in the body of the let-expression. Indeed, it is hard to see what polymorphism would mean if we insisted that variables introduced by a let definition should have the same type, as with variables bound by λ.

To examine the type structure of this expression, we need to extend the tree notation to represent it:

```
                                 S :: T6 -> T7 -> T8   K :: T6
                                 ----------------------------@
                                         T7 -> T8       K :: T7
 Tree-S          Tree-K                  -----------------------@
 S :: TS         K :: TK                                T8
 ------------------------------------------------------------- let S,K.
                                       T9
```

Since we already know how to type-check the right-hand sides of the definitions of S and K, we have merely indicated their type trees, to save space. Moreover, we have skipped a few steps in representing the type structure of (S K K). The equations for the type structure of the right-hand sides of the definitions of S and K can be solved to yield:

```
TS = (T0 -> T1 -> T2) -> (T0 -> T1) -> T0 -> T2
TK = T3 -> T4 -> T3
```

The new constraints we have to consider are those relating T8 to T9, and the types TS and TK to the types of their occurrences in the body of the let-expression.

For the first constraint, plainly we should require that T8=T9. As for the second, the constraint is that the type of the occurrence of S should be an instance of the type TS, and the types of the two occurrences of K should each be an instance of the type TK. But how should we represent such a requirement by means of an equation?

When working out the equations by hand, it is quite natural to proceed as follows: *refrain* from making any such representation at the outset. Instead, obtain first a fully evaluated expression for the type of TS and TK (as we have done). Then introduce new type labels for the instantiated variables at each occurrence of S and K in the body of the let-expression. (In this case, there are three such variables in the type for S, namely T0, T1 and T2; and two in the type of K, namely T3 and T4.) If we use a fresh set of variables for each occurrence, then we can still work with equations, and leave the values of those fresh variables to be worked out while we are exploring the type structure of the body. So in this case we should add new variables T10, T11, T12 to instantiate TS at its first occurrence, T13 and T14 to instantiate TK at the first occurrence of K, and T15 and T16 to instantiate TK at the second occurrence of K. We then add the equations

```
T6 -> T7 -> T8 =     (T10 -> T11 -> T12)
                  -> (T10 -> T11) -> T10 -> T12
            T6 = T13 -> T14 -> T13
            T7 = T15 -> T16 -> T15
```

From the first of these we derive:

```
T6 = T10 -> T11 -> T12
T7 = T10 -> T11
T8 = T10 -> T12
```

reasoning that if (T1 -> T2) = (T1′ -> T2′), then T1 = T1′ and T2 = T2′. By the same reasoning, we have

```
T10 = T13 = T12
T11 = T14
T10 = T15
T11 = T16 -> T15
```

which allows us to express the types of the two occurrences of K as

```
T6 = T10 -> (T16 -> T10) -> T10
T7 = T10 -> T16 -> T10
```

and the type of the whole expression as

```
T9 = T8 = T10 -> T10
```

So the rule we adopt as the type-constraint for let-expressions is that the types of the occurrences of the defined names in the body must be instances of the types of the corresponding right-hand sides. The procedure we adopt to compute those instances is to instantiate the variables in the types of those right-hand sides with new variables, making a fresh instance for each occurrence of the defined name in the body of the let. In fact, we shall not in general be able to instantiate *all* the type variables, as we shall see shortly.

8.5.4 Top-level letrecs

Turning now to letrecs, it seems clear that a variable introduced by a letrec definition should be capable of taking on different types in the body of the program governed by the letrec, just as in the case of let-definitions. So in

```
letrec f = (...)
in (...f...f...f...)
```

we expect f to be capable of taking on different types throughout the expression body. However, there is a new question we must answer. The variable introduced by a recursive definition can also have many occurrences in the right-hand side of its definition, as it were ‘while’ it is being defined, as well as ‘after’. In general, when there are several mutually recursive definitions, as in

$$
\begin{aligned}
&\text{letrec } x_1 = (\ldots x_1 \ldots x_i \ldots x_k \ldots)\\
&\qquad\quad \ldots\\
&\qquad\quad x_k = (\ldots x_1 \ldots x_j \ldots x_k \ldots)\\
&\text{in } (\ldots x_1 \ldots x_i \ldots x_j \ldots x_k \ldots)
\end{aligned}
$$

any one of the defined names x_i can occur many times in many right-hand sides, as well as in the body. Should we insist that all these occurrences have the same type, in the sense of requiring equality to hold between the type labels for the variable occurrences in the definitions? Or should we treat them as we treat them in the body, and require only that at each such occurrence, the type be an instance of the type of the corresponding right-hand side? Unfortunately, in the nature of things, there is no obvious answer. Nevertheless, to see what the question means, consider the example

```
letrec Y = (λf. f (Y f)) in ...
```

Written out as a tree, the first definition is

```
                Y :: T0   f :: T1
                ─────────────────@
        f :: T2          T3
        ─────────────────────@
                 T4
           ───────────────λf.
               Y::T5
```

The constraints we can write down straight away are these:

```
T1 = T2
T0 = T1 -> T3
T2 = T3 -> T4
T5 = T1 -> T4
```

from which it follows that

```
T0 = (T3 -> T4) -> T3
```

and

```
T5 = (T3 -> T4) -> T4
```

The question is, should we ask that T0 = T5, or only that T0 be an instance of T5? In the former case, the only solution is T5 = ((T4 -> T4) -> T4), as we would expect of a fixed-point function. On the other hand, the alternative requires only that T3 be an instance of T4, so again T5 = ((T4 -> T4) -> T4) is a solution.

We shall adopt the (usual) approach according to which 'during' such definitions all occurrences of the defined variables must share the same type as the right-hand side of their definitions. On the other hand, 'after' the definitions, the defined variables are polymorphic, and the type of such a variable can be instantiated differently to satisfy the local constraints on different occurrences of the variables in the body of the definition. If nothing else, this approach has at least the merit of simplicity.

Some different approaches to the type-checking of recursive definitions have been explored by Mycroft [1984]. In some (but not all) of these approaches the problem of whether an expression is well typed becomes only semi-decidable.

8.5.5 Local Definitions

We have presented type-checking as the search for the solution of a system of constraints, represented by equations T′ = T between type expressions. So far, we know that when type-checking an expression of let or letrec form, we should impose the constraint that the types of the occurrences of the defined variables in the body should equal new instances of the types derived for their right-hand sides. But just which type variables may be instantiated?

To understand this issue, we have to probe a little into the reason for our conviction that a defined name can take on different types in the body of its definition. The reason seems to be this:

> An expression (let x = E in E′) is well typed just in case the expression E′[E/x] is well typed, which is the expression obtained by substituting E for the free occurrences of x in E′.

For each occurrence of x in E′, we should be able to instantiate the type variables in the type tree for E in such a way that it forms a subtree of the type tree for E′[E/x]. This instantiation is only possible if we do not thereby violate the law that occurrences of a λ-bound variable must have the same type, or the corresponding law for letrecs.

Consider the expression (λx.let y = x in y y). By the principle above, this is well typed just in case (λx.x x) is well typed, which it blatantly is not. The problem is that the type expression for y contains (is!) a variable occurring in the type of a more global λ-bound variable. We cannot instantiate that variable differently at the different occurrences of y in (y y).

Consider the partial expression

```
λx.
   let I    = λz. z
       prxI = λc. (c x I)
       p1   = λx.λy. x
       p2   = λx.λy. y
   in ...
```

Informally, the types of the defined names are

```
I    :: A -> A
prxI :: (X -> (A -> A) -> B) -> B
p1   :: A -> B -> A
p2   :: A -> B -> B
```

where A and B are schematic variables, and X is the type of x. If we take the body of the let-expression to be the expression

```
prxI p1 (prxI p1)
```

then it cannot be typed. For to satisfy the type constraints of this body, we would have to instantiate X differently at the different occurrences of prxI. On the other hand, if the body were

```
prxI p2 (prxI p2)
```

then the expression is well typed. For the structure of that expression does not constrain X to be instantiated differently at the different occurrences of prxl.

When we are type-checking the body B of a let or letrec definition, we must therefore distinguish the type variables in the type derived for a defined name according to whether they may or may not be differently instantiated at the various occurrences of the name. Variables of the former kind are those that do not occur in the type of any *constrained* variable in the definition of the name. A constrained variable is one which is a bound variable of a lambda abstraction enclosing B, or one defined in a letrec-expression enclosing B in one of its right-hand sides.

This is one of the points at which the type regime of Miranda differs from that of the type checker described here. The Miranda compiler requires that all occurrences of a variable bound in a local definition share a single type. This has the effect that local definitions cannot introduce new polymorphism into a program. We will not explore the implications of this difference here – the type checking rules given in this and the following chapter are for a standard implementation of the Milner type discipline.

We have used the notion of type trees to help elucidate the type structure of expressions, and guide us towards a sharper view of the rules we use when constructing and checking the types of expressions. In the next section we summarize those rules. With luck, the device will have served its purpose, and we can then consider how to turn our intuitions into algorithms.

8.6 Summary of Rules for Correct Typing

The following rules are intended to describe the local 'look' of the type structure of a well-typed expression. To lighten the notational burden, we shall sometimes simplify the expression whose type tree is depicted in the figures. The simplifications are indicated in the commentary.

8.6.1 Rule for Applications

```
A -> B        A
--------------- @
       B
```

8.6.2 Rule for Lambda Abstractions

```
. . . x :: A . . . x :: A . . .
  . . . . . . . . . . . . . . . . .
              B
        ------------ λx.
          A -> B
```

Note that all occurrences of the variable x bound by the abstraction must have the same type.

8.6.3 Rule for let-expressions

```
{...y :: C...}
      ......            ...x :: A' ... x :: A'' ...
       ....              ..............
       x::A                    B
      ---------------------------------------- let x.
                          B
           {              ...                }
           {          ----- λy.              }
           {              ...                }
```

Here we have shown only the case where just one definition is made in the let-expression: let x = E in E′.

Restriction: A′ and A″ are instances of A. No variable may be instantiated which occurs in the type of a variable bound in a more global lambda abstraction or letrec-expression (i.e. one further down the tree). The portions of the figure in curly brackets indicate such a situation. Any type variables in A shared with C may not be instantiated in forming A′ and A″.

8.6.4 Rule for letrec-expressions

```
...x :: A ... x :: A ...
      ......            ...x :: A' ... x :: A'' ...
       ....              ..............
       x::A                    B
---------------------------------------------- letrec x.
                     B
```

Here we have shown only the case where just one definition is made in the letrec-expression: letrec x = E in E′. Note that the occurrences of x within the right-hand side of the definition must have the same type.

Restriction: just as in the let rule.

8.7 Some Cautionary Remarks

There is a beguiling similarity between the notion of type which we use in mathematics, and the notion which we use in functional programming. It is all too easy to transfer intuitions concerning the mathematical notion of type to the notion used in programming. There are at least two important differences.

First, the types in a functional language are types of partial objects, whose evaluation may not terminate. In contrast, the mathematical notion of type, whose study began with Frege [Gaeck and Black, 1970] and Whitehead and Russell [1910–1913], concerns total objects, whose definitions are well founded. The purpose of the mathematical notion of type is to elucidate the foundations of mathematics. The purpose of the notion in functional programming is to assure us at compile-time that a program will not 'go wrong', where we do not count a program to have gone wrong if it does not terminate, or a function is applied to arguments for which it has not been defined.

Second, in functional programming 'recursion' is interpreted in a very liberal sense, going far beyond recursion on well-founded structures, or positive inductive definitions. As a direct result of this, the notion of a type in functional programming cannot be the same notion that we use in mathematics. For example, in a functional program we can define an integer omega, where

```
omega = omega + 1
```

and this cannot belong to the (mathematical) type of integers. Another symptom of this liberal attitude to recursion is exhibited by the definition of the algebraic type

```
D ::= LAMBDA (D -> D)
```

in which the defined type occurs negatively (to the left of the arrow) on the right-hand side of the definition. This is not to say that there is no mathematical sense in the functional programming notions. On the contrary, there is a rich and sophisticated theory (domain theory) which aims to give a mathematical interpretation to just such constructs. But while constructing that theory, and reasoning about the mathematical structures it involves, we are using on the metalevel the ordinary mathematical notion of type.

We hope that this chapter has shown that a naive understanding of the notion of type certainly gives us plenty to go on. We also hope to have achieved another goal: that of showing that there are limits to the questions we can settle on a naive basis alone.

References

Gaeck, P., and Black, M. (editors) 1970. Function and concept. In *Translations from the Philosophical Writings of Gottlob Frege*. Basil Blackwell.

Milner, R. 1978. A theory of type polymorphism in programming. *Journal of Computer and System Science*. Vol. 17, pp. 348–75.

Mycroft, A. 1984. Polymorphic type schemes and recursive definitions. In *Proceedings of the International Symposium on Programming, Toulouse*, pp. 217–39. LNCS 167. Springer Verlag.

Strachey, C. 1967. Fundamental concepts in programming languages. In *Notes for the International Summer School in Computer Programming, Copenhagen*.

Whitehead, A.N., and Russell, B.A.W. 1910–1913. *Principia Mathematica*, 3 volumes. Cambridge University Press.

Nine

A TYPE-CHECKER

Peter Hancock

In this chapter we will construct a type-checker in Miranda, taking the rules developed in the previous chapter as the basis for the type discipline.

Sections 9.1 and 9.2 show how the expressions of the intermediate language and its type expressions can be represented as Miranda data types. Sections 9.3 to 9.6 are concerned with the basic mechanisms of the type-checker, which is itself defined in Section 9.7.

9.1 Representation of Programs

Since we propose to write a type-checker in Miranda, we will have to represent the program to be type-checked as a Miranda data structure, which is passed as an argument to the type-checking function.

The program to be checked will be represented by an object of the structured type vexp, defined below. Each line of the type definition is derived directly from the corresponding construct in the concrete syntax.

```
vname == [char]
vexp   ::=   VAR vname
           | LAMBDA vname vexp
           | AP vexp vexp
           | LET [vname] [vexp] vexp
           | LETREC [vname] [vexp] vexp
```

In a sense, this type encompasses slightly too much. We shall suppose that the program is not 'trivially' malformed: in a LET or LETREC construct, the list of variables must have the same length as the light of right-hand sides; the variable list in a LET or LETREC construct must not be empty, and should contain no repetitions. Moreover, the free variables in an expression must be among those associated with predeclared types, either because they are supplied by the system, or because their types can be deduced from type definitions in the program. We can assure ourselves that these restrictions are met in a simple recursive scan through the program.

To understand the representation, let us take for an example the following trivial program:

```
let S = λx.λy.λz. x z (y z)
    K = λx.λy. x
in  S K K
```

Considered as an object in the type vexp, the program becomes:

```
LET ["S","K"] [rhs_S, rhs_K] main
where
   var_S    = VAR "S"
   var_K    = VAR "K"
   var_x    = VAR "x"
   var_y    = VAR "y"
   var_z    = VAR "z"
   main     = AP (AP var_S var_K) var_K
   rhs_S    = plambda ["x","y","z"] body_S
   rhs_K    = plambda ["x","y"] body_K
   body_S   = AP (AP var_x var_z) (AP var_y var_z)
   body_K   = var_x
   plambda vs e = foldr LAMBDA e vs
```

which the reader may write out without using 'where' if so inclined.

9.2 Representation of Type Expressions

To construct the type-checker, we will need to represent type expressions by Miranda data structures. We need a type for the names of type variables and, for the moment, we will take this to be the type of lists of characters. (For technical convenience, we will revise this definition in Section 9.6.)

```
tvname    ==  [char]
type_exp  ::=  TVAR tvname
               | TCONS [char] [type_exp]
```

This definition says that a type expression must be either a type variable or a compound type (such as (A -> B), [A] or (A,B)). We represent such compound types by the name of the operator (e.g. "arrow" for (A -> B), "cross" for (A,B)), and a list of the operands.

Whatever other type-forming operators we have, we will certainly need the function type operator. So let us define:

```
arrow :: type_exp -> type_exp -> type_exp
arrow t1 t2      = TCONS "arrow" [t1,t2]
```

If t1 and t2 are of type type_exp, and we know what types they represent, then (arrow t1 t2) will represent the type of functions from t1 to t2. Using Miranda's dollar notation for infixes, we may write this in the form (t1 $arrow t2), which adheres more closely to the informal notation.

The other type-forming operations we have mentioned could be represented in a similar way:

```
int     :: type_exp
int          = TCONS "int" []

cross :: type_exp -> type_exp -> type_exp
cross t1 t2 = TCONS "cross" [t1,t2]

list   :: type_exp -> type_exp
list t       = TCONS "list" [t]
```

The function tvars_in returns a list of the variable names that occur in a type expression. (The list may contain repetitions.)

```
tvars_in :: type_exp -> [tvname]
tvars_in t = tvars_in' t []
             where
                tvars_in' (TVAR x) l        = x:l
                tvars_in' (TCONS y ts) l  = foldr tvars_in' l ts
```

9.3 Success and Failure

Since type-checking is something that can succeed or fail, we have to choose a mechanism for representing success and failure within Miranda.

We shall use the type (reply *) for the type of the values of a function which may succeed (returning an object of type *) or fail (returning no indication as to why).

```
reply *   ::= OK *   |   FAILURE
```

It would not be acceptable for a practical type-checker to return no indication as to why a check has failed. One might then use a slightly more complicated operator, such as

```
reply' * **   ::= OK' *   |   FAILURE' **
```

which is capable of returning error information. It is notoriously difficult to write error-handling code without obscuring the code to handle correct cases, so we will use instead the simpler, less informative operator. Any error detected while type-checking will be propagated up to the top level without further examination of the program. Here, too, there may be grounds for complaint, which we counter with the same excuse.

(There is more than one way to represent success and failure. An alternative approach to the one taken here is described by Wadler [1985].)

9.4 Solving Equations

Consider type-checking an application (AP e1 e2), where we have worked out the type t1 for e1 and the type t2 for e2. To do this, we try to 'solve the equation'

```
t1 = t2 -> (TVAR n)
```

where n is a type variable name that has not been used before. As we have seen, the structure of an expression gives rise to a system of such equations.

How should we represent solutions of systems of type equations? In mathematics, the solution of simultaneous equations

$$a_{1,1} \times x_1 + a_{1,2} \times x_2 = b_1$$
$$a_{2,1} \times x_1 + a_{2,2} \times x_2 = b_2$$

is expressed by giving values for each of the unknowns x_1 and x_2 which satisfy the equations. Analogously, an alleged solution of a system of type equations can be expressed as a function from type variables (the unknowns) to type expressions (their values). The allegation is that the equations are satisfied when we replace (i.e. substitute) the unknowns by their values under the function. We therefore take

```
subst == tvname -> type_exp
```

to be the type of substitutions. We shall see how to determine whether a set of equations between type expressions has a solution, and if so how to construct a substitution that satisfies them. We shall use identifiers such as phi, phi', psi, as variables over substitutions.

9.4.1 Substitutions

Given a substitution function phi and a type expression te, we define (sub_type phi te) to be the type expression obtained by performing the phi substitution on all the type variables in te:

```
sub_type :: subst -> type_exp -> type_exp
sub_type phi (TVAR tvn)       = phi tvn
sub_type phi (TCONS tcn ts) = TCONS tcn (map (sub_type phi) ts)
```

Here map is the function that applies a function to each entry in a list:

```
map :: (* -> **) -> [*] -> [**]
map f []      = []
map f (x:xs) = f x : map f xs
```

Two substitutions can be composed to give a further substitution:

```
scomp :: subst -> subst -> subst
scomp sub2 sub1 tvn = sub_type sub2 (sub1 tvn)
```

The crucial property of scomp is that

```
sub_type (scomp phi psi) = (sub_type phi) . (sub_type psi)
```

(Remember that function composition is represented by an infix dot.)

The identity substitution id_subst has the property that

```
sub_type id_subst t = t
```

for all t::type_exp. It can be defined by:

```
id_subst :: subst
id_subst tvn = TVAR tvn
```

A *delta substitution* is one that affects one variable only. We define:

```
delta :: tvname -> type_exp -> subst
delta tvn t tvn' = t,                  tvn = tvn'
                 = TVAR tvn'
```

Hence, (sub_type (delta tvn t)) is the function that maps a type expression to one that contains t where before it had (TVAR tvn).

In fact, all the substitutions we need will be built up from the identity substitution id_subst by composition on the left with substitutions of delta form.

In general, a substitution may associate a variable with a value which itself contains variables. If those variables in turn are given values different from themselves, then the substitution is not 'fully worked out'. When we work out a set of equations

$$x_1 = t_1; \ldots; x_k = t_k$$

by substituting t_i for x_i at all of its occurrences in $t_1, \ldots, t_k$, we may have to iterate the substitution many times before the equations stabilize to their final forms. (Of course, this iterative process does not terminate if there is a circularity in the equations.) In general, we are interested in obtaining 'fully worked out' substitutions, which do not have to be re-applied. The next definition is intended to capture what we mean by such a substitution.

A substitution phi is *idempotent* if

```
(sub_type phi) . (sub_type phi) = sub_type phi
```

or equivalently, if (phi $scomp phi) = phi. In other words, if you apply the substitution twice, you get nothing different the second time. A type expression t is a *fixed point* of a substitution phi if

```
sub_type phi t = t
```

In particular, if (TVAR x) is a fixed point of phi, then we say that x is *unmoved* by phi.

Note that if phi is idempotent, and phi moves tvn, then

```
sub_type phi (VAR tvn)
```

is a fixed point of phi, and hence cannot contain tvn.

9.4.2 Unification

In this section we will show how to construct a substitution which solves a given set of type equations, using a process called *unification*.

A system of type equations can be represented by a list of pairs of type expressions, where each pair (t_1,t_2) represents the equation

$$t_1 = t_2$$

To solve the equations, we have to find a substitution phi which *unifies* the left- and right-hand sides of all equations in the system, where phi unifies the pair (t_1,t_2) if

$$\text{sub\_type phi } t_1 = \text{sub\_type phi } t_2$$

If this equation holds, phi is said to be a *unifier* of t_1 and t_2. If phi is a unifier of each pair in the list representing a set of equations, we may think then of phi as a simultaneous solution of the equations.

If the substitution phi solves a system of equations, then clearly any substitution psi′ of the form (psi $scomp phi) is also a solution, but phi will usually be a more general solution than psi′. A substitution phi is *no less general* than a substitution psi if there is a substitution rho such that

```
psi = rho $scomp phi
```

If such an equation holds, then psi is said to be an *extension* of phi.

If we have constructed a solution phi of a system of type equations, and we have done no more than is necessary to satisfy the equations, we will have a solution which is *maximally general*, in the sense that it is no less general than any other solution.

For an example (in informal terms), consider the type expressions

```
T1 = (A -> B) -> C
T2 = (B -> A) -> (A -> B)
```

The substitutions phi1 and phi2, where

```
phi1 A = B, phi1 C = (B -> B)
phi2 B = A, phi2 C = (A -> A)
```

are both unifiers of T1 and T2. In fact, they are examples of maximally general unifiers: they each do (one version of) the minimum necessary to make T1 and T2 equal, so that any other unifier of T1 and T2 is an extension of each of them.

The problem of unification is to find a maximally general idempotent unifier of a set of pairs of expressions. The method we use is Robinson's [1965] unification algorithm. It is convenient when coding the algorithm to concentrate on the problem of *extending* a given substitution, which solves a set of equations

$$t_1 = t_1'; \ldots ; t_k = t_k'$$

to one that solves an extended set

$$t_1 = t_1'; \ldots ; t_k = t_k' ; t_{k+1} = t_{k+1}'$$

So we shall pose the problem in the following way. Given a pair (t_1,t_2) of type expressions, and an idempotent substitution phi, our algorithm should return FAILURE if there is no extension of phi which unifies (t_1,t_2), and it should return (OK psi), where psi is an idempotent unifier of (t_1,t_2) which extends phi. (In fact, the one we construct will be maximally general among such extensions of phi.)

The simplest equation we can consider is one of the form

```
TVAR tvn = t
```

To handle such cases in the unification algorithm, we will make use of the following function:

```
extend :: subst -> tvname -> type_exp -> reply subst
extend phi tvn t      = OK phi,            t = TVAR tvn
                      = FAILURE,           tvn $in tvars_in t
                      = OK ((delta tvn t) $scomp phi)
```

An expression (extend phi tvn t) will be evaluated only when:

(i) phi is an idempotent substitution (the solution we are trying to extend);
(ii) t is a fixed point of phi;
(iii) tvn is unmoved by phi (tvn does not already have a value under phi).

The value of the expression is either FAILURE, or of the form (OK phi′), where phi′ is an idempotent substitution extending phi, such that

```
sub_type phi' t' = t                  if t' = TVAR tvn
                 = sub_type phi t'    otherwise
```

In fact, phi′ is maximally general among extensions of phi which solve the equation:

```
TVAR tvn = t
```

Note that if phi is idempotent, t is a fixed point of phi and tvn *is* moved by phi, then tvn can occur in neither (phi tvn) nor t.

We can code the unification algorithm as follows:

```
unify :: subst -> (type_exp, type_exp) -> reply subst

unify phi ((TVAR tvn),t)
      = extend phi tvn phit,                  phitvn = TVAR tvn
      = unify phi (phitvn,phit)
        where
          phitvn = phi tvn
          phit   = sub_type phi t

unify phi ((TCONS tcn ts),(TVAR tvn))
      = unify phi ((TVAR tvn),(TCONS tcn ts))

unify phi ((TCONS tcn ts),(TCONS tcn' ts'))
      = unifyl phi (ts $zip ts'),              tcn = tcn'
      = FAILURE
```

The function zip, which is generally useful, turns a pair of lists into a list of pairs, whose length is the same as that of the shorter of the lists:

```
zip :: [*] -> [**] -> [(*,**)]
zip [] xs          = []
zip (x:xs) []      = []
zip (x:xs) (y:ys) = (x,y):zip xs ys
```

The function unifyl is defined such that (unifyl phi pts) constructs a substitution extending phi which unifies corresponding entries in the list of pairs pts. This function is also generally useful, so it is defined globally too.

```
unifyl :: subst -> [(type_exp,type_exp)] -> reply subst

unifyl phi eqns = foldr unify' (OK phi) eqns
                  where
                       unify' eqn (OK phi)  = unify phi eqn
                       unify' eqn FAILURE = FAILURE
```

This completes the definition of the unification algorithm.

It is important to see why the unification algorithm terminates. After all, in the definition above we have defined the value of (unify (TVAR tvn) t) in terms of (unify phitvn phit) where phitvn = (phi tvn) and phit = (sub_type phi t), which may be very much larger expressions than (TVAR tvn) and t. However, we only use that clause of the definition in circumstances when tvn cannot occur in phitvn or phit. Define the *solution set* of phi to be the set of variables which occur in an expression (phi tvn'), where tvn' is moved by phi. We can prove that (unify phi (t1,t2)) terminates, by a nested induction: the outer induction is on the number of variables in t1 and t2 which are not in the solution set of phi, and the inner induction is on the combined length of t1 and t2.

The unification algorithm has many applications other than type-checking. In particular it is a key algorithm in the implementation of programming languages such as Prolog.

9.5 Keeping Track of Types

When type-checking an expression with free variables, there are two ways to proceed.

9.5.1 Method 1: Look to the Occurrences

We can find the constraints imposed on the types of the free variables by the manner in which they occur in the expression. In a complete program, the free variables must stand for the system's built-in functions or functions associated with type definitions. We would then look to see whether the types deduced for *each occurrence* of a free variable can be instances of the type supplied a priori for that variable. When type-checking a lambda abstraction (λx . E), we would check that the types deduced for the various occurrences of x within E can be unified to the same type expression, and we would handle occurrences of defined variables in the right-hand sides of a letrec-expression in the same way.

It is quite possible to develop a type-checker along these lines: one is presented in Damas [1985].

9.5.2 Method 2: Look to the Variables

It is technically rather a nuisance that distinct *occurrences* of the same variable in an expression are associated with different type expressions. Is there something which we can associate with each *variable* instead?

Suppose we wish to type-check a let-expression. First of all we type-check the definitions of the let, thus deducing a type for each variable defined by the let. Then it seems that we could associate each variable with its type, and proceed to type-check the body of the let-expression. At each occurrence of one of these defined variables in the body, we should construct an *instance* of its associated type, substituting fresh type variables for the *schematic* variables in the type (see Section 8.5.3). However, as we discovered in Section 8.5.5, some of the variables in the type are *constrained* and should not be substituted for, and the instantiation mechanism must take account of this.

What is needed, therefore, is to associate with each variable a kind of type *template*, in which the schematic variables are distinguished from the non-schematic variables. Then the template can be instantiated by copying it, substituting a fresh type variable for each occurrence of a schematic variable (but copying non-schematic variables unchanged). This type template is called a *type scheme*. To summarize:

(i) The *schematic* type variables in a type scheme associated with a variable are those that may be freely instantiated to conform with the type constraints on the various occurrences of that variable.

(ii) All the other (non-schematic) variables in a type scheme are constrained, and must not be instantiated when instantiating the type scheme. As we remarked in Section 9.4, they behave in a similar way to the unknowns of a mathematical equation. For example, consider the simultaneous equations

$$a_{1,1} \times x_1 + a_{1,2} \times x_2 = b_1$$
$$a_{2,1} \times x_1 + a_{2,2} \times x_2 = b_2$$

We seek values for the unknowns x_1 and x_2, by solving the equations, but they must be consistently instantiated, so that x_1 stands for the same value wherever it occurs (and likewise x_2).

By analogy, we will refer to the non-schematic variables of a type scheme as *unknowns*. They are the type variables whose values we seek by solving the system of type constraints implied by the structure of an expression.

(In papers about type-checking, schematic variables are often called *generic* variables, and unknowns are called *non-generic*. We mention this only to make it easier to link up with the literature, and will not use that terminology here.)

There is a partial analogy between type schemes and lambda abstractions. The schematic variables of a type scheme correspond to the formal parameter of a lambda abstraction, and the unknowns of a type scheme correspond to the free variables of a lambda abstraction. Applying a lambda abstraction to an argument involves constructing an instance of its body, substituting the argument for occurrences of the formal parameter (but copying free variables unchanged). This is very similar to the process of instantiating a type scheme, which involves constructing an instance of the type scheme template, substituting fresh type variables for occurrences of the schematic variables (but copying unknowns unchanged).

We will represent type schemes by objects of the type

```
type_scheme ::= SCHEME [tvname] type_exp
```

A type variable occurring in a type scheme (SCHEME scvs e) is schematic if its name occurs in the list scvs, otherwise it is an unknown.

```
unknowns_scheme :: type_scheme -> [tvname]
unknowns_scheme (SCHEME scvs t) = tvars_in t $bar scvs
```

where

```
bar :: [*] -> [*] -> [*]
bar xs ys = [ x <- xs | ~ (x $in ys) ]
in :: * -> [*] -> bool
in x' []      = False
in x' (x:xs) = True,        x = x'
             = x' $in xs
```

During the course of type-checking we will have occasion to apply a substitution to a type scheme, to reflect additional information we have on its unknowns. When doing this, we should take care that only the unknowns are affected (remember that the schematic variables function like the formal parameter of a lambda abstraction, and have only local significance):

```
sub_scheme :: subst -> type_scheme -> type_scheme
sub_scheme phi (SCHEME scvs t)
        = SCHEME scvs (sub_type (exclude phi scvs) t)
```

where

```
exclude phi scvs tvn = TVAR tvn,        tvn $in scvs
                     = phi tvn
```

In Section 2.2.6 we demonstrated the irritating problem of 'name-capture', whereby a free variable of a lambda abstraction could become bound by being substituted inside another lambda abstraction. There is a similar problem here with substitution into type schemes. We must take care that the expression

```
sub_scheme phi (SCHEME scvs t)
```

is only evaluated when the schematic variables scvs are distinct from any variables occurring in the result of applying the substitution phi to any of the unknowns of t. Otherwise a type variable in the range of the substitution (which is always an unknown) might surreptitiously be changed into a schematic variable. The way in which we ensure this is to guarantee that the names of the schematic type variables in the type scheme are always distinct from those which can occur in the range of the substitution (which are always unknowns).

9.5.3 Association Lists

Having decided to associate a type scheme with each free variable in an expression, rather than a type expression with each occurrence of a free variable, we now have to decide how this information should be provided to the type-checker. There are two requirements on the data structure we use:

(i) It should provide a mapping from the free variables of the expression to type schemes.
(ii) We should be able to determine the *range* of that mapping.

To understand the second point, consider type-checking (let x=E in E′). We start by deriving a type t for E, in a type environment

$$x_1 :: ts_1, \ldots, x_k :: ts_k$$

which associates a type scheme ts_i with each variable x_i free in E (the ts_i thus constitute the range of the type environment). In other words, we attempt to build a solution phi to the type equations implied by the structure of E, such that

E :: t   provided that x_1 :: ts_1', . . . , x_k :: ts_k'

where ts_i' is the image of ts_i under the substitution phi. We then form the type scheme ts to be associated with x when type-checking E', in the extended environment

x_1 :: ts_1', . . . , x_k :: ts_k' , x :: ts

The schematic variables of ts are all of the type variables of t except those that are unknown (non-schematic) in any of the schemes ts_1', . . . ,ts_k'. So whatever data structure we choose to represent the environment of the type-checker, it should give us ready access to the set of unknowns in its range (the ts_i').

An association list provides us with a suitable data structure.

```
assoc_list * ** == [(*,**)]
```

Here * stands for the type of keys, and ** for the type of associated values. A key k is associated with a value v by means of the pair (k,v). The partial function itself is represented by a list of such associations. We shall use al, al', etc. as variables over association lists.

```
dom :: assoc_list * ** -> [*]
dom al = [ k | (k,v) <- al]
```

(dom al) returns a list (possibly with duplications) of the keys associated with values in the list, which is how we shall represent the domain of a partial function.

```
val :: assoc_list * ** -> * -> **
val al k = hd [ v | (k',v) <- al ; k = k' ]
```

If k is a key in (dom al), then (val al k) returns the first value in the list which is associated with k. When using this function, we should be careful to ensure that the second argument belongs to the domain of the association list.

```
install al k v = (k,v):al
```

(install al k v) returns an association list which implements the same partial function as al, except that the key k is now mapped to the value v.

```
rng :: assoc_list * ** -> [**]
rng al = map (val al) (dom al)
```

The property which rng is intended to satisfy is that every entry in (rng al) is a value of (val al).

We shall represent the information passed to the type-checker about the types of the free variables of an expression by means of an object of the following type:

```
type_env == assoc_list vname type_scheme
```

We shall use gamma, gamma′, etc. as variables standing for type environments. The functions unknowns_scheme and sub_scheme can be extended to act on type environments, in the obvious way:

```
unknowns_te :: type_env -> [tvname]
unknowns_te gamma = appendlist (map unknowns_scheme (rng gamma))

appendlist :: [ [*] ] -> [*]
appendlist lls = foldr (++) [] lls

sub_te :: subst -> type_env -> type_env
sub_te phi gamma
    = [ (x,sub_scheme phi st) | (x,st) <- gamma ]
```

9.6 New Variables

When type-checking a closed expression, we first assigned a distinct type variable to each subexpression, and then wrote down equations expressing the constraints on those variables imposed by the structure of the expression. When type-checking an expression containing variables defined in a let- or letrec-expression, we chose first to work out the schematic types of those variables (i.e. we checked the definitions first). We then assigned to each occurrence of such a variable a type expression obtained by substituting new unknown variables for the schematic variables, using a distinct set of unknowns for each distinct occurrence.

So we will need a mechanism that enables us to 'make up' new type variables, and guarantees that they are distinct from type variables we may introduce in the future. There are many ways to provide such a mechanism. The one we adopt here is to postulate that there is a type name_supply, and functions

```
next_name :: name_supply -> tvname
deplete   :: name_supply -> name_supply
split     :: name_supply -> (name_supply,name_supply)
```

such that if ns is a name supply, then (next_name ns) is distinct from any name supplied by (deplete ns), and if (ns0,ns1) = split ns, then any name supplied from ns0 is distinct from any name supplied by ns1. One way to implement such a type is to (re)define tvname, thus:

```
tvname        == [num]
name_supply   == tvname
next_name ns  = ns
deplete (n:ns) = (n+2:ns)
split ns      = (0:ns,1:ns)
```

For example, if we start with the name supply [0], then the names it will supply are [0], [2], [4], ..., while the names supplied by splitting the supply into [0,0] and [1,0] will be [0,0], [2,0], [4,0], ..., and [1,0], [3,0], [5,0], ..., respectively. (The +2 in the definition of deplete is only an artifice to ensure that the two halves of a split name supply are forever distinct.)

The function name_sequence returns from a name supply an infinite sequence of distinct names derived from that supply:

```
name_sequence :: name_supply -> [tvname]
name_sequence ns = next_name ns : name_sequence (deplete ns)
```

In practice, it is probably better to adopt an approach other than the supply of new variables, according to which variables are named by integers, and the name supply represented by the name of the next variable to be allocated. The type-checker would then take the name supply as an argument, and return the depleted supply as part of its value. We have adopted an approach which wastes large portions of the variable name space, in order not to encumber the type-checker code with a further avoidable detail.

9.7 The Type-checker

Finally, we are in a position to define the type-checker. This will take the form of a function (tc gamma ns e) where

(i) gamma is a type environment, associating type schemes with each of the free variables of e. When the type-checker is invoked upon a complete program, this type environment should be initialized to contain declarations of the types of the built-in system-supplied identifiers.
(ii) ns is a supply of type variable names.
(iii) e is the expression to be checked.

The value returned will be a reply, which in the case of success will return a pair of the form (phi,t) where

(i) phi is a substitution defined on the unknown type variables in gamma.
(ii) t is a type derived for the expression e, in the type environment (sub_te phi gamma). It will in fact be a fixed point of the substitution phi.

In other words, if

```
tc gamma ns e = OK (phi,t)
```

then e::t can be derived from gamma, provided that each unknown tvn in gamma has the value given it by phi.

We shall define the function tc by induction on the structure of the expression, with a different clause for each form which an expression can take:

```
tc :: type_env -> name_supply -> vexp -> reply (subst, type_exp)
tc gamma ns (VAR x)            = tcvar     gamma ns x
tc gamma ns (AP e1 e2)         = tcap      gamma ns e1 e2
tc gamma ns (LAMBDA x e)       = tclambda gamma ns x e
tc gamma ns (LET xs es e)      = tclet     gamma ns xs es e
tc gamma ns (LETREC xs es e) = tcletrec  gamma ns xs es e
```

We will describe each of these cases in a separate section, beginning at Section 9.7.2. First, however, we define a useful auxiliary function tcl.

9.7.1 Type-checking Lists of Expressions

It is convenient to define a function (tcl es gamma n) which applies to a list of expressions es, and will return in the case of success a similar result OK (phi,ts), where ts is a list of types derived for corresponding components of the list es in the type environment (sub_te phi gamma). phi embodies all the constraints on gamma necessary to derive those types simultaneously. The function is defined from tc by the equations:

```
tcl :: type_env -> name_supply -> [vexp] -> reply (subst, [type_exp])
tcl gamma ns []       = OK (id_subst,[])
tcl gamma ns (e:es) = tcl1 gamma ns0 es (tc gamma ns1 e)
                         where (ns0,ns1) = split ns

tcl1 gamma ns es FAILURE      = FAILURE
tcl1 gamma ns es (OK (phi,t)) = tcl2 phi t (tcl gamma' ns es)
                                   where gamma' = sub_te phi gamma

tcl2 phi t FAILURE       = FAILURE
tcl2 phi t (OK (psi,ts)) = OK (psi $scomp phi, (sub_type psi t) : ts)
```

The substitution can be thought of as built up in two stages. In the first stage, we type-check each entry in the list, in the type environment 'seen' through the substitutions derived for previous entries. Then in the second stage, we form the substitution by cumulative composition, and ensure that each type returned for an expression is a fixed point of the composite substitution.

9.7.2 Type-checking Variables

When type-checking a variable x in a given type environment gamma, with name supply ns, we look up the type scheme associated with that variable by gamma. Recall that in a type scheme, a type variable is *either schematic*, in which case we substitute a fresh type variable for it, *or unknown*, in which case we leave it as it is.

So we return a new instance of the schematic type associated with the variable, in which the schematic variables have been replaced by fresh type variables. In this way, the type constraints on different occurrences of a variable x can be resolved independently, as indicated by the schematic variables in the type scheme associated with x.

```
tcvar :: type_env -> name_supply -> vname
                  -> reply (subst,type_exp)
tcvar gamma ns x
      = OK (id_subst, newinstance ns scheme)
        where scheme = val gamma x
```

where

```
newinstance :: name_supply -> type_scheme -> type_exp
newinstance ns (SCHEME scvs t)
        = sub_type phi t
          where al  = scvs $zip (name_sequence ns)
                phi = al_to_subst al
```

Here we have built an association list between the schematic variables and an initial segment of the name sequence built on the given name supply. Such an association list can be made into a substitution, by means of the function:

```
al_to_subst :: assoc_list tvname tvname -> subst
al_to_subst al tvn     = TVAR (val al tvn),    tvn $in (dom al)
                       = TVAR tvn
```

9.7.3 Type-checking Application

When type-checking an expression (AP e1 e2) with respect to a type environment gamma, we first of all try to construct a substitution phi which solves the type constraints on e1 and e2 together. Suppose that the types t1 and t2 are derived for e1 and e2. We then try to construct an extension of phi which satisfies the additional constraint

```
t1 = t' -> t2
```

where t′ is a new type variable. We obtain this extension, as usual, by unifying t1 with t′ -> t2.

```
tcap :: type_env -> name_supply -> vexp -> vexp
                 -> reply (subst,type_exp)
tcap gamma ns e1 e2
       = tcap1 tvn (tcl gamma ns' [e1,e2])
         where tvn = next_name ns
               ns' = deplete ns

tcap1 tvn FAILURE
       = FAILURE
tcap1 tvn (OK (phi,[t1,t2]))
       = tcap2 tvn (unify phi (t1,t2 $arrow (TVAR tvn)))

tcap2 tvn FAILURE = FAILURE
tcap2 tvn (OK phi)  = OK (phi, phi tvn)
```

9.7.4 Type-checking Lambda Abstractions

When type-checking (LAMBDA x e), we know nothing at the outset about the type of x. So we associate x with a scheme of the form (SCHEME [] (TVAR tvn)), where tvn is a new type variable. Because this scheme has no schematic type variables, the various occurrences of the variable will be assigned the value of the same type variable. This is the formal counterpart of our decision to insist that all occurrences of the same LAMBDA-bound variable should have the same type.

```
tclambda :: type_env -> name_supply -> vname -> vexp
                     -> reply (subst,type_exp)
tclambda gamma ns x e
      = tclambda tvn (tc gamma' ns' e)
            where ns'    = deplete ns
                  gamma' = new_bvar (x,tvn) : gamma
                  tvn    = next_name ns

tclambda1 tvn FAILURE
      = FAILURE
tclambda1 tvn (OK (phi,t))
      = OK (phi, (phi tvn) $arrow t)

new_bvar (x,tvn) = (x,SCHEME [] (TVAR tvn))
```

9.7.5 Type-checking let-expressions

When type-checking an expression (LET xs es e), we first of all type-check the right-hand sides in the list es. We then have to update the environment so that it associates the appropriate schematic types with the names in the list xs, and type-check the body e. The details of constructing the 'appropriate' schematic types are slightly involved, so we shall hide them in the definition of a function add_decls.

```
tclet :: type_env -> name_supply
         -> [vname] -> [vexp] -> vexp
         -> reply (subst, type_exp)
tclet gamma ns xs es e
   = tclet1 gamma ns0 xs e (tcl gamma ns1 es)
     where (ns0,ns1) = split ns

tclet1 gamma ns xs e FAILURE
    = FAILURE
tclet1 gamma ns xs e (OK (phi,ts))
    = tclet2 phi (tc gamma'' ns1 e)
      where gamma'' = add_decls gamma' ns0 xs ts
                gamma' = sub_te phi gamma
             (ns0,ns1) = split ns
```

```
tclet2 phi FAILURE
      = FAILURE
tclet2 phi (OK (phi',t))
      = OK (phi' $scomp phi, t)
```

The purpose of add_decls is to update a type environment gamma so that it associates schematic types formed from the types ts with the variables xs. The variables which become schematic variables are those that are not unknowns in gamma. The definition is slightly complicated by our obligation to ensure that the names of the schematic variables are distinct from the names of any unknown variables which can occur in the range of a substitution. We use the name sequence ns to supply new names for the schematic variables.

```
add_decls :: type_env -> name_supply
              -> [vname] -> [type_exp] -> type_env
add_decls gamma ns xs ts
        = (xs $zip schemes) ++ gamma
          where schemes   = map (genbar unknowns ns) ts
                unknowns  = unknowns_te gamma

genbar unknowns ns t
        = SCHEME (map snd al) t'
          where al   = scvs $zip (name_sequence ns)
                scvs = (nodups (tvars_in t)) $bar unknowns
                t'   = sub_type (al_to_subst al) t
```

Here snd is a function which projects a pair to its second coordinate. The projection functions for pairs are defined by

```
fst :: (*,**) -> *
fst (x,y) = x

snd :: (*,**) -> **
snd (x,y) = y
```

The function nodups returns a list with the same set of entries as its argument list, but without duplicates:

```
nodups :: [*] -> [*]
nodups xs = f [] xs
            where
              f acc []     = acc
              f acc (x:xs) = f acc xs,  x $in acc
                           = f (x:acc) xs
```

9.7.6 Type-checking letrec-expressions

The definition of the function invoked to type-check expressions (LETREC xs es e) is rather intricate, as there are many things to do. In outline, they are these:

(i) Associate new type schemes with the variables xs. These schemes will have no schematic variables, in accordance with our decision to insist that all occurrences of a defined name in the right-hand sides of a recursive definition should have the same type.

(ii) Type-check the right-hand sides. If successful, this will yield a substitution and a list of types which may be derived for the right-hand sides if the type environment is constrained by the substitution.

(iii) Unify the types derived for the right-hand sides with the types associated with the corresponding variables, in the context of that substitution. This is in accordance with our decision that the right-hand sides of recursive definitions must receive the same types as occurrences of the corresponding variables. Should the unification succeed, that constraint can be met.

(iv) We are now in much the same situation as we were in with expressions of LET form, when the definitions had been processed, and it remained to type-check the body e, after updating the type environment with appropriate schematic types.

```
tcletrec :: type_env -> name_supply
            -> [vname] -> [vexp] -> vexp
            -> reply (subst, type_exp)
tcletrec gamma ns xs es e
     = tcletrec1 gamma ns0 nbvs e (tcl (nbvs ++ gamma) ns1 es)
       where (ns0,ns') = split ns
             (ns1,ns2) = split ns'
             nbvs      = new_bvars xs ns2

new_bvars xs ns = map new_bvar (xs $zip (name_sequence ns))

tcletrec1 gamma ns nbvs e FAILURE
     = FAILURE
tcletrec1 gamma ns nbvs e (OK (phi,ts))
     = tcletrec2 gamma' ns nbvs' e (unifyl phi (ts $zip ts'))
       where ts'    = map old_bvar nbvs'
             nbvs'  = sub_te phi nbvs
             gamma' = sub_te phi gamma

old_bvar (x,SCHEME [] t) = t

tcletrec2 gamma ns nbvs e FAILURE
     = FAILURE
tcletrec2 gamma ns nbvs e (OK phi)
     = tclet2 phi (tc gamma'' ns1 e)
       where ts        = map old_bvar nbvs'
             nbvs'     = sub_te phi nbvs
             gamma'    = sub_te phi gamma
             gamma''   = add_decls gamma' ns0 (map fst nbvs) ts
             (ns0,ns1) = split ns
```

The definition of the type-checker is now complete.

References

Damas, L. 1985. *Type Assignment in Programming Languages*. CST-33-35. Department of Computer Science, University of Edinburgh. April.

Robinson, J.A. 1965. A machine-oriented logic based on the resolution principle. *Journal of the ACM*. Vol. 12, no. 1, pp. 23–41.

Wadler, P. 1985. How to replace failure by a list of successes. In *Conference on Functional Programming Languages and Computer Architecture, Nancy*. Jouannaud (editor). LNCS 201. Springer Verlag.

Part II

GRAPH REDUCTION

Ten

PROGRAM REPRESENTATION

At this stage, we assume that we have successfully translated the functional program into a lambda expression. In the next few chapters we will show how to execute the program, reducing the lambda expression to normal form.

First of all we have to establish some *representation* for the lambda expression, as it is held in the computer's memory. This chapter outlines the possibilities.

10.1 Abstract Syntax Trees

In all implementations of graph reduction, the expression to be evaluated is held in the machine in the form of its *syntax tree*.

The leaves of the tree are constant values (such as 0, 'a', TRUE), built-in functions (such as +, −, ∗), or variable names.

The application of a function f to an argument x is represented thus:

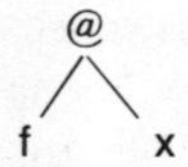

The '@' sign is called the *tag* of the node, and indicates that the node is an application. We deal with functions of several arguments by currying:

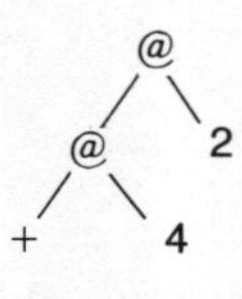

This tree denotes the expression (+ 4 2), which shows the function + applied to the argument 4, giving a function (+ 4), which is then applied to the argument 2. Figure 10.1 shows a slightly more complicated example.

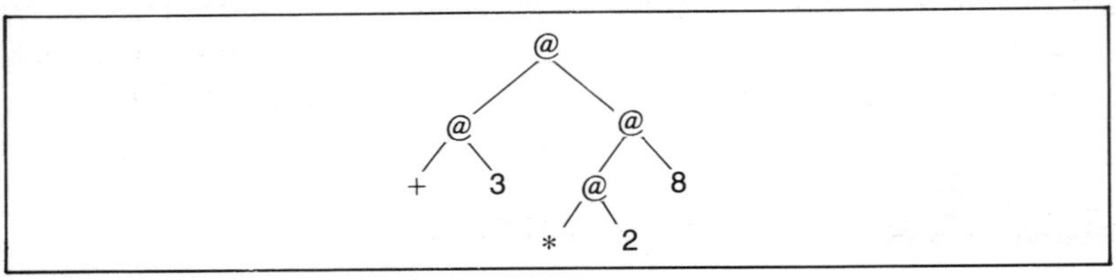

Figure 10.1 The tree of (+ 3 (* 2 8))

A lambda abstraction (λx . body) is represented thus:

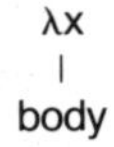

The λx tells that the node is a lambda abstraction and gives the formal parameter.

The graph of the expression (CONS E_1 E_2) will look like this

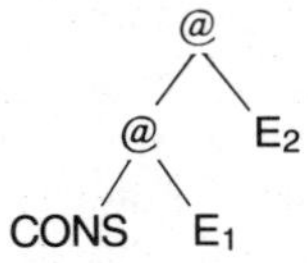

(E_1 and E_2 stand for arbitrary expressions, as usual.) The result of evaluating it will be a CONS cell, which we depict like this:

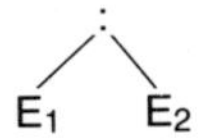

where the ':' tag labels the node as a CONS cell (just as @ labels a node as an application).

10.2 The Graph

The process of reduction performs successive transformations on the syntax tree. During this process the *tree* becomes a *graph*, for reasons that will become clear in Chapter 12. We use the term 'graph' here in the sense of 'network', a collection of *nodes* connected together by some *directed edges*. Figure 10.2 shows an example graph.

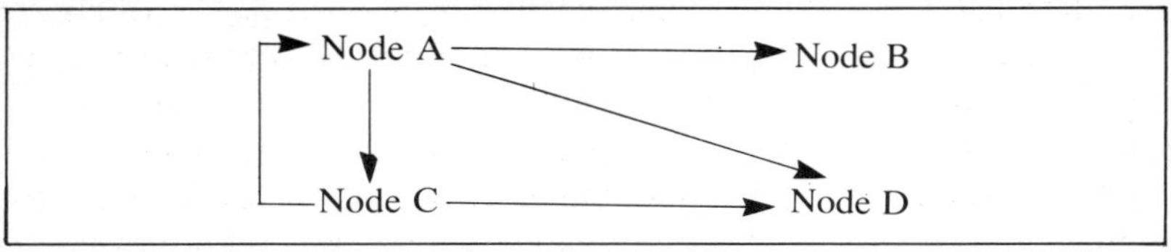

Figure 10.2 An example graph

A graph differs from a tree in that two edges can point to the same node. For example, in Figure 10.2 node D is a descendant of nodes A and C (we say that it is *shared*). A graph is said to be *acyclic* if there is no path from a node back to itself (Figure 10.2 is *not* acyclic, since there is a path from node A to itself, via node C). A directed acyclic graph is often abbreviated DAG.

10.3 Concrete Representations of the Graph

The pictures we have shown are still somewhat abstract. In a typical implementation each node of the tree would be represented by a small contiguous area of store, called a *cell*. A cell holds a *tag* which tells the type of the cell (application, number, built-in operator, lambda abstraction, CONS cell, etc.), and two or more *fields*. The number of fields in a cell varies between implementations. Many implement fixed-size cells with two fields, but some have variable-sized cells. This issue is further discussed below. We may draw a cell thus:

Tag	Field 1	Field 2

A field may contain the address of another cell, in which case we say that it is a *pointer*, and that it *points to* the cell. We draw a pointer field like this:

[Address ——►] Another cell

Alternatively, a field may contain an *atomic* (non-pointer) data value. We draw a non-pointer field like this:

[A data value]

Each node of the abstract syntax tree (or graph) corresponds to a cell of the concrete representation. The tag on the node goes in the tag field of the cell. Possible concrete representations for the syntax tree nodes we have met are given in Figure 10.3, and, using these, our (+ 4 2) tree, for example, would be represented as in Figure 10.4. Such pictures are rather laborious to draw, so we will normally use the abstract version.

10.3.1 Representing Structured Data

We recall from Chapter 4 that an implementation of Miranda has to support a family of *constructor functions*, of which NIL and CONS are particular examples. A constructor function builds a structured data object, which is simply an aggregate of values together with a *structure tag* to distinguish it from other constructors of the same data type. Typically the structure tag will be a small integer, between 1 and the number of constructors of the type (but see below, where tags and type-checking are discussed).

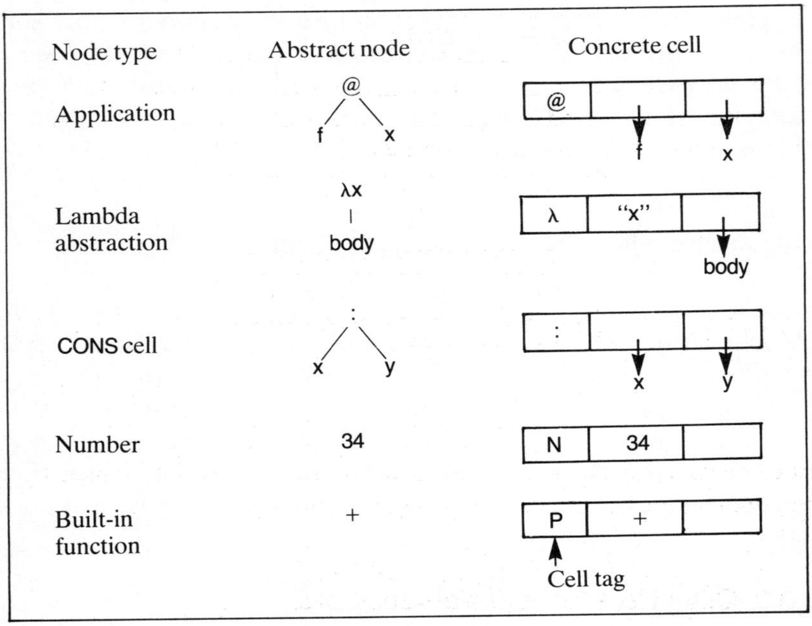

Figure 10.3 Possible concrete representations

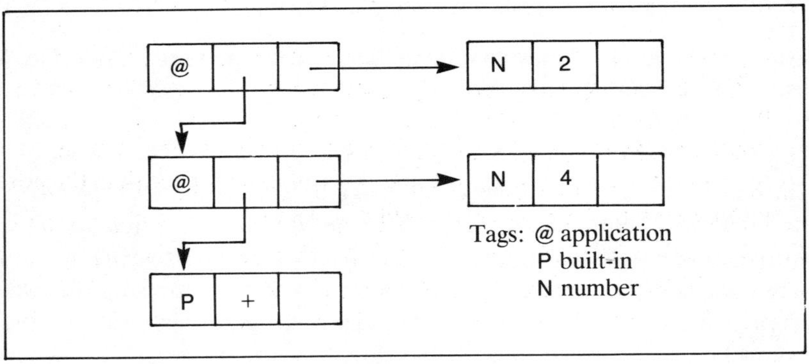

Figure 10.4 The concrete tree of (+ 4 2)

If the implementation supports variable-sized cells then we can implement these structures directly:

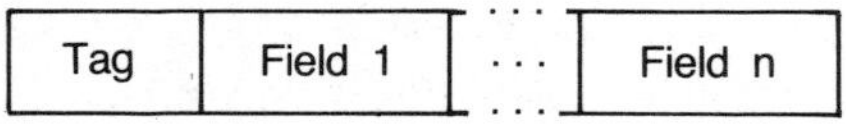

If the implementation supports fixed-size cells only, with two fields, then the structure will have to be implemented as a linked collection of cells:

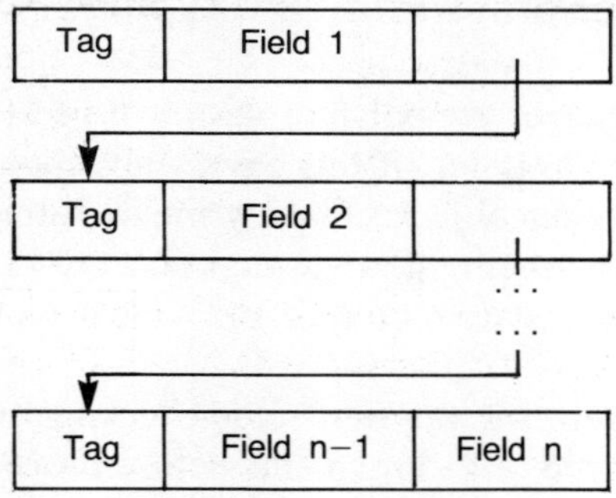

Notice that, since the size of the structured object is determined by the structure tag, the last cell can contain the last *two* fields.

10.3.2 Other Uses for Variable-sized Cells

As we have seen, the provision of variable-sized cells gives a much more efficient representation of structured data objects. However, variable-sized cells may also be useful to contain other objects such as:

(i) arrays;
(ii) arbitrary precision integers;
(iii) blocks of compiled code;
(iv) multiple applications; for example, we could represent (f a b) as a single three-field cell containing f, a and b. This takes less space than the normal method, which requires two two-field cells.

Unfortunately, variable-sized cells carry an implementation cost, as we will see in Chapter 17.

10.4 Tags and Type-checking

In what follows we will find it convenient to distinguish two families of tags. The *structure tags* identify data objects, and distinguish them from one another. For example, a CONS cell and NIL would have distinct structure tags. *System tags* identify cells holding *system objects*, such as application nodes, lambda abstractions, built-in operators, and so on. The '. . . and so on' is highly implementation-dependent. For example, some implementations may tag an application node differently if it is discovered to be irreducible, so that repeated efforts to reduce it can be avoided.

10.5 Compile-time versus Run-time Typing

Some functional languages are polymorphically typed (see Chapter 8), and type-checked at compile-time. In this case, only enough distinct tags are required to identify system objects uniquely and to distinguish data objects of a given type from each other (e.g. to distinguish a CONS cell from NIL). Thus relatively few distinct tags are required, and a tag is typically represented in eight bits or fewer.

Other languages rely on run-time type-checking, where each built-in operator checks the type of its arguments before proceeding. This requires that each data type be distinguishable from all the others used in the program. Such run-time type-checked languages normally have only a fixed set of types, and do not allow the user to introduce new types, so a fixed-size tag is still sufficient.

Even in a type-checked system it is often considered desirable to carry around type information at run-time to aid in system debugging. This is problematic in languages that allow the programmer to introduce new types, because there is no bound to the number of types which have to be distinguishable. In this case an escape mechanism is normally used for user-defined types, whereby the first field of the cell representing the object carries a unique type identification.

10.6 Boxed and Unboxed Objects

In Figure 10.4 each number seems to require a cell to itself. This seems rather profligate, since a field of a cell is normally large enough to contain a number. Thus, instead of a field pointing to a cell which contains a number, it would be better to put the number directly in the field. For example, the tree representing (+ 4 2) using unboxed representations would look like Figure 10.5 (compare Figure 10.4).

Data objects which can be completely described by a *single field* are called *unboxed*, while those which are represented by *one or more cells* are called *boxed* (the cell 'boxes' the data object). Typical candidates for an unboxed representation are integers, booleans, characters and built-in operators (which can be identified by a small integer or code pointer). For example, Figure 10.4 incorporates boxed representations of integers and built-in functions, while Figure 10.5 gives them unboxed representations. It is clear that significant savings in the number of cells allocated can be achieved by using unboxed representations.

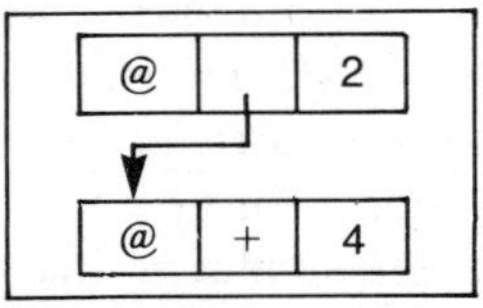

Figure 10.5 The concrete tree of (+ 4 2) (unboxed representations)

In a boxed system, the tag of a cell completely determines which fields of the cell are pointers and which are not; for example, the two fields of an application cell are always pointers (see Figure 10.4).

In contrast, in an unboxed system, any field which may contain a pointer may also contain an unboxed object. For example, a field of an application cell may either be a pointer or an unboxed (i.e. non-pointer) object (see Figure 10.5). Hence, all such fields must have an extra bit, called the *pointer-bit*, to distinguish pointers from unboxed objects. Fields now look like this:

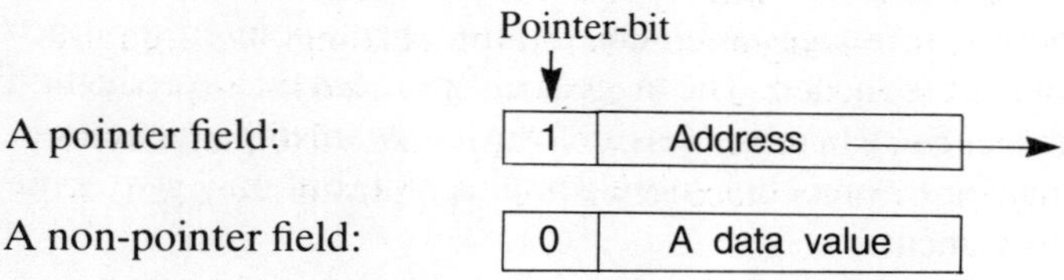

A minor shortcoming of unboxed objects for run-time type-checked systems is that unboxed objects are not tagged (since tags are attached to cells not fields). In Figure 10.4, the N tag on numbers enables the + built-in operator to check that its arguments are indeed numbers, whereas this is not possible with a basic unboxed system. However, an unboxed system can still incorporate run-time type-checking by reducing the number of bits in the unboxed object sufficiently to fit a tag into the field as well. Non-pointer fields would then look like this:

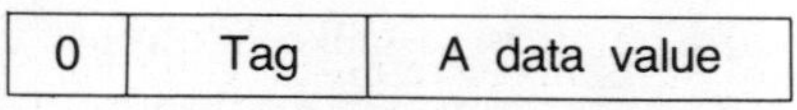

Even for compile-time type-checked systems it is vital that built-in functions (such as +) are able to distinguish evaluated operands from unevaluated ones (so that an unevaluated operand can first be evaluated). Fortunately this is easy because if the operand is a pointer the tag on the cell pointed to will show whether it is evaluated or not; and if the operand is a non-pointer then it is an unboxed object which requires no further evaluation.

10.7 Tagged Pointers

Some implementations put a tag into pointer fields also, thus

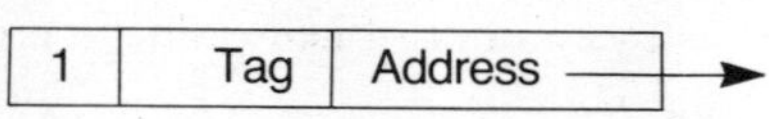

For example, both the SKIM [Clarke *et al.*, 1980] and NORMA [Richards, 1985] reduction machines do this, though they use the tag in different ways. NORMA regards the pointer tag as a *cache* for the tag of the cell pointed to. Thus if the pointer tag is valid (one value of the pointer tag is reserved for INVALID) it contains the tag of the cell to which the pointer points. Like any cache, this technique should be regarded purely as an optimization of the ordinary tagged-cell approach.

In SKIM, however, there are no tags on cells at all. The only tags are in the fields. This has the advantage that a cell now consists of two identical fields (instead of two identical fields plus a tag), which allows a more uniform hardware design for SKIM. However, it means that a cell cannot change its tag; for example, an application cell must remain an application cell, because it would be impossible to change the tags of all pointers to the cell at once. This makes reduction slightly more awkward.

In summary, both a pure tagged cell and a pure tagged pointer approach can adequately support reduction. The tagged cell approach makes reduction rather easier, but gives rise to a rather less uniform hardware implementation. The NORMA cacheing approach is more complex still, but may give some performance improvement.

10.8 Storage Management and the Need for Garbage Collection

As reduction proceeds we will need to build new pieces of graph. In order to do so we have to *allocate* new cells. Cells are allocated from a (large) area of storage called the *heap*, which is simply an unordered collection of cells. The term 'heap' emphasizes that the physical adjacency of two cells is purely coincidental; what matters is which cells point to which.

As well as allocating new cells, the reduction process will also discard cells, or rather it will discard pointers to cells. We must re-use cells whenever possible, because if we never did so we would soon run out of heap space. Unfortunately, in a graph there may be many pointers to the same cell, and we can only re-use a cell when there are no further pointers to it. So long as there are further pointers to a cell from elsewhere in the graph, it cannot be re-used because it is still in use. Cells with no pointers to them are said to be *garbage*. It is quite tricky to identify garbage cells, and all implementations of functional languages include a *garbage collector* whose purpose is to identify and recycle garbage cells.

The whole activity of cell allocation and garbage collection is called storage management, and is further discussed in Chapter 17. As we will see there, fixed-size cells allow for a rather more simple garbage collector than variable-sized cells.

References

Clarke, T.J.W., Gladstone, P.J.S., Maclean, C., and Norman, A.C. 1980. SKIM – The SKI reduction machine. *Proceedings of the ACM Lisp Conference, Stanford*, Calif. 95044.

Richards, H. 1985. *An Overview of Burroughs NORMA*. Austin Research Center, Burroughs Corp., Austin, Texas. January.

Eleven

SELECTING THE NEXT REDEX

When the graph of a functional program has been loaded into a computer, an *evaluator* is called to reduce the graph to normal form. It does this by performing successive reductions on the graph, which involves two distinct tasks:

(i) selecting the next redex to be reduced;
(ii) reducing it.

In this chapter we shall address the first issue, before turning our attention to the second issue in the next chapter.

As Section 2.3 has shown, the order in which reductions take place has a profound effect on the behavior of the program. We begin by discussing the nature of this effect.

11.1 Lazy Evaluation

In an ordinary imperative language (such as Pascal), arguments to a function are evaluated before the function is called (*call by value*). However, it is possible that the argument thus passed is never used in the body of the function, so that the work done in evaluating it is wasted. This suggests that a better scheme might be to postpone the evaluation of the argument until its value is actually required (*call by need*). Call by need is in fact rarely implemented in imperative languages for two main reasons:

(i) The evaluation of an argument may cause some side-effects to take place, and may produce a result which depends on the side-effects (such as assignments) of other parts of the program. Hence, the exact time at which the argument is evaluated is crucial to the correct behavior of the program. However, it can be quite tricky to work out exactly when the argument will first be needed (and hence evaluated).

(ii) Call by need is hard to implement in a stack-based implementation.

In the context of functional languages, call by need is often called *lazy evaluation*, since it postpones work until it becomes unavoidable. Conversely, call by value is often called *eager evaluation*.

11.1.1 The Case for Lazy Evaluation

In the context of functional programming, there are strong reasons for providing lazy evaluation in the language.

It adds a new dimension of expressive power to the language, allowing, in particular, the construction and manipulation of *infinite data structures* and *streams*. A full justification of this point of view is outside the scope of this book, since it lies in the area of software engineering rather than implementations, and the reader is referred to Chapter 8 of Henderson's book [1980], Section 3.4 of Abelson and Sussman [1985] and the author's paper [Peyton Jones, 1986].

Not all functional languages have lazy semantics. For instance, ML and Hope are strict, while SASL, KRC, LML, Miranda, Orwell and Ponder are lazy.

11.1.2 The Case Against Lazy Evaluation

There is only one argument against lazy evaluation, but it is a very persuasive one: the price of lazy evaluation is execution speed. There seems to be no avoiding this in practice. Faster implementations are possible when the arguments to functions can be evaluated before the function is applied.

Languages like ML and Hope have strict (call by value) semantics, but support lazy evaluation where it is explicitly requested by the programmer (particularly in data constructors). The argument is that the price for lazy evaluation should only be paid where it is actually required.

11.1.3 Normal Order Reduction

Any implementation of lazy evaluation has two ingredients:

(i) Arguments to functions should be evaluated only when their value is needed, not when the function is applied.

(ii) Arguments should only be evaluated once; further uses of the argument within the function should use the value computed the first time. Since the language is functional we can be sure that this scheme gives the same result as re-evaluating the argument.

In a nutshell, arguments should be evaluated *at most once* and, if possible, not at all.

Any implementation of a lazy language must somehow support these two ingredients. We will have to wait until the next chapter before we see how to support the second ingredient, but the first is rather easy – it is directly implemented by normal order reduction!

Recall from Section 2.3 that normal order reduction specifies reducing the leftmost outermost redex first. Given an application of a function to an argument, the outermost redex is the function application itself, so a normal order reducer will reduce this prior to reducing the argument to normal form. For example, in the expression

```
(λx.3) <bomb>
```

where <bomb> does not terminate, normal order chooses to apply the lambda abstraction (giving the result 3) rather than first evaluating the argument <bomb>. Hence normal order reduction directly implements the first ingredient of a lazy evaluator.

In terms of reduction order, strict semantics means reducing the argument to a lambda expression *before* reducing the application of the lambda expression to the argument. This is called *applicative order* reduction.

As we will see in this chapter, normal order is actually an extremely natural and easily implemented reduction order, since the rule for identifying the next redex turns out to be rather simple. Thus graph reduction gives a 'good fit' with lazy evaluation.

11.1.4 Summary

There are strong arguments for and against lazy evaluation, but a detailed discussion of the question is beyond the scope of this book. (The author is, however, convinced that lazy evaluation is a crucially important feature for functional programming.)

It seems undeniable, however, that graph reduction is a particularly effective implementation technique for lazy languages. Since graph reduction is the subject of this book, we will henceforth restrict our attention to languages with lazy semantics, implemented using normal order reduction.

Arvind *et al.* [1984] give a more detailed description of some of these issues.

11.2 Data Constructors, Input and Output

Suppose that the result of evaluating our program is an infinite list. We want this list to be printed out *as it is generated*. We certainly do not want to wait until it has all been evaluated before printing anything, because we would have to wait forever! Similarly, we do not want the program to evaluate its entire input before producing any output. These observations focus our attention on the mechanisms available for input and output.

Input and output are regarded as side-effects in imperative programming languages, so functional systems have to take a different view since they do not support side-effects. The accepted solution is to regard the functional program as a function from input data to output data:

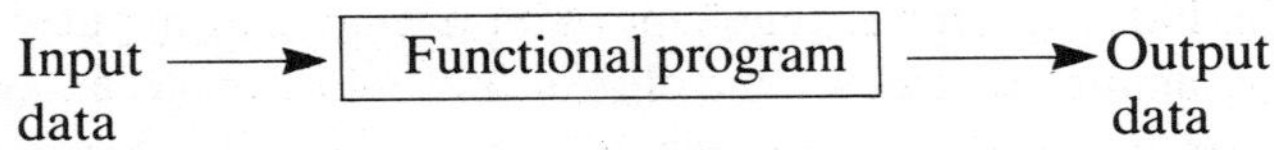

The input data are normally presented to the program as an infinite list of characters, which might, for example, come from the user's keyboard. The output data are the result of applying the program to the input list, and are normally some kind of data structure which might, for example, be displayed on the user's screen.

As well as getting the correct results to the program, however, we also want it to have 'nice' operational behavior, namely that output is printed as soon as it is available, and that input is not consumed until it is needed. In the next two sections we discuss how this operational behavior can be achieved, beginning with the printing mechanism.

11.2.1 The Printing Mechanism

Since we want to print out a data structure as it is generated, we see that the evaluation of a functional program is driven by the need to print its result, and that the evaluator is called from the printing program. The printing program calls the evaluator, and then looks at the root of the result (i.e. the root of the evaluated graph). If it is a number (or boolean, character, etc.), the printer prints it and evaluation is complete. If, on the other hand, the result is a data constructor (such as a CONS cell), the printing program can call the evaluator successively to evaluate the components of the data structure, printing out the results as it goes. The whole printing process can be repeated recursively on the components of the data structure.

Assuming that our functional program always evaluates to a number or a CONS cell, we might write a pseudo-code printing program like this:

```
Print( E )
begin
        E′ := Evaluate( E )

        if (IsNumber( E′ )) then Output( E′ )
        else begin
                Print( Head( E′ ) )
                Print( Tail( E′ ) )
        end
end
```

When Evaluate(E) yields a CONS cell it is vital that its head and tail are not yet evaluated. If they were evaluated immediately then the entire data structure would be evaluated before any of it could be printed. This is achieved by using *lazy* constructors; that is, constructors that do not evaluate their arguments.

It has become quite common for printing mechanisms to print the components of a data constructor one after the other, with no separating characters. This hides the underlying shape of the data structure, but gives the functional programmer complete control over the character stream actually output to the printer. SASL, for example, behaves in this way [Turner, 1983], though Miranda does not.

So far we have assumed that the result of a program will be printed, but there is no reason why it should not be put in a file, or fed into some other program instead. This routing of output would be controlled by the 'printing mechanism', possibly directed by routing information contained in the output data structure itself.

11.2.2 The Input Mechanism

In order to extract characters from the input list, the program will need to evaluate the list, element by element. Just as in the case of the printer, it is vital that the first evaluation does not force evaluation of the entire list, otherwise the entire input list would have to be evaluated (that is, read in) before any of it could be used. This would effectively rule out interactive programs, in which later input data depend on earlier output data.

11.3 Normal Forms

Our consideration of both input and output have led us to the same conclusion, namely that

> evaluating an expression whose result is a CONS cell should not entail evaluating its head and tail.

This means that we should stop reduction when there may still be some redexes left in the graph (in the head and the tail). None of these redexes will be reduced by a normal order reduction scheme until the whole expression has been evaluated to a CONS cell, because until then there will always be a top-level redex which normal order will select.

Hence, what we need to do is to pursue normal order reduction, but *stop* when there is no top-level redex (even though there may be inner redexes left in the graph).

11.3.1 Weak Head Normal Form

To express this idea precisely we need to introduce a new definition:

> DEFINITION
>
> A lambda expression is in *weak head normal form* (WHNF) if and only if it is of the form
>
> F E_1 E_2 ... E_n
>
> where n ≥ 0;
> and either F is a variable or data object
> or F is a lambda abstraction or built-in function
> and (F E_1 E_2 ... E_m) is not a redex for any m≤n.
>
> An expression has no *top-level redex* if and only if it is in weak head normal form.

For example, the following expressions are in weak head normal form:

3	
A CONS cell	
+ (− 4 3)	top-level + does not have enough arguments
(λx.+ 5 1)	not applied to anything

The last two examples are in weak head normal form, but not in normal form, since they contain inner redexes. Weak head normal form is often confused with *head normal form*; this point is discussed at the end of the section.

Our reduction order is therefore to *reduce* the top-level redex (there can only be one such) until weak head normal form is reached. We can think of it like this:

> Original expression
> ↓ Normal order reductions of top-level redexes
> Weak head normal form (no top-level redexes)
> ↓ Normal order reductions of inner redexes
> Normal form (no redexes at all)

We pursue normal order reduction, but stop at WHNF rather than proceeding all the way to normal form. This is an essential ingredient of lazy evaluation, since reducing through to normal form risks performing unnecessary reductions.

11.3.2 Top-level Reduction is Easier

The result of a functional program never has any free variables. For example, (+ x 1) is not a valid functional program since it has the free variable x, whose value is not specified.

Since we only ever reduce the top-level redex, which has no free variables, it follows that the arguments of the redex have no free variables either. This means that the name-capture problem described in Section 2.2.6 can never arise in our implementations, which is a considerable relief. It is also an essential property if we are to compile our programs (see Chapter 13).

11.3.3 Head Normal Form

Head normal form is often confused with weak head normal form, so it merits some discussion. The content of this section is, however, largely academic since for most purposes head normal form is the same as weak head normal form. Nevertheless, we will stick to the term WHNF for the sake of precision.

> DEFINITION
>
> A lambda expression is in *head normal form* (HNF) if and only if it is of the form
>
> $\lambda x_1.\lambda x_2 \ldots \lambda x_n.(v\ M_1\ M_2\ \ldots\ M_m)$
>
> where $n, m \geq 0$;
> v is a variable (x_i), a data object, or a built-in function;
> and ($v\ M_1\ M_2\ \ldots\ M_p$) is not a redex for any $p \leq m$.

Anything in HNF is also in WHNF, but not vice versa. For example, the following expression is in WHNF but not HNF:

```
λx.((λy.y) 3)
```

To reach HNF the inner redex should be reduced.

The difference between HNF and WHNF is only significant when the result is a lambda abstraction, since for data objects and built-in functions they are identical. For the purists, though, the question is whether we should perhaps reduce to HNF rather than WHNF. This raises some practical difficulties, since it will involve performing inner reductions where the argument may have free variables, so the name-capture problem of Section 2.2.6 comes back.

Taking this idea further, Barendregt *et al.* [1986] advocate a reduction order called *innermost spine reduction*. This is a modification of normal order which evaluates the body of a lambda expression *before* applying it to an argument. For example

```
   (λx.((λy.y) 3)) 4
→  (λx.3) 4
→  3
```

This is based on the insight that the body of the lambda expression will subsequently be evaluated anyhow, so we do not risk non-termination by evaluating it before applying it. Thus Barendregt *et al.* show that innermost spine reduction never takes more reductions than normal order, and sometimes takes fewer. As mentioned above, the serious problem with innermost spine reduction is that it entails performing reduction in the presence of free variables. From an implementation point of view (only), this objection is so serious (see Section 11.3.2) that we abandon innermost spine reduction forthwith.

This view is not universally held; see, for example, Watson *et al.* [1986].

11.4 Evaluating Arguments of Built-in Functions

Some built-in functions, such as + and HEAD, need to evaluate their arguments before they can execute. For example, consider

```
+ (- 4 3) 5
```

The inner redex (- 4 3) must be evaluated before the + can proceed. We say that + is *strict* in both arguments (see Section 2.5.4).

When the evaluator finds that the top-level redex is an application of a built-in function which evaluates its argument(s), it has to check whether the appropriate argument(s) are already in WHNF. If they are not, it must *recursively invoke itself* to reduce them to WHNF before proceeding with the application of the function. For example, in the expression

```
IF (NOT TRUE) f g h
```

we will select the redex (IF (NOT TRUE) f g) for reduction. Now, the function IF must evaluate its first argument (only), and that argument is not yet in WHNF. So the evaluator recursively invokes itself on the (NOT TRUE) expression, which returns FALSE, at which point the IF can proceed.

As another example, consider

```
HEAD (CONS 2 NIL)
```

The outer level redex is the application of HEAD, and HEAD must evaluate its argument to WHNF (that is, until it is a CONS cell). So the evaluator invokes itself recursively to evaluate

```
CONS 2 NIL
```

This evaluation produces a CONS cell in one reduction, from which HEAD extracts the result, 2.

To summarize, the evaluator has to invoke itself recursively to evaluate the arguments of strict built-in functions.

11.5 How to Find the Next Top-level Redex

Having decided to implement normal order reduction of top-level redexes only, we must ask how to find the appropriate redex given a graph to reduce. Our expression can only be of the form

f E_1 E_2 ... E_n

whose graph looks like this:

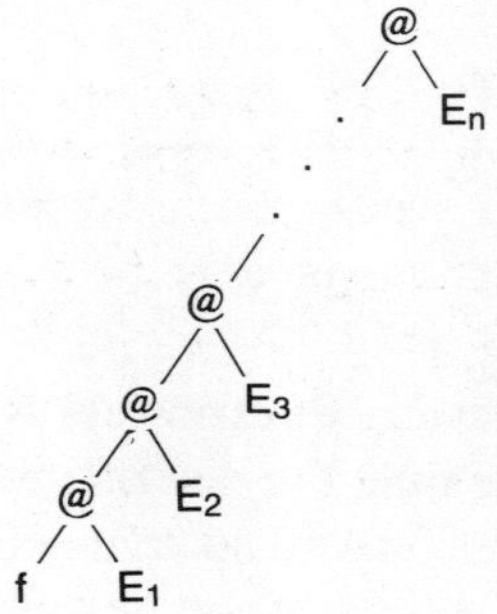

Here, f is a data object, a built-in function or a lambda abstraction (but not an application or we would have drawn another level in the picture), and there may be zero or more arguments (E_i), which are arbitrarily complicated expressions. There are now various possibilities:

(i) f may be a *data object* such as a number or a CONS cell, in which case the expression is in weak head normal form and we are done. However, in this case n should be 0; if not, the data object is being applied to an argument. This corresponds to a type error in the original program, such as using a number as a function, and will never occur if the program has been type-checked.

(ii) f may be a *built-in function* taking, say, k arguments. In this case we must check to see whether there are enough arguments available (i.e. $n \geq k$); if so, (f E_1 ... E_k) is the outermost redex which normal order will select. For example, in Figure 11.1(a) the redex is (IF E_1 E_2 E_3) and the $ marks the root of this subgraph.

If there are too few arguments ($n < k$) then the expression is in weak head normal form.

(iii) f may be a *lambda abstraction*. If it has an argument available ($n \geq 1$) the redex we should reduce next is (f E_1). For example, in Figure 11.1(b) the redex is ((λx.body) E_1), and the $ marks this application node.

If there are no arguments ($n = 0$) then the expression is in weak head normal form.

According to our abstract expression syntax there is one other possibility for f: it could be a *variable name*. However, in this case the variable must occur free in the entire expression, so we may justifiably give an error.

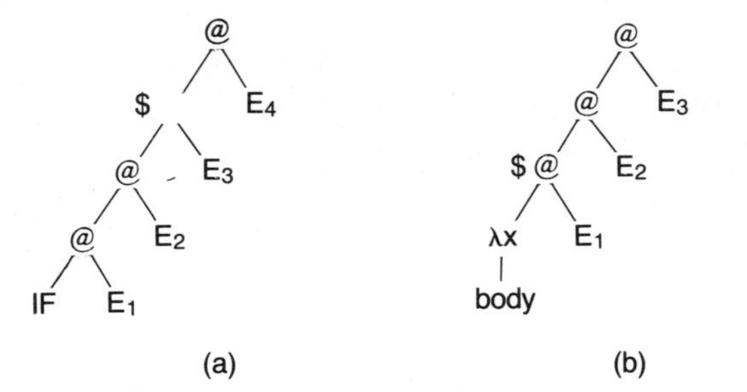

Figure 11.1 Finding the next redex (marked $)

Some evaluators insist that an expression always reduces to a data object in the end. They will therefore treat the case of a built-in function with too few arguments or lambda expression with no arguments as an error. If in addition the program is type-checked the test can be omitted altogether, since there will always be enough arguments for a function. (Note: this is not true for other reduction orders. For example, an applicative order reducer will evaluate the argument to a function before applying a function, and the argument might itself be a partially applied function.)

Thus to find f we just go down the left branch of each application node from the root. This left-branching chain of application nodes is called the *spine* of the expression, and the act of 'going down' the spine is sometimes called *unwinding* the spine. Continuing the analogy, the *vertebrae* of the spine are the application nodes encountered during unwinding, the *ribs* are the arguments of the vertebrae (the E_i in Figure 11.1), and the *tip* of the spine is the extreme bottom of the spine (IF is at the tip of the spine in Figure 11.1(a)).

It is therefore rather easy to find the next redex to reduce. We just unwind the spine until we find a function, and then, based on the function we find, we go back up the spine to find the root of the redex.

Notice that the most natural way to proceed is to reduce the top-level redex, so there is a good 'fit' between normal order reduction and graph reduction. We have to go to extra trouble to evaluate arguments to functions before applying the function.

11.6 The Spine Stack

So far we have said that we should 'unwind the spine' and 'go back up the spine', without saying how to do so. In particular, as we unwind the spine we pass by the arguments that we will subsequently require during the reduction of the function (built-in or lambda abstraction) found at the tip. This suggests that we should keep a *stack* of pointers to the vertebrae as shown in Figure

11.2. Now the arguments are all readily available, and the number of arguments is given by the depth of the stack. Furthermore, the vertebrae themselves are also accessible from the stack. This will prove to be crucially important once we start to consider how to perform a reduction (in Chapter 12), since the root of the redex is *overwritten* with the result of performing the reduction.

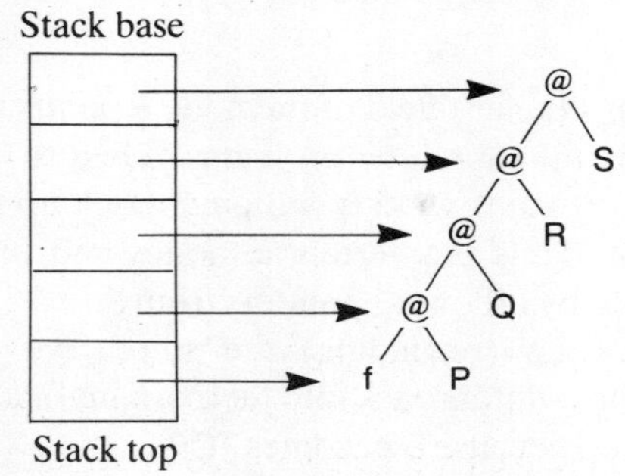

Figure 11.2 The spine stack

When we recursively evaluate the arguments to a built-in function, we need a brand new stack. Fortunately,

(i) the existing stack will not change until the argument evaluation is complete,
(ii) the new stack can be discarded when the argument evaluation is complete,

so the new stack can be built directly on top of the old one. We must, however, take care to save the depth of the old stack first, so that we can restore it when evaluation of the argument is completed. Most implementations have a separate stack, called the *dump*, for this purpose. Alternatively, the depth of the old stack can be saved on the stack itself. This technique is rather reminiscent of the *stack frames* of imperative languages.

11.6.1 Pointer-reversal

In some ways the stack is rather a nuisance because its size has no convenient bound, so it is not clear how much space to allocate to it. This problem is particularly pressing in machines specifically designed to do reduction, where the stack might have to be embodied in hardware.

It turns out that a clever trick, known as *pointer-reversal*, allows us to get away without a separate stack at all. It is borrowed from a well-known garbage collection technique (the Deutsch–Schorr–Waite algorithm [Schorr and Waite, 1967]), and consists of simply *reversing* the pointers in the spine as we unwind it.

Specifically, we hold two pointers, F and B (for forward and backward). To begin with, F points to the root of the expression, and B points to a unique cell called TOP. This initial set-up is shown in the left-hand column of Figure 11.3, where we have depicted the spine vertically on the page. Then to unwind one level, we set

```
F        = Left( F )  )
Left( F ) = B          } simultaneously
B        = F          )
```

where Left(F) means the left field of the node F points to. This operation is shown taking place in the subsequent columns of Figure 11.3. When we reach the tip, F will point to the tip and B will point back up the trail of reversed pointers to the root. Thus the vertebrae nodes and the arguments to the function can be found by following pointers from B.

When going back up (rewinding) the spine, we simply reverse the operation, putting the pointers back into their original state. We can easily tell when we reach the top because B becomes TOP.

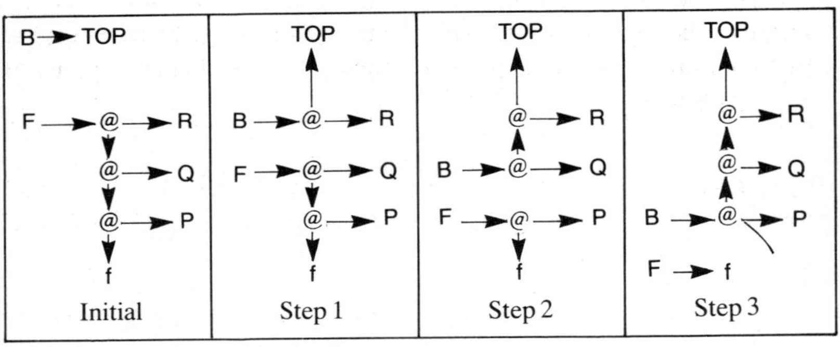

Figure 11.3 Pointer-reversal in action on (f P Q R)

11.6.2 Argument Evaluation using Pointer-reversal

There is a slight problem when we need to evaluate the arguments to a strict built-in function. Consider the expression (IF (= x 0) P Q). When we have unwound the spine to find the IF, the graph looks like the left column of Figure 11.4. Now we need to evaluate the argument, so we must unwind the spine of the argument. Unfortunately, we cannot initialize B with TOP, because we would then not be able to find our way back to the parent spine. Instead we simply pointer-reverse our way into the argument spine, but *marking the parent spine vertebrae*, in some way. To 'turn the corner' into the argument spine, we perform the following operations:

```
F         = Right( B )  )
Right( B ) = F           } simultaneously
Mark( B )               )
```

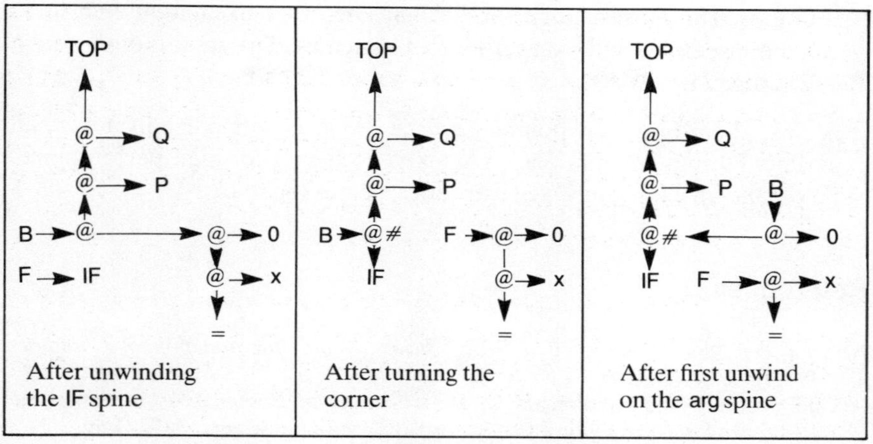

Figure 11.4 Pointer-reversal for argument evaluation

In the diagram we have marked the vertebra with #. Now when rewinding the argument spine, we know we have reached the top when we encounter a node marked with #, at which point we know that we have completed evaluation of the argument, and can resume evaluation of the parent spine.

This technique was discovered by a number of researchers independently, and is described by Stoye *et al.* [1984].

11.6.3 Stacks versus Pointer-reversal

Given the alternative, then, is pointer-reversal better than a stack?

(i) A stack is significantly faster than the pointer-reversing scheme. The stack gives instant access to arguments and vertebrae, without having to follow chains of pointers. This is particularly important in a parallel machine, where there are much higher overheads associated with accessing the (global) heap than the (local) stack. Furthermore, all reversed pointers have to be un-reversed later, resulting in heap accesses which a stacking implementation may not have to make.

(ii) Pointer-reversal uses very little extra storage. All that is required is a bit in each cell to control the evaluation of arguments to strict built-in functions. There is no (reasonable) bound to the possible length of a spine, so not only does a separate stack require some extra storage, but also (more seriously) we cannot know in advance how much extra storage to allocate. This is a significant complication for machines which implement the stack in hardware (e.g. NORMA [Richards, 1985]).

(iii) It turns out that the stack offers a large number of further opportunities for performance improvement, and we address this topic more fully in Chapters 20 and 21.

(iv) For a pointer-reversing implementation, the complete state of the evaluation is described by the two pointers F and B (together with the graph). This is useful for a parallel machine, when evaluations may need to be suspended and their state saved somehow. This topic is discussed in Chapter 24.

It seems, therefore, that pointer-reversal alone is suitable only for small experimental implementations. A stack is necessary for high performance, but a parallel machine may well use both schemes together.

References

Abelson, H., and Sussman, G.J. 1985. *Structure and Interpretation of Computer Programs*. MIT Press.

Arvind, Kathail, V., and Pingali, K. 1984. *Sharing of Computation in Functional Language Implementations.* Laboratory for Computer Science, MIT. July.

Barendregt, H.P., Kennaway, J.R., Ixlop, J.W., and Sleep, M.R. 1986. *Needed reduction and spine strategies for the lambda calculus.* Report CS-R8621. Centre for Mathematics and Computer Science, Amsterdam. May.

Henderson, P. 1980. *Functional Programming – Application and Implementation.* Prentice-Hall.

Peyton Jones, S.L. 1986. Functional programming languages as a software engineering tool. In *Software Engineering – The Critical Decade.* Ince (editor). Peter Peregrinus.

Richards, H. 1985. *An Overview of Burroughs NORMA*. Austin Research Center, Burroughs Corp., Austin, Texas. January.

Schorr, H., and Waite, W. 1967. An efficient machine independent procedure for garbage collection. *Communications of the ACM*. Vol. 10, no. 8, pp. 501–6.

Stoye, W.R., Clarke, T.J.W., and Norman, A.C. 1984. Some practical methods for rapid combinator reduction. In *Proceedings of the ACM Symposium on Lisp and Functional Programming, Austin*, pp. 159–66. August.

Turner, D.A. 1983. *The SASL Language Manual.* University of Kent. November.

Watson, P., Watson, I., and Woods, V. 1986. *A Model of Computation for the Parallel Evaluation of Functional Languages.* PMP/MU/PW/000001. Department of Computer Science, University of Manchester. February.

Twelve

GRAPH REDUCTION OF LAMBDA EXPRESSIONS

We have now dealt with the issue of which redex to reduce next, and how to find it. In this chapter we will complete the implementation by showing how to perform a reduction.

Performing a reduction constitutes a *local transformation* of the graph representing the expression, so the process of reduction successively modifies the graph until it reaches its final form, the result of the computation.

As we have seen in the previous chapter, the function at the tip of the spine may be either a lambda abstraction, or a built-in function (if, that is, the graph has a top-level redex at all). We will deal with these two cases separately.

12.1 Reducing a Lambda Application

Suppose the redex consists of a lambda abstraction applied to an argument. Then we must apply the β-reduction rule to the graph. That is, we must construct an instance of the body of the lambda abstraction, substituting the argument for free occurrences of the formal parameter.

We will sometimes refer to this process as 'constructing a new instance of the body of the lambda abstraction', but we will often abbreviate this to 'instantiating the lambda body'. Figure 12.1 gives an example.

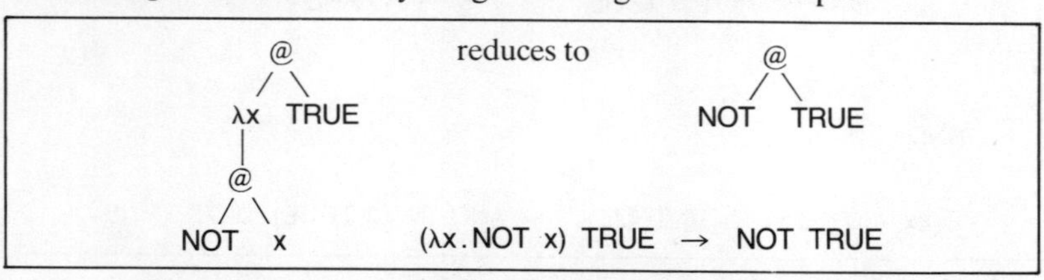

Figure 12.1 Instantiating the body of a lambda abstraction

Three important issues of implementation arise here:

(i) The argument may be bulky and/or contain redexes, so we should substitute *pointers* to the argument for the formal parameter (see Section 12.1.1).
(ii) The redex may be shared, so we must *physically overwrite* the root of the redex with the result (see Section 12.1.2).
(iii) The lambda abstraction may be shared, so we must construct a *new instance* of the lambda body, rather than substituting in the original body directly (see Section 12.1.3).

We will deal with these issues in the following sections.

12.1.1 Substituting Pointers to the Argument

When substituting the argument for the formal parameter, we could just *copy* the argument whenever the formal parameter occurred. But copying the argument may be very wasteful, because

(i) the argument might be a very large expression, in which case we are wasting space by making multiple copies of the same object;
(ii) the argument might contain redexes, in which case we are wasting work by duplicating redexes which may subsequently have to be separately reduced (if they are needed).

Both of these problems can be avoided by substituting *pointers* to the argument for the formal parameter. This gives rise to *sharing*, whereby there may be many pointers to the same expression, and it is for precisely this reason that the expression tree becomes a graph. Figure 12.2 is an example of this process in action, in which the (NOT TRUE) expression becomes shared.

Sharing by means of pointers was first suggested by Wadsworth [1971], who called it *graph reduction*. It is the key idea that turns reduction into a practical technique. The alternative, of copying the argument wherever it is used, is called *tree reduction* or *string reduction* and is normally considered pro-

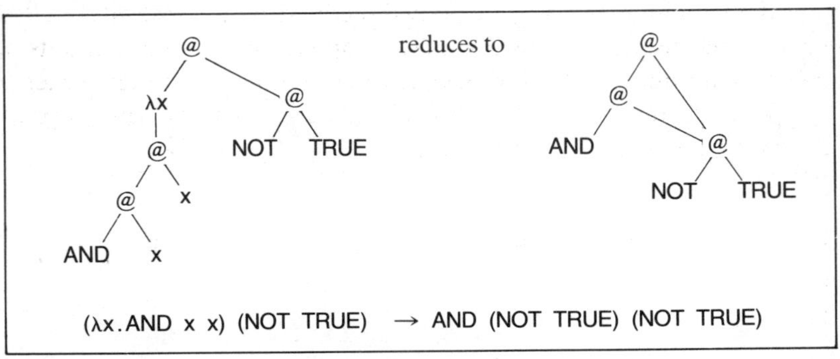

Figure 12.2 Pointer substitution

hibitively expensive (though Mago's parallel reduction machine uses it [Mago, 1980], relying on massive parallelism to overcome the inefficiency).

12.1.2 Overwriting the Root of the Redex

If we are to exploit sharing successfully we must ensure that when an expression is reduced we modify the graph to reflect the result. This will ensure that shared expressions will only be reduced once. For instance, in Figure 12.2 the (NOT TRUE) expression will be reduced next (since AND requires its arguments to be evaluated), and we would like to arrange that this reduction is only done once.

We can achieve this by the simple expedient of physically *overwriting* the root of the redex with the (root of) the result. Here is an example in which the node marked '$' is the root of the redex, and is physically overwritten with the result of the reduction:

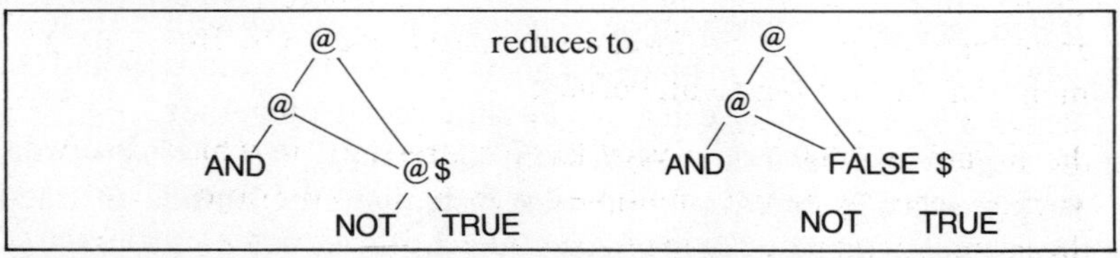

Notice that fragments of the redex (in this case just the NOT and TRUE nodes) are not affected by the overwriting, and become completely detached from the part of the graph we are considering. They cannot be recovered and re-used immediately because they may be shared with other nodes not in the picture. If not, then they will eventually be recovered by the garbage collector.

There is an important complication associated with overwriting the root of the redex, which we discuss later, in Section 12.4.

12.1.3 Constructing a New Instance of the Lambda Body

As the word 'instance' implies, when applying a lambda abstraction we must make substitutions within a *new copy* of the body of the lambda abstraction rather than updating the original body directly with the substitutions. This is necessary because the abstraction may be applied many times, and its body serves as a 'master template' from which an instance is constructed each time it is applied; the master template should not be altered by the copying process. Thus the example in Figure 12.1 should really look like this:

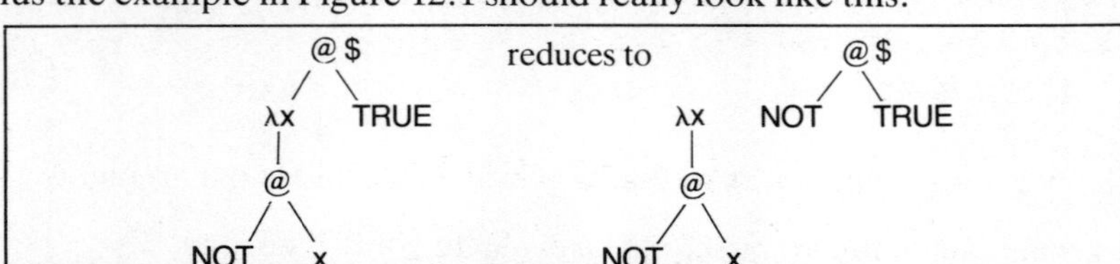

The original lambda abstraction remains intact in case it is shared.

We may describe the instantiation operation by a recursive function Instantiate(Body,Var,Value), which copies Body substituting Value for free occurrences of Var. This function implements precisely the substitution operation described in Figure 2.3. Specifically:

Instantiate(Body,Var,Value) constructs Body[Value/Var]

Instantiate proceeds by case-analysis on the root node of Body, and each case is a direct transcription of the corresponding line of Figure 2.3:

(i) *if* Body is a variable x and Var = x *then* return Value (here we substitute Value for an occurrence of Var),
(ii) *if* Body is a variable x and Var ≠ x *then* return Body,
(iii) *if* Body is a constant or built-in function *then* return Body,
(iv) *if* Body is an application (E_1 E_2) *then* return the application (Instantiate(E_1,Var,Value) Instantiate(E_2,Var,Value)),
(v) *if* Body is a lambda abstraction λx.E and Var = x *then* return Body – the new lambda abstraction binds Var anew, so no substitutions should occur inside it, and hence we can avoid instantiating it altogether,
(vi) *if* Body is a lambda abstraction λx.E and Var ≠ x *then* return λx. Instantiate(E,Var,Value) – we must instantiate the lambda abstraction in case there are free occurrences of Var inside it.
This case is much simpler than the corresponding rule of Figure 2.3, because we are assuming that Value has no free variables (see Section 11.3.2).

Figure 12.3 gives a possible definition of Instantiate in the C language.

The instantiation process is simple enough, but it risks copying large expressions in which Var does not occur free at all, and hence which could be shared. We could alleviate this by adding a new first clause to the definition of Instantiate:

if Body does not contain any free occurrences of Var *then* return Body.

This would, however, be an expensive test to make. We might imagine some sort of annotation scheme whereby we could precompute such information, but it is hard to do in general (even Wadsworth did not give an algorithm!). An implementation which manages to perform this test, or which does something equivalent, is said to be *fully lazy*. We discuss full laziness in detail in Chapter 15, but ignore it until then.

12.1.4 Summary

In the previous chapter we saw that lazy evaluation had two ingredients:

(i) arguments to functions should be evaluated only if needed;
(ii) once evaluated, they should never be re-evaluated.

```
Instantiate( Body, Var, Value )
expression *Body, *Var, *Value;
{
    if (IsAp( Body ))    /* Is Body an application node? */
        return( MakeAp( Instantiate( GetFun( Body ), Var, Value ),
                        Instantiate( GetArg( Body ), Var, Value ) );

    if (IsVar( Body )) /* Is Body a variable? */
    {
        if (Body == Var)       /* Is Body the variable Var? */
            return( Value );
        else
            return( Body );
    }
    if (IsLam( Body )) /* Is Body a lambda abstraction? */
    {
        if (GetVar( Body ) == Var)     /* Same formal parameter? */
            return( Body );
        else
            return( MakeLam( GetVar( Body ),
                             Instantiate( GetBody( Body ), Var, Value )));
    }
/* So Body must be a constant or built-in function */
    return( Body );
}
```

Note: IsAp(B) tests whether B is an application node
GetFun(B) gets the function from an application node
GetArg(B) gets the argument from an application node
MakeAp(F,A) makes a new application node

IsVar(B) tests whether B is a variable node

IsLam(B) tests whether B is a lambda abstraction node
GetVar(B) gets the formal parameter from an abstraction
GetBody(B) gets the body from an abstraction node
MakeLam(V,B) makes a new lambda abstraction node

Figure 12.3 The Instantiate function in C

We saw that normal order evaluation implemented the first ingredient. We can now see that the second ingredient is implemented by the combination of two things:

(i) substituting pointers to the argument rather than copying it avoids duplicating the (unevaluated) argument;
(ii) updating the root of the redex with the result ensures that further uses of the argument will get the benefit of the work done.

To summarize:

Normal order evaluation to weak head normal form
+
Substitute pointers
+
Update redex root with result

= Lazy evaluation

This implementation strategy is called *lazy graph reduction.*

12.2 Reducing a Built-in Function Application

Suppose the redex consists of a built-in function applied to the correct number of arguments. First of all, any arguments whose values are needed must be evaluated by recursively invoking the evaluator. Then the built-in function can be executed, and the result physically overwrites the root of the redex.

For example, consider the expression (+ 6 (∗ 3 4)), which has the graph

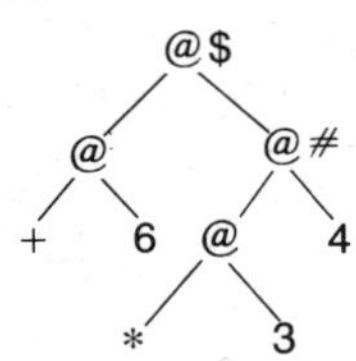

We first select node $ for reduction, but discover that + needs to evaluate its arguments. So we recursively invoke the evaluator on the first argument, only to discover that it is already in WHNF. Then we invoke the evaluator on the second argument, which causes node # to be selected for reduction. Again, we recursively reduce the arguments of the ∗ (they are already in WHNF), and now we can execute the ∗. The result of this multiplication overwrites node #, thus

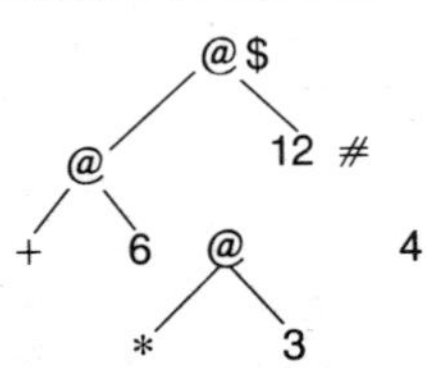

As always, we see that fragments of the original graph remain, subsequently

to be recovered by the garbage collector. Now the evaluation of the arguments of + is complete, and it executes, giving

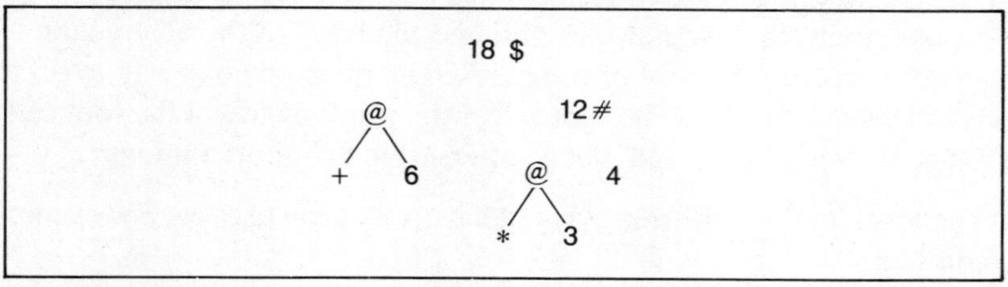

The node $, the root of the original expression, is the result, the other fragments being garbage. From now on we will no longer draw the garbage nodes in our pictures.

12.3 The Reduction Algorithm So Far

We now review our reduction algorithm, putting together the material of the previous two sections.

REPEAT

- (1) Unwind the spine until something other than an application node is encountered.
- (2) Examine the objects found at the tip of the spine (see Section 11.5).
  - (a) *A data object.* Check that it is not applied to anything. If not, the expression is in WHNF so STOP, otherwise there is an ERROR.
  - (b) *A built-in function.* Check the number of arguments available. If there are too few arguments the expression is in WHNF so STOP. Otherwise evaluate any arguments required, execute the built-in function and overwrite the root of the redex with the result.
  - (c) *A lambda abstraction.* Check that there is an argument; if not the expression is in WHNF so STOP. Otherwise instantiate the body of the lambda abstraction, substituting pointers to the argument for the formal parameter, and overwrite the root of the redex with the result.

END

12.4 Indirection Nodes

In Section 12.1 we described how to reduce an application of a lambda abstraction by constructing an instance of the body of the lambda abstraction, substituting pointers to the argument for the formal parameter, and updating the root of the redex with the result. The final operation, updating the root of the redex, contains a hidden danger, which this section will expose.

Suppose, then, that we have instantiated the body of the abstraction and are about to update the root of the redex. The most obvious way to do this seems to be simply *to copy* the root cell of the result on top of the root cell of the redex. This is all very well, but it suffers from two shortcomings:

(i) The result of the reduction may not have a root cell to copy. For example, consider

    (λx.4) 5

In an unboxed implementation the result, 4, is represented as a non-pointer, and hence does not occupy a cell at all.

(ii) It is slightly inefficient, because the root cell of the result is constructed (by Instantiate), copied over the root of the redex, and then *discarded*, because there are no further pointers to it.

It would be more efficient to build the root cell of the result directly *on top* of the root cell of the redex, thus avoiding ever constructing the root cell of the result in the first place.

However, in a reduction such as

    (λx.x) (f 6)

the root cell of the result is *not a newly constructed cell* so we cannot construct the root cell of the result on top of the root of the redex.

It appears, therefore, that lambda abstractions in which the body consists of an unboxed constant or a single variable, form a special case. We consider the former possibility first.

12.4.1 Updating with Unboxed Objects

We recall from Chapter 10 that an unboxed object is one which is represented as a non-pointer, rather than as a pointer to a cell. How can we update the root of the redex with such an object?

We are forced to introduce a new type of cell, an *indirection cell*. An indirection cell has a tag, IND say, which identifies the cell as an indirection, and a single field which is the contents of the cell. When updating an application cell with an unboxed object we overwrite the application with an indirection cell whose content is the unboxed object. For example:

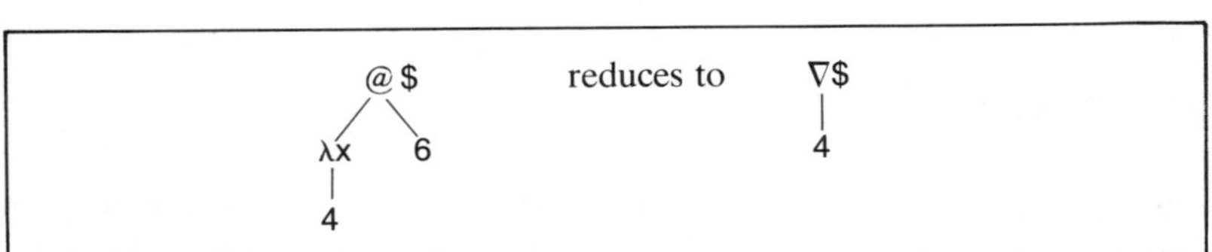

where we use ∇ to identify indirection nodes.

This expedient seems not to be necessary in an implementation in which everything is boxed, since we can just copy the top node of the object over the root of the redex. However, we still need to take care as the next section shows.

12.4.2 Updating where the Body is a Single Variable

Consider our example, the expression ((λx.x) (f 6)):

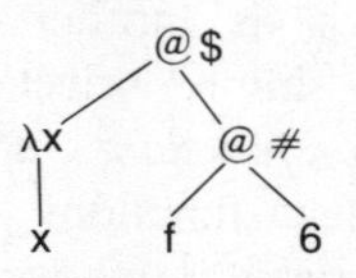

There are two ways in which we can update the root of the redex:

(i) We could *copy the root cell of the result* on top of the root cell of the redex thus:

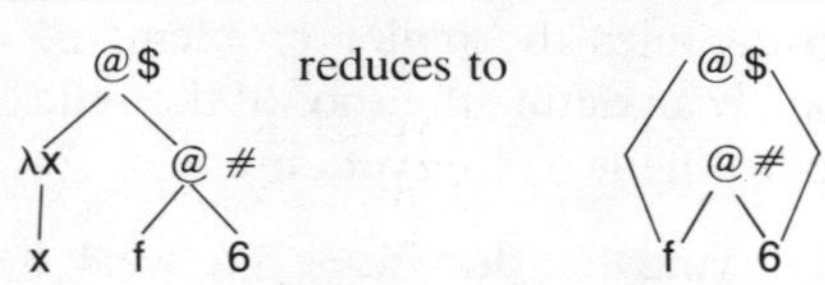

Now the result (seen from the point of view of node $) is quite correct (viz. (f 6)). However, now the application of f to 6 has been duplicated, (f 6) *may be evaluated twice* if node # happens to be shared. This would be wasted work if (f 6) were expensive; we have lost laziness. Notice that this problem can only arise if the body of the lambda abstraction consists of a single variable. If the body is an application, then the root of the result will be a newly constructed application cell, and hence cannot be shared.

Even if this were not the case, and the (f 6) were already in normal form, node $ is a duplicate of node #, which is a waste of storage space.

Furthermore, this alternative might not be possible in an implementation supporting variable-sized cells, if the root cell of the argument was bigger than the root cell of the redex.

(ii) We could take the hint from Section 12.4.1, and use an indirection node. We would then overwrite node $ with an indirection to node #, thus:

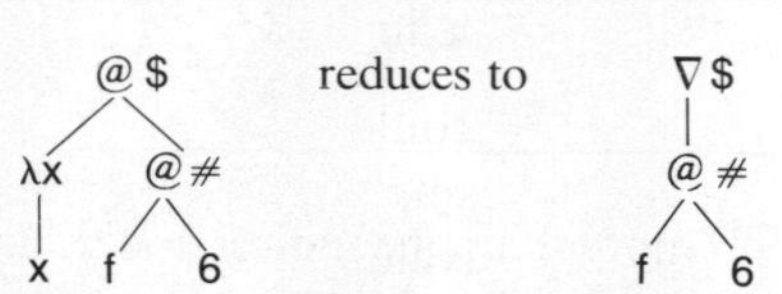

The trouble with introducing indirection nodes is that they can then appear at any point in the graph, so the reduction machine must contain tests for indirection nodes in many places.

Furthermore there is a danger that long chains of indirection nodes might build up (for example, suppose (f 6) evaluated to an indirection node), which would clog up the machine.

The issue of whether to copy or to use indirection nodes arises in other cases also. For example, HEAD selects the head of its argument (which it first evaluates to a CONS cell), and meets the same problem in overwriting the root of the redex with the result. IF is another example of such a function. Functions like these which simply select some component of their argument(s) are called *projection functions*.

All the arithmetic and boolean functions will suffer too in an unboxed implementation, because their result is unboxed.

In general, any function whose result is not a cell constructed during the reduction will raise the question of how to update the root.

12.4.3 Evaluating the Result before Updating

A solution which overcomes the major problems of either method is *to evaluate* the result *before* updating the root of the redex. We can justify this approach with the following two observations:

(i) We are currently trying to reduce node $ to weak head normal form. So the first thing we are going to do once this reduction is complete is to reduce the result of the reduction ((f 6) in this case) to WHNF.

Hence we can safely reduce node # to WHNF *before* overwriting node $ with the result.

(ii) Once an expression is in WHNF its root is never again overwritten, because it is never again selected as the root of a redex.

Observation (i) means that if the result of the reduction of node # was an indirection to a CONS cell *, we could overwrite node $ with an indirection to node * (not node #).

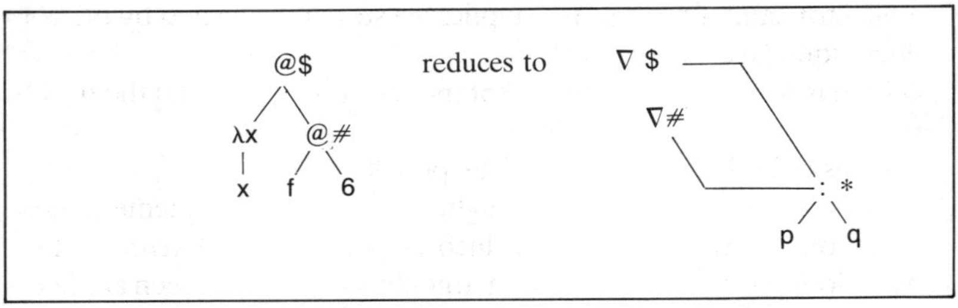

Thus we would never get more than one indirection node in a chain.

Observation (ii) tells us that it is safe to copy node # once it is in WHNF since it will never again be overwritten; by copying it we still waste space, but we no longer risk duplicated reductions. For example, if the (f 6) evaluated to a CONS cell, copying would give this:

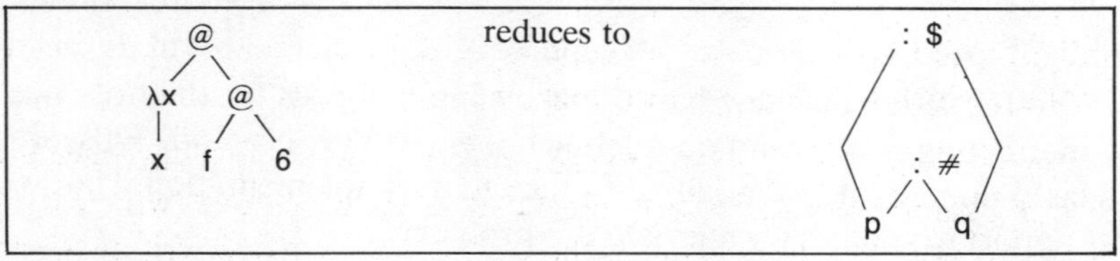

12.4.4 Summary: Indirection Nodes versus Copying

This is a slightly tricky section, and we shall summarize our conclusions.

(i) When the root of the result is constructed during the reduction, and is sufficiently small, it should be constructed directly on top of the root of the redex, rather than being allocated elsewhere, copied and discarded.

(ii) If the root of the result was not constructed during the reduction, then we can overwrite the root of the redex *either* with a copy of the root of the result, *or* with an indirection to the result.

(iii) The cases covered by (ii) arise for
  (a) functions (both lambda abstractions and built-in functions) returning unboxed results,
  (b) lambda abstractions whose body consists of a single variable,
  (c) built-in projection functions, which include HEAD, TAIL and IF.

(iv) In the cases covered by (ii), the result should be evaluated to WHNF before overwriting the root of the redex. If this is done, no sharing is lost and the number of reductions performed is the same either way.

There are the following arguments in favor of using indirections:

(i) There is no alternative if the result is an unboxed object.

(ii) They use no fewer cells at the time the reduction takes place. However, indirection nodes can be 'shorted out' and recovered by the garbage collector, thus recovering the storage they occupy, whereas the garbage collector cannot recover the duplicated storage allocated by the copying technique (see Chapter 17).

(iii) There is no problem if the root of the result is bigger than the root of the redex.

(iv) Chains of indirection nodes can be prevented.

(v) It has been suggested by Hughes [1985] that implementations of functional languages should incorporate *memo functions*; that is, functions which remember what arguments they have been applied to so far, together with the corresponding results, and when reapplied to one of these arguments deliver the corresponding result directly. This idea works better in a system based on indirection nodes, since if we make copies of nodes then identical arguments may look different to the memo function.

There is only one argument against indirection nodes, but it is rather persuasive:

(i) The reduction machine has to make continual tests for the presence of indirection nodes, and de-reference them as they crop up. This adds a large number of potentially slow tests to the implementation. Hardware support would largely alleviate this problem.

On balance it looks as if copying has a short-term advantage of speed, but the generality of indirection will probably win out in the end.

12.5 Implementing Y

We have said in Chapter 2 that Y is always implemented directly, and we now discuss how this is done. The reduction rule for Y is

```
Y f  →  f (Y f)
```

and there are two ways of implementing this:

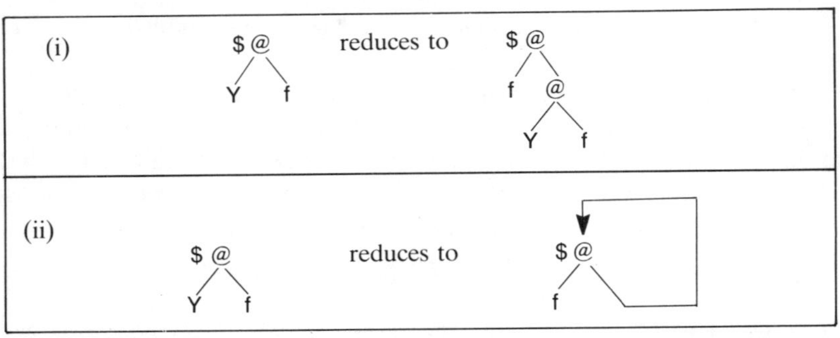

The first is straightforward, but the second is more interesting. The right branch of the result node $ points back at node $. To see that this is a correct implementation, consider the reduction rule for Y. On the right-hand side of the rule, the thing f is applied to is (Y f), but the *original* redex was (Y f) and so f can be applied to the root of the original redex.

Another way to see this is to try taking the reduction sequence for Y further:

```
Y f  →  f (Y f)
     →  f (f (Y f))
     →  f (f (f (Y f)))
     . . .
     →  f (f (f (f. . .)))
```

which is just what the suggested graph represents.

This is the first time our graphs have incorporated *cycles* and this is indeed the only source of cycles in many implementations. This form of Y is therefore sometimes called *cyclic* Y or *knot-tying* Y.

Cyclic graphs give important economies in the use of storage. Using the acyclic version of Y means that the graph representing (Y f) grows without limit as each recurrent (Y f) redex is evaluated. In contrast, using a cyclic version of Y means that (Y f) is represented by a single cell. Hence cyclic graphs give finite representations of some infinite objects (such as recursive functions and some infinite data structures).

The principal disadvantage of a cyclic Y is that the presence of cycles prevents the use of simple reference-counting garbage collection (see Chapter 17).

References

Hughes, R.J.M. 1985. Lazy memo functions. In *Proceedings of the IFIP Conference on Functional Programming Languages and Computer Architecture, Nancy*, pp. 129–46. Jouannaud (editor). LNCS 201. Springer Verlag. September.

Mago, G.A. 1980. A cellular computer architecture for functional programming. *IEEE Computer Society COMPCON*, pp. 179–87.

Wadsworth, C.P. 1971. Semantics and pragmatics of the lambda calculus, Chapter 4. PhD thesis, Oxford.

Thirteen

SUPERCOMBINATORS AND LAMBDA-LIFTING

Since the operation of constructing an instance of a lambda body while substituting for the formal parameter is the fundamental operation of our implementation, we will now consider how to make it more efficient.

In this chapter and the next we will show how to transform a lambda expression into a form in which the lambda abstractions are particularly easy to instantiate. These special lambda abstractions are called *supercombinators*, and the transformation is called *lambda-lifting*. Then, in Chapter 15, we will show how to enhance the lambda-lifting transformation to be *fully lazy*, a property alluded to in Section 12.1.3. The terms 'supercombinator' and 'fully lazy' were both coined by Hughes, who was the first to combine full laziness with lambda-lifting [Hughes, 1984].

13.1 The Idea of Compilation

The operation of instantiating the body of a lambda abstraction was called Instantiate in the previous chapter, and was performed by a recursive tree-walk over the lambda body. Such an Instantiate operation is rather inefficient for the following reasons:

(i) at each node of the body, Instantiate has to do a case analysis on the tag of the node;
(ii) at each variable node Instantiate has to test if the node is the formal parameter; a similar test has to be made at each lambda node;
(iii) new instances of subexpressions containing no free occurrences of the formal parameter will be constructed when they could safely and

beneficially be shared (we discuss this point in more detail in Chapter 15).

A more efficient alternative to this is *compilation*, whereby we associate with each lambda body a *fixed sequence of instructions* which will construct an instance of the lambda body. Then the operation of instantiating a lambda body would consist simply of obeying the sequence of instructions associated with the lambda body.

This instruction sequence can be constructed in advance by a compiler, and contains implicitly the knowledge about the shape of the body and where the formal parameter occurs. Hence we would expect the compiled code to run much faster than the Instantiate method, for just the same reasons that compiled code runs faster than interpreted code in conventional languages. In effect, all the tests in Instantiate are made in advance by the compiler. Furthermore, it turns out that compilation opens up many new avenues for optimization, which offer considerable further efficiency increases.

Unfortunately, not all lambda abstractions are amenable to compilation in this way. Consider, for example, the lambda abstraction

```
λx.(λy.- y x)
```

When we apply the λx abstraction to an argument, 3 say, we instantiate its body, thus creating a brand new lambda abstraction (λy.- y 3). Furthermore, each application of the λx abstraction to a different argument will create a new and different λy abstraction, thus making a nonsense of our hope to compile a single fixed code sequence for each lambda abstraction.

The problem is that x occurs free in the body of the λy abstraction, so that we have to make a new instance of the λy abstraction whenever x is bound to a new value by an application of the λx abstraction. In the case of lambda abstractions which have no free variables there is no problem, and we can compile a code sequence for it as outlined above.

One way around this problem would be to allow the code sequence to access the values of the free variables in some way, thus parameterizing the code sequence on the values of the free variables. This approach leads us to the SECD machine [Landin, 1964; Henderson, 1980], in which the code sequence for a lambda abstraction has access to an *environment* which contains values for each of the free variables, thus allowing a single code sequence for each lambda abstraction. It is also the route followed by all block-structured languages, in which the values of free variables are found by looking in the appropriate stack frame.

In this book, however, we will study a totally different approach, called *supercombinator graph reduction*, which does not require the addition of an environment to our model of graph reduction. The idea is to *transform* the program into an equivalent one in which all the lambda abstractions are amenable to compilation. This transformation algorithm, which is called *lambda-lifting*, is of considerable interest in its own right, and we devote the rest of this chapter and the next to it. After this, we spend a chapter discussing an important optimization to lambda-lifting, called *full laziness*, and Chapter 16 then digresses to describe an important alternative transformation, into *SK combinators*. Finally, the bulk of the third part of the book (Chapters 18–21) is spent in an extended discussion of how to compile the transformed program into a linear instruction sequence, and the optimizations which this opens up.

13.2 Solving the Problem of Free Variables

In this section we outline our strategy for dealing with the problem of free variables. We do so by using a modified form of β-reduction, in which we may effectively perform several β-reductions at once.

Consider our current example

```
λx.λy.- y x
```

Suppose we applied it to two arguments, thus:

```
(λx.λy.- y x) 3 4
```

The lambda reducer described in Chapter 12 would proceed like this:

```
   (λx.λy.- y x) 3 4
→  (λy.- y 3) 4
→  - 4 3
```

There is no reason, however, why we should not perform the λx and λy reductions *simultaneously*, thus:

```
   (λx.λy.- y x) 3 4
→  - 4 3
```

This ‘multi-argument’ reduction entails constructing an instance of the body (- y x) whilst substituting 3 for free occurrences of x, and 4 for free occurrences of y. The following observations are crucial:

(i) Much is gained by performing the reductions simultaneously. Firstly, doing so builds less intermediate structure in the heap, since the intermediate result of the λx reduction is never constructed. Second (and more important), no problems are presented by the free occurrence of x in the λy abstraction.

(ii) Nothing is lost by performing the λx and λy reductions simultaneously. The result of performing the λx reduction alone is a λy abstraction, and (assuming that we perform normal order reduction until WHNF is reached) no further work can be done on the λy abstraction until it is given another argument.

Hence we may as well wait until both arguments are present and then perform both reductions at once. This applies even if the application of the λx abstraction to a single argument is shared.

13.2.1 Supercombinators

What sort of lambda abstractions are amenable to this sort of multi-argument reduction? Simply lambda abstractions of the form $(\lambda x_1.\lambda x_2 \ldots \lambda x_n.E)$. This motivates a new definition:

> DEFINITION
>
> A *supercombinator*, $S, of *arity* n is a lambda expression of the form
>
> $\lambda x_1.\lambda x_2 \ldots \lambda x_n.E$
>
> where E is not a lambda abstraction (this just ensures that all the 'leading lambdas' are accounted for by $x_1 \ldots x_n$) such that
>
> (i) $S has no free variables,
> (ii) any lambda abstraction in E is a supercombinator,
> (iii) $n \geq 0$; that is, there need be no lambdas at all.
>
> A *supercombinator redex* consists of the application of a supercombinator to n arguments, where n is its arity. A *supercombinator reduction* replaces a supercombinator redex by an instance of the supercombinator body with the arguments substituted for free occurrences of the corresponding formal parameter.

For example,

```
3
(+ 2 5)
λx.x
λx.+ x 1
λx.+ x x
λx.λy.- y x
λf.f (λx.+ x x)
```

are all supercombinators, while the following are not:

λx.y	(y occurs free)
λy.- y x	(x occurs free)
λf.f (λx.f x 2)	(inner λx abstraction is not a supercombinator, since f occurs free)

13.2.1.1 Supercombinators of non-zero arity

Supercombinators of non-zero arity (that is, having at least one λ at the front) are important because they will be our *unit of compilation*. Since they have no free variables (clause (i)) we can compile a fixed code sequence for them. Furthermore, clause (ii) ensures that any lambda abstractions in the body have no free variables, and hence do not need to be copied when instantiating the supercombinator body.

Such a supercombinator is somewhat analogous to a Pascal function which takes several (value) parameters, which does not refer to any global variables, and which has no side-effects.

13.2.1.2 Supercombinators of arity zero and CAFs

A supercombinator of arity zero (that is, having no λs at the front) is just a constant expression (remember that it has no free variables). These supercombinators are often called *constant applicative forms* or CAFs. For example,

```
3
+ 4 5
+ 3
```

are all CAFs. The last example makes the point that CAFs can still be functions.

Since a CAF has no λs at the front, they are never instantiated. Hence, no code need be compiled for it, since a single instance of its graph can freely be shared.

13.2.1.3 Combinators

A 'supercombinator' sounds like a special sort of 'combinator' and indeed this is the case:

> DEFINITION
>
> A *combinator* is a lambda expression which contains no occurrences of a free variable [Barendregt, 1984].

A combinator is a 'pure' function in the sense that the value of a combinator applied to some arguments depends only on the values of the arguments, and not on any free variables. The term 'combinator' has a long pedigree [Curry and Feys, 1958].

Thus some lambda expressions are combinators, and some combinators are supercombinators.

13.2.2 A Supercombinator-based Compilation Strategy

If only all the lambda abstractions in our program were supercombinators! Then it would be easy to compile them all, for the reasons mentioned in the last section. Real programs, of course, have many lambda abstractions which are not supercombinators, but it turns out to be relatively straightforward to transform the program so that it contains only supercombinators. This will be our strategy, and we embark on the transformation in Section 13.3.

For the sake of clarity we will often give names to supercombinators. These names are entirely arbitrary, since the lambda abstractions are anonymous, and we will normally begin them with a $ to make them distinctive. Thus we could write

```
$XY = λx.λy.- y x
```

but to emphasize their special status further we will write the definition like this:

```
$XY x y = - y x
```

Our strategy is therefore to transform the lambda expression we wish to compile into:

(i) a set of supercombinator definitions, plus
(ii) an expression to be evaluated.

To emphasize the inseparability of these two components we use a box, just as we did in the case of Miranda programs (Section 3.3), thus:

Supercombinator definitions . . . . . .
Expression to be evaluated

For example, we could represent the expression

```
(λx.λy.- y x) 3 4
```

as

$XY x y = - y x
$XY 3 4

A crucial point in the definition of a supercombinator given above is that a supercombinator reduction only takes place when all the arguments are present. For example,

```
($XY 3)
```

is not a supercombinator redex, and will not be reduced. We can therefore regard the supercombinator definitions as a set of *rewrite rules*. A reduction consists of rewriting an expression which matches the left-hand side of a rule with an instance of the corresponding right-hand side. Such systems are called *term rewrite systems* and have been much studied in their own right [O'Donnell, 1977; Klop, 1980; Hoffman and O'Donnell, 1982].

13.3 Transforming Lambda Abstractions into Supercombinators

To summarize our progress so far, we have seen that certain sorts of lambda abstractions, the supercombinators, are particularly easy to compile. Our implementation effort now breaks into two parts:

(i) a translation algorithm which transforms all the lambda abstractions in the program into supercombinators;
(ii) an implementation of supercombinator reduction.

First of all we consider how to transform lambda abstractions into supercombinators. Here is an example program (in which neither lambda abstraction is a supercombinator):

```
--------------------------
(λx.(λy.+ y x) x) 4
```

Consider first the innermost lambda abstraction (λy.+ y x).

It has a free variable, x, so it is not a supercombinator. However, a simple transformation will make it into one:

> make each free variable into an extra parameter (we sometimes call this *abstracting* the free variable).

Thus we would transform

```
(λy.+ y x)
```

to

```
(λx.λy.+ y x) x
```

(This operation is simply β-abstraction.) To see that these two expressions are equivalent, just perform a β-reduction on the second to get the first. To make it slightly clearer we could perform an α-conversion on the λx abstraction to give

```
(λw.λy.+ y w) x
```

This clarifies the distinction between the two xs which occurred in the previous version. Now the lambda abstraction (λw.λy.+ y w) is a supercombinator! Performing this transformation on our original program gives

```
--------------------------
(λx.(λw.λy.+ y w) x x) 4
```

Next we give the supercombinator a name, $Y say, like this

```
$Y w y = + y w
--------------------------
(λx.$Y x x) 4
```

Now we see that the λx abstraction also fulfills the conditions for supercombinatorhood, and we give it the name $X, thus

```
$Y w y = + y w
$X x = $Y x x
-----------------------------
$X 4
```

We can now execute our program by performing supercombinator reductions:

```
   $X 4
→  $Y 4 4
→  + 4 4
→  8
```

To review the algorithm so far:

UNTIL there are no more lambda abstractions:

(1) Choose any lambda abstraction which has no inner lambda abstractions in its body.
(2) Take out all its free variables as extra parameters.
(3) Give an arbitrary name to the lambda abstraction (e.g. $X34).
(4) Replace the occurrence of the lambda abstraction by the name applied to the free variables.
(5) Compile the lambda abstraction and associate the name with the compiled code.

END

It is easy to see that we suffer an increase in the size of the program during this transformation, but it is a price we pay willingly in exchange for the easier reduction rules.

When we have completed the algorithm we arrive at a program of the form

```
. . . supercombinator definitions . . .
-----------------------------------------
E
```

But what about the expression E? It must have no free variables, since it is the top-level expression to be evaluated, so we can make it into a zero-parameter supercombinator (a CAF) thus

```
. . . supercombinator definitions . . .
$Prog = E
-----------------------------------------
$Prog
```

thus completing the transformation of the program into supercombinators.

So far we have not made any explicit mention of recursion. This topic is so important that we devote the whole of the next chapter to it.

Following Johnssòn [1985], we call the transformation from lambda expressions to supercombinators 'lambda-lifting' since all the lambda abstractions are lifted to the top level.

13.3.1 Eliminating Redundant Parameters

In this section and the next we will consider two simple optimizations to the lambda-lifting algorithm. Consider the expression

```
λx.λy.- y x
```

It is actually a supercombinator as it stands, but suppose we blindly applied our algorithm as described above. First we choose the λy abstraction, noting that x is free, and transform it to

```
$Y x y = - y x
--------------------------
λx.$Y x
```

(Here we have chosen to use x instead of w as the name of the extra parameter to the $Y supercombinator. This choice is arbitrary, but we will normally choose the same name as the free variable being abstracted.) Now dealing with the λx abstraction, we get

```
$Y x y = - y x
$X x = $Y x
--------------------------
$X
```

It is clear that we can simplify the definition of $X to

```
$X = $Y
```

(This is just η*-reduction*, of course.) Having done this we see that $X itself is redundant, and $X can be replaced wherever it occurs by $Y, giving

```
$Y x y = - y x
--------------------------
$Y
```

So there are two optimizations to consider:

(i) Remove redundant parameters from definitions by η-reduction.
(ii) Where this produces redundant definitions, eliminate them.

These optimizations together exploit supercombinators that appear naturally in the original program, and sometimes catch other η-reductions as well.

Caveat: it turns out that, for more sophisticated implementations, performing such η-reductions is actually *undesirable*, unless they succeed in eliminating a definition, which is always desirable. For a full explanation of this point, see Section 20.3.4.

13.3.2 Parameter Ordering

When we take out several free variables from a lambda abstraction as extra parameters the order in which we put them seems rather arbitrary. For example, consider the program

```
------------------------------------
(...
    (λx.λz.+ y (* x z))
    ...)
```

where the '...' stands for some expression enclosing the λx abstraction. It could be transformed to

```
$S x y z = + y (* x z)
------------------------------------
(...
    (λx.$S x y)
    ...)
```

or alternatively it could be transformed to

```
$S y x z = + y (* x z)
------------------------------------
(...
    (λx.$S y x)
    ...)
```

Both x and y are free, and it does not seem to matter which order we take them out in. However, let us take the second possibility one stage further, by lifting the λx abstraction:

```
$S y x z = + y (* x z)
$T y x   = $S y x
------------------------------------
(...
    ($T y)
    ...)
```

Now we can remove the redundant parameters from the definition of $T, and eliminate the definition of $T altogether (since it is the same as $S). This would not have been possible had we put the extra parameters x and y for $S in the other order. Hence we should *order the free variables*, with those bound at inner levels coming last in the parameter list of the supercombinator.

This suggests that we could associate a *lexical level-number* with each lambda abstraction, so that the lexical level-number of a lambda abstraction is defined to be one more than the number of textually enclosing lambdas (the experienced reader will recognize these level-numbers as de Bruijn numbers [de Bruijn, 1972]). For example, consider

```
(λx.λy.+ x (* y y))
```

The λx abstraction is at level 1, while the λy abstraction is at level 2 (since it is enclosed by a λx abstraction).

The lexical level of a variable is now defined to be the lexical level of the lambda abstraction which binds it. If the level of x is less than y we say that x is *freer* than y, since it is bound further out.

Constants (including built-in functions such as +, and previously generated supercombinators) can be regarded as being bound at the top level, and so should be at level 0. There is, of course, no need to abstract out constants as extra parameters during lambda-lifting.

To summarize:

(i) The level-number of a *lambda abstraction* is one more than the number of lambda abstractions which textually enclose it. If there is none, then its level-number is 1.
(ii) The level-number of a *variable* is the level-number of the lambda abstraction which binds it.
(iii) The level-number of a *constant* is 0.

It is simple to determine the lexical levels of all variables in a single tree-walk over the expression. On the way down the tree the level-numbers of the lambdas are recorded in a sort of environment, while on the way up the level of each variable is computed, using the environment.

Now to maximize the chances of being able to apply η-reduction we can simply sort the extra parameters in increasing order of lexical level.

13.4 Implementing a Supercombinator Program

All the preceding work has shown how to compile our program into a set of supercombinator definitions. What happens now? We have spoken of the supercombinators being compiled in some way, but in fact there is a spectrum of possible implementations:

(i) We could keep the body of the supercombinator as a tree, and instantiate it using a function similar to Instantiate. This is the supercombinator equivalent of the lambda reducer in the last chapter, and all the mechanisms described in the previous chapters concerning how to find the next redex, how to perform a reduction, indirection nodes, the stack and so on are still valid. The only change required is in the implementation of Instantiate. It is simplified because all lambda abstractions are known to be supercombinators (which have no free variables, and hence need never be copied), but is made more complicated because it has to substitute for several variables at once.

We call this the template-instantiation implementation.

(ii) We could keep the body of the supercombinator as a tree, but held in a contiguous block of store. Now the instantiation can be done with a modified block move, which can be implemented much more efficiently than a tree-walking instantiation. This idea is used by Keller [1985]. It is possible because supercombinators are constructed once and for all at compile-time, rather than being generated on the fly at run-time.

(iii) We could compile the body to a linear sequence of instructions which will create an instance when executed. This is the idea behind the G-machine [Johnsson, 1984], which we discuss in Chapters 18–21. This is faster still, and also opens the way to many further optimizations, as we shall see.

The fundamental point is that all we can do with a supercombinator is to apply it, and hence we are free to choose a representation for the supercombinator that makes this operation efficient.

References

Barendregt, H.P. 1984. *The Lambda Calculus: its syntax and semantics*, 2nd edition, p. 24. North-Holland.

Curry, H.B., and Feys, R. 1958. *Combinatory Logic*, Vol. I. North-Holland.

De Bruijn, N.G. 1972. Lambda calculus notation with nameless dummies. *Indagationes Mathematicae*. Vol. 34, pp. 381–92.

Henderson, P. 1980. *Functional Programming: application and implementation*. Prentice-Hall.

Hoffman, C.M., and O'Donnell, M.J. 1982. Programming with equations. *ACM TOPLAS*. Vol. 4, no. 1, pp. 83–112.

Hughes, R.J.M. 1984. The design and implementation of programming languages. PhD thesis, PRG-40, Programming Research Group, Oxford. September.

Johnsson, T. 1984. Efficient compilation of lazy evaluation. In *Proceeding of the ACM Symposium on Compiler Construction, Montreal*, pp. 58–69. June.

Johnsson, T. 1985. Lambda lifting: transforming programs to recursive equations. In *Conference on Functional Programming Languages and Computer Architecture, Nancy*. Jouannaud (editor). LNCS 201. Springer Verlag.

Keller, R.M. 1985. Distributed graph reduction from first principles. Department of Computer Science, University of Utah.

Klop, J.W. 1980. Combinatory reduction systems. PhD thesis, Mathematisch Centrum, Amsterdam.

Landin, P.J. 1964. The mechanical evaluation of expressions. *Computer Journal*. Vol. 6, pp. 308–20.

O'Donnell, M.J. 1977. *Computing in Systems Described by Equations*. LNCS 58. Springer Verlag.

Fourteen

RECURSIVE SUPERCOMBINATORS

So far we have made no explicit mention of how our lambda-lifter should handle recursive definitions. One way to do so is to translate all our recursive definitions into non-recursive ones, using the fixpoint combinator Y, as described in Chapter 2. This is inefficient and slow for the following reasons:

(i) There is no reason why the *supercombinators* should not be explicitly recursive since, unlike lambda abstractions, they have names so they can refer to themselves. For example

```
$F x = $G ($F (- x 1)) 0
```

(ii) To make $F non-recursive using Y would require an auxiliary definition, thus:

```
$F = Y $F1
$F1 F x = $G (F (- x 1)) 0
```

Defining $F in this way will require more reductions than the explicitly recursive version, since the Y has to be reduced.

(iii) In Chapter 6 the translation into the ordinary lambda calculus of a letrec involving mutual recursion was handled by first grouping the definitions into a tuple, and then making this definition non-recursive with Y. Not only is it annoying to have to introduce tuples to handle mutual recursion of functions, but it is also very inefficient since the tuple has to be constructed and then taken apart.

We conclude that explicitly recursive definitions of supercombinators will give a better performance. We now describe the techniques required to obtain a set of mutually recursive supercombinator definitions without using Y.

14.1 Notation

Since we want to treat recursion directly, we do not want it to be compiled into applications of the Y combinator. Hence we assume that the high-level functional program is instead translated into the lambda notation augmented with the simple let and letrec constructs, as was described in Chapter 3.

In passing we observe that the notation

```
$S1 x y = B1
$S2 f = B2
etc.
------------------------
E
```

is precisely equivalent to

```
letrec
        $S1 = λx.λy.B1
        $S2 = λf.B2
        etc.
in
        E
```

so that the lambda-lifting process can be regarded as a source to source transformation of the enriched lambda calculus.

14.2 Lets and letrecs in Supercombinator Bodies

Suppose we wanted to write a textual description for the graph

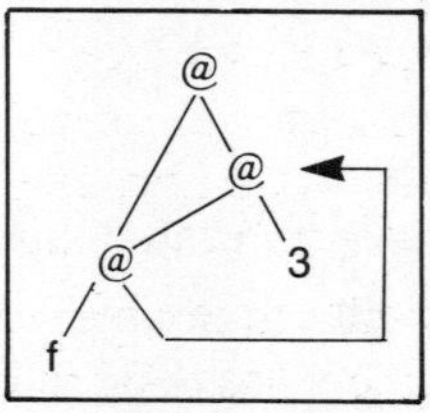

Whilst expressions such as (f (g a) b) can describe trees, they cannot express the sharing and cycles embodied in the above graph. One solution would be to name the nodes (a, b and c, say, working top to bottom) and express the graph thus:

```
a = c b
b = c 3
c = f b
```

We would also want to identify a as being the root of the graph. But we have just reinvented the letrec! The graph can be described by the letrec expression

```
letrec a = c b
       b = c 3
       c = f b
in a
```

This gives us the idea that letrec expressions can be regarded as *textual descriptions of a cyclic graph*. Hence a letrec in a supercombinator body can be regarded as the description of a graphical portion of the supercombinator body.

Up to now we have considered a supercombinator body to be a *tree*, and applying the supercombinator involves constructing a new instance of the tree. Now we see that allowing letrecs in a supercombinator body allows the body to be a *graph*, and applying such a supercombinator involves constructing a new instance of this graph. We say that such a supercombinator has a *graphical body*.

For example, consider the following supercombinator definition:

```
$Y f = letrec yf = f yf
       in yf
```

This is a definition of the cyclic version of the familiar Y combinator, whose body is a graph. When $Y is applied, we make an instance of the graph, substituting for occurrences of the formal parameter, f. During the instantiation we must be careful to preserve the cycles of the original graph.

A compiling implementation would compile code which would, when executed, construct the graph with the appropriate substitutions made. The way in which this is done is described in Chapter 18.

In a similar way we can allow supercombinator bodies to contain let-expressions, regarding them as descriptions of (acyclic) graphs. This will actually save us reductions, because we can now describe directly expressions such as

```
let x = 3 in E
```

where we would previously have translated this to

```
(λx.E) 3
```

which requires a reduction to explicate.

To summarize, we see that

(i) it is quite easy to extend supercombinators to allow them to have bodies which are general graphs, rather than being restricted to trees;
(ii) graphical supercombinator bodies can easily be described using a letrec (or a let in the case of acyclic bodies);
(iii) to instantiate a letrec (or let), we simply construct the graph described by the letrec (or let);
(iv) using graphical bodies can save us reductions.

We now discuss how to transform recursive programs into supercombinators with graphical bodies.

14.3 Lambda-lifting in the Presence of letrecs

Our lambda-lifting algorithm will work as before, lifting the lambda abstractions to the top level. No special note need be taken of letrecs; they can be treated just like any other expression. In particular, lambda-lifting still applies only to lambda abstractions, not to letrecs as well. Some lambda abstractions will have letrecs in their bodies, which will give rise to supercombinators with graphical bodies.

The question arises, however, of what lexical level-number to assign to variables bound in a letrec.

The variables bound in a letrec will be instantiated when the *immediately (textually) enclosing lambda abstraction* is applied to an argument, since that is when we construct the instance of the letrec, substituting for all the free variables. Hence the variables bound in a letrec should be given the lexical level-number of the immediately enclosing lambda abstraction.

What if there is no enclosing lambda abstraction? In this case the natural level-number for such variables should be 0. But this gives us a hint, since 0 is the level-number we assign to constants and supercombinators. If there is no enclosing lambda abstraction, then the definition bodies of the letrec can have no free variables (other than the variables defined in the letrec); in other words, they are combinators. All that is needed to turn them into supercombinators is to lambda-lift them to remove any inner lambdas. Notice that the variables bound in such level 0 letrecs will not be taken out as free variables because constants (level 0) are not taken out.

Suppose we have to lambda-lift this program, which computes the infinite list of 1s.

```
-----------------------------------
letrec x = CONS 1 x
in x
```

The letrec is at level 0, and there are no lambda abstractions, so x is a supercombinator already, and we get

```
$x = CONS 1 $x
-----------------------------------
$x
```

As an example of a recursive function, consider the factorial function:

```
letrec fac = λn.IF (= n 0) 1 (* n (fac (- n 1)))
in fac 4
```

The letrec is at level 0, and there are no lambda abstractions inside the body of the λn abstraction. Hence, fac is already a supercombinator and we get

```
$fac n = IF (= n 0) 1 (* n ($fac (- n 1)))
$Prog = $fac 4
------------------------------------------
$Prog
```

14.4 Generating Supercombinators with Graphical Bodies

So far none of our supercombinators has had a graphical body. This occurs when a letrec has some free variables. Consider, for example, the program

```
let
        Inf = λv.(letrec vs = CONS v vs in vs)
in
        Inf 4
```

(Inf v) returns the infinite list of vs. Again, Inf is at level 0 and contains no inner lambda abstractions, so it is already a supercombinator, and we get

```
$Inf v = letrec vs = CONS v vs in vs
$Prog = $Inf 4
------------------------------------------
$Prog
```

Notice that the graphical body of the supercombinator preserves the (finite) cyclic representation of the (infinite) data structure.

14.5 An Example

We shall now work through an example to show the lambda-lifting algorithm in action. Here is a Miranda program to sum the first 100 integers. It is written in a slightly odd style in order to demonstrate various aspects of the algorithm:

```
sumInts m = sum (count 1)
            where
                count n = [],                 n>m
                        = n : count (n+1)

sum []     = 0
sum (n:ns) = n + sum ns
--------------------------------------------------------
sumInts 100
```

Translating this into the enriched lambda calculus gives

```
--------------------------------------------------------
letrec
   sumInts
   = λm.letrec
            count = λn.IF (> n m)
                          NIL
                          (CONS n (count (+ n 1)))
         in
            sum (count 1)
   sum = λns.IF (= ns NIL) 0 (+ (HEAD ns) (sum (TAIL ns)))
in
   sumInts 100
```

(Note: this is not exactly the translation that will be produced by the pattern-matching compiler described in Chapter 5, but it is a correct translation, and will suffice for present purposes.) The variables sumInts and sum are defined at level 0, but sumInts has an inner lambda abstraction. This λn abstraction has the free variables m and count. We lift them out to generate a super-combinator, which we arbitrarily name $count, thus

```
$count count m n = IF (> n m) NIL (CONS n (count (+ n 1)))
--------------------------------------------------------
letrec
   sumInts
   = λm.letrec
            count = $count count m
         in
            sum (count 1)
   sum = λns.IF (= ns NIL) 0 (+ (HEAD ns) (sum (TAIL ns)))
in
   sumInts 100
```

Now sumInts and sum have no inner abstractions, and they are at the top level, so they are supercombinators. Lifting them directly, and adding the final $Prog supercombinator, gives

```
$count count m n = IF (> n m) NIL (CONS n (count (+ n 1)))
$sum ns = IF (= ns NIL) 0 (+ (HEAD ns) ($sum (TAIL ns)))
$sumInts m = letrec count = $count count m
             in $sum (count 1)
$Prog = $sumInts 100
------------------------------------------------------------
$Prog
```

We are done.

14.6 Alternative Approaches

The technique described earlier is not the only way of lambda-lifting recursive functions. For example, Johnsson [1985] describes an algorithm which constructs graphical supercombinator bodies for data structures, but not for functions.

Briefly, his technique works like this. Suppose we have a program with a recursive function f containing a free variable v:

```
------------------------------------
(...
    letrec f = λx.(...f...v...)
    in (...f...)
...)
```

We generate a recursive supercombinator $f from f by abstracting the free variables (just v in this case) *but not* f *itself.* Instead, all uses of f are replaced with ($f v), including those in the body of $f itself. This yields

```
$f v x = ...($f v)...v...
------------------------------------
(...
    (...($f v)...)
...)
```

To illustrate the method we will recompile the sumInts example given earlier. Recall that we begin with the program

```
----------------------------------------------------------------
letrec
   sumInts
   = λm.letrec
          count = λn.IF (> n m)
                        NIL
                        (CONS n (count (+ n 1)))
        in
          sum (count 1)

    sum = λns.IF (= ns NIL) 0 (+ (HEAD ns) (sum (TAIL ns)))
in
    sumInts 100
```

First we lambda-lift the λn abstraction, abstracting out the free variable m, *but not* count. Instead, we replace all calls to count with ($count m), which gives

```
$count m n = IF (> n m) NIL (CONS n ($count m (+ n 1)))
----------------------------------------------------------------
letrec
   sumInts
   = λm.sum ($count m 1)
   sum = λns.IF (= ns NIL) 0 (+ (HEAD ns) (sum (TAIL ns)))
in
   sumInts 100
```

There were two calls to count, one in the body of the λn abstraction and one in the definition of sumInts, both of which were replaced with ($count m). Notice that this substitution could equally well be carried out using a let-definition to bind count to ($count m).

Now sumInts and sum are supercombinators, so we lift them out to give

```
$count m n = IF (> n m) NIL (CONS n ($count m (+ n 1)))
$sum ns = IF (= ns NIL) 0 (+ (HEAD ns) ($sum (TAIL ns)))
$sumInts m = sum ($count m 1)
$Prog = $sumInts 100
----------------------------------------------------------------
$Prog
```

Notice that (unlike our previous method) no supercombinator has a graphical body; all the recursion is handled by direct recursion of supercombinators. However, it turns out that cyclic data structures have to be treated in a different way, and do require supercombinators with graphical bodies.

The new method has one major advantage. In our previous approach the recursive call to count in the $count supercombinator was made to a function passed in as a parameter (called count). In contrast, the new method makes the recursive call directly to the supercombinator $count. This means that the compiler can see which function is being called, and this information can make the compiled code considerably more efficient (see Chapter 20).

On the other hand, the $count supercombinator generated by the new method is larger than that generated by the previous method. It contains an extra application node ($count m), and a new instance of this application node will be constructed on every application of $count, which will consume more store.

In the case of mutually recursive functions, it turns out that each function needs to be passed the free variables of all the other functions in the mutually recursive set, as well as its own. This involves doing the sort of dependency analysis described in Section 6.2.8. Furthermore, as mentioned above, data structures and functions must be treated in different ways by the new method, which makes the compiler more complicated.

The trade-off between the two techniques is not yet clear.

14.7 Compile-time Simplifications

Once lambda-lifting has been completed there are some simple optimizations that further improve the lambda-lifted program. These take the form of compile-time simplifications of the program.

14.7.1 Compile-time Reductions

It may be advantageous to perform certain reductions at compile-time. For example, consider the definitions

```
$F x y = + ($G y) x
$G p = * p p
```

The ($G y) in the body of $F is a redex which will be created every time $F is applied. We could, however, reduce it at compile-time, giving

```
$F x y = + (* y y) x
```

thus performing the $G reduction once and for all at compile-time. This process is directly analogous to expanding out the code for a procedure call in-line, a common optimization in conventional compilers. In order to preserve sharing we should replace the redex with a let-expression:

```
$G E  →  let p = E in * p p
```

Sometimes we can evaluate subexpressions completely, as in the definition

```
$H x = + x (* 3 4)
```

where we can safely evaluate the (* 3 4) once and for all at compile-time. This is called constant folding in conventional compiler technology.

The question of exactly which redexes to reduce is not completely straightforward, especially in the case of recursive functions, because indiscriminate use of the technique may cause the code size to increase significantly. The decision is not clear-cut, because it depends on the relative priorities of speed and code size. Hudak and Kranz [1984] give an interesting discussion of a particularly thorough-going use of compile-time reduction.

14.7.2 Common Subexpression Elimination

Sometimes (for clarity) the programmer may write an expression such as

```
* ($F x) ($F x)
```

Rather than compute ($F x) twice, we can replace the expression with

```
let fx = $F x in * fx fx
```

Identifying common subexpressions may be done by a hashing algorithm which checks to see if an expression already exists before building a new one. This simplification seems always to be beneficial, but see Chapter 23 for a warning about some possible drawbacks.

14.7.3 Eliminating Redundant lets

Sometimes lets of the form

```
let x = y in E
```

arise, in which the right-hand side of the definition is a single variable. These can safely be eliminated by replacing occurrences of x by y in E.

It is also quite common to encounter code in which a variable defined in a let is used only once in its scope. For example, consider the supercombinator

```
$sumSq x y = let xsq = * x x
                 ysq = * y y
             in
                 + xsq ysq
```

In this case we may as well substitute the right-hand side of the definition for the (single) occurrence of the variable, giving

```
$sumSq x y = + (* x x) (* y y)
```

This is simpler and, it turns out, slightly more efficient. It may be achieved simply by accumulating information on the number of textually distinct occurrences of each variable in the body of a let.

References

Hudak, P., and Kranz, D. 1984. A combinator based compiler for a functional language. In *Proceedings of the 11th ACM Symposium on Principles of Programming Languages*, pp. 122–32. January.

Johnsson, T. 1985. Lambda-lifting – transforming programs to recursive equations. In *Conference on Functional Programming and Computer Architecture, Nancy*, pp. 190–203. Jouannaud (editor). LNCS 201. Springer Verlag.

Fifteen

FULLY LAZY LAMBDA-LIFTING

As we discussed in Chapter 11 our implementations support lazy evaluation. However, there is one major way in which an implementation based on lambda-lifting can be made still lazier than the version we have described so far. The purpose of this chapter is to describe the opportunity and the modifications required to exploit it.

15.1 Full Laziness

As we remarked in Section 12.1.3, a straightforward implementation of the template-instantiation procedure risks constructing *multiple instances of the same expression*, rather than sharing a single copy of them. This wastes space because each instance occupies separate storage, and it wastes time because the instances will be reduced separately. This waste can be arbitrarily large; for example, the duplicated instances might each separately perform some large calculation.

The loss of sharing can best be seen using an example. Consider the function

```
f = λy.+ y (sqrt 4)
```

Whenever this function is applied to an argument we will slavishly construct a new instance of the subexpression (sqrt 4) in its body, despite the fact that all instances of the (sqrt 4) reduce to 2. It would be better not to construct a new instance of such constant subexpressions, but to share a single instance instead. This can do no harm, since the constant subexpression does not contain any occurrences of the formal parameter, and hence its value cannot change between one application and another.

It looks as if these constant subexpressions could be spotted and marked by a compiler, but they can be generated 'on the fly'. Consider the Miranda program

```
f = g 4
g x y = y + (sqrt x)
------------------------------
(f 1) + (f 2)
```

This compiles to the lambda expression:

```
------------------------------------------
letrec f = g 4
       g = λx.λy.+ y (sqrt x)
in + (f 1) (f 2)
```

Therefore, when evaluating the expression, we get

```
   + (f 1) (f 2)
```

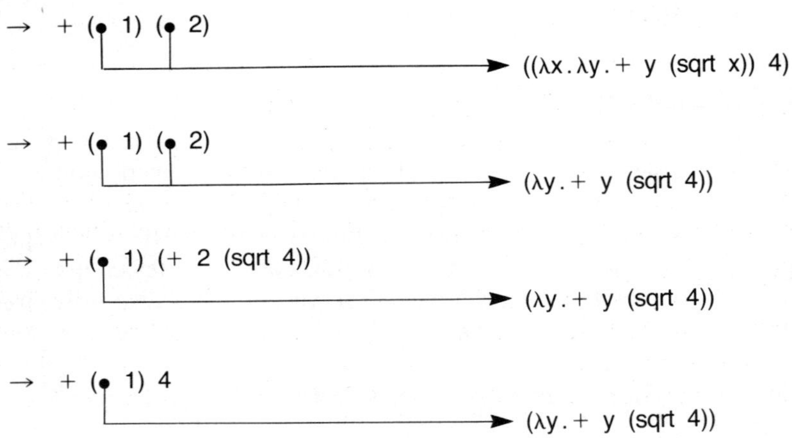


```
→  + (+ 1 (sqrt 4)) 4
→  + 3 4
→  7
```

The crucial point is that the (sqrt 4) is evaluated twice, because a fresh instance of it is made each time the λy is applied. The reason for this is that it is a *dynamically created* constant subexpression of the λy abstraction.

Not surprisingly, just the same problem occurs with supercombinators. Our example compiles to

```
$g x y = + y (sqrt x)
$f = $g 4
$Prog = + ($f 1) ($f 2)
-----------------------------------
$Prog
```

The reduction proceeds as follows:

```
   $Prog
```

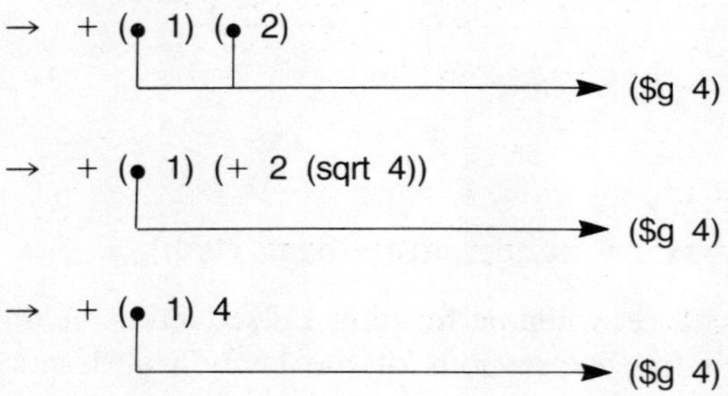


```
→  + (+ 1 (sqrt 4)) 4
→  + 3 4
→  7
```

Again we see that the (sqrt 4) has been evaluated twice.

To be as lazy as possible we would like to share even these dynamically created constant expressions. Specifically, the effect we want to achieve is that every expression is evaluated *at most once* after the variables in it have been bound. This is called *full laziness*. It corresponds closely to an optimization sometimes performed by conventional compilers on loops, in which expressions not involving the loop variable (i.e. free expressions) are moved out of the loop so that they are not repeatedly evaluated.

15.2 Maximal Free Expressions

The problem we have discovered is that laziness can be lost if we instantiate too much of the body of a lambda abstraction.

Which parts should not be instantiated? The parts of the body that should not be instantiated are those subexpressions which contain no (free) occurrences of the formal parameter, because if the formal parameter does not occur then the value of the subexpression will be the same between all instances, and hence may be shared. To formalize this we need a new definition.

> **DEFINITION**
>
> A subexpression E of a lambda abstraction L is *free* in L if all variables in E are free in L. A *maximal free expression* or *MFE* of L is a free expression which is not a proper subexpression of another free expression of L. (E is a proper subexpression of F if and only if E is a subexpression of F and E ≠ F.)

Examples

In the following lambda abstractions the maximal free expressions of the λx abstractions are underlined.

(1) (λx.sqrt x)
(2) (λx.x (sqrt 4))
(3) (λy.λx.± x (* y y))
(4) (λy.λx.+ (* y y) x)
(5) (λx.(λx.x) x) (here the (λx.x) is free despite the name clash)

To achieve full laziness, therefore, when performing a β-reduction we must not instantiate the maximal free expressions of the lambda abstraction. Instead of instantiating them we must substitute a pointer to the single shared instance in the body of the lambda abstraction. This key idea was first recognized by Wadsworth [1971]. To illustrate, recall our example from the previous section

```
---------------------------------
letrec f = g 4
       g = λx.λy.+ y (sqrt x)
in + (f 1) (f 2)
```

The reduction sequence begins in the same way

+ (f 1) (f 2)

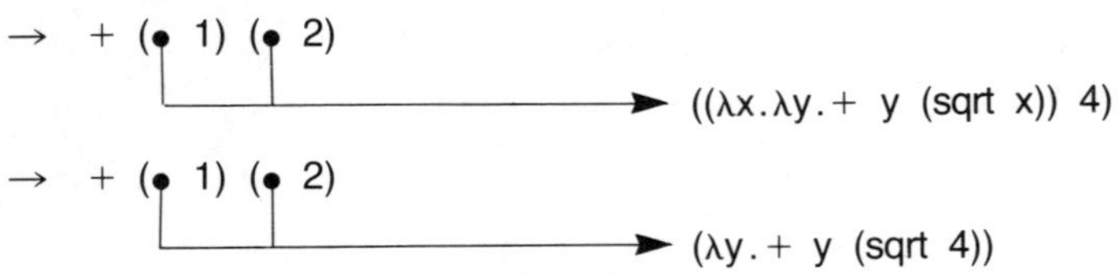

But now we see that (sqrt 4) is free in the λy abstraction, and hence should not be instantiated when the abstraction is applied. Thus we get

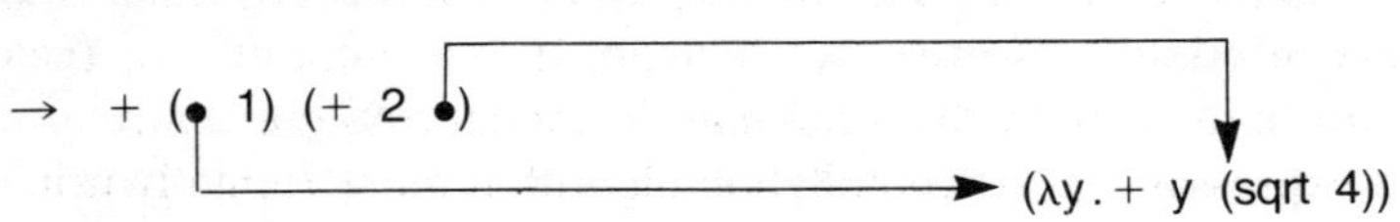

The instance contains a pointer back to the (sqrt 4) in the body of the abstraction.

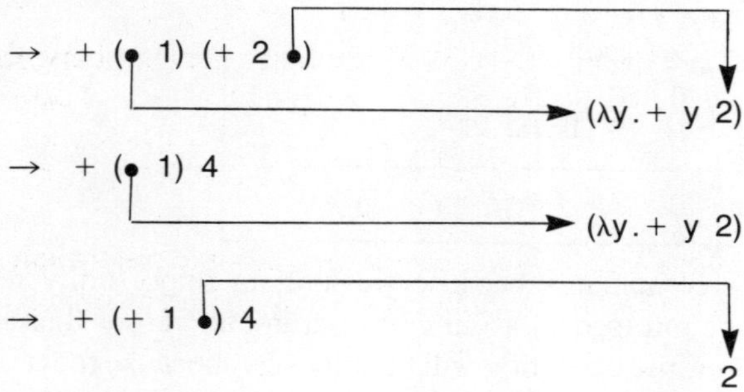


```
→  + 3 4
→  7
```

Now the (sqrt 4) is only evaluated once, as we had hoped.

15.3 Lambda-lifting using Maximal Free Expressions

In order to achieve full laziness in the lambda reducer of Chapter 12 we appear to need to identify maximal free expressions dynamically. As we noted there, this is rather difficult to do efficiently

Fortunately, it turns out that we can modify the lambda-lifting algorithm so that a straightforward implementation of the resulting supercombinator program is automatically fully lazy. The algorithm was invented by Hughes [1984].

15.3.1 Modifying the Lambda-lifting Algorithm

The modification we need is to *abstract the maximal free expressions*, rather than free variables, when lambda-lifting a lambda abstraction.

In our running example, the function g has the lambda abstraction

```
λx.λy.+ y (sqrt x)
```

When doing lambda-lifting on the λy abstraction, we abstracted x out as an extra parameter, since it occurs free. Instead we should abstract out the entire (free) subexpression (sqrt x) as an extra parameter, thus generating the supercombinator

```
$g1 sqrtx y = + y sqrtx
```

The name 'sqrtx' is an arbitrary name invented for the extra parameter. We replace the λy abstraction with the supercombinator $g1 applied to the subexpression, thus:

```
λx.$g1 (sqrt x)
```

Completing the compilation in the normal way gives

```
$g1 sqrtx y = + y sqrtx
$g x = $g1 (sqrt x)
$f = $g 4
$Prog = + ($f 1) ($f 2)
-----------------------------------
$Prog
```

We get an extra supercombinator because we lose an opportunity for η-reduction when we take out (sqrt x) as an extra parameter rather than x. However, in compensation, the execution will be fully lazy, because the uses of (sqrt x) will be shared. Now we can follow the reduction sequence again:

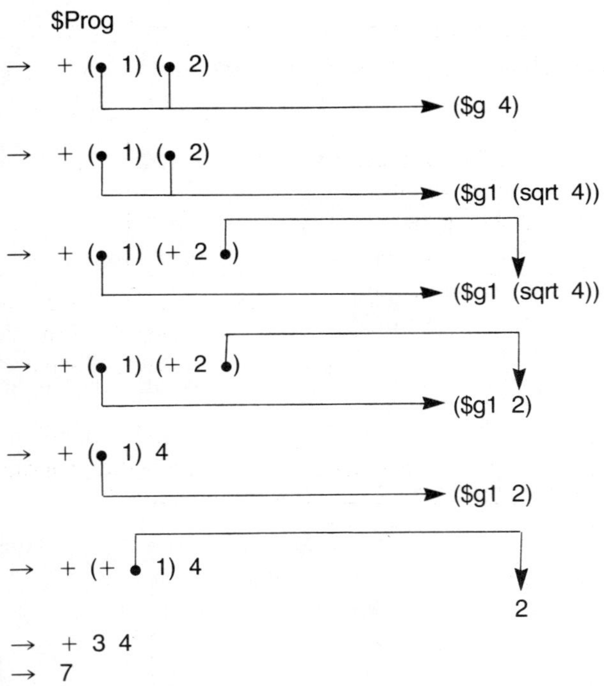

The (sqrt 4) is shared, and hence only evaluated once.

So to preserve full laziness we should, during lambda-lifting,

> abstract out the maximal free expressions (rather than only the free variables) of a lambda abstraction as extra parameters.

This modification is sufficient to preserve full laziness. We call it *fully lazy lambda-lifting*.

One slight optimization is that if a maximal free expression turns out to have no free variables at all (so it is a CAF), then instead of abstracting it out as an extra parameter, it can simply be given a name and made into a supercombinator. The name can then be used instead of the expression. This is illustrated in the next section.

15.3.2 Fully Lazy Lambda-lifting in the Presence of letrecs

As in Chapter 14, our strategy needs to take account of letrecs. Consider the program

```
-----------------------------------------
let
    f = λx.letrec fac = λn.(...)
            in + x (fac 1000)
in
    + (f 3) (f 4)
```

The algorithm of Chapter 14 will compile it to

```
$fac fac n = (...)
$f x = letrec fac = $fac fac
       in + x (fac 1000)
-----------------------------------------
+ ($f 3) ($f 4)
```

The function fac is defined locally in the body of f, and hence (fac 1000) cannot be lifted out as a free expression from the body of f. Unfortunately, this means that (fac 1000) will be recomputed each time $f is applied, so we have lost full laziness.

The solution is to recognize that the definition of fac does not depend on x. With this in mind we can 'float' the letrec for fac outwards, giving this program

```
-----------------------------------------
letrec
    fac = λn.(...)
in let
    f = λx.+ x (fac 1000)
in
    + (f 3) (f 4)
```

Now our fully lazy lambda-lifter will produce a fully lazy program:

```
$fac n = (...)
$fac1000 = $fac 1000
$f x = + x $fac1000
$Prog = + ($f 3) ($f 4)
-----------------------------------------
$Prog
```

This example also illustrates the utility making a maximal constant expression into a supercombinator ($fac1000 in this case), rather than abstracting it out as a parameter.

Our strategy now breaks into two phases:

(i) Float out letrec (and let) definitions as far as possible.
(ii) Perform fully lazy lambda-lifting.

How far out can a letrec definition be floated? The value of a variable bound in a letrec will generally depend on the values of certain free variables. We call the set of free variables on which a variable x depends, x's *free variable set*. Once we know x's free variable set we can float the definition of x outwards until the next enclosing lambda abstraction binds one of the variables in the free variable set.

This step has the additional benefit that definitions which have no free variables at all will be floated out to the top level, where they will be turned into supercombinators directly.

15.4 A Larger Example

We shall now work through a larger example to show the lambda-lifting algorithm with full laziness modifications in action.

The example is the function 'foldl', being used to add up the numbers between 1 and 100.

```
sumInts n = foldl (+) 0 (count 1 n)

count n m = [],                    n>m
count n m = n : count (n + 1) m

foldl op base []     = base
foldl op base (x:xs) = foldl op (op base x) xs
----------------------------------------------
sumInts 100
```

Translating the example into the enriched lambda calculus, we get

```
----------------------------------------------
letrec
   sumInts = λn.foldl + 0 (count 1 n)

   count = λn.λm.IF (> n m) NIL (CONS n (count (+ n 1) m))

   foldl
   = λop.λbase.λxs.IF (= xs NIL)
                      base
                      (foldl op (op base (HEAD xs)) (TAIL xs))
in sumInts 100
```

(Note: as before, this is not exactly the translation that would be produced by the pattern-matching compiler, but it suffices for present purposes.) Applying the algorithm to foldl, we choose the innermost lambda abstraction, (λxs...), and look for maximal free expressions, which are (foldl op), (op base) and base. We take these out as extra parameters, p, q and base respectively, giving

```
$R1 p q base xs = IF (= xs NIL) base (p (q (HEAD xs)) (TAIL xs))
----------------------------------------------------------------
letrec
   sumInts = λn.foldl + 0 (count 1 n)
   count = λn.λm.IF (> n m) NIL (CONS n (count (+ n 1) m))
   foldl = λop.λbase.$R1 (foldl op) (op base) base
in
   sumInts 100
```

Now the innermost lambda abstraction is λbase, and its maximal free expressions are ($R1 (foldl op)) and op, which we will take out as r and op respectively, giving

```
$R1 p q base xs = IF (= xs NIL) base (p (q (HEAD xs)) (TAIL xs))
$R2 r op base = r (op base) base
----------------------------------------------------------------
letrec
   sumInts = λn.foldl + 0 (count 1 n)
   count = λn.λm.IF (> n m) NIL (CONS n (count (+ n 1) m))
   foldl = λop.$R2 ($R1 (foldl op)) op
in
   sumInts 100
```

Now all the definitions in the top-level letrec are supercombinators, because we have lifted out all the inner lambdas, so after lifting out any constant expressions we can lift them directly to get

```
$sumInts n = $foldlPlus0 ($count1 n)
$foldlPlus0 = $foldl + 0
$count1 = $count 1
$count n m = IF (> n m) NIL (CONS n ($count (+ n 1) m))
$foldl op = $R2 ($R1 ($foldl op)) op
$Prog = $sumInts 100
$R1 p q base xs = IF (= xs NIL) base (p (q (HEAD xs)) (TAIL xs))
$R2 r op base = r (op base) base
----------------------------------------------------------------
$Prog
```

Notice that we *cannot* eliminate the op parameter of $foldl, since it is used twice on the right-hand side.

15.5 Implementing Fully Lazy Lambda-lifting

We now turn our attention to algorithms for achieving the transformations required by fully lazy lambda-lifting.

15.5.1 Identifying the Maximal Free Expressions

How can we identify the maximal free expressions of a lambda abstraction? We can use the concept of *lexical level-number* introduced in Section 13.3.2, and compute the lexical level of expressions as well as variables. The lexical level of an expression should be the maximum of the levels of the free variables within it. Then when lambda-lifting a lambda abstraction at level *n*, we should take out as extra parameters any subexpressions within the body whose level is less than *n*.

For example, in the base of the lambda abstraction for g, which is

```
λx.λy.+ y (sqrt x)
```

the λx abstraction is at level 1 and the λy abstraction is at level 2. Hence the various subexpressions have level-numbers as follows

```
+                  level 0
(+ y)              level 2
sqrt               level 0
(sqrt x)           level 1
(+ y (sqrt x))     level 2
```

To summarize:

(i) The level-number of a *constant* is 0.
(ii) The level-number of a *variable* is the textual nesting depth of the lambda which binds it.
(iii) The level-number of an *application* (f x) is the maximum of the level-numbers of f and x.

Given an expression E, its *native lambda abstraction* is the enclosing lambda abstraction whose level-number is the same as that of E. Looking 'outwards from E' it is the first lambda abstraction which binds any variable in E.

All the maximal free expression information can be determined, and lambda-lifting performed, in a single tree-walk over the expression:

(i) On the way down the tree, the level-number of each lambda abstraction is recorded.
(ii) On the way up, the level of each expression is computed, using the environment and the levels of its subexpressions. If it is applied to another expression with the same level-number, then the two are

merged, otherwise they are given new unique names (since they will be maximal free expressions of distinct lambda abstractions). The merging is the mechanism whereby free expressions are combined to form *maximal* free expressions.

(iii) When a lambda is encountered on the way up, it is transformed into a supercombinator, and the lambda abstraction is replaced by the supercombinator applied to the maximal free expressions. The maximal free expressions are those subexpressions with level-number less than that of the lambda abstraction, after the merging has taken place.

15.5.2 Lifting CAFs

The maximal constant expressions (level 0) need slightly different treatment. It would be correct to take them out as extra parameters, but there is an easier way. We can simply define a new supercombinator of zero arguments to be the constant expression, and use the name of the supercombinator instead of the expression. No benefit is obtained, however, by doing this with constant expressions consisting of a single constant (such as 3 or $F), so they can be left as they are.

For example, in the expression

```
λx.+ 1 x
```

the (+ 1) is a maximal free expression at level 0, and can be made into a supercombinator $Inc:

```
$Inc = + 1
```

Now the expression becomes

```
λx.$Inc x
```

In this case all that we achieve is the sharing of the (+ 1) graph for each application of the lambda abstraction, but if the constant expression is itself a redex (like (+ 1 3), for example) then we also save repeated evaluation of the redex. There was an example of the utility of this in the $fac1000 supercombinator of Section 15.3.2. (Note: there is actually a strong case to be made for not lifting out a constant expression unless it is in fact a redex – see Section 15.6.1.)

15.5.3 Ordering the Parameters

In Section 13.3.2 we put the parameters of a supercombinator in order of increasing level-number, to maximize the opportunities for η-reduction. The same ordering is useful for maximal free expression parameters, for two reasons.

The first is the same as before. A maximal free expression will often be just a single free variable, and in this case, we should still like to have a chance of η-reduction.

The second reason concerns the *size* of the MFE. To maximize sharing (which is the object of the exercise) we should like to make our MFEs as large as possible.

Suppose we have the lambda abstraction

```
λx.(...G...F...E...)
```

where E, F and G are MFEs of the λx abstraction, and

level of F < level of G < level of E

It would be best to define the supercombinator

```
$S f g e x = (...g...f...e...)
```

and replace the abstraction with

```
$S F G E
```

because then ($S F G) will have a smaller level-number than E, and hence will be taken out of E's native lambda abstraction as a single MFE. If we had arranged the parameters in the reverse order, G and F would have had to be taken out separately.

This will not affect the amount of computation involved (since ($S F G) cannot be reducible), but it will mean that there is only one instance of the ($S F G) tree rather than one for each application of E's native lambda abstraction. Thus, correctly ordering the parameters should make the maximal free expressions *larger* and *fewer*.

The example in the Section 15.4 showed an example of this optimization in action. We abstracted (foldl op), (op base) and base from the body of the λxs abstraction, calling them p, q and base respectively. Though we did not mention this at the time, we put p first, since (foldl op) is freer than (op base) and base. This subsequently enabled us to abstract ($R1 (foldl op)) from the λbase abstraction.

We conclude that ordering the parameters by increasing level-number is better in both these respects.

15.5.4 Floating Out the lets and letrecs

We recall that to maintain full laziness we must 'float' definitions given in lets and letrecs outwards. In this section we discuss the algorithm in more detail.

Since we will float out all the definitions in a letrec together, we assume that the dependency analysis described in Chapter 6 has already been performed. If it were not performed, then a definition might not be floated out as far as possible, merely because it happened to be defined in the same letrec as a definition which could not be floated out so far. For the same reason we assume that lets contain only a single definition.

In practice, the algorithm of this section could probably be combined with the dependency analysis algorithm.

How far out should a let(rec) be floated? We can compute the 'correct' level-number of its variables, by computing the level-numbers of their definition bodies. This level-number is correct in the sense that it identifies the innermost lambda abstraction on which the definition depends. The let(rec) should then be floated out until the nearest enclosing lambda abstraction has this level-number.

This still leaves some freedom in choosing exactly how far out a let(rec) can be floated. The algorithm which we describe below specifies that:

(i) The immediately enclosing lambda abstraction has the same level-number as that of the variables bound in the let(rec).
(ii) The let(rec) does not appear in the function position of an application.
(iii) It should be floated out as little as possible subject to the constraints (i) and (ii).

The second condition rejects expressions such as:

```
(let v = E in E₁) E₂
```

in favor of the following equivalent expression, in which the let is floated out one more stage:

```
let v = E in (E₁ E₂)
```

(and similarly for letrecs). This has no effect on laziness, but allows an important simplification in Chapter 20.

The final condition specifies that a let(rec) should be floated out no further than is necessary to meet the first two conditions. To see why this may be important, consider the expression

```
IF E (λx.let v = F in G) H
```

where E, F, G and H are arbitrary expressions, and F does not contain x. The algorithm will transform this to

```
IF E (let v = F in (λx.G)) H
```

A sophisticated implementation may be able to avoid constructing the graph of H if E turns out to be TRUE, and vice versa (see Chapter 20). If we were to float the let out further, we would get the expression

```
let v = F in (IF E (λx.G) H)
```

which is less good, because then the graph of F would have to be constructed whatever value E turned out to have.

We can now outline the algorithm as follows. Working from the outside inwards, for each let(rec) perform the following steps:

(1) Compute the level-numbers of each definition body. While doing so for a letrec, assume that the level-number of the variables defined in the

letrec is zero. The reason for this is that the level-number of a recursive definition depends only on its free variables, and not on the (as yet unknown) level-number of the recursive definition itself.

(2) For a letrec, compute the maximum of the level-numbers of the definitions' bodies. This is the correct level-number for the variables bound in the letrec. For lets, the correct level-number is that computed in Step 1. This level-number should be used for the variables bound in the let(rec) when processing its body.

(3) Float out the definitions until the next enclosing lambda abstraction has the same level-number as that of the variables defined in the let(rec), which was computed in Step 2.

(4) Finally, if the let(rec) now appears in the function position of an application, continue to float it out until it does not.

Note: if a letrec re-binds a variable that is already in scope, then it cannot be floated outwards without risk of capturing occurrences of the outer variable. The solution is to systematically rename one of the variables.

15.6 Eliminating Redundant Full Laziness

The transformations required to achieve full laziness have a price. There are at least three ways in which we pay:

(i) Supercombinators with many arguments (for all the MFEs) are generated. This increases the size of the redex and slows down reduction.

(ii) More seriously, more supercombinators may be generated because of the loss of opportunities for η-optimization. To see this, refer back to the example in Section 15.4, where three combinators were generated for foldl where one would have sufficed for a non-fully lazy implementation. More supercombinators mean more reductions.

(iii) Most serious of all, the program is broken up into small fragments, fragments of the bodies of functions being exported piecemeal. For a straightforward template-instantiation implementation this is not a problem, but if the bodies of supercombinators are compiled then many opportunities for optimization may be lost. This will become clearer in Chapter 20, but consider for example the lambda abstraction

```
λv.λx.IF (= v 0) (+ x 1) (+ x 2)
```

The non-fully lazy lambda-lifter will generate a single supercombinator:

```
$R v x = IF (= v 0) (+ x 1) (+ x 2)
```

An optimizing compiler will produce code for $R which first tests the value of v, and then evaluates either the (+ x 1) or (+ x 2), to compute a numerical value. No heap will be consumed. A fully lazy lambda-lifter will produce two combinators:

```
$S1 if-v-zero x = if-v-zero (+ x 1) (+ x 2)
$S v            = $S1 (IF (= v 0))
```

and will replace the λv abstraction with $S. The compiler will now have to generate code for $S1 to construct (+ x 1) *and* (+ x 2) *in the heap* before unwinding the spine of the if-v-zero function, about which it now has no information.

These objections are substantial, but on the other hand full laziness can save very large amounts of time and space in some cases. Further study reveals, however, that the fully lazy lambda-lifter often abstracts out an expression when *nothing is gained* by so doing. Hence we could improve the transformation by selectively performing ordinary (rather than fully lazy) lambda-lifting where nothing is gained by the fully lazy method. This section is therefore devoted to identifying certain situations where fully lazy lambda-lifting gains nothing, and is based on work by Fairbairn [1985] and Hudak and Goldberg [1985].

15.6.1 Functions Applied to Too Few Arguments

In the example above, the fully lazy lambda-lifter took out (IF (= v 0)) as an extra parameter. However, IF requires 3 arguments to reduce, so no work is saved by sharing this expression. More precisely, just as much work would be saved by taking out (= v 0) as an extra parameter, thus

```
$T1 v-zero x = IF v-zero (+ x 1) (+ x 2)
$T v         = $T1 (= v 0)
```

and replacing the λv abstraction with $T. In a straightforward template-instantiation implementation some space would be saved by taking out the larger expression (since the application of IF to (= v 0) would only be built once), but even this is not always true in a compiled implementation (see Chapter 20).

The conclusion is that no work is saved by abstracting out expressions which consist of a built-in operator or supercombinator applied to too few arguments. As the example shows, however, the arguments of the function may be considered for abstraction.

This applies equally to constant expressions which might otherwise be candidates for a new supercombinator definition (see Section 15.5.2). As an illustration of this, consider the example in Section 15.4, where the $foldlPlus0 and $count1 supercombinators are irreducible; nothing is gained by treating them as separate supercombinators.

15.6.2 Unshared Lambda Abstractions

Continuing with the same example, suppose the lambda abstraction under consideration appeared in a context like this:

```
let
    f = λv.λx.IF (= v 0) (+ x 1) (+ x 2)
in
    ...(f 4 5)...
```

and suppose that the (f 4 5) is the only use of f. In this case, the partial application (f 4) *cannot be shared*, since it is used immediately. Using the $S combinator for f, the reduction (f 4 5) would go like this:

```
f 4 5  =  $S 4 5
       →  $S1 (= 4 0) 5
       →  IF (= 4 0) (+ 5 1) (+ 5 2)
       →  + 5 2
       →  7
```

Since the partial application cannot be shared, neither can the painstakingly abstracted expression (= 4 0). No sharing would be lost by using the original $R combinator instead. From this example we can derive a general rule:

> given a lambda abstraction λx.E in a context in which it cannot be shared, we should not abstract free expressions from E because they will not be shared. Instead we should abstract only the free variables.

We can justify this rule by observing that free expressions abstracted from E cannot be shared because:

(i) they are not shared inside E, since they are abstracted from a single place in E;
(ii) they are not shared outside E, because the whole lambda abstraction λx.E is not shared.

The sharing of partial applications is just a specific instance of this general rule. Notice that for the first time our lambda-lifting strategy becomes *context-dependent*. The trick is to work out when a lambda abstraction might be shared. This is not at all obvious. For a start, it might be passed as an argument to another function, in which case a complete analysis would involve looking at the body of that function. More subtly, consider an extension of our example:

```
let
    f = λv.λx.IF (= v 0) (+ x 1) (+ x 2)
    g = λx.λy.+ 1 (f x y)
in
   ...expression not mentioning f...
```

It does not look as if a partial application of f can be shared. But if a partial application of g is shared we will abstract (f x) as an MFE from the λy abstraction in g, so then the partial application of f is shared.

Discovering information about sharing is potentially very difficult (it seems to be another application of *abstract interpretation*; see Chapter 22), but the saving grace is that we can give up at any time and assume that a partial application may be shared. The details are beyond the scope of this book but Fairbairn [1985] and Hudak and Goldberg [1985] each describe their algorithms.

References

Fairbairn, J. 1985. The design and implementation of a simple typed language based on the lambda calculus, pp. 59–60. PhD thesis, *Technical Report 75*. University of Cambridge. May.

Hudak, P., and Goldberg, B. 1985. Serial combinators. In *Conference on Functional Programming Languages and Computer Architecture, Nancy*, pp. 382–99. Jouannaud (editor). LNCS 201. Springer Verlag.

Hughes, R.J.M. 1984. The design and implementation of programming languages. PhD thesis, PRG-40. Programming Research Group, Oxford. September.

Wadsworth, C.P. 1971. Semantics and pragmatics of the lambda calculus, Chapter 4. PhD thesis, Oxford.

Sixteen

SK COMBINATORS

In this chapter we shall examine another graph reduction technique based on a *fixed set of supercombinators*. The most important members of this set are called S and K; hence the title of this chapter. The idea of having a fixed set of supercombinators contrasts with the approach previously described, in which the supercombinator definitions are generated from the program.

The method is appealing because it gives rise to an extremely simple reduction machine which, in effect, only has to support built-in operators and needs no template-instantiation mechanism. In addition it turns out that the implementation is, in a certain sense, lazier than our best efforts so far, but as we shall see, these benefits are won at a price.

(Note: in this chapter we shall use lower-case letters to stand for expressions, to avoid confusion with the combinators, which are written in upper case.)

16.1 The SK Compilation Scheme

Our strategy is to transform the program into one containing only the built-in operators and constants, together with the combinators S, K and I. These combinators are described by the reduction rules

```
S f g x  →  f x (g x)
K x y    →  x
I x      →  x
```

The motivation for choosing this particular set should become clearer as we proceed. S, K and I are all supercombinators, since they satisfy the definition given in Chapter 13, but for the purposes of this chapter, and for compatibility with other published work, we will use the more general term ‘combinator’.

16.1.1 Introducing S, K and I

Consider the lambda abstraction Fun, where

Fun = (λx.e_1 e_2)

where e_1 and e_2 are arbitrary expressions. Given the reduction rule for S, an equivalent expression is Fun′, where

Fun′ = S (λx.e_1) (λx.e_2)

We can demonstrate that Fun and Fun′ are equivalent by applying them to the same argument:

```
Fun arg   =  (λx.e1 e2) arg
          →  (e1[arg/x]) (e2[arg/x])

Fun' arg  =  S (λx.e1) (λx.e2) arg
          →  ((λx.e1) arg) ((λx.e2) arg)
          →  (e1[arg/x]) (e2[arg/x])
```

Hence Fun = Fun′ by extensional equality.

We call the transformation from Fun to Fun′ the S-*transformation*, and denote it using a '⇛' arrow, in the following way:

λx.e_1 e_2 ⇛ S (λx.e_1) (λx.e_2)

Notice the difference between the arrows '⇛' and '→'. Both denote the transformation of one expression into an equivalent one, but the former denotes a compile-time transformation and the latter denotes a run-time reduction.

As an example of the use of the S-transformation, consider the expression

h = λx.OR x TRUE

Applying the S-transformation twice, we get

```
       λx.OR x TRUE
S  ⇛  S (λx.OR x) (λx.TRUE)
S  ⇛  S (S (λx.OR) (λx.x)) (λx.TRUE)
```

(We use an 'S' in the left margin to indicate that the S-transformation rule is being used.)

As we perform the S-transformation, the λx gets pushed down one level each time, because so long as its body is an application we can apply the S-transformation again. Each time we apply the S-transformation we produce two new λx abstractions, but with smaller bodies. In the end the body will be an atomic object, and there are two cases to consider:

(i) The expression is (λx.x). This is just the identity function, which we call I, with the definition

    I x → x

The I-transformation replaces (λx.x) with I, thus:

```
λx.x  ⇒  I
```

There was an instance of this in the previous example, and applying the I-transformation, we would get

```
        S (S (λx.OR) (λx.x)) (λx.TRUE)
I   ⇒   S (S (λx.OR) I) (λx.TRUE)
```

(ii) The expression is (λx.c), where c is a constant or a variable other than x. This is a function which takes one argument, discards it, and returns c, so we can replace it with (K c), where

```
K c x  →  c
```

The K-transformation rule is therefore:

```
λx.c  ⇒  K c
```

where c is any constant, or a variable other than x. As in the case of S, the equivalence of (λx.c) and (K c) can be shown by extensional equality.

There are two instances of this in our example, (λx.OR) and (λx.TRUE). Replacing these with (K OR) and (K TRUE) we get

```
        S (S (λx.OR) I) (λx.TRUE)
K   ⇒   S (S (K OR) I) (K TRUE)
```

To summarize, we have developed the *transformation rules* and the *reduction rules* for the combinators S, K and I shown in Figure 16.1.

S-reduction:	S f g x	→ f x (g x)	
K-reduction:	K c x	→ c	
I-reduction:	I x	→ x	
I-transformation:	λx.x	⇒ I	
K-transformation:	λx.c	⇒ K c	(c ≠ x)
S-transformation:	λx.e_1 e_2	⇒ S (λx.e_1) (λx.e_2)	

Figure 16.1 The SKI rules

We can use the reduction rules to evaluate the transformed program:

```
        h x
    =   S (S (K OR) I) (K TRUE) x
S   →   S (K OR) I x (K TRUE x)
S   →   K OR x (I x) (K TRUE x)
K   →   OR (I x) (K TRUE x)
I   →   OR x (K TRUE x)
K   →   OR x TRUE
```

(We use an S, K or I in the left margin as a reminder of which reduction rule is being applied.)

16.1.2 Compilation and Implementation

The S, K and I transformations together constitute a complete compilation algorithm (the *SK compilation algorithm*), which will transform *any* lambda expression into an expression involving only S, K, I and constants!

Here, then, is the SK compilation algorithm to compile an expression e:

```
WHILE e contains a lambda abstraction DO

    (1) Choose any innermost lambda abstraction of e.
    (2) If its body is an application, apply the S-transformation.
    (3) Otherwise its body must be a variable or constant, so apply
        the K or I transformation as appropriate.

END
```

By transforming the innermost lambda abstractions first we ensure that the body of the chosen lambda abstraction contains no lambdas. This, incidentally, means that we do not run into any α-conversion problems, either during compilation or evaluation of the combinator expression; a very desirable property in view of the subtle problems encountered in Chapter 2.

As an example, let us compile the expression ((λx.+ x x) 5).

```
          (λx.+ x x) 5
S    =>   S (λx.+ x) (λx.x) 5
S    =>   S (S (λx.+) (λx.x)) (λx.x) 5
I    =>   S (S (λx.+) I) (λx.x) 5
I    =>   S (S (λx.+) I) I 5
K    =>   S (S (K +) I) I 5
```

The successive lines show the state of the expression at successive iterations of the algorithm's WHILE loop. To reassure ourselves that the algorithm has produced an equivalent expression, we can evaluate the result using the reduction rules for the combinators:

```
     S (S (K +) I) I 5
 →   S (K +) I 5 (I 5)
 →   K + 5 (I 5) (I 5)
 →   + (I 5) (I 5)
 →   + 5 (I 5)
 →   + 5 5
 →   10
```

To summarize, we have developed a compilation algorithm which will compile any expression into an expression involving only S, K, I and constants (including built-in functions). All the variables have disappeared! Recursion may be dealt with using Y, as previously explained in Chapter 6. Y is then treated as a built-in function by the combinator compilation algorithm.

Figure 16.2 expresses the SK compilation algorithm more formally using

Name	Syntactic object
e, e_1, e_2	Expressions
f, f_1, f_2	Expressions with no inner λs
x	A variable
cv	A constant (including function constants, such as +, Y, etc.), or a variable

C⟦ e ⟧ Compiles e to SK combinators

C⟦ e_1 e_2 ⟧ = **C**⟦ e_1 ⟧ **C**⟦ e_2 ⟧
C⟦ λx.e ⟧ = **A** x ⟦ **C**⟦ e ⟧ ⟧
C⟦ cv ⟧ = cv

A x ⟦ f ⟧ Abstracts x from f

A x ⟦ f_1 f_2 ⟧ = S (**A** x ⟦ f_1 ⟧) (**A** x ⟦ f_2 ⟧)
A x ⟦ x ⟧ = I
A x ⟦ cv ⟧ = K cv

Figure 16.2 SK compilation algorithm

the ⟦ ⟧ notation. We give it here because it is easy to express optimizations to the method using the ⟦ ⟧ notation, which we shall do in later sections.

The **C** function compiles an expression into combinators, while the **A** function (which **C** calls) compiles the body of a lambda abstraction by abstracting the variable from the body. The only notational addition is that the function **A** takes two parameters instead of just one: a variable and an expression in ⟦ ⟧ brackets.

Notice that we apply **C** to the body of a lambda abstraction before applying **A**; this ensures that any inner lambdas are dealt with first, so that **A** only has to deal with atoms and applications. Unfortunately, this also means that the algorithm is quadratic, because the expression has **A** applied to it once for each enclosing lambda.

Let us compile the same expression ((λx.+ x x) 5) using the new notation:

C⟦ (λx.+ x x) 5 ⟧
= **C**⟦ (λx.+ x x) ⟧ **C**⟦ 5 ⟧
= **A** x ⟦ **C**⟦ + x x ⟧ ⟧ 5
= **A** x ⟦ + x x ⟧ 5
= S (**A** x ⟦ + x ⟧) (**A** x ⟦ x ⟧) 5
= S (S (**A** x ⟦ + ⟧) (**A** x ⟦ x ⟧)) I 5
= S (S (K +) I) I 5

16.1.3 Implementations

The combinators S, K, I, etc. are simply particular examples of supercombinators, so the reduction machine required to execute them is a cut-down version of the supercombinator reduction machine. The method of finding the next redex by sliding down the spine, the choice of a spine stack or pointer reversal, the implementation of Y, the use of indirection nodes, and so on, all apply exactly as described in Chapter 12. The main differences are that

(i) the combinators are implemented directly as built-in functions by the reduction machine, rather than indirectly via a general supercombinator body instantiation mechanism;
(ii) the reduction machine does not need to implement the template-instantiation mechanism described in Section 12.1, since there are no lambda abstractions to instantiate.

This means that a graph reducer based on SK reduction is one of the simplest implementations of graph reduction.

The implementations of Turner's languages SASL [Turner, 1976] and Miranda are based on SK combinators, exactly as described above, with some minor enhancements (especially to assist pattern-matching).

The family of SK combinators can be thought of as the built-in instruction set of a graph reduction machine, and thus amenable to direct implementation in hardware. This idea has been taken up in two machines designed specifically to implement SK reduction, the Cambridge SKIM machine [Stoye, 1985 and 1983] and Burroughs' NORMA machine [Richards, 1985].

16.1.4 SK Combinators Perform Lazy Instantiation

A program compiled into SK combinators executes even more lazily than a supercombinator program. For example, consider the supercombinator definition

$$\$F\ x = IF\ e_c\ e_t\ e_f$$

where e_t and e_f are textually large expressions. When $F is applied, new instances of e_t and e_f are constructed, despite the fact that one or other will certainly be discarded. Let us instead compile it using SK combinators:

```
            λx.IF ec et ef
S     ⇒    S (λx.IF ec et) (λx.ef)
S     ⇒    S (S (λx.IF ec) (λx.et)) (λx.ef)
S     ⇒    S (S (S (K IF) (λx.ec)) (λx.et)) (λx.ef)
```

Suppose that $(\lambda x.e_c)$ compiles to a combinator expression c_c, $(\lambda x.e_t)$ compiles to c_t, and $(\lambda x.e_f)$ compiles to c_f. Then the whole expression compiles to

$$S\ (S\ (S\ (K\ IF)\ c_c)\ c_t)\ c_f$$

When we apply this compiled expression to an argument x, the reduction sequence begins like this:

$$
\begin{array}{ll}
 & S\ (S\ (S\ (K\ IF)\ c_c)\ c_t)\ c_f\ x \\
\rightarrow & S\ (S\ (K\ IF)\ c_c)\ c_t\ x\ (c_f\ x) \\
\rightarrow & S\ (K\ IF)\ c_c\ x\ (c_t\ x)\ (c_f\ x) \\
\rightarrow & K\ IF\ x\ (c_c\ x)\ (c_t\ x)\ (c_f\ x) \\
\rightarrow & IF\ (c_c\ x)\ (c_t\ x)\ (c_f\ x)
\end{array}
$$

Notice that we have not constructed an instance of e_t or e_f as we did in the supercombinator case. Instead we have postponed this instantiation by building the expressions (c_t x) and (c_f x). Only the branch selected by the IF will be evaluated any further.

The effect of S is to push the argument down one level (only) into the body of the function. This is advantageous if any parts of the body are discarded.

The price paid for this laziness is the allocation of intermediate nodes to hold the partially instantiated branches of the IF. For example, the application node (c_t x) would not have been allocated by a supercombinator implementation. In addition, the reduction steps are rather small. This question is further discussed at the end of the chapter.

16.1.5 I is Not Necessary

Curiously enough, S and K are sufficient on their own, because the expression (S K K) is extensionally equal to I:

$$
\begin{array}{llcl}
 & S\ K\ K\ x & & I\ x \\
\rightarrow & K\ x\ (K\ x) & \rightarrow & x \\
\rightarrow & x & & \\
 & \text{Hence } I = S\ K\ K & &
\end{array}
$$

It is for this reason that this chapter is entitled 'SK combinators', rather than 'SKI combinators'. However, it is only of theoretical interest; all reasonable implementations include I.

16.1.6 History

This remarkable and counter-intuitive transformation of lambda expressions into combinators was first developed by Curry and Feys [1958], but was thought to be of more mathematical than practical interest until David Turner used it as the basis of an implementation of the functional language SASL [Turner, 1979a and 1979b]. In these papers he described a number of optimizations to the basic compilation scheme which we will examine in the next section.

16.2 Optimizations to the SK Scheme

The examples given above show that the basic compilation algorithm tends to produce rather large combinator expressions from quite innocuous-looking lambda abstractions. In fact, in the form given above it is virtually unusable, because the combinator expressions become so large, and require so many reductions to reduce to normal form.

Fortunately there are some optimizations which render the technique quite practicable, which we will develop in this section. To perform these optimizations we shall need to introduce five new combinators (B, C, S′, B′ and C′).

16.2.1 K Optimization

Consider the expression

```
λx.+ 1
```

When we compile it, we get

```
S (K +) (K 1)
```

This is very stupid, because x is not used at all in the body of the lambda abstraction. A far better result would be

```
K (+ 1)
```

This optimization is easily achieved, by the optimization rule

```
S (K p) (K q)  ⇒  K (p q)
```

It is a simple matter to prove the extensional equality of these expressions:

```
   S (K p) (K q) x            K (p q) x
→  K p x (K q x)           →  p q
→  p (K q x)
→  p q
   Hence  S (K p) (K q) = K (p q)
```

When applied to an argument (K (p q)) requires only one reduction, instead of three for (S (K p) (K p)), so the optimized version is indeed more efficient.

The effect of applying this rule consistently is that

```
A x ⟦ e ⟧ = K e    if and only if   x is not used in e
```

This property shows that the K optimization is just what is needed to preserve *full laziness*. To illustrate this, suppose that f = (λx.p q), where p and q do not use x. We can now produce two combinator translations for f, with and without the K optimization:

```
f = λx.p q  ⇒  S (K p) (K q)    (unoptimized version)
            ⇒  K (p q)          (optimized version)
```

Now if we use the unoptimized version of f, whenever we apply f to a new argument x, we get

```
   S (K p) (K q) x
→  K p x (K q x)
→  p (K q x)
→  p q
```

and this application of p to q, (p q), is brand new. However, if we use the optimized version, we get

```
   K (p q) x
→  p q
```

and this (p q) is the original shared instance in the (K (p q)) expression. Thus, not only does it take fewer reductions to get to (p q), but we will only compute (p q) once; that is, we have a fully lazy implementation.

16.2.2 The B Combinator

Consider the lambda abstraction

```
λx.- x
```

This compiles to

```
S (K -) I
```

which wastes time and effort passing x into the left branch (K –) where it is promptly discarded. What we would like is a version of S which passes x to the right only; let us call it B. The reduction rule for B is

```
B f g x  →  f (g x)
```

The appropriate optimization rule is

```
S (K p) q  ⇒  B p q
```

which says 'if x is not used in the left branch (as shown by the K), then use B instead of S'. This rule would optimize our example thus

```
S (K -) I  ⇒  B - I
```

Notice that this optimization saves work at compile-time (because the resulting program is smaller) and at run-time (because there are fewer reductions to be done). In fact, this particular example can be optimized further. The expression

```
(B p I)
```

is the same as

```
p
```

For, applying (B p I) to any argument x, we see

```
     B p I x
  →  p (I x)
  →  p x
```

So we can use another optimization rule

```
B p I  ⇛  p
```

which optimizes our example further:

```
B – I  ⇛  –
```

This is a very good translation for (λx. – x), which is the same as that obtained by η-conversion. In fact the (B p I) optimization is just η-conversion in a new guise.

16.2.3 The C Combinator

Just as (B f g x) sends x into g but not f, so it is convenient to have a combinator C, which sends x into f but not g, thus

```
C f g x  →  f x g
```

The optimization rule for C is

```
S p (K q)  ⇛  C p q
```

Figure 16.3 summarizes the extra reduction and optimization rules we have developed so far. The validity of these rules can readily be proved using extensional equality. For example:

```
     S (K p) q x            B p q x
  →  K p x (q x)         →  p (q x)
  →  p (q x)
     Hence  S (K p) q = B p q
```

Reduction rules

```
B f g x  →  f (g x)
C f g x  →  f x g
```

Optimization rules

```
S (K p) (K q)  ⇛  K (p q)
S (K p) I      ⇛  p
S (K p) q      ⇛  B p q
S p (K q)      ⇛  C p q
```

Figure 16.3 B, C and K optimizations

A x ⟦ f ⟧	Abstracts x from f
A x ⟦ f_1 f_2 ⟧	= **Opt**⟦ S (**A** x ⟦ f_1 ⟧) (**A** x ⟦ f_2 ⟧) ⟧
A x ⟦ x ⟧	= I
A x ⟦ cv ⟧	= K cv

Opt⟦ e ⟧	**Opt**imizes e
Opt⟦ S (K p) (K q) ⟧	= K (p q)
Opt⟦ S (K p) I ⟧	= p
Opt⟦ S (K p) q ⟧	= B p q
Opt⟦ S p (K q) ⟧	= C p q
Opt⟦ S p q ⟧	= S p q

Figure 16.4 Modifications to SK compilation algorithm to include B and C

We can formalize the optimizations in the ⟦ ⟧ notation by introducing a new function **Opt**, which optimizes a combinator expression. Figure 16.4 shows the definition of **Opt** and a modified version of **A** which uses it.

Let us apply the new algorithm to the example in Section 16.1.2. We omit some of the steps, which are rather laborious.

C⟦ (λx. + x x) 5 ⟧
= **A** x ⟦ + x x ⟧ 5
= **Opt**⟦ S (**A** x ⟦ + x ⟧) I ⟧ 5
= **Opt**⟦ S **Opt**⟦ S (K +) I ⟧ I ⟧ 5
= **Opt**⟦ S + I ⟧ 5
= S + I 5

We can now evaluate the expression thus

S + I 5
→ + 5 (I 5)
→ 10

The compiled expression is much smaller, and the reduction sequence much shorter, than before.

16.2.4 The S′ Combinator

There remains one major opportunity for improving the code produced by the compilation algorithm. It occurs when abstracting many variables from an expression. Suppose we were compiling

$\lambda x_n \ldots \lambda x_2 . \lambda x_1 . p\ q$

where p and q are complicated expressions, which both use $x_1, x_2, \ldots, x_n$. We define

${}^1p$ = **A** x_1 ⟦ p ⟧
${}^2p$ = **A** x_2 ⟦ ${}^1p$ ⟧

and so on.

Now, we are going to have to abstract x_1, x_2, . . ., x_n in turn from (p q). This gives the following results:

Original expression	p q
First abstraction (x_1)	S ^{1}p ^{1}q
Second abstraction (x_2)	S (B S ^{2}p) ^{2}q
Third abstraction (x_3)	S (B S (B (B S) ^{3}p)) ^{3}q
Fourth abstraction (x_4)	S (B S (B (B S) (B (B (B S)) ^{4}p))) ^{4}q

The size of the expression expands *quadratically* with the number of variables abstracted. This happens because the combinators introduced by one abstraction complicate subsequent abstractions.

We would like to deal with the general problem of abstracting a variable, x_1, from

<combinator expression> p q

where <combinator expression> contains no variables. At the moment the abstraction goes like this:

A x_1 ⟦ <combinator expression> p q ⟧
= S (B <combinator expression> ^{1}p) ^{1}q

and it is the fact that we introduce *two* new combinators (S and B), one of which is nested, that causes the problem. Suppose we invent a new combinator, S′, with the following optimization rule

S (B x y) z ⇒ S′ x y z

Now we get a simpler abstraction:

A x_1 ⟦ <combinator expression> p q ⟧
= S′ <combinator expression> ^{1}p ^{1}q

We must choose the reduction rule for S′ to make this optimization valid, so

S′ c f g x
= S (B c f) g x (to make optimization valid)
→ B c f x (g x)
→ c (f x) (g x)

which gives us the reduction rule for S′, namely

S′ c f g x → c (f x) (g x)

Thus S′ is like S, but ‘reaches over’ one extra argument.

Let us see what effect the S′ optimization has on multiple abstraction:

Original expression	p q
First abstraction (x_1)	S ^{1}p ^{1}q
Second abstraction (x_2)	S′ S ^{2}p ^{2}q
Third abstraction (x_3)	S′ (S′ S) ^{3}p ^{3}q
Fourth abstraction (x_4)	S′ (S′ (S′ S)) ^{4}p ^{4}q

Now there is only a *linear* build-up of combinators as we perform successive abstractions. This key optimization renders the whole system practicable.

16.2.5 The B′ and C′ Combinators

Sometimes the variable being abstracted will only be used in p or q, so we need companion combinators B′ and C′, with reduction rules

```
B′ c f g x  →  c f (g x)
C′ c f g x  →  c (f x) g
```

each of which is like its undashed counterpart, except that it 'reaches over' one extra argument. We also need the corresponding optimization rules

```
B (c f) g     ⇛  B′ c f g
C (B c f) g   ⇛  C′ c f g
```

We can, as usual, show the correctness of these rules by showing that the two sides are extensionally equal, which follows directly from the definitions of the combinators.

The optimization rule for B′ is slightly surprising, since it does not look quite like the optimization rules for S′ and C′. Furthermore, the 'optimized' version requires no fewer reductions to evaluate than the 'unoptimized' version, and worse still, experiments show that this B′ optimization actually degrades performance!

This seems to have something to do with the B′ optimization rule. We gain nothing when introducting a B′, because the sizes of the two graphs are the same, and we actually lose an opportunity for optimization at an outer level, because we destroy a (B c f) pattern that might be useful in building an S′ or C′. For example, the expression

```
C (B (c f) g) h
```

will become

```
C (B′ c f g) h
```

if the B′ optimization is used, but will become

```
C′ (c f) g h
```

if not. A different combinator, B∗, has been suggested by Mark Sheevel of Burroughs Corp. It has the reduction rule

```
B∗ c f g x  →  c (f (g x))
```

and optimization rule

```
B c (B f g)  ⇛  B∗ c f g
```

This rule looks more like the optimization rules for S′ and C′, and experiments show that this B∗ does indeed give a performance improvement. This little tale serves to show that the choice of a set of combinators is by no means an entirely systematic process.

Figure 16.5 gives the final compilation algorithm, including all the optimizations we have discussed. The only point to notice is that the optimization rules for B∗ and C′ are expressed in terms of S, rather than going via the intermediate B and C forms. Figure 16.6 gives a summary of the reduction rules for each combinator.

```
      C[[ e ]]  Compiles e to SK combinators

C[[ e1 e2 ]] = C[[ e1 ]] C[[ e2 ]]
C[[ λx.e ]]  = A x [[ C[[ e ]] ]]
C[[ cv ]]    = cv
-----------------------------------------------------------------

      A x [[ f ]]  Abstracts x from f

A x [[ f1 f2 ]]    = Opt[[ S (A x [[ f1 ]]) (A x [[ f2 ]]) ]]
A x [[ x ]]        = I
A x [[ cv ]]       = K cv
-----------------------------------------------------------------

      Opt[[ e ]]  Optimizes e

Opt[[ S (K p) (K q) ]]        = K (p q)
Opt[[ S (K p) I ]]            = p
Opt[[ S (K p) (B q r) ]]      = B* p q r
Opt[[ S (K p) q ]]            = B p q
Opt[[ S (B p q) (K r) ]]      = C' p q r
Opt[[ S p (K q) ]]            = C p q
Opt[[ S (B p q) r ]]          = S' p q r
```

Figure 16.5 Final SK compilation algorithm

```
I x           →  x
K c x         →  c
S f g x       →  f x (g x)
B f g x       →  f (g x)
C f g x       →  f x g
S' c f g x    →  c (f x) (g x)
B* c f g x    →  c (f (g x))
C' c f g x    →  c (f x) g
```

Figure 16.6 Summary of combinator reduction rules

16.2.6 An Example

We conclude with an example of the compilation algorithm in action. The example is a function that implements Euclid's algorithm for finding the greatest common divisor (gcd) of two integers, a and b, where b≤a. In Miranda, the function is

```
gcd a b = a,       b=0
gcd a b = gcd b (a rem b)
```

where 'rem' is the built-in remainder function. Compiling to lambda expressions, we get

```
gcd = λa.λb.IF (= 0 b) a (gcd b (REM a b))
```

This is cheating slightly, because we should have dealt with the recursive call to gcd using Y, which would give

```
gcd = Y (λgcd.λa.λb.IF (= 0 b) a (gcd b (REM a b)))
```

However, the work is laborious enough without doing this, so we shall use the previous version. Abstracting first b and then a gives

```
gcd =   λa.λb.IF (= 0 b) a (gcd b (REM a b))
    ⇛   λa.S (C (B IF (= 0)) a) (S gcd (REM a))
    ⇛   S′ S (C (B IF (= 0))) (B (S gcd) REM)
```

We can test this by evaluating (gcd 35 7):

```
    gcd 35 7
=   S′ S (C (B IF (= 0))) (B (S gcd) REM) 35 7
→   S (C (B IF (= 0)) 35) (B (S gcd) REM 35) 7
→   C (B IF (= 0)) 35 7 (B (S gcd) REM 35 7)
→   B IF (= 0) 7 35 (B (S gcd) REM 35 7)
→   IF (= 0 7) 35 (B (S gcd) REM 35 7)
→   IF FALSE 35 (B (S gcd) REM 35 7)
→   B (S gcd) REM 35 7
→   S gcd (REM 35) 7
→   gcd 7 (REM 35 7)
=   S′ S (C (B IF (= 0))) (B (S gcd) REM) 7 (REM 35 7)
...
→   IF (= 0 (REM 35 7)) 7 (B (S gcd) REM 7 (REM 35 7))
→   IF (= 0 0) 7 (B (S gcd) REM 7 0)
→   IF TRUE 7 (B (S gcd) REM 7 0)
→   7
```

Combinator compilation and reduction is very simple but very laborious – a task well suited to a computer!

16.3 Director Strings

It seems at first that combinator compilation totally destroys the structure of the original expression, leaving a tangle of Ss and Ks, but this is not the case. Gaining insight into the structure of a combinator expression will lead us to a more efficient implementation.

16.3.1 The Basic Idea

Suppose we are abstracting a variable x_1 from an application (p q) where p and q are complicated expressions, and suppose it compiles to (S ^{1}p ^{1}q). (Recall that ^{1}p denotes the result of abstracting x_1 from p, and similarly ^{1}q.) The syntax trees of (p q) and (S ^{1}p ^{1}q) are

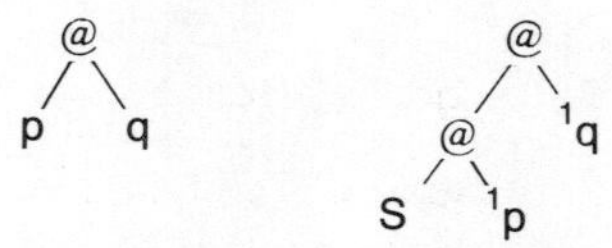

We could, however, regard the S as an *annotation* of the expression (^{1}p ^{1}q), and draw it thus:

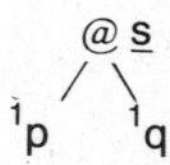

(S ^{1}p ^{1}q)

This annotated syntax tree is intended to be no more than an *alternative representation* for (S ^{1}p ^{1}q). The $\underline{s}$ annotates the application node, saying 'this node is a function expecting one argument, which should be sent into both branches'.

Suppose that we now abstracted another variable x_2 from (S ^{1}p ^{1}q), and got (C′ S ^{2}p ^{1}q); that is, x_2 is used in p but not in q. Then we could draw the annotated syntax tree like this:

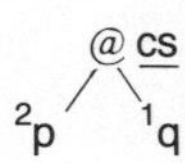

(C′ S ^{2}p ^{1}q)

The $\underline{cs}$ annotation says 'this node is a function of two arguments, the first of which should be sent to the left branch, and the second of which should be sent to both branches'. These annotations are called *director strings*, and consist of a string of *directors* which direct the flow of successive arguments into the graph. In addition to the $\underline{s}$ and $\underline{c}$ directors we also need a $\underline{b}$ director which directs the argument to the right branch only.

Director strings were developed by Kennaway and Sleep [1982a and 1982b], who used the more mnemonic symbols '^', '\' and '/' for $\underline{s}$, $\underline{b}$ and $\underline{c}$ respectively. The advantage of this representation is that it obviously preserves the original structure of the expression, and yet has a simple equivalent combinator form. In particular,

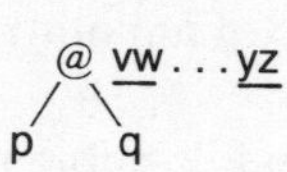

is equivalent to (V′ (W′ (...(Y′ Z)...)) p q)

where $\underline{v}$, $\underline{w}$... are chosen from {$\underline{s}$, $\underline{b}$, $\underline{c}$}, and V′, W′ ... Z are the corresponding combinators. To give a concrete example, consider the lambda abstraction

```
λx.λy.+ (+ x y) x
```

This has the syntax tree

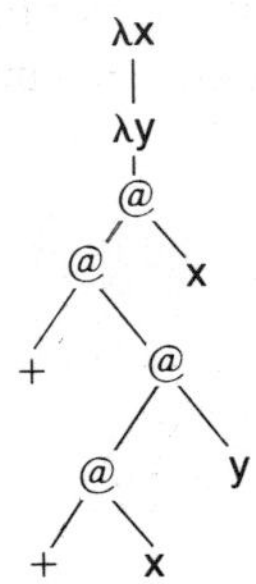

The annotated syntax tree, together with its associated combinator representation, looks like this:

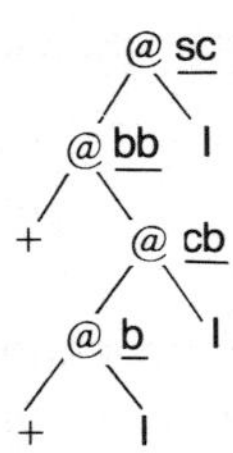

Annotated syntax tree

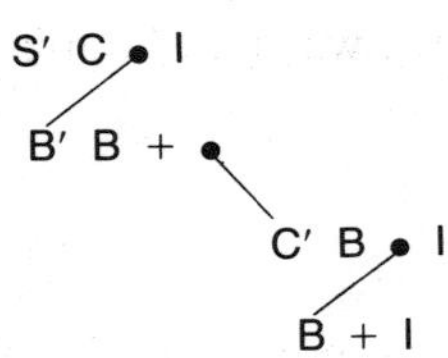

Combinator representation

The combinator representation is diagrammatic, and when flattened out looks like this:

```
S′ C (B′ B + (C′ B (B + I) I)) I
```

The Is in the left-hand tree indicate leaf nodes (they are *bona fide* I combinators). Some of these Is would not be present in the compiled combinator form because of η-optimization, so if we convert the annotated syntax tree to combinators we would get a slightly suboptimal combinator expression. Notice that not all nodes have the same number of annotations; the bottom node has only one because only x gets sent to it.

The simple equivalence between director strings and combinators mentioned above gives a more systematic basis for the choice of combinators we made in the first part of this chapter.

16.3.2 Minor Refinements

Consider the lambda abstraction

```
λx.λy.+ y 1
```

This does not use x at all, so we need a director which says 'the argument is not needed in either branch'. We call this director j. It can only occur at the root of a lambda abstraction, because in the rest of the expression the arguments are only sent where they are needed. Thus the lambda abstraction would have the annotated tree

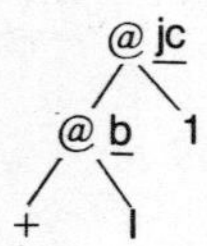

Corresponding to the director are the J and J′ combinators

```
J f g x    →  f g
J′ k f g x →  k f g
```

Another awkward problem is what to do when given a lambda abstraction such as

```
λx.λy.3
```

Here the body is not even an application, so we cannot annotate it. In this case we use the old K combinator for the λy abstraction, transforming it to

```
λx.K 3
```

Now the body is an application, so the annotation for x can go as before.

16.3.3 Director Strings as Combinators

We now turn our attention to the implementation of director strings.

So far we have two representations for programs, namely SK combinator expressions, and syntax trees annotated with directors. To each director there corresponds exactly one combinator in the combinator representation, each of which takes a whole node. Since there are only four directors (j, s, b and c), we could encode each director in two bits. Encoding a string of directors as a bit-string would give a dramatic decrease in program size over the combinator representation, since we would need only two bits instead of a whole node to store each combinator. This would make the program execute faster, too, since there would be less of it to fetch from store.

This suggests a third representation of the program:

Represent 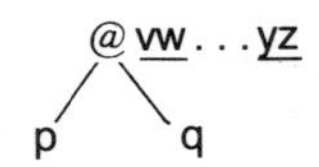 as 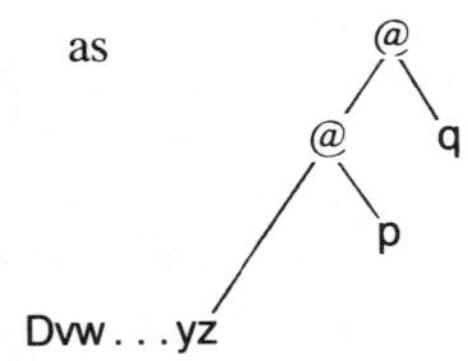

where Dvw...yz is one of a family of combinators with the following reduction rules:

```
Djvw...yz  p q x  →  Dvw...yz p q
Dsvw...yz  p q x  →  Dvw...yz (p x) (q x)
Dbvw...yz  p q x  →  Dvw...yz p (q x)
Dcvw...yz  p q x  →  Dvw...yz (p x) q
D                 →  I
```

This new representation, together with the D reduction rules, is a perfectly executable combinator program, except that it is represented much more compactly than the original. The only cost is a slight increase in the complexity of the reduction machine. An escape mechanism is also required to deal with the case where there are too many directors in the string to fit in the D combinator family. Stoye [1985] describes an implementation of director strings on SKIM.

16.4 The Size of SK Combinator Translations

One obvious feature of the examples given in this chapter is that the translated program is often much larger than in its lambda form; in fact Kennaway [1982] shows that the size of the combinator expression can be proportional to the square of the size of the lambda expression in the worst case. To become convinced of this, the reader is encouraged to construct the director string form of the lambda abstraction

$\lambda x_n \ldots \lambda x_2 . \lambda x_1 . (x_1\ x_2\ \ldots\ x_n)$

A closely related observation is that the SK combinator compiler repeatedly re-scans the code it has already partially compiled. This can be seen in the compilation rule

C⟦ λx.e ⟧ = **A** x ⟦ **C**⟦ e ⟧ ⟧

in Figure 16.5.

Burton [1982] describes a method for balancing the expression tree, at the expense of introducing extra redexes; this gives a complexity of $0(N \log N)$, but with a larger constant. Joy *et al.* [1985] summarize these and other related results.

By way of comparison, Hughes [1984] shows that the supercombinator technique has a worst case complexity of $0(N \log N)$, but is typically linear.

To conclude, for a lambda expression of size N, SK combinator compilation time and code size is worst case $0(N^2)$ and typically $0(N \log N)$, while supercombinator compilation time and code size is worst case $0(N \log N)$ and typically linear.

16.5 Comparison with Supercombinators

SK combinators represent one extreme of graph reduction techniques. Complex reductions are reduced to the composition of many fast, simple reductions, so the 'grain' of execution steps is about as small as it can conceivably be. This is a mixed blessing, and we attempt a summary of the pros and cons at this point.

16.5.1 In Favor of SK Combinators

(i) A small, fixed set of combinators can be implemented directly in hardware, thus bypassing a level of interpretation. This is analogous to moving from machine code to microcode.

(ii) The instantiation of lambda bodies is done lazily, thus avoiding instantiating sections of graph which are subsequently to be discarded.

(iii) The technique is fully lazy.

(iv) The reduction machine is relatively simple to implement.

16.5.2 Against SK Combinators

(i) The 'grain' of execution steps is too small. Since the arguments to a function are pushed down into its body one level at a time, many intermediate application nodes are created and almost immediately taken apart again. This means that an SK combinator reducer consumes a lot of transient storage, which increases the load on the garbage collector.

(ii) The translation to combinators is expensive compared with supercombinator techniques, and the resulting program is larger (see Section 16.4).

(iii) With SK combinators, the larger program increases the number of storage accesses required, as does the creation and subsequent examination of intermediate application nodes.

(iv) Any scheme for improving performance using cacheing must operate with a unit of cacheing of a single node. A supercombinator machine can cache whole supercombinator bodies, another consequence of the coarser grain of supercombinators.

References

Burton, F.W. 1982. A linear space translation of functional programs to Turner combinators. *Information Processing Letters*. Vol. 14, no. 5, pp. 202–4.

Curry, H.B., and Feys, R. 1958. *Combinatory Logic*, Vol. 1. North-Holland.

Hughes, R.J.M. 1984. The design and implementation of programming languages. PhD thesis, PRG-40. Programming Research Group, Oxford.

Joy, M.S., Rayward-Smith, V.J., and Burton, F.W. 1985. Efficient combinator code. *Computer Languages*. Vol. 10, no. 3/4, pp. 211–24.

Kennaway, J.R. 1982. *The Complexity of a Translation of Lambda Calculus to Combinators*. Department of Computer Science, University of East Anglia.

Kennaway, J.R., and Sleep, M.R. 1982a. *Director Strings as Combinators*. Department of Computer Science, University of East Anglia.

Kennaway, J.R., and Sleep, M.R. 1982b. *Counting Director Strings*. Department of Computer Science, University of East Anglia.

Richards, H. 1985. *An Overview of Burroughs NORMA*. Austin Research Center, Burroughs Corp., Austin, Texas. January.

Stoye, W.R. 1983. The SKIM microprogrammer's guide. *Technical Report 31*. University of Cambridge. October.

Stoye, W.R. 1985. The implementation of functional languages using custom hardware. PhD thesis, Computer Lab., University of Cambridge. May.

Turner, D.A. 1976. *SASL Reference Manual*. University of St Andrews.

Turner, D.A. 1979a. A new implementation technique for applicative languages. *Software – Practice and Experience*. Vol. 9, pp. 31–49.

Turner, D.A. 1979b. Another algorithm for bracket abstraction. *Journal of Symbolic Logic*. Vol. 44, no. 2, pp. 67–270.

Seventeen

STORAGE MANAGEMENT AND GARBAGE COLLECTION

As mentioned in Chapter 10, a graph reducer requires the support of a storage management system which allocates cells on request, and recovers garbage cells for subsequent re-use. Storage management and garbage collection is a subject on which there is a large literature. Cohen [1981] gives an excellent survey with a comprehensive list of references.

The purpose of this chapter is to sketch the standard algorithms, to give an assessment of their characteristics, and to make a brief survey of more recently developed techniques.

17.1 Criteria for Assessing a Storage Manager

When considering a garbage collection technique it is helpful to keep in mind the criteria against which it should be assessed. The main ones are:

(i) *What are its overheads* (in space and time)*?* All garbage collection systems consume resources, both in the form of per-cell extra storage requirements and in the CPU cycles taken to perform the collection.

(ii) *Does it support compaction?* If a storage manager repeatedly allocates, recovers and re-allocates variable-sized cells, the free storage tends to become fragmented into many small separate blocks. This can mean that a cell cannot be allocated because no free block is large enough, even though the total free storage is adequate. This phenomenon is known as *storage fragmentation* [Knuth, 1976], and it can only be avoided by periodically *compacting* all the cells together at one end of the address space, so as to produce a large contiguous free area from which to allocate new cells. Compaction also has a beneficial effect on virtual memory performance.

(iii) *How well does it support a sparsely used heap and virtual memory?* There has been much recent interest in very large *persistent* heaps. The idea of persistence is that a functional operating system, for example, could incorporate a filing system as part of its data structures in a very large heap, rather than treating the filing system as something external to the program (an idea first implemented in Multics). In such a system, only a small fraction of the heap will be in active use at any time, and a virtual memory system is essential to cache the active portion in fast memory.

(iv) *Can it operate on a parallel machine, or in real time?* One of the attractions of functional languages is that they offer a natural way to exploit the power of parallel architectures (see Chapter 24), which requires storage managers that are capable of running on such a distributed system.

Some garbage collection techniques require the computation to be stopped while garbage collection takes place, leading to an 'embarrassing pause' during which the system appears to do nothing. This is unacceptable in real-time applications, and garbage collectors have been proposed which work in parallel with the useful computation. Such parallel collectors may also be suitable for parallel architectures.

(v) *What is the effect of heap occupancy?* The performance of some algorithms drops sharply when the heap gets full.

(vi) *Can it recover cyclic structures?*

These issues are all discussed by Cohen.

17.2 A Sketch of the Standard Techniques

There are several well-known garbage collection techniques. Among these are *mark-scan*, *copying* and *reference-counting* garbage collectors. In this section we will give a brief sketch of the algorithms and their characteristics. Cohen [1981] is the reference where no reference is given explicitly.

Mark-scan algorithms operate in two phases. First, all accessible cells are *marked* by traversing the entire accessible structure. Then a linear scan through memory recovers all unmarked cells.

Copying algorithms work by copying the entire accessible structure from one portion of the address space (*from-space*) into another (*to-space*), thereby leaving all the garbage behind in from-space. Cells being copied into to-space are placed contiguously, beginning at one end of the space, and hence when copying is complete there is a contiguous area in to-space from which new cells can be allocated. When to-space fills up with new cells, the spaces are *flipped* (i.e. to-space becomes from-space and vice versa) and the process is repeated. The algorithm is surprisingly simple, and is well described in Baker's classic paper [1978].

Reference-counting relies on keeping an extra field, called the *reference-count*, in each cell. The reference-count field holds the number of references to the cell (i.e. the number of pointers to the cell). This count is incremented whenever a pointer is duplicated, and decremented whenever a pointer is discarded. When the reference-count drops to zero the cell must be garbage, since no other cells point to it.

Against our criteria, the techniques have the following characteristics.

(i) *Overheads.* A *mark-scan* collector requires a *mark bit* in each cell to indicate that the cell has been visited. In addition it appears at first that the mark phase will require an auxiliary *stack* to guide its recursive tree-walk. Furthermore, the only bound on the size of this stack is the number of cells in the heap, though this bound would only be attained in pathological cases. This would be a heavy price to pay, but fortunately the Deutsch–Schorr–Waite pointer-reversing algorithm [Schorr and Waite, 1967] reduces the space overheads of the mark phase algorithm to a single bit per cell (in addition to the mark bit). This algorithm was explained in a different context in Section 11.6.1.

Copying collectors appear to have a 100% space overhead, but in a virtual memory system the semi-space that is not in use will be paged out, so there is very little overhead in fast memory. Even during copying, activity only takes place at two sites in the target semi-space (to-space), so only two pages of to-space need to be paged in.

Reference-counting collectors require a reference-count field in every cell. In principle this field should be as wide as an address, since every cell in the heap could point to a single cell, but in practice reference-counts are almost always small. Hybrid systems have therefore been proposed, which have a limited-width reference-count field. When there are too many references to a cell and the reference-count field overflows it is set to a special value meaning 'infinity', which is never decremented (so the cell is then irrecoverable). Cells irrecoverable by reference-counting are subsequently recovered by an occasional invocation of a mark-scan or copying collector.

Reference-counting collectors are also somewhat less easy to use. Great care must be taken in the implementation never to duplicate a reference without incrementing the reference-count, though this is not, of course, a criticism of the adequacy of the algorithm itself. More seriously, many extra storage accesses are required to update the reference-counts.

(ii) *Compaction.* Compaction can be combined with the scanning phase of a *mark-scan* collector. This is usually done using *sliding compaction*, in which cells are slid down to one end of the address space, maintaining their address order. This means that cells which point to each other will not normally end up physically adjacent.

A *copying* collector is inherently compacting, since the cells are copied into a contiguous area in to-space. Furthermore, it is fairly easy to arrange that cells that point to one another get copied into physically adjacent locations, which significantly improves *locality* and gives opportunities for extra-compact list representations (*cdr-coding*) [Baker, 1978]. This process is sometimes called *linearizing* since linked lists get copied into a contiguous linear area of store, and it further reduces the storage overheads of a copying collector. The improvement in locality may also give improved paging performance in a virtual memory system.

Reference-counting does not inherently perform any compaction, but there is no reason why a compactor could not run concurrently with a reference-counting garbage collector.

(iii) *Sparsely used heap/virtual memory. Mark-scan* and *copying* collectors visit all accessible cells, not just those in immediate use. In contrast, *reference-counting* collectors visit only cells in current use. For heaps in which only a small fraction of the accessible data is in active use, this represents a strong advantage for reference-counting.

Without compaction the accessible cells get thinly spread through the address space, giving appalling paging behavior. The locality-improving possibilities of copying collectors (or reference-counting plus a copying compactor), mentioned above, thus make them preferable to sliding compaction.

(iv) *Parallel machines and real-time performance.* Since garbage collection began, researchers have tried to find ways to run garbage collection in parallel with useful computation, in an endeavor to eliminate the 'embarrassing pause'. For *mark-scan* collectors this may be achieved by arranging that garbage collection is performed by a process (or processor) *in parallel with* useful computation. The algorithm is, of course, more complicated [Steele, 1975; Kung and Wong, 1977; Dijkstra *et al.*, 1978].

For *copying* collectors, an ingenious scheme allows the copying process to take place incrementally, a fixed small amount being performed whenever a cell is allocated [Baker, 1978]. This scheme increases the overheads of the useful computation somewhat, in both time and space, and fails completely if to-space fills up before copying is completed.

Reference-counting collectors are inherently distributed in time, and hence need no modification for real-time performance.

(v) *Effect of heap occupancy.* The performance of *mark-scan* and *copying* collectors degrades sharply as the heap gets full, since all the accessible data have to be visited in order to recover the few unused cells. *Reference-counting*, on the other hand, is unaffected by heap occupancy.

(iv) *Cyclic structures. Mark-scan* and *copying* collectors have no problem with cyclic structures, but *reference-counting* cannot recover them. The reason is that when a cell refers to itself it may have a non-zero reference-count even though it is not accessible from anywhere else (and hence is garbage). Recent developments in this area are discussed below.

17.3 Developments in Reference-counting

The overheads of reference-counting, and its inability to recover cyclic structures, have often led to its dismissal as a garbage collection technique, except in specialized contexts. However, recent work has made progress towards alleviating these problems, and the inherently real-time and distributed nature of reference-counting is becoming increasingly attractive as parallel architectures gain in importance.

17.3.1 Reference-counting Garbage Collection of Cyclic Structures

Hughes [1982] has suggested an extension to the conventional reference-counting algorithm that would allow it to reclaim circular structures, based on previous work by Bobrow [1980].

The key idea is simple and elegant. We regard the accessible data in the heap as a *directed graph*, and divide this graph into its *strongly connected components*. In this context we recall that

(i) a graph is *strongly connected* if, for any two nodes A and B, there is a path from A to B, and vice versa;
(ii) a *strongly connected component* of a graph is a maximal strongly connected subgraph.

Now, it is clear that

(i) if one node of a strongly connected component is accessible, then all its nodes are (and vice versa);
(ii) if we coalesce all the nodes in each strongly connected component, then the resulting *derived graph* is acyclic.

But now, since the derived graph is acyclic, it is amenable to conventional reference-counting garbage collection; and when a node of the derived graph becomes unreferenced, all the nodes of the corresponding strongly connected component have become unreferenced.

Hughes therefore suggests adding a second reference-count field to each node, which either contains the *shared reference-count* for the strongly connected component of which the node is a part, or is used to point at the node which does hold the shared reference-count. He gives algorithms for incrementally maintaining the information about which components are strongly connected, and shows that they are rather cheap, except where a strongly connected component is broken up.

It appears that this technique can successfully alleviate the ‘circular data structure problem', and thus allow exploitation of the other desirable characteristics of reference-counting. Aertes [1981] describes an essentially identical system. Brownbridge [1985] describes a different reference-counting technique, also claimed to be capable of recovering circular structures.

Interestingly, all of these techniques will only work for implementations free of side-effects. In other words, they will work for implementations of functional languages, but not for Lisp (at least, not if the program uses RPLACs). Perhaps this is a new point in favor of functional languages!

17.3.2 One-bit Reference-counts

The logical extreme of the limited width reference-count idea is a one-bit reference-count field. This is not a new idea [Wise and Friedman, 1977].

Recently, however, a number of researchers noticed that instead of storing a one-bit reference-count *in the cell* it would be possible to store the reference-count *in the pointer*. A single bit in each pointer identifies the pointer as being a *unique reference* or a *shared reference*. Cells are created with a unique reference to them; when a unique reference is duplicated, *both* copies become shared references. When a unique reference is discarded the cell to which it points can be immediately re-used; when a shared reference is discarded no recovery is possible. Like all elegant ideas it is marvellously obvious in retrospect.

The principal advantage of storing the reference-count in the pointer is that it completely eliminates the extra store accesses required to increment and decrement reference-counts.

The benefits of even such a narrow reference-count are dramatic. Stoye *et al.* [1984] report that up to 70% of all garbage cells are recovered immediately they become unused in the SKIM SK combinator reduction machine. Further performance improvement is gained in the SKIM implementation because reclaimed cells are often re-used immediately, rather than being attached to the free list.

17.3.3 Hardware Support for Reference-counting

Much of the time overhead of reference-counting would be alleviated if hardware support were available. Wise [1985] describes hardware for a 'smart' memory module, capable of detecting when one pointer is overwritten with another. When this occurs, the module sends a 'decrement' message to the module which holds the cell pointed to by the old pointer, and an 'increment' message to the module which holds the cell pointed to by the new pointer.

17.4 Shorting out Indirection Nodes

In Chapter 12 we discussed the introduction of *indirection nodes* to preserve sharing when updating the root of a redex with its result. This is the only purpose of indirection nodes, and in all other respects they are a burden on the implementation, since they take up storage, and have to be 'jumped over' when traversing the graph.

It turns out that a rather simple modification to the garbage collector can 'short out' all the indirection nodes in a graph, so they are no longer required. Consider a mark-scan collector. When it reaches an indirection node during the mark phase, it does not mark the indirection node. Instead it overwrites the pointer to the indirection node with the contents of the indirection, effectively shorting it out. Thus:

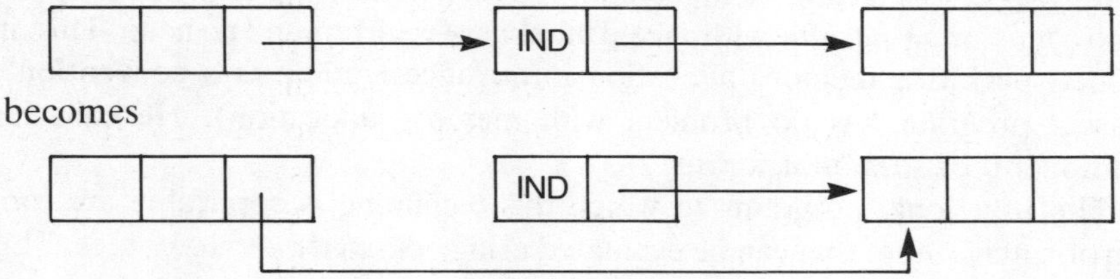

Since all pointers to indirection nodes will be updated in this way it follows that the indirection nodes themselves will be unreferenced (and unmarked), so they can be collected with the rest of the garbage. Not only does this save store, but it also saves time when following the pointers that have been updated. A very similar technique will work for a copying collector.

17.5 Exploiting Cell Lifetimes

Another approach recently suggested by Lieberman and Hewitt [1983] is based on the observation that

> The longer a cell has lived,
> the longer it is likely to live.

Consider, for example, a heap which includes a filing system. Many files will be unused for long periods, while data structures that are currently being processed will have relatively short lifetimes. A conventional copying collector will copy the entire filing system each time it runs – a very wasteful activity, since it is unlikely to recover any space from the inactive majority of the filing system.

Hewitt and Lieberman therefore suggest dividing the address space into *regions* of increasing age. Most pointers point backwards in time (that is, if they cross region boundaries, they will mostly point from younger regions to older ones). Where pointers point from an older region into a younger one (only update operations can cause this), they are constrained to go via an *entry table* associated with the younger region.

Now the youngest region can be garbage-collected *independently*, using Baker's algorithm, so long as we preserve all cells referenced from its entry table. In general, any region can be garbage-collected without touching any older information. So all we have to do is to garbage-collect young regions (where garbage collection will be fruitful) more often than older ones (where it will be less fruitful, but eventually necessary).

17.6 Avoiding Garbage Collection

Another approach to garbage collection is to try to avoid it altogether. Wadler [1984] suggests a technique for compiling a certain class of functional program into a *finite state machine* with a fixed number of registers and no heap. This, in effect, performs memory allocation in advance (rather as a conventional Pascal program has no problem with memory allocation). He calls his compiler the *listless transformer.*

The functional programs to which this technique is applicable are, not surprisingly, those that can be evaluated using *bounded internal storage*. This includes, for example, functions that find the length of a list, add up a list, concatenate or merge two lists, or divide a list into two lists of odd and even elements. It excludes, however, functions that sort a list, append a list to itself, or work on tree-shaped data.

Clearly the applicability of the method is limited, but where appropriate it is extremely effective, since the finite state machine can be made very fast.

Wadler has a working implementation of his listless transformer, written in KRC.

17.7 Garbage Collection in Distributed Systems

Efforts to develop garbage collectors which work in parallel with useful computation have gained new impetus with the advent of parallel architectures, where the problem generalizes to many computation and garbage collection processes.

Most work has been addressed to architectures with a single large address space (*closely coupled* systems), for example Hudak [1983a and 1983b] and Ben-Ari [1984].

Other efforts have been directed towards *loosely coupled* systems in which the heap is distributed between a number of processing elements, and accessing a cell held by another processing element is recognized as a relatively expensive operation. Examples include Mohamed-Ali [1984] and Hughes [1985].

References

Aertes, J.P.H. 1981. *Implementing SASL without Garbage Collection*. EUT-Report 81-WSK-05. Eindhoven Univ. of Technology. November.

Baker, H. 1978. List processing in real time on a serial computer. *Communications of the ACM*. Vol. 21, no. 4, pp. 280–94.

Ben-Ari, M. 1984. Algorithms for on-the-fly garbage collection. *ACM TOPLAS*. Vol. 6, no. 3, pp. 333–44.

Bobrow, D.G. 1980. Managing reentrant structures using reference-counts. *ACM TOPLAS*. Vol. 2, no. 3, pp. 269–73.

Brownbridge, D. 1985. Cyclic reference-counting for combinator machines. In *Proceedings of the IFIP Conference on Functional Programming and Computer Architecture, Nancy*. September.

Cohen, J. 1981. Garbage collection of linked data structures. *ACM Computing Surveys*. Vol. 13, no. 3, pp. 341–67.

Dijkstra, E.W., Lamport, L., Martin, A.J., Scholten, C.S., and Steffens, E.F.M. 1978. On-the-fly garbage collection – an exercise in cooperation. *Communications of the ACM*. Vol. 21, no. 11, pp. 966–75.

Hudak, P. 1983a. *Distributed Graph Marking*. Research report 268, Computer Science Dept, Yale. January.

Hudak, P. 1983b. Distributed task and memory management. In *Proceedings of the ACM Symposium on Principles of Distributed Computing*, pp. 277–89. August.

Hughes, R.J.M. 1982. *Reference-counting with Circular Structures in Virtual Memory Applicative Systems*. Programming Research Group, Oxford.

Hughes, R.J.M. 1985. A distributed garbage collection algorithm. In *Proceedings of the IFIP Conf. on Functional Programming and Computer Architecture, Nancy*, pp. 256–72. Jouannaud (editor). LNCS 201, Springer Verlag. September.

Knuth, D. 1976. *The Art of Computer Programming*. Vol. I, Section 2.5. Addison Wesley.

Kung, H.T., and Wong, S.W. 1977. *An Efficient Parallel Garbage Collection System, and its Correctness Proof*. Dept of Comp. Sci., Carnegie-Mellon Univ. September.

Lieberman, H., and Hewitt, C. 1983. A real time garbage collector based on the lifetimes of objects. *Communications of the ACM*. Vol. 26, no. 6, pp. 419–29.

Mohamed-Ali, K.A. 1984. Object oriented storage management and garbage collection in distributed processing systems. PhD Thesis, report TRITA-CS-8406. Royal Institute of Technology, Stockholm. December.

Schorr, H., and Waite, W. 1967. An efficient machine independent procedure for garbage collection. *Communications of the ACM*. Vol. 10, no. 8, pp. 501–6.

Steele, G.L. 1975. Multiprocessing compactifying garbage collection. *Communications of the ACM*. Vol. 18, no. 9, pp. 495–508.

Stoye, W.R., Clarke, T.J.W., and Norman, A.C. 1984. Some practical methods for rapid combinator reduction. In *Proceedings of the ACM Symposium on Lisp and Functional Programming, Austin*, pp. 159–66. August.

Wadler, P. 1984. Listlessness is better than laziness: lazy evaluation and garbage collection at compile-time. In *Proceedings of the ACM Symposium on Lisp and Functional Programming, Austin*, pp. 45–52. August.

Wise, D. 1985. Design for a multiprocessing heap with on-board reference-counting. In *Functional Programming and Computer Architecture, Nancy*, pp. 289–304. Jouannaud (editor). LNCS 201. Springer Verlag.

Wise, D.S., and Friedman, D.P. 1977. The one-bit reference-count. *BIT*. Vol. 17, no. 3, pp. 351–9.

Part III

ADVANCED GRAPH REDUCTION

Eighteen

THE G-MACHINE

The heart of any graph reducer is the implementation of function application. In Chapter 12 we saw that a lambda abstraction can be applied to an argument by constructing an instance of the body of the abstraction with substitutions made for occurrences of the formal parameter. Unfortunately, this involved an inefficient traversal of the tree representing the body of the abstraction, and the presence of free variables seemed to make a more efficient implementation rather difficult.

With this in mind, we developed the supercombinator transformation in Chapter 13, which yielded particularly simple lambda abstractions (the supercombinators), which had no free variables. This simplified the process of instantiating the body of such an abstraction, but at the (minor) price of having to substitute for several variables at once. However, the principal incentive for developing the supercombinator transformation was the hope of compiling the body of a supercombinator to a fixed sequence of instructions which, when executed, would construct an instance of its body.

The payoff comes in this chapter, in which we will examine the G-machine, an extremely fast implementation of graph reduction based on supercombinator compilation. The G-machine was developed at the Chalmers Institute of Technology, Göteborg, Sweden, by Johnsson and Augustsson. This chapter and the subsequent three chapters draw heavily on the G-machine papers [Johnsson, 1984; Augustsson, 1984]. Many of the ideas in these chapters are theirs, and not all of them have appeared in the published literature.

The development of the G-machine is presented informally, but it would be an interesting exercise to give a formal proof of its correctness [Lester, 1985].

18.1 Using an Intermediate Code

Once we have decided to compile supercombinator bodies to a sequence of instructions we have to decide on the language in which the instructions should be written. It would be possible to produce, say, VAX machine code directly, but this approach suffers from two disadvantages. Firstly, we would have to start all over again if we want to generate code for some other machine, and, secondly, we would be in danger of mixing up the issues of how to compile supercombinators to a sequential code with issues of how best to exploit particular features of the VAX.

This is not a new problem, and a common solution is to define an *intermediate code*, which can be regarded as the machine code for an abstract sequential machine. Then the compilation process can be split into two parts: first generate the intermediate code, and then generate target code for a particular machine from the intermediate code. Changing the code generator to generate code for a different target machine is then relatively easy, and improvements made in the compilation to intermediate code benefit all such code generators. Examples of this approach include Pascal's P-code [Clark, 1981], BCPL's O-code [Richards, 1971] and Portable Standard Lisp's C-macros [Griss and Hearn, 1981].

18.1.1 G-code and the G-machine Compiler

For these reasons, the designers of the G-machine defined an intermediate code called G-code, into which supercombinator bodies are compiled. The compiler for the G-machine follows a sequence similar to that described in the first two parts of this book. In particular:

(i) The source language is a variant of ML with lazy evaluation semantics, called Lazy ML (or LML).
(ii) Early phases of the compiler perform type-checking, compile pattern-matching and do dependency analysis. At this stage the program has been translated to the lambda calculus (augmented with let and letrec).
(iii) A lambda-lifter transforms the program to supercombinator form. The full laziness optimization is not performed, but his feature could easily be added.
(iv) Now the supercombinators are compiled to G-code.
(v) Finally, machine code for the target machine is generated from the G-code.

Figure 18.1 shows the structure of the G-machine compiler.

Our description of the G-machine compiler falls into three parts:

(i) a description of the compilation algorithm which translates the source language into the intermediate code;
(ii) a description of the intermediate code itself, giving a precise description of what each instruction does;

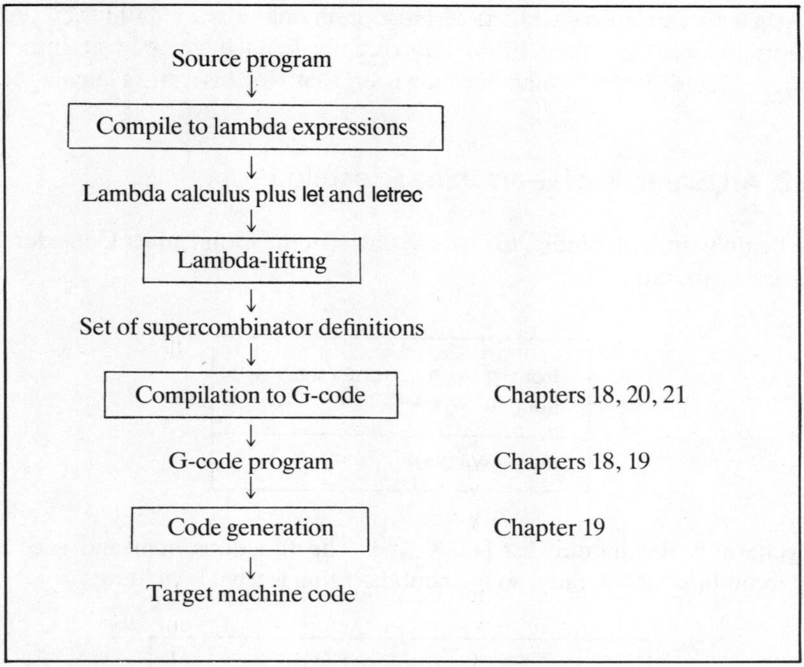

Figure 18.1 Structure of the G-machine compiler

(iii) a description of the code generator.

We will discuss the first of these parts in this chapter and the latter two in the next chapter. First, however, we will mention some related work.

18.1.2 Other Fast Sequential Implementations of Lazy Languages

The implementation of Ponder [Fairbairn, 1982], developed by Fairbairn and Wray, is based on a similar approach to the G-machine. The Ponder Abstract Machine (PAM) is at least as sophisticated as the G-machine, though they were developed independently, and is described in Fairbairn's thesis [Fairbairn, 1985; Fairbairn and Wray, 1986]. An interesting development of this work is a cross-compiler which compiles Ponder abstract machine instructions into SKIM microcode [Elworthy, 1985].

A related approach, though one which diverges from graph reduction, is to use a lexically scoped dialect of Lisp, such as Scheme [Steele and Sussman, 1978] or T [Rees and Adams, 1982], as an intermediate code. This takes advantage of the immense amount of effort which has been spent on building fast Lisp implementations, and is the approach taken by Hudak [Hudak and Kranz, 1984].

A fast VAX implementation of Hope [Burstall *et al.*, 1980] based on an intermediate code called FP/M has recently been developed at Imperial College [Field, 1985] (remember, however, that Hope is a strict language).

18.2 An Example of G-machine Execution

We begin with an example, to give the flavor of the G-machine. Consider the Miranda program

```
from n = n : from (succ n)
succ n = n+1
-------------------------
from (succ 0)
```

It generates the infinite list [1,2,3,. . .,]. The functions from and succ are supercombinators already, so the lambda-lifting is trivial, yielding

```
$from n = CONS n ($from ($succ n))
$succ n = + n 1
$Prog = $from ($succ 0)
------------------------------
$Prog
```

The G-machine uses a stack, and execution begins with a pointer to the initial graph on top of the stack (Figure 18.2(a)). The spine is then unwound, exactly as previously discussed in Section 11.6, without using pointer-reversal. The difference comes when the spine has been completely unwound, so that there is a pointer to $from on the stack (see Figure 18.2(b)). By following this pointer the machine extracts

(i) the number of arguments expected by $from (one in this case);
(ii) the starting address for the code for $from.

First it checks that there are enough arguments on the stack for $from to execute, and finds that there are. It then rearranges the top of the stack slightly (see the transition from (b) to (c) in Figure 18.2) and then jumps to the code for $from. The rearrangement of the top of the stack puts a pointer to the argument to $from on top of the stack. We will discuss the stack rearrangement in more detail later. Notice also that the machine *jumps* to $from rather than *calling* it. An instruction at the end of $from will complete evaluation of the graph after the $from reduction is done.

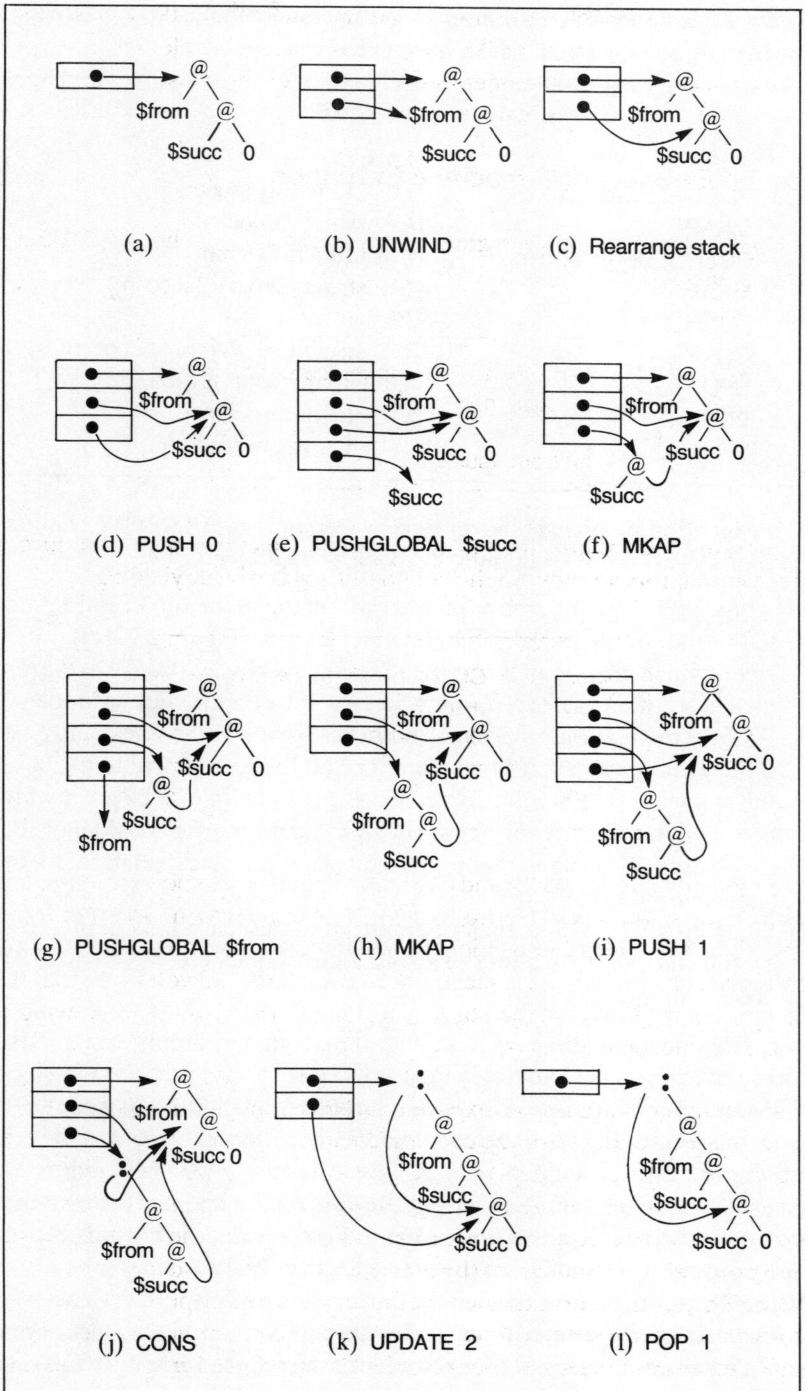

Figure 18.2 Evaluation of ($from ($succ 0))

Control has now passed to $from. A G-machine compiler will produce the following G-code for $from, which is executed in sequence:

G-code for function $from

```
PUSH 0;               Push n
PUSHGLOBAL $succ;     Push function $succ
MKAP;                 Construct ($succ n)
PUSHGLOBAL $from;     Push function $from
MKAP;                 Construct ($from ($succ n))
PUSH 1;               Push n
CONS;                 Construct (n : ($from ($succ n)))
UPDATE 2;             Update the root of the redex
POP 1;                Pop the parameter n
UNWIND;               Initiate next reduction
```

The execution of $from is shown step by step in Figure 18.2. We can make several observations by examining the code given above:

(i) At the point of entry, the parameter n is on top of the stack, and a pointer to the root of the redex is immediately below it (Figure 18.2(c)).

(ii) Items which are not on top of the stack are addressed *relative to the top of the stack*, with the top element having offset zero. For example, the PUSH 1 instruction takes the element next to top in the stack, and pushes it onto the stack. Stack items cannot be addressed relative to the base of the stack because a reduction takes place at the tip of the spine, with an unknown number of vertebrae above. (An alternative would have been to assume a frame pointer, and relegate offset calculation to code generation time.)

(iii) Some instructions take their operands from the stack and put their result on the stack in the manner of a zero address machine. MKAP and CONS are examples of such instructions.

Apart from the last three instructions, the sequence simply constructs an instance of the body of $from (see Figure 18.2(l)).

The UPDATE 2 instruction updates the root of the redex with a copy of the root of the result (there is a slight inefficiency here, since the root of the result is discarded almost immediately it is constructed; we will address this efficiency question later). Notice that the G-machine updates the root of the redex using copying, rather than using indirection nodes (but this is not an inherent property of the G-machine – see Section 19.4.4).

The POP 1 instruction removes the parameters (only one in this case) from the stack, leaving a pointer to the reduced graph on top of the stack. Finally UNWIND examines the tag of the root node of the reduced graph. In this case it is a CONS cell, so evaluation is complete.

This concludes our example, for now. (Note: in order to reduce the number of execution steps, the example contains some optimizations which we will not study until Chapter 20.)

We will now develop the G-machine in a stepwise fashion, beginning with a very simple implementation, and developing the compilation algorithm and the G-code together. First, however, we will specify the language from which we are compiling.

18.3 The Source Language for the G-compiler

The compilation to G-code begins with a program consisting of a number of supercombinator definitions of the form

```
$S x1 x2 ... xn = E
```

where E is an expression containing no lambdas, but which may contain lets and letrecs. Figure 18.3 gives a reminder of the syntax of expressions. Notice

```
<E> ::= <constant>
     |  <identifier>
     |  <let> <E>
     |  let <identifier> = <E> in <E>
     |  letrec <identifier> = <E>
                ...
              <identifier> = <E>
        in <E>
```

Figure 18.3 BNF for syntax of expressions

that the left-hand side of a definition in a let or letrec can consist only of a single variable; local function definitions have been removed by lambda-lifting. For example,

```
let f x = + x 1
in E
```

cannot occur. Notice also that we allow only one definition in a let. Multiple definitions can be handled by nested lets, and the restriction slightly simplifies the compiler.

It is worth having a formal description of the syntax, because our compiler will need to contain a case for each construct. Referring to the syntax enables us to confirm that all cases have been covered.

To save repetitive work in this chapter we will use a stripped-down set of built-in functions and constants, shown in Figure 18.4. The stripped-down set has been chosen to illustrate all the features of the compiler. The operators in the right-hand column behave exactly like those in the left-hand column.

Assuming that we implement lists with structure tag 1 for NIL and 2 for

Stripped-down set	*Others which behave similarly*
integer constants	boolean, character constants
NEG (unary negation)	NOT
+	−, *, /, REM $<, \leq, =, \geq, >$
IF	CASE-n
FATBAR	
CONS	PACK-SUM-d-r, PACK-PRODUCT-r
HEAD	TAIL, SEL-r-i, SEL-SUM-r-i

Figure 18.4 Built-in functions and constants

CONS, we use CONS, HEAD and TAIL as abbreviations for PACK-SUM-2-2, SEL-SUM-2-1 and SEL-SUM-2-2 respectively. These abbreviations are easier to remember, and are used in the G-machine papers.

We do not treat UNPACK, since it is eliminated by the transformation described in Chapter 6.

We will postpone a treatment of the FATBAR function until Chapter 20.

18.4 Compilation to G-code

For the rest of this chapter we will discuss the compilation of supercombinator definitions to G-code, leaving the code generation for the next chapter.

The compilation of a program to G-code and its execution by the G-machine are purely optimizations to the simpler template-instantiation implementation. We begin with the simplest possible G-machine, where the connection with template-instantiation is very direct. Later on, in Chapters 20 and 21, we will develop a number of optimizations which considerably speed up the operation of the machine.

The G-code compilation algorithm behaves like this:

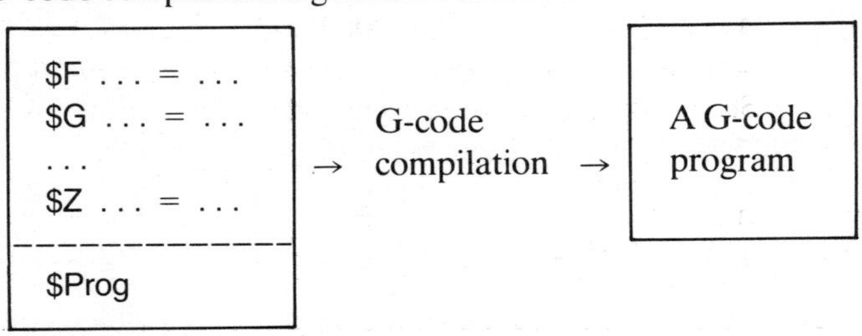

The compilation algorithm takes a set of supercombinator definitions, together with a distinguished one ($Prog), and produces a G-code program. The G-code program will consist of the following parts:

(i) A segment of initialization code, which will perform any run-time initialization necessary.
(ii) A segment of G-code which evaluates the distinguished supercombinator $Prog and prints its value. This will probably follow immediately after (i).
(iii) A segment of G-code corresponding to each supercombinator definition. Each of these will be identified by an initial label.
(iv) Labelled segments of G-code corresponding to each built-in function (such as + or CONS). This constitutes the run-time library, since it is the same for all programs.

The code segments for (i) and (ii) can be fairly simple. All we need for (i) is a G-code instruction BEGIN which labels the beginning of the program and initializes anything necessary. Then to evaluate $Prog we will first push it onto the stack (using a G-code instruction PUSHGLOBAL), then evaluate it (using the EVAL instruction) and then print it (using the PRINT instruction). Here is a code sequence that could be generated to initialize the system and print $Prog:

```
BEGIN;                    Beginning of program

PUSHGLOBAL $Prog;         Push $Prog onto stack
EVAL;                     Evaluate it
PRINT;                    Print the result

END                       End of program
```

We have felt free to invent G-code instructions out of thin air to perform the steps of the program. We will continue to do this, and will wait until the next chapter before giving them a more precise meaning. The EVAL instruction is discussed in Section 18.8.1.

We now turn our attention to (iii), compiling code for supercombinators, leaving (iv) for Section 18.8.

18.5 Compiling a Supercombinator Definition

We may depict the compilation of a supercombinator definition like this:

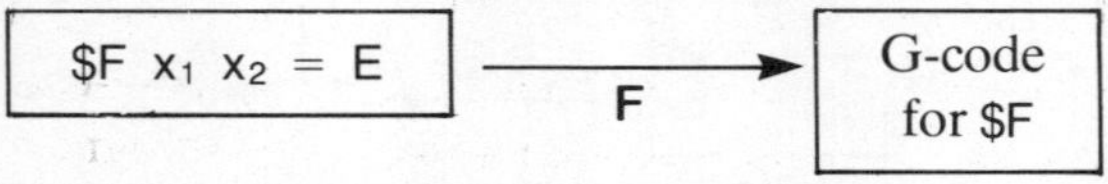

We can regard the compiler as a *function* F, which takes a supercombinator definition as its argument, and returns the compiled G-code as its result. Using the [[ ]] notation:

$$F[\![\ \$F\ x_1\ x_2 = E\ ]\!] = \ldots \text{G-code for \$F} \ldots$$

We call the function **F** a *compilation scheme*, and we will use a number of other compilation schemes as auxiliary functions to **F**. Using this notation will allow us to express quite subtle compilation techniques in a compact and elegant way.

Now we will 'turn up the magnification' still more, and consider what the G-code for $F might look like. Before we can do this we must establish the context in which the code for $F will execute, and in particular the configuration of the stack which $F expects.

18.5.1 Stacks and Contexts

Suppose the G-machine was evaluating the expression ($F p q r s), and $F was a supercombinator of two arguments. After the spine of the graph has been unwound, the stack would look like this:

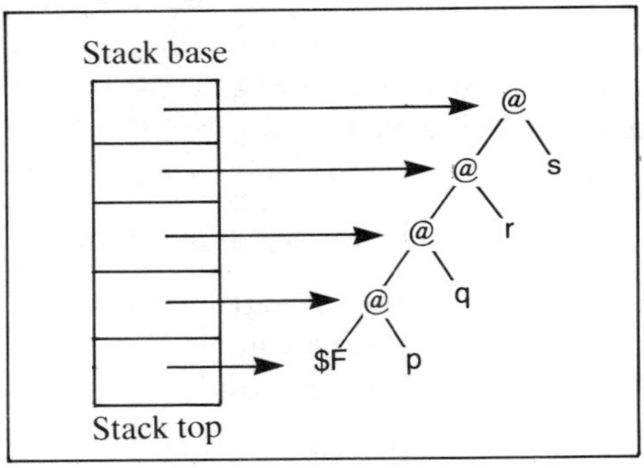

(In all the pictures the stack grows downwards.) This is not the most convenient configuration during execution of $F, because in order to access the arguments p and q it needs to do an indirect access via the vertebrae. The solution is to rearrange the stack after unwinding is complete, and before the supercombinator is executed, so that the elements on the stack point directly to the arguments, thus:

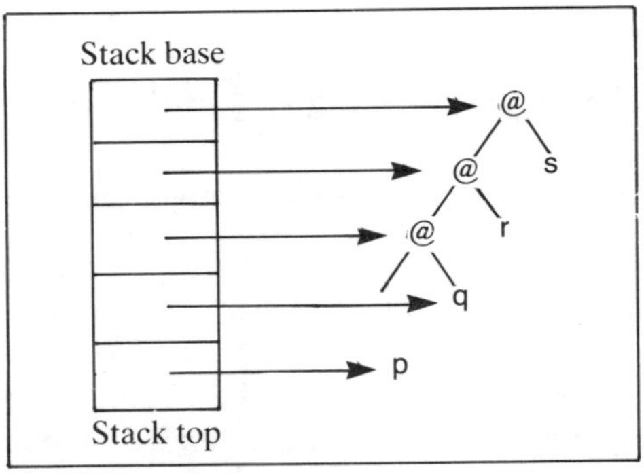

The rest of the spine is still there, of course, but it has not been drawn. Notice that we do retain a pointer to the root of the redex, because we will subsequently need to update it. Now the arguments p and q are conveniently accessible. The supercombinator $F itself has been popped off, because this stack rearrangement is actually carried out by a prelude to the target code for $F.

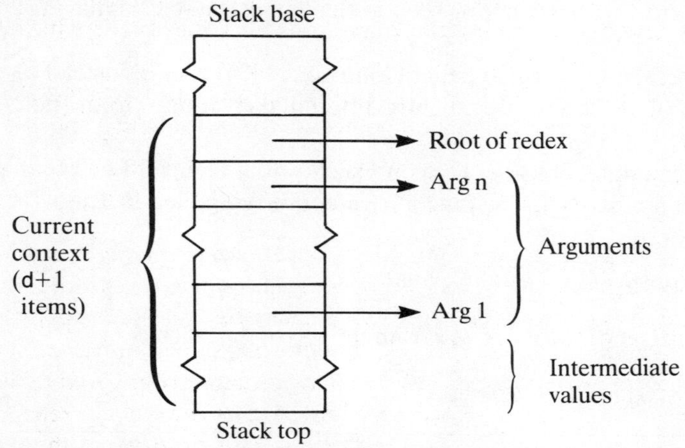

Figure 18.5 The stack during G-code execution

We see, therefore, that during the execution of the G-code for a supercombinator, the stack looks like Figure 18.5. The section at the top of the stack, including the pointer to the root of the current redex, the arguments and the intermediate values, is called the *current context*. It always sits at the top end of the stack, but there may be other stack elements between the stack base and the base of the current context. At the end of the execution of a function, the root of the redex will be updated and all the items in the context will be popped, leaving only the pointer to the root of the redex.

To summarize, here are two ground rules, which will hold throughout:

(1) When execution of (the code corresponding to) a supercombinator body begins, the arguments are on top of the stack, and underneath them is a pointer to the root of the redex.
(2) When execution of the supercombinator completes, only the pointer to the reduced graph remains on the stack. The reduced graph is not necessarily in WHNF, so the last instruction in the supercombinator initiates the next reduction.

During compilation of a supercombinator the compiler needs to maintain a model of what the stack looks like. In particular, it needs to know where the value of each variable is held, relative to the top of the stack. For all our compilation functions this information will be held as:

(i) ρ, a function which takes an identifier and returns a number giving the offset of the corresponding argument from the base of the current context, counting the bottom element of the context as having an offset of

0. The pointer to the root of the current redex therefore has an offset of 0, and the last argument has an offset of 1 (see Figure 18.5).

(ii) d, the depth of the current context minus one.

From these we can calculate the offset of a variable, x, from the top of the stack as $(d - \rho\ x)$, counting the top element of the stack as having an offset of 0.

(Note: the G-machine paper [Johnsson, 1984] uses 'r' instead of 'ρ' and 'n' instead of 'd'. It also uses slightly different conventions for n and r ($n = d+1$ and $r\ x = 1 + \rho\ x$).)

For example, consider the context shown in Figure 18.6. The depth of the context is 5, so d=4. The function ρ maps the variable x to 2 and y to 1, and we write

ρ = [x=2, y=1]

The offset of the value of x from the top of the stack is

$(d - \rho\ x) = (4 - 2) = 2$

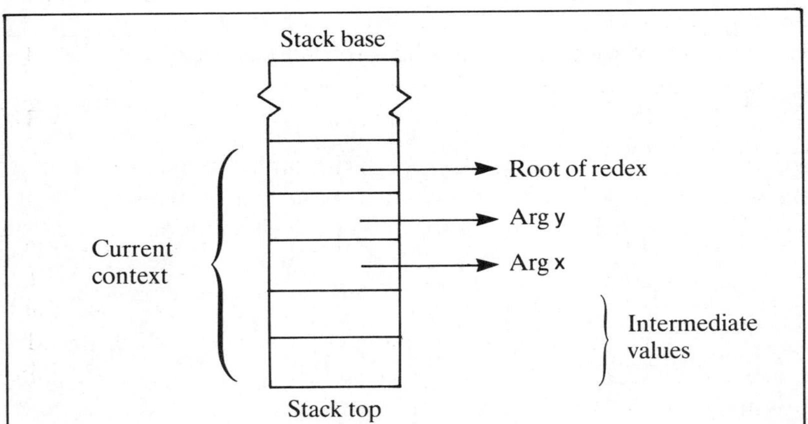

Figure 18.6 An example context

18.5.2 The **R** Compilation Scheme

We can now give the complete definition of the compilation scheme **F** we referred to above:

F[[f x_1 x_2 . . . x_n = E]]
= GLOBSTART f,n; **R**[[E]] [x_1=n, x_2=n−1,. . .,x_n=1] n

where f stands for a supercombinator name. The 'GLOBSTART f,n' is a G-code pseudo-instruction which labels the beginning of a function called f, which takes n arguments. Then **F** calls a function **R** to compile code for the body, E, of the supercombinator, passing it the correct ρ and d (in that order).

We must now describe what **R** does. As we saw in our example, the code for a supercombinator has to do four things:

(i) construct an instance of the supercombinator body, using the parameters on the stack;
(ii) update the root of the redex with a copy of the root of the result (note: there are the usual complications if the body consists of a single variable, which we deal with later);
(iii) remove the parameters from the stack;
(iv) initiate the next reduction.

This translates directly into a compilation scheme for **R**:

R⟦ E ⟧ ρ d = **C**⟦ E ⟧ ρ d; UPDATE (d+1); POP d; UNWIND

We use another auxiliary function, **C** (for Construct Instance), which produces code to construct an instance of E and put a pointer to it on the stack, which constitutes step (i). The UPDATE instruction overwrites the root of the redex (which is now at offset (d+1) from the top of the stack) with the newly created instance, which is currently on top of the stack (step (ii)); UPDATE then pops it from the stack. Then the POP instruction pops the arguments (step (iii)), and the UNWIND instruction initiates the next reduction (step (iv)). Figure 18.7 summarizes the **F** and **R** compilation schemes.

Warning: while it will give the correct results, the code generated by **R** may give bad performance for projection functions, such as

```
f x y z = y
```

where the body of the function consists of a single variable. The reasons for this were explained in Section 12.4. As given, the UPDATE instruction generated by the **R** scheme will copy the root of the argument y, without first evaluating it. This risks duplicating the root of a redex, which would lose laziness. We will fix this problem in the next version of **R**, at the beginning of Chapter 20.

All we have left to do is to describe the **C** compilation scheme.

F⟦ SCDef ⟧

generates code for a supercombinator definition SCDef.

F⟦ f x_1 x_2 ... x_n = E ⟧ = GLOBSTART f n;
R⟦ E ⟧ [x_1=n, x_2=n−1, ..., x_n=1] n

R⟦ E ⟧ ρ d

generates code to apply a supercombinator to its arguments.
Note: there are d arguments.

R⟦ E ⟧ ρ d = **C**⟦ E ⟧ ρ d; UPDATE (d+1); POP d; UNWIND

Figure 18.7 The **R** compilation scheme

18.5.3 The C Compilation Scheme

The **C** compilation scheme compiles code to construct an instance of an expression. It is a function with the following behavior:

(i) *Arguments*: the expression to be compiled, plus ρ and d, which specify where the arguments of the supercombinator are to be found in the stack.
(ii) *Result*: a G-code sequence which, when executed, will construct an instance of the expression, with pointers to the supercombinator arguments substituted for occurrences of the corresponding formal parameters, and leave a pointer to the instance on top of the stack.

To define **C** fully, we must specify the result of the call

C⟦ E ⟧ ρ d

for every possible expression E. The expression E can take a number of forms (see Figure 18.3), and we define **C** by specifying it separately for each form of E. The cases are described in the following sections.

18.5.3.1 E is a constant

There are actually two cases to consider here. First, suppose E is an integer, i (or a boolean, or other built-in constant value). All we need do is to push a pointer to the integer onto the stack (or the integer itself in an unboxed implementation), an operation which is carried out by the G-code instruction

PUSHINT i

We may write the compilation rule like this:

C⟦ i ⟧ ρ d = PUSHINT i

Secondly, suppose E is a supercombinator or built-in function, called f. We must push a pointer to the function onto the stack, using the G-code instruction

PUSHGLOBAL f

We write the rule in the same way as before:

C⟦ f ⟧ ρ d = PUSHGLOBAL f

18.5.3.2 E is a variable

The next case to consider is that of a variable, x. The value of the variable is in the stack, at offset (d − ρ x) from the top, and the G-code instruction

PUSH (d − ρ x)

will copy this item onto the top of the stack. Hence we may write the rule

C⟦ x ⟧ ρ d = PUSH (d − ρ x)

18.5.3.3 E is an application

If E is an application (E_1 E_2), where E_1 and E_2 are arbitrary expressions, then the expression to be constructed is the application of E_1 to E_2. It is easy to do this: first construct an instance of E_2 (leaving a pointer to the instance on top of the stack), then construct an instance of E_1 (likewise), then make an application cell from the top two items on the stack, and leave a pointer to the application cell on top of the stack. This can be achieved by the following rule:

$$\mathbf{C}[\![\ E_1\ E_2\ ]\!]\ \rho\ d = \mathbf{C}[\![\ E_2\ ]\!]\ \rho\ d;\ \mathbf{C}[\![\ E_1\ ]\!]\ \rho\ (d+1);\ \text{MKAP}$$

Notice that the current context is one deeper during the second call to **C**, so we passed it (d+1) instead of d.

MKAP is an instruction which takes the top two items on the stack, pops them, forms an application node in the heap, and pushes a pointer to this node onto the stack. If MKAP took its arguments in the other order, we could construct first E_1 and then E_2. This might seem to be a more logical order, but we will see later that it is more convenient to construct E_2 first.

18.5.3.4 E is a let-expression

Next, consider the rule for let-expressions

$$\mathbf{C}[\![\ \text{let } x = E_x \text{ in } E_b\ ]\!]\ \rho\ d$$

where x is a variable and E_x, E_b are expressions (we consider only the case of a single definition). We recall that a let in a supercombinator body is just a way of describing a graph (with sharing) rather than a tree. We can deal with let in a very straightforward way.

(i) First we construct an instance of E_x, leaving a pointer to it on the stack.
(ii) Then we augment ρ to say that x is to be found at offset (d+1) from the base of the context (which is true, since it is on top of the stack).
(iii) Then we construct an instance of E_b, using the new values of ρ and d, leaving a pointer to the instance on top of the stack.
(iv) Now a pointer to the instance of E_b is on top of the stack, and underneath it is a pointer to the instance of E_x. We no longer want the latter, so we squeeze it out by sliding down the top element of the stack on top of it.

Figure 18.8 shows the execution of a let after these four stages.

In symbols:

$$\begin{aligned}&\mathbf{C}[\![\ \text{let } x = E_x \text{ in } E_b\ ]\!]\ \rho\ d\\ &= \mathbf{C}[\![\ E_x\ ]\!]\ \rho\ d;\ \mathbf{C}[\![\ E_b\ ]\!]\ \rho[x=d+1]\ (d+1);\ \text{SLIDE } 1\end{aligned}$$

Remembering that ρ is a function taking a variable as its argument, the notation 'ρ[x=d+1]' means 'a function which behaves just like ρ except when it is applied to x, in which case it delivers the result (d+1)'. In other words,

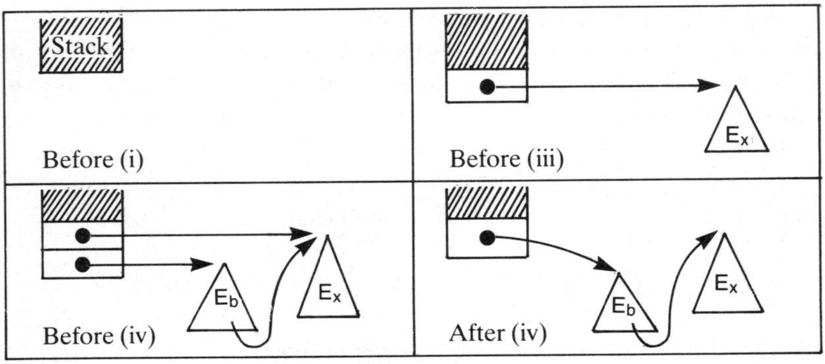

Figure 18.8 Execution of a let

ρ[x=d+1] is just ρ augmented with information about where to find x. Symbolically,

```
ρ[x=n] x = n
ρ[x=n] y = ρ y        if x ≠ y
```

The 'SLIDE 1' instruction squeezes out one element from the stack.

The job was fairly easy to do because we could access the graph constructed by the let definition in just the same way as we access the parameters of a supercombinator. This is another strong reason for performing the stack rearrangement described in Section 18.5.1.

18.5.3.5 E is a letrec-expression

Finally, we consider the rule for

C[[letrec D in E_b]] ρ d

where D is a set of definitions and E_b is an expression. Recall that a letrec in a supercombinator body is just a description of a *cyclic graph*. The way to construct such a graph is:

(i) First allocate some empty cells, one for each definition, putting pointers to them on the stack. These empty cells are called *holes*.

(ii) Now augment the context ρ and d to say that the values of the variables bound in the letrec can be found in the stack locations just allocated.

(iii) Then for each definition body:

  (a) construct an instance of it, leaving a pointer to the instance on top of the stack, and

  (b) then update its corresponding hole with the instance (using the UPDATE instruction; this also removes the pointer on top of the stack).

During the instantiation process, occurrences of names bound in the letrec will be replaced by pointers to the corresponding hole, because we have augmented the context in stage (ii).

(iv) Now instantiate E_b, leaving a pointer to it on the stack.

(v) Lastly, squeeze out the pointers to the definition bodies. This is why the SLIDE instruction has an argument, telling it how many elements to squeeze out.

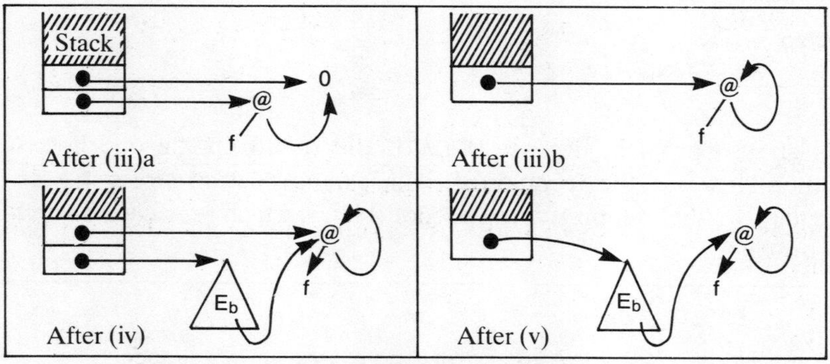

Figure 18.9 Execution of letrec x = f x in E_b

Figure 18.9 shows various stages in the execution of

C⟦ letrec x = f x in E_b ⟧ ρ d

In symbols, we write:

C⟦ letrec D in E_b ⟧ ρ d
= **CLetrec**⟦ D ⟧ ρ' d'; **C**⟦ E_b ⟧ ρ' d'; SLIDE (d'−d)
where
(ρ', d') = **Xr**⟦ D ⟧ ρ d

This uses two new auxiliary functions **CLetrec** and **Xr**, which are defined as follows.

$$\textbf{CLetrec}\left[\!\!\left[\begin{array}{l} x_1 = E_1 \\ x_2 = E_2 \\ \ldots \\ x_n = E_n \end{array}\right]\!\!\right] \rho\ d = \begin{array}{l} \text{ALLOC } n; \\ \textbf{C}[\![E_1]\!]\ \rho\ d;\ \text{UPDATE } n; \\ \textbf{C}[\![E_2]\!]\ \rho\ d;\ \text{UPDATE } n{-}1; \\ \quad\ldots \\ \textbf{C}[\![E_n]\!]\ \rho\ d;\ \text{UPDATE } 1; \end{array}$$

CLetrec performs the first two steps of the process. The 'ALLOC n' instruction allocates n holes in the heap and pushes pointers to them onto the stack. Then the instances of the definition bodies are constructed and the UPDATE instruction overwrites a hole with the root of the corresponding instance.

$$\textbf{Xr}\left[\!\!\left[\begin{array}{l} x_1 = E_1 \\ x_2 = E_2 \\ \ldots \\ x_n = E_n \end{array}\right]\!\!\right] \rho\ d = \left(\rho \left[\begin{array}{l} x_1{=}d{+}1 \\ x_2{=}d{+}2 \\ \ldots \\ x_n{=}d{+}n \end{array}\right],\ d{+}n\right)$$

Xr just computes the augmented ρ and the new value of d, returning them as a pair (ρ', d'). The [] bracket updates ρ to include all the new information.

The final 'SLIDE (d'−d)' slides down the top element of the stack, squeezing out the pointers to the E_i.

Warning: there will be a problem if a definition body consists of a single variable name bound in the same letrec; for example

```
letrec x = y
       y = CONS 1 y
in E
```

This gives a problem because UPDATE will try to update one hole with another. However, the definition of x will be removed at an earlier stage in the compiler, by the optimization of Section 14.7.3, which replaces occurrences of x by y in E.

```
C⟦ E ⟧ ρ d
```

Constructs the graph for an instance of E in a context given by ρ and d. It leaves a pointer to the graph on top of the stack.

```
C⟦ i ⟧ ρ d                    = PUSHINT i
C⟦ f ⟧ ρ d                    = PUSHGLOBAL f
C⟦ x ⟧ ρ d                    = PUSH (d − ρ x)
C⟦ E1 E2 ⟧ ρ d                = C⟦ E2 ⟧ ρ d; C⟦ E1 ⟧ ρ (d+1); MKAP
C⟦ let x=Ex in E ⟧ ρ d        = C⟦ Ex ⟧ ρ d;
                                C⟦ E ⟧ ρ[x=d+1] (d+1); SLIDE 1
C⟦ letrec D in E ⟧ ρ d        = CLetrec⟦ D ⟧ ρ' d'; C⟦ E ⟧ ρ' d'; SLIDE (d'−d)
                                where
                                (ρ', d') = Xr⟦ D ⟧ ρ d
```

Figure 18.10 The C compilation scheme

```
CLetrec⟦ D ⟧ ρ d
```

Takes a mutually recursive set of definitions D, constructs an instance of each body, and leaves the pointers to the instances on top of the stack.

```
CLetrec⟦ x1 = E1 ⟧ ρ d = ALLOC n;
       ⟦ x2 = E2 ⟧       C⟦ E1 ⟧ ρ d; UPDATE n;
       ⟦ . . .   ⟧       C⟦ E2 ⟧ ρ d; UPDATE n−1;
       ⟦ xn = En ⟧       . . .
                         C⟦ En ⟧ ρ d; UPDATE 1;
```

```
Xr⟦ D ⟧ ρ d
```

Returns a pair (ρ', d') which gives the context augmented by the definitions D.

```
Xr⟦ x1 = E1 ⟧ ρ d = ( ρ [ x1=d+1 ], d+n )
  ⟦ x2 = E2 ⟧           [ x2=d+2 ]
  ⟦ . . .   ⟧           [ . . .  ]
  ⟦ xn = En ⟧           [ xn=d+n ]
```

Figure 18.11 Auxiliary compilation schemes **CLetrec** and **Xr**

18.5.3.6 Summary

We are done! The **C** compilation scheme has been described in considerable detail because the same ideas will be used again and again in what follows. It is worth some study to ensure that you understand what is going on. Figures 18.10 and 18.11 summarize the **C** scheme.

18.6 Supercombinators with Zero Arguments

The lambda-lifting algorithm given in earlier chapters may produce some supercombinators with no arguments. The most obvious example of this is the $Prog supercombinator.

Such supercombinators are simply *constant expressions* (sometimes called *constant applicative forms* or CAFs), since they have no parameters at all. The presence of CAFs raises two issues, compilation and garbage collection, which we now discuss.

18.6.1 Compiling CAFs

How should we compile CAFs? There are two alternatives:

(i) Do not compile them at all. Instead keep them as pieces of graph. Since they are not functions they will never be copied, so they can be shared without further ado. This is a perfectly acceptable solution, but it does mean that the compiled program is a mixture of target machine code and graph.

(ii) Treat them as supercombinators with zero arguments and compile them to G-code which will, when executed, construct an instance of their graph. Since we want to share this graph (and not make repeated copies of it) the instance should overwrite the compiled code in some way.

This is easily achieved. We allocate a single graph node, tagged as a function, which holds a pointer to the compiled code. This node is shared by anyone who uses the supercombinator. When the compiled code executes, the current context will contain a pointer to that node as its only element (since there are no arguments), so the node will be updated with the result, and this update will be seen by anyone else sharing the node. The **F** scheme is therefore quite adequate to compile the code for the body.

The advantage of this is that the compiled program consists almost entirely of target machine code, plus some individual graph nodes, one per supercombinator. In the Chalmers G-machine these nodes are allocated space physically adjacent to the target machine code of the supercombinator, outside the main heap. Such CAF nodes should not be in read-only memory, however, since they must be updated after their code is executed.

18.6.2 Garbage Collection of CAFs

Supercombinators which have one or more arguments need not be garbage-collected at all, since they cannot grow in size. CAFs, on the other hand, can grow in size without bound. For example, consider the program:

```
$from n = CONS n ($from (+ n 1))
$Ints = $from 1
$F x y = ...$Ints...
$Prog = ...$F...
-----------------------------
$Prog
```

$Ints is the infinite list of integers, and we would like to recover the space this list occupies when it is no longer needed. Unfortunately, we will be unable to reclaim this space if we decide that all supercombinators should not be subject to garbage collection.

$Ints can be recovered when there are no references to it, directly or indirectly, from $Prog. However, $Prog may refer to $Ints indirectly, by using $F which uses $Ints, so we cannot recover $Ints just because $Prog does not refer to it directly.

The only clean way around this is to associate with each supercombinator (of any number of arguments, including zero) a list of CAFs to which it refers directly or indirectly. Then, for mark-scan garbage collection, to mark a supercombinator of one or more arguments we simply mark all the CAFs in its associated CAF list. To mark an unreduced CAF we mark its CAF list, while a reduced CAF is indistinguishable from any other heap structure and is marked as usual.

Another way to understand this is to see that in a template-instantiating implementation, the template for $F would refer to that for $Ints. Hence, $Ints would be reached by the mark phase of garbage collection during the normal marking traversal of $F. In a compiled implementation, however, the reference to $Ints is buried in the code for $F, and the CAF list for $F makes this dependency sufficiently explicit for the garbage collector to understand it.

This technique, or something similar, is essential to prevent ever-expanding CAFs from filling up the machine.

18.7 Getting it all Together

We can now put all the pieces together to describe how to compile a complete program. Consider the program:

```
$F x = NEG x
$Prog = $F 3
-------------
$Prog
```

(Note: such a program will never be generated by the lambda-lifter due to η-optimization, but it serves here as the smallest feasible example program.) This will compile to the following G-code:

```
BEGIN;                      Beginning of program
PUSHGLOBAL $Prog;           Load $Prog
EVAL; PRINT;                Evaluate and print it
END;

GLOBSTART $F, 1;            Beginning of $F (one argument)
PUSH 0;                     Push x
PUSHGLOBAL $NEG;            Push $NEG
MKAP;                       Construct ($NEG x)
UPDATE 2;                   Update the root of the redex
POP 1;                      Pop the parameter
UNWIND;                     Continue evaluation

GLOBSTART $Prog, 0;         Beginning of $Prog (no arguments)
PUSHINT 3;                  Push 3
PUSHGLOBAL $F;              Push $F
MKAP;                       Construct ($F 3)
UPDATE 1;                   Update the $Prog
UNWIND;                     Continue evaluation
```

We have now described a complete compilation scheme for compiling a program into G-code. It is far from optimal, as we will soon see, but even in its present form it should work faster than a template-instantiation implementation.

The only mysterious feature of the above code is the function $NEG. It is one of the built-in functions in the run-time system, and we now describe the G-code for these functions.

18.8 The Built-in Functions

The names of built-in functions will appear in our implementation in three distinct ways. For example, CONS can appear in the following ways:

(i) As a (built-in) function in the supercombinator program. For example

```
$S x y = CONS y x
```

(ii) As a G-code instruction, which takes the top two elements on the stack, forms a CONS cell from them, and puts a pointer to the result on top of the stack (see Section 18.2).

(iii) As a built-in run-time function. For example, at run-time the machine may have to evaluate a graph like this

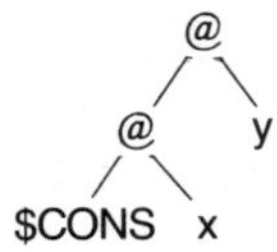

The spine will be unwound and the function $CONS will be found at the tip. Just as in the $from example (Section 18.2) the code for $CONS will be entered to perform the reduction. This means that there should be a G-code sequence for the $CONS function, and for all other built-in functions.

It is for this reason that we prefix this form of CONS with a $. At run-time it appears just like any user-defined supercombinator; that is as a (boxed) G-code sequence. In the next few chapters, therefore, we will not make any distinction between built-in functions and supercombinators. Sometimes we will call them *globals*; this is the origin of the PUSHGLOBAL instruction.

No confusion between the first two cases should arise, because the meaning should be clear from its context. One slight annoyance is that now we have

C⟦ CONS ⟧ ρ d = PUSHGLOBAL $CONS

which makes it look as if **C** 'sticks the $ on a global', but this is contradicted by the case of a supercombinator:

C⟦ $X ⟧ ρ d = PUSHGLOBAL $X

We content ourselves with the general rule as given in the **C** scheme, namely

C⟦ f ⟧ ρ d = PUSHGLOBAL f

and remember that a $ is added to built-in functions. (This is, of course, a purely notational point.)

The third case above raises the question of what the G-code sequences for CONS and the other built-in functions are, and we will develop them in this section. The built-in functions we will consider are those given in the left-hand column of Figure 18.4; those in the right-hand column are analogous. In doing this we will also develop some new G-code instructions.

18.8.1 $NEG, $+, and the EVAL Instruction

NEGate is an example of a function which has to evaluate its argument. As we have seen before (Sections 11.4 and 12.2) this always seems to require a new mechanism for recursive argument evaluation, and the G-machine is no exception. The new mechanism we introduce is the G-code instruction EVAL, which evaluates the top item on the stack, leaving the evaluated object on the stack. With the aid of this instruction we can give the following sequence for $NEG:

```
EVAL;        Evaluate the argument
NEG;         Negate it
UPDATE 1;    Update the root of the redex
UNWIND;      Continue
```

The code for $+ is similar, complicated only by having to get the appropriate parameter on top of the stack before calling EVAL:

```
PUSH 1;      Get first argument
EVAL;        Evaluate it
PUSH 1;      Get second argument
EVAL;        Evaluate it
ADD;         Add them
UPDATE 3;    Update root of redex
POP 2;       Pop parameters
UNWIND;      Evaluation is complete
```

The EVAL instruction does the following:

(i) Examines the object on top of the stack. If it is a CONS cell, an integer (boolean, character), a supercombinator or a built-in function, EVAL does nothing.
(ii) If it is an application cell, EVAL creates a new stack, pushes the top item of the old stack, saves the current program counter (which now points to the instruction after the EVAL), and then executes the UNWIND instruction.

After each reduction an UNWIND instruction is executed. If this UNWIND discovers that the expression is in WHNF, it restores the old stack and jumps to the saved return address.

As we saw in Section 11.6, we can build the new stack directly on top of the old stack. Indeed they can overlap by one item, since the top element of the old stack is the same as the bottom element of the new stack. We need to save two items on another stack, called the *dump*:

(i) the old stack depth, or (equivalently) the old stack pointer;
(ii) the old program counter.

The UNWIND instruction at the end of the code for $NEG or $+ will always discover that evaluation is complete, because we know that the result of a negation or addition is an integer. It is wasteful, therefore, for UNWIND to test the result for being in WHNF. We can encode this information by using a new instruction, RETURN, instead of UNWIND. RETURN assumes that the expression being evaluated is now in WHNF, but otherwise behaves just like UNWIND; that is, it restores the old stack and jumps to the saved program counter.

The new code for $NEG would therefore be:

```
EVAL;          Evaluate the argument
NEG;           Negate it
UPDATE 1;      Update the root of the redex
RETURN;        Evaluation is complete
```

18.8.2 $CONS

When the code for $CONS is entered, the two objects to be CONSed are on top of the stack, and below them is a pointer to the root of the redex. We can therefore produce the following code sequence for $CONS:

```
CONS;          Form the CONS cell
UPDATE 1;      Update the root of the redex
RETURN;        Result guaranteed to be in WHNF
```

CONS is a G-code instruction which CONSes together the top two items on the stack, pops them and pushes a pointer to the CONS cell. The CONS cell is then copied over the root of the redex by UPDATE. The CONS cell cannot be applied to anything (or the type-checker would have complained), so the expression being evaluated must now be in WHNF; we can thus use RETURN instead of UNWIND.

The treatment of $PACK-SUM-d-r is similar, except that we need a new G-code instruction PACKSUM d,r which constructs a structured data object with structure tag d and r fields, whose values are found on the stack. CONS is then equivalent to PACKSUM 2,2. $PACK-PRODUCT-r can be treated similarly, using a new G-code instruction PACKPRODUCT r. If sum types and product types are represented in the same way, then a single G-code instruction would suffice.

18.8.3 $HEAD

$HEAD is a function which evaluates its argument (to WHNF); it expects the result to be a CONS cell, from which it can extract the head (that is, the first field). Then, for the reasons we discussed in Section 12.4, it must evaluate the head of the cell before overwriting the root of the redex with it. Failing to do this final evaluation would result in the duplication of work.

The code for $HEAD is:

```
EVAL;          Evaluate to WHNF
HEAD;          Take its head
EVAL;          Evaluate the head
UPDATE 1;      Update root of redex
UNWIND;        Continue
```

Notice that we cannot use RETURN at the end, even though the result of the

HEAD must be in WHNF (since it has been EVALuated). Consider, for example, the expression

```
($HEAD E) 3
```

where E is some expression. Here, $HEAD evaluates E, takes its head, evaluates it, updates the ($HEAD E) redex and then *applies the result* to 3. Evaluation of the whole expression is not complete merely because the result of the ($HEAD E) reduction is in WHNF.

$TAIL and $SEL-SUM-r-i are precisely analogous to $HEAD, except that we need a new G-code instruction SELSUM r,i which selects the ith component of a structured data object of sum type and of size r. Similarly, $SEL-r-i (the selector functions for product types) requires the introduction of a new G-code instruction SELPRODUCT r,i. If sum and product types use the same representation, then only one new G-code instruction is required.

18.8.4 $IF, and the JUMP Instruction

In order to generate code for $IF we need to introduce two jump instructions (JUMP and JFALSE), and a label pseudo-instruction (LABEL).

The code for $IF is:

```
PUSH 2;          Get first argument
EVAL;            Evaluate it
JFALSE L1;       Jump to L1 if false
PUSH 1;          Get second argument
JUMP L2;

LABEL L1;        Pseudo-instruction; a label
PUSH 0;          Get third argument

LABEL L2;
EVAL;            Evaluate before overwriting
UPDATE 4;        Overwrite root
POP 3;           Pop arguments
UNWIND;          Continue
```

(L1 and L2 are unique labels.)

The reason for the last EVAL instruction was mentioned in the previous section, as was the reason for using UNWIND rather than RETURN.

In order to implement $CASE-n we need an n-way jump instruction,

```
CASEJUMP L1,L2,...,Ln
```

which examines the structure tag of the object on top of the stack, and jumps to one of n labels depending on its value. Apart from this, its treatment is identical to $IF, so we will not mention it any further.

18.9 Summary

This chapter has presented the payoff for the hard work earlier in the book. We have developed:

(i) a compilation algorithm which takes a supercombinator program and compiles it into G-code;
(ii) G-code sequences for a representative range of built-in functions.

The next chapter completes the picture by giving a precise description of G-code and a discussion on how to implement it.

References

Augustsson, L. 1984. A compiler for lazy ML. In *Proceedings of the ACM Symposium on Lisp and Functional Programming, Austin*, pp. 218–27, August.

Burstall, R.M., MacQueen, D.B., and Sanella, D.T. 1980. HOPE: an experimental applicative language. In *Proceedings of the ACM Lisp Conference*, pp. 136–43, August.

Clark, R. (editor) 1981. *UCSD P-system and UCSD Pascal Users' Manual*, 2nd edition. Softech Microsystems, San Diego.

Elworthy, D. 1985. Implementing a Ponder cross compiler for the SKIM processor. Dip. Comp. Sci. Dissertation, Computer Lab., Cambridge. July.

Fairbairn, J. 1982. Ponder and its type system. *Technical Report 31*. Computer Lab., Cambridge. November.

Fairbairn, J. 1985. Design and implementation of a simple typed language based on the lambda calculus. *Technical Report 75*. Computer Lab., Cambridge. May.

Fairbairn, J., and Wray, S.C. 1986. Code generation techniques for functional languages. In *Proceedings of the ACM Conference on Lisp and Functional Programming, Boston*, pp. 94–104, August.

Field, A. 1985. *The Compilation of FP/M Programs into Conventional Machine Code*. Dept Comp. Sci., Imperial College. June.

Griss, M.L., and Hearn, A.C. 1981. A portable Lisp compiler. *Software – Practice and Experience*. Vol. 11, pp. 541–605.

Hudak, P., and Kranz, D. 1984. A combinator based compiler for a functional language. In *Proceedings of the 11th ACM Symposium on Principles of Programming Languages*, pp. 122–32, January.

Johnsson, T. 1984. Efficient compilation of lazy evaluation. In *Proceedings of the ACM Conference on Compiler Construction, Montreal*, pp. 58–69, June.

Lester, D. 1985. The correctness of a G-machine compiler. MSc dissertation, Programming Research Group, Oxford. December.

Rees, J.A., and Adams, N.I. 1982. T – a dialect of LISP. In *Proceedings of the ACM Symposium on Lisp and Functional Programming*, pp. 114–22, August.

Richards, M. 1971. The portability of the BCPL compiler. *Software – Practice and Experience*. Vol. 1, no. 2, pp. 135–46.

Steele, G.L., and Sussman, G.J. 1978. *The Revised Report on Scheme*. AI Memo 452, MIT. January.

Nineteen

G-CODE

Definition and Implementation

So far we have described a basic compilation algorithm from supercombinators into G-code. The next step, code generation, is to compile the G-code program into target machine code.

The basic idea is that to each G-code instruction there corresponds a simple sequence of target machine instructions, so that we can generate target code for a G-code program simply by generating these sequences for each instruction:

G-code	*Target machine code*
PUSH 3	<Target code for PUSH 3>
UPDATE 4	<Target code for UPDATE 4>

Typically the output of the code generator would be a program in the assembly code of the target machine, which would then be assembled, linked with any run-time libraries, and run.

In order to perform code generation in this way we need to know:

(i) exactly what each G-code instruction is supposed to do;
(ii) how the various bits of the abstract G-machine are mapped on to the target machine.

We will address these two issues in order.

19.1 What the G-code Instructions Do

The G-machine is a finite-state machine, with the following components:

(i) S, the stack.

(ii) G, the graph.
(iii) C, the G-code sequence remaining to be executed.
(iv) D, the dump. This consists of a stack of pairs (S, C), where S is a stack and C is a code sequence.

Thus the entire *state* of the G-machine is a 4-tuple <S, G, C, D>. We will describe the *operation* of the G-machine by means of *state transitions*. First, however, we need some notation for each component of the state.

19.1.1 Notation

A stack whose top item is n is written n:S, where S is a stack. An empty stack is written [].

A code sequence whose first instruction is I is written I:C, where C is a code sequence. An empty code sequence is written [].

A dump whose top pair is (S,C) is written (S,C):D, where D is a dump. An empty dump is written [].

The possible types of nodes in the graph are written like this:

INT i	an integer.
CONS n_1 n_2	a CONS node.
AP n_1 n_2	an application node.
FUN k C	a function (supercombinator or built-in) of k arguments, with code sequence C.
HOLE	a node which is to be filled in later. This is used for constructing cyclic graphs.

The notation G[n=AP n_1 n_2] stands for a graph in which node n is an application of n_1 to n_2 (n is just a name for this node). The notation G[n=G n′] stands for a graph in which node n has the same contents as node n′ (we will need this only to describe the UPDATE instruction).

The *graph* is a logical concept, implemented by the *heap*. A *node* in the logical graph need not necessarily occupy a *cell* in the physical heap. In the case of CONS, AP, FUN and HOLE a logical node will indeed occupy a physical cell, but an INT node (i.e. an integer) will occupy a cell in a boxed implementation but will not in an unboxed implementation (see Section 10.6).

19.1.2 State Transitions for the G-machine

To illustrate the way in which we can use state transitions to describe the effect of instructions, consider the instruction PUSHINT i. We can write the following transition:

<S, G, PUSHINT i:C, D> ⇒ <n:S, G[n=INT i], C, D>

This says that when PUSHINT i is the first instruction, the G-machine makes a transition (denoted by ⇒) to a new state in which

(i) a new node n is pushed onto the stack,
(ii) the graph is updated with the information that node n is INT i,
(iii) the code to be executed is everything after the PUSHINT i,
(iv) and the dump is unchanged.

Notice that the name n, which is introduced on the right-hand side, is intended to be a new and unique node name.

More complicated instructions can be described using pattern-matching. EVAL is an example of this:

```
<n:S, G[n=AP n1 n2], EVAL:C, D>
⇒  <n:[], G[n=AP n1 n2], UNWIND:[], (S,C):D>

<n:S, G[n=FUN 0 C′], EVAL:C, D>
⇒ <n:[], G[n=FUN 0 C′], C′:[], (S,C):D>

<n:S, G[n=INT i], EVAL:C, D>
⇒ <n:S, G[n=INT i], C, D>
```

and similarly for CONS and non-CAF FUN nodes.

The appropriate state transition for EVAL is selected depending on what kind of node is found on top of the stack (the node n):

(i) The first equation describes what EVAL does if the node on top of the stack is an application. The current stack and code are pushed onto the dump, a new stack is formed with the top of the old stack as its only element, and UNWIND is executed.
(ii) The second equation describes what EVAL does if the node on top of the stack is a compiled supercombinator of arity zero (that is, a CAF; see Section 18.6). In this case the machine saves its state on the dump, forms a new stack with the CAF as its only element, and executes the code associated with the CAF (which will subsequently update the FUN node with its reduced value).
(iii) The third equation describes what EVAL does if the node on top of the stack is an integer: it does nothing! The same applies if the node on top of the stack is a CONS or non-CAF function node.

An omitted transition indicates a run-time machine error (e.g. n is a HOLE).

Notice that in the first rule for EVAL we have (strictly speaking) to repeat the ‘G[n=AP n_1 n_2]’ on the right-hand side of the rule, since G alone would imply that node n was no longer in the graph. This is clumsy and hard to read, since the reader has to check that node n is the same on both sides of the rule. Accordingly we abbreviate the rule to

```
<n:S, G[n=AP n1 n2], EVAL:C, D>
⇒  <n:[], G, UNWIND:[], (S,C):D>
```

and imply that nodes not explicitly mentioned in the G field on the right-hand side are unchanged from the left-hand side.

Using this notation we can now give a complete description of the G-code instructions (Figures 19.1 and 19.2). The transitions for UNWIND are a little complicated, so we will explain them briefly. There are four cases:

(i) The item on top of the stack is an integer or a CONS node. In this case it must be the only element of the stack, and the expression being evaluated is in WHNF. UNWIND therefore completes evaluation by restoring the saved stack and code from the dump, and putting the result of the evaluation on the top of the restored stack.

(ii) The item on top of the stack is (a pointer to) an application node. In this case we just push the head of the application on the stack and repeat the UNWIND instruction.

(iii) The item on top of the stack is a function, and there are enough arguments on the stack. In this case we rearrange the stack as described in Section 18.5.1, and begin executing the code for the function. The v_i are the vertebrae on the spine, while the n_i are the arguments to the function.

(iv) The item on top of the stack is a function, but there are too few arguments for it to execute (this is described by the $\{a<k\}$ condition). In this case the expression being evaluated is in WHNF, so UNWIND completes evaluation by restoring the saved stack and code from the dump, and putting the result of the evaluation on the top of the restored stack.

19.1.3 The Printing Mechanism

The G-code instructions developed so far are intended to reduce an expression to WHNF. As we saw in Section 11.2, though, we also need a printing mechanism which repeatedly invokes the evaluator to reduce expressions to WHNF and prints them. It would be nice if we could describe the printing mechanism within the same framework, and we now do so.

We introduce one new instruction, PRINT, which prints the top element on the stack. In order to describe its action we need to add one new component in the G-machine state: O, the output produced by the machine. The empty output is denoted by [ ], and O;x denotes the output O followed by the output x. Now we can define PRINT:

```
<O, n:S, G[n=INT i], PRINT:C, D>  =>  <O;i, S, G, C, D>

<O, n:S, G[n=CONS n1 n2], PRINT:C, D>
=>  <O, n1:n2:S, G, EVAL:PRINT:EVAL:PRINT:C, D>
```

All the other instructions leave O unchanged.

```
EVAL        <v:S, G[v=AP v' n], EVAL:C, D>
            ⇒ <v:[], G, UNWIND:[], (S,C):D>

            <n:S, G[n=FUN 0 C'], EVAL:C, D>
            ⇒ <n:[], G, C':[], (S,C):D>

            <n:S, G[n=INT i], EVAL:C, D>  ⇒  <n:S, G, C, D>
            and similarly for CONS and non-CAF FUN nodes.

UNWIND      <n:[], G[n=INT i], UNWIND:[], (S,C):D>
            ⇒ <n:S, G, C, D>
            and similarly for CONS nodes.

            <v:S, G[v=AP v' n], UNWIND:[], D>
            ⇒ <v':v:S, G, UNWIND:[], D>

            <v0:v1:...:vk:S, G[v0=FUN k C                 ], UNWIND:[], D>
                              [vi=AP vi-1 ni, (1≤i≤k)]
            ⇒ <n1:n2:...:nk:vk:S, G, C, D>

            <v0:v1:...:va:[], G[v0=FUN k C'], UNWIND:[], (S,C):D>
  {a<k}     ⇒ <va:S, G, C, D>

RETURN      <v0:v1:...:vk:[], G, RETURN:[], (S,C) :D>  ⇒  <vk:S, G, C, D>

JUMP        <S, G, JUMP L:...:LABEL L:C, D>  ⇒  <S, G, C, D>

JFALSE      <n:S, G[n=BOOL true], JFALSE L:C, D>  ⇒  <S, G, C, D>
            <n:S, G[n=BOOL false], JFALSE L:...:LABEL L:C, D>
            ⇒ <S, G, C, D>
```

Figure 19.1 G-machine state transitions (control)

```
PUSH          <n0:n1:...:nk:S, G, PUSH k:C, D>
              ⇒ <nk:n0:n1:...:nk:S, G, C, D>

PUSHINT       <S, G, PUSHINT i:C, D>  ⇒  <n:S, G[n=INT i], C, D>
PUSHGLOBAL    similarly

POP           <n1:n2:...:nk:S, G, POP k:C, D>  ⇒  <S, G, C, D>

SLIDE         <n0:n1:...:nk:S, G, SLIDE k:C, D>  ⇒  <n0:S, G, C, D>

UPDATE        <n0:n1:...:nk:S, G, UPDATE k:C, D>
              ⇒ <n1:...:nk:S, G[nk=G n0], C, D>

ALLOC         <S, G, ALLOC k:C, D>
              ⇒ <n1:n2:...:nk:S, G[n1=HOLE, ..., nk=HOLE], C, D>

HEAD          <n:S, G[n=CONS n1 n2], HEAD:C, D>
              ⇒ <n1:S, G, C, D>

NEG           <n:S, G[n=INT i], NEG:C, D>
              ⇒ <n':S, G[n'=INT (−i)], C, D>

ADD           <n1:n2:S, G[n1=INT i1, n2=INT i2], ADD:C, D>
              ⇒ <n:S, G[n=INT (i1+i2)], C, D>

MKAP          <n1:n2:S, G, MKAP:C, D>  ⇒  <n:S, G[n=AP n1 n2], C, D>
CONS          similarly
```

Figure 19.2 G-machine state transitions (stack and data)

Finally, we say what the BEGIN instruction does, which initializes the machine:

<O, S, G, BEGIN:C, D> ⇒ <O, [], [], C, []>

BEGIN simply initializes the stack, graph and dump to be empty, and then runs the rest of the code C.

19.1.4 Remarks about G-code

This way of defining the meaning of G-code is very similar to that used by Landin [1964] to describe the SECD machine; indeed, the G-machine could almost be called the SGCD machine. This is our first hint that the execution of functional programs by graph reduction (as in the G-machine) and by delayed substitution (as in the SECD machine) is not as different as at first appears; a topic we will return to later.

19.2 Implementation

We now begin a discussion of how to implement the abstract machine defined by G-code on a concrete machine (the target machine). To start with, we have to provide concrete representations for each of the four components of the G-machine state <S, G, C, D>, which we do in this section.

For the sake of definiteness we will study the Chalmers G-machine implementation, which generates machine code (the target code) for a VAX. Some familiarity with VAX machine code is useful in what follows, so we digress briefly to summarize the knowledge required.

19.2.1 VAX Unix Assembler Syntax

Here is an example of a typical instruction we may generate:

```
movl 12(%EP),-(%EP)
```

The movl is the VAX instruction to move a four-byte word. The source is 12(%EP), and uses indexed addressing, so that the address of the operand is the contents of register EP plus 12. The destination is –(%EP) and uses indirect addressing with pre-decrement.

The notation %EP stands for a register, and the symbol EP should be previously defined by an assembler directive:

```
.set EP,10
```

Registers can also be referred to by the notation r0 for register 0, r1 for register 1 and so on.

The moval instruction (Move Address) moves the *address* of the source operand into the destination, rather than moving the source operand itself as movl does. For example,

```
moval 4(%EP),r0
```

adds 4 to register EP and puts the result in register 0. It can also be used to move literal constants:

```
moval 4,r0
```

loads 4 into r0.

The subroutine call and return instructions are jsb and rsb.

19.2.2 The Stack Representation

The G-machine stack is represented by a data area to hold the stack, together with a stack pointer held in a register, called EP. The stack grows downwards, and each element of the stack is a 32-bit VAX word. EP points to the top element of the stack, so elements can be pushed onto the stack using pre-decrement of EP, and popped off with post-increment. For example,

```
movl r0,-(%EP)        Push register 0
movl (%EP)+,r0        Pop register 0
```

As with any stack we must be careful to check for stack overflow. At first it looks as if we must perform this check (if the target machine's hardware does not) on every push. A much cheaper solution is available, however, because the amount of stack used by a function is totally predictable at compile-time (apart from EVAL and UNWIND instructions). All we need do is compute the amount of stack needed by a function (excluding any EVALs or UNWINDs), and check at the beginning of the function that sufficient stack space is available.

An UNWIND at the end of the function can consume an unpredictable amount of stack, so it must check for overflow on each push. An EVAL causes an UNWIND followed by a function call, both of which are now dealt with, so EVAL need only check for dump overflow.

19.2.3 The Graph Representation

The graph is represented by a large heap area of storage. Each node of the graph is represented by a *cell* in the heap. Each cell consists of a *tag* and one or more *fields*. The tag and each field occupy one VAX machine word (four bytes), and the words constituting a cell are arranged contiguously. A two-field cell would look like this:

Byte offset	
0	Tag
4	Field 1
8	Field 2

It may seem rather wasteful to use four bytes to store a tag, but it gives considerable uniformity to heap allocation, and offers the opportunity for an ingenious optimization (see Section 19.4).

AP n m	AP	n	m
CONS n m	CONS	n	m
INT i	INT	i	
HOLE	HOLE		
FUN k C	See Section 19.4.3		

Figure 19.3 Node representations in the G-machine

Boxed representations of basic values are used. The various types of node are represented as shown in Figure 19.3.

A copying garbage collector is used, so only half the heap area is in use at any time. Cells are allocated contiguously in the current heap area, and a register called HP points to the next free word. Cells can then be allocated simply by incrementing HP; indeed this can be done at the same time as the contents of the cell are filled in by using the VAX auto-increment instruction.

It appears at first that HP should be checked after each increment to see if the heap is exhausted (which initiates garbage collection), which would require an extra instruction for each allocation. Instead, however, the compiler computes how much heap will be allocated by each supercombinator, and inserts code at the beginning of the supercombinator to check that enough heap is available. If not enough is available, garbage collection is invoked. Hence, during execution of a supercombinator there is no danger of heap exhaustion, so cells can be allocated with a simple auto-increment on HP.

19.2.4 The Code Representation

The code is the VAX machine code, together with the program counter.

19.2.5 The Dump Representation

The dump is the VAX system stack, together with its stack pointer held in the (special) SP register. This stack is addressed in the same way as the other stack.

19.3 Target Code Generation

Having established concrete representations for the four components of the G-machine state, we now turn our attention to the task of generating target code from the G-code instruction sequence. We begin with a simple method, and then demonstrate a simple but effective optimization technique.

19.3.1 Generating Target Code from G-code Instructions

In this section we will show how to perform simple code generation from G-code into VAX assembler code.

To each G-code instruction there should correspond a short sequence of VAX machine instructions. For example, using the representations described in Section 19.2 for the VAX, we could generate code for the PUSH instruction like this:

```
PUSH n          movl 4*n(%EP),-(%EP)
```

The source is 4*n(%EP), and uses indexed addressing to fetch the word 4*n bytes from the top of the stack, which is pointed to by register EP. We must multiply n by 4 to get a byte offset (rather than a word offset). The destination is the top of the stack, and we pre-decrement the stack pointer to push the new word onto the stack.

As a longer illustration, we will generate code for the function

```
g f = NEG (f 5)
```

With our present compilation algorithm this compiles to

```
PUSHINT 5; PUSH 1; MKAP; PUSHGLOBAL $NEG; MKAP;
UPDATE 2; POP 1; UNWIND
```

A simple code generation would go like this:

G-code	HP	VAX assembler code	Comments
PUSHINT 5	0	moval I_5,-(%EP)	Push 5
PUSH 1		movl 4(%EP),-(%EP)	Push f
MKAP	4	moval APPLY,(%HP)+	Tag of apply node to heap
	8	movl (%EP)+,(%HP)+	Function of apply node (f)
	12	movl (%EP)+,(%HP)+	Argument of apply node (5)
		moval -12(%HP),-(%EP)	Result on stack (f 5)
PUSHGLOBAL $NEG		moval C_NEG,-(%EP)	Push NEG
MKAP	16	moval APPLY,(%HP)+	Tag of apply node to heap
	20	movl (%EP)+,(%HP)+	Function of apply ($NEG)
	24	movl (%EP)+,(%HP)+	Argument of apply (f 5)
		moval -12(%HP),-(%EP)	Result on stack
UPDATE 2		movl (%EP)+,r1	Result in register r_1
		movl 4(%EP),r2	Root of redex in r_2
		movl (r1)+,(r2)+	Copy tag
		movl (r1)+,(r2)+	Copy first field
		movl (r1)+,(r2)+	Copy second field
POP 1		moval 4(%EP),%EP	Decrement stack pointer

APPLY is the tag word for an apply node.
I_5 is the address of a boxed integer 5.
C_NEG is the address of the NEG function cell.

We will see later how to implement the UNWIND instruction.

Notice the way in which cell allocation in the heap takes place by loading data into the heap at the point pointed to by the HP register using auto-increment addressing. This neatly combines the operations of allocating a cell and loading data into it.

The second column shows that it is possible to keep track of the value of HP at code generation time. This will prove useful in performing optimizations.

This code is adequate, but not especially intelligent, because it has many redundant pushes and pops. For example, the last instruction of the second MKAP sequence could be merged with the first instruction of the UPDATE sequence to give

```
moval  -12(%HP),r1
```

This kind of optimization has been well studied elsewhere [Wulf *et al.*, 1975; Bauer and Eickel, 1976; Aho and Ullman, 1977], but one of the basic ideas is so simple and gives such good results that we describe it in the next section.

19.3.2 Optimization Using a Stack Model

The idea of this optimization is that during code generation we should maintain a model of what is on the stack at any given time. We call this the *simulated stack*. The simulated stack is a compile-time stack, which holds the specification of values that would have been in the run-time stack if we had used a straightforward code generation scheme (as in the previous section). For example, possible entries in the simulated stack, together with the values they specify, are:

(i) 5, the literal value 5;
(ii) NEG, the address of the $NEG function cell;
(iii) heap 20, the address of the cell at offset 20 from the HP pointer value at the start of execution of the supercombinator;
(iv) stack 2, the value at offset 2 from the EP stack pointer value at the start of execution of the supercombinator.

Figure 19.4 illustrates by redoing our example, which shows a considerable reduction in the number of VAX machine instructions generated. Notice how important it is that garbage collection does not take place during a supercombinator execution. If it did so, all the heap offsets might be rendered erroneous.

The simulated stack will be empty at the end of the execution of a supercombinator. The EVAL instruction needs special treatment, which we discuss in the next section.

As a by-product of this code generation we get the amount of heap used by the supercombinator, so the compiler can generate the code to check for heap exhaustion at the beginning of the supercombinator (but see EVAL, below).

G-code	HP VAX assembler code	Simulated stack	Comments
	0	[]	Begin
PUSHINT 5		5:[]	Push 5
PUSH 1		stack 0:5:[]	Push f
MKAP	4 moval APPLY,(%HP)+		Tag to heap
	8 movl 0(%EP),(%HP)+	5:[]	Fun to heap
	12 moval I_5,(%HP)+	[]	Arg to heap
		heap 0:[]	Result on stack
PUSHGLOBAL $NEG		NEG:heap 0:[]	Push NEG
MKAP	16 moval APPLY,(%HP)+		Tag to heap
	20 moval C_NEG,(%HP)+	heap 0:[]	Fun to heap
	24 moval −20(%HP),(%HP)+	[]	Arg to heap
		heap 12:[]	Result on stack
UPDATE 2	moval −12(%HP),r1	[]	Result in r_1
	movl 4(%EP),r2		Root in r_2
	movl (r1)+,(r2)+		Copy tag
	movl (r1)+,(r2)+		Copy first
	movl (r1)+,(r2)+		Copy second
POP 1	moval 4(%EP),%EP		Pop arguments

Figure 19.4 Code generation using a simulated stack

19.3.3 Handling EVALs and JUMPs

EVAL is a considerable nuisance because it may cause an arbitrary amount of computation to occur. This means that the amount of heap consumed has no simple bound, and garbage collection may occur during such evaluation, thus completely disrupting the simulated stack and HP.

We can deal with this by treating the segments of code between EVALs separately, each with its own code to check for heap exhaustion. All stack and heap offsets in the simulated stack are calculated relative to the values of EP and HP at the beginning of the segment (not the supercombinator, as stated above). Furthermore, before EVAL is called, the simulated stack must be flushed out onto the real stack.

Similar remarks apply to sections of code broken with JUMP instructions. If there are two different routes leading to a given place in the code then different amounts of heap may have been allocated along the two routes, and the contents of the simulated stack may be different. Accordingly, the simulated stack must be flushed before JUMPs also.

What all this amounts to is that we can generate good code for straight-line segments of code ('basic blocks' in conventional compiler terminology), but have to take more care when the flow of control can be broken.

19.4 More on the Graph Representation

We may think of the G-machine in the following way:

G-code execution mechanism
----------Graph interface----------
The graph

The G-code execution mechanism manipulates nodes in the graph, using a certain limited set of operations which we call the *graph interface*. Once we have specified the graph interface we are at liberty to alter the concrete implementation of the graph so long as the implementation supports all the operations in the graph interface.

In practice, such a clean separation of concerns is hard to achieve without suffering a considerable performance penalty. We may distinguish, however, between two kinds of graph operation:

(i) *Node-specific operations* are only used on a specific type of node. For example, the G-code instruction HEAD is only executed when the node on top of the stack is known to be a CONS node. Node-specific operations can normally compile to a single target machine instruction.

Other examples of node-specific operations are ADD and JFALSE.

(ii) *Generic operations* are used on a variety of types of node. For example, when the UNWIND instruction is executed, nothing is known about the node on top of the stack. The first thing UNWIND has to do is to perform case analysis on the node type. Generic operations are considerably more expensive than node-specific operations because of this case analysis.

Other examples of generic operations are EVAL, PRINT, CASEJUMP and some garbage collection operations.

The Chalmers G-machine has a rather fast and elegant implementation of the generic operations, which contributes significantly to its performance and extensibility. We will discuss this technique in the succeeding sections.

19.4.1 Implementing Tag Case Analysis

As noted earlier, in the Chalmers G-machine the tag of a cell is a *word*, and it points to a small table of code entry points, one entry point for each generic operation.

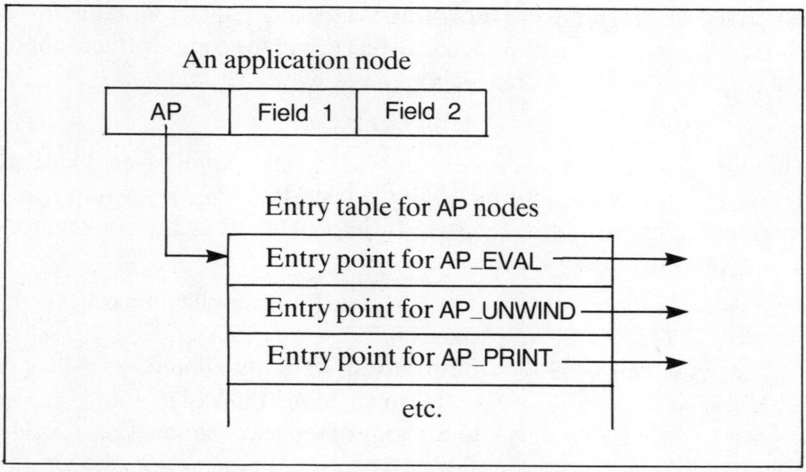

The AP_EVAL code, for example, performs the appropriate operations to evaluate an application node. Each distinct node type has a different entry table, so that case analysis on a cell can now be performed simply by jumping to the appropriate entry of the table pointed to from the tag of the cell.

Naturally, the EVAL entry must occupy the same position in the entry table for each node type.

19.4.2 Implementing EVAL

In this section we will consider the implementation of the EVAL instruction. This comes in two parts:

(i) the code that is generated in-line for an EVAL G-code instruction;
(ii) the code for the EVAL entry of each tag's entry table.

First of all, here is the VAX target code which might be generated in-line for an EVAL G-code instruction:

```
movl (%EP),r0          Top of stack to r0
movl (r0),r1           Tag to r1
jsb *O_Eval(r1)        Call Eval code
```

The element on top of the stack is fetched into r0 (without popping the stack), its tag is fetched into r1, and the final instruction is an indexed subroutine call, where O_Eval is the offset of the Eval entry in the entry table. Notice that by using a jsb instruction we push the return address (the code pointer C) onto the system stack (the dump D), so that we can return to the instruction following EVAL when evaluation is complete.

We now consider the Eval code thus entered. Suppose that the cell in question is an integer cell (we assume a boxed implementation for the moment). Then no evaluation need take place, and the code is rather simple:

```
INT_EVAL:                      The Eval code for an integer cell.
          rsb                  Return from Eval
```

The same applies to function cells and CONS cells. Application nodes are a different story, however. In this case we need to push the current stack S (implemented by EP) onto the dump D (implemented by the system stack), and then UNWIND the application.

```
AP_EVAL                        The Eval code for an application cell.
          <Test for SP stack overflow>
          movl %EP,-(SP)       Push current stack onto dump
AP_UNWIND:                     Fall through to AP_UNWIND
                               r0 is a copy of top stack element
                               r1 is its tag
```

First we save the current stack on the dump, checking first for dump overflow, and then behave like UNWIND (see next section). Notice that to save the current stack on the dump we need only save the current stack *pointer* on the system stack. Logically, the new stack only contains a single element, which is the top element of the old stack, so we do not need to alter the stack pointer itself. The depth of the current stack can be found by comparing the old stack pointer (found on top of the system stack) with the current stack pointer (in EP).

19.4.3 Implementing UNWIND

Here is the VAX machine code sequence that might be generated for an UNWIND G-code instruction:

```
movl (%EP),r0                  Top of stack to r0
movl (r0),r1                   Tag to r1
jmp *0_Unwind(r1)              Jump to Unwind code
```

The element on top of the stack is fetched into r0 (without popping the stack), its tag is fetched into r1, and an indexed jump to the Unwind code is made (not a jsb).

Now suppose that the cell in question is an application cell. What should the AP_UNWIND code do? It should simply push the head of the cell on the stack and UNWIND it again. Remembering that r0 points to the cell in question, we get:

```
AP_UNWIND:                     The Unwind code for an application cell
          <Check for EP stack overflow>
          movl Head(r0),r0     Get head
          movl r0,-(%EP)       Push it
          movl (r0),r1         Get tag in r1
          jmp *0_Unwind(r1)    Unwind it
```

As noted in Section 19.2.2, we should first check for stack overflow, unless the machine's hardware is capable of doing so automatically.

Suppose, instead, that the cell is an integer cell. Then the specification for UNWIND says that the integer cell must be the only thing on the stack, and we should return to the caller, restoring the old stack but putting the top element of the current stack on top of it. Fortunately, it is already in the right place! Hence, all that is required is the following:

```
INT_UNWIND:                   The Unwind code for an integer cell
        movl (SP)+,%EP        Restore stack pointer
        rsb                   Return to caller
```

Suppose now that we are unwinding a global function cell. Then the specification for UNWIND (see Figure 19.1) requires a test to check whether there are enough arguments on the stack for the function to execute. The Chalmers G-machine actually uses a separate tag for each function, complete with a separate entry table (remember that a tag takes a whole word, so there are plenty of tags available). This means that instead of having code for FUN_UNWIND we have a piece of code F_UNWIND for each global function F (supercombinator or built-in function). Suppose that F takes two arguments. Then the code for F_UNWIND might look like this:

```
F_Return:                          We get here if there are too
                                   few args. Return to caller.
        movl (SP)+,%EP             Restore stack pointer
        rsb                        Return to caller

F_UNWIND:                          Unwind code for function F
                                   NB: pointer to FUN node is still on stack
        moval 8(%EP),r0            r0 points to base of context
        cmpl (SP),r0               Is this below stack base?
        jlss F_Return              Return if too few args

                                   Now rearrange the stack
        movl 4(%EP),r0             Top vertebra in r0
        movl Tail(r0),(%EP)        Push its tail (overwrites FUN pointer)
        movl 8(%EP),r0             Next vertebra in r0
        movl Tail(r0),4(%EP)       Tail into stack

F_EXEC:                            Now comes the code for F
        ...
```

The code immediately after F_UNWIND first makes a test to see whether there are enough arguments. It does so by computing the address of the base of the context in the stack, assuming that enough arguments are present. In this case, two arguments and four bytes per stack element give an offset of eight from the top of the current stack. It then compares this context base address with the saved stack pointer, found on the dump, which points to the base of the current stack. If the former is less than the latter, there are too few arguments, so it jumps to F_Return where the old stack is restored and the current evaluation completes with a return to the caller (just as for INT_UNWIND).

If there are enough arguments, the next four instructions rearrange the current context ready for the main body of code for F, which begins at F_EXEC. This entry point will be used in Chapter 21.

A 'FUN k C' node is therefore represented as a cell with a tag but no fields. The tag gives access to the entry points which know about k and C.

19.4.4 Indirection Nodes

A major advantage of this method of implementing generic operations is that new node types can be added without changing anything except to provide an entry table for the new node type. As an example of this, we will now describe how to introduce indirection nodes into the implementation.

Thus far we have described an implementation of the G-machine which performs the update at the end of a reduction by *copying* the root of the result of the reduction over the root of the redex. As we described at length in Section 12.4, we could instead overwrite the root of the redex with an *indirection* to the result. The section also discussed the trade-offs between the two approaches, but we will now show how some minor and local changes to our implementation can change the G-machine from using copying to using indirection nodes.

We need to perform only two changes:

(i) We must introduce a new cell type, an indirection cell, complete with its entry table. It will only have one field, which contains the indirection pointer.
(ii) We must change the implementation of the UPDATE instruction.

The only work associated with the first change is to provide target code sequences for each generic operation. They are all rather easy. For example, IND-UNWIND – the Unwind code for an indirection cell – looks like this:

```
movl 4(r0),r0          Get the indirection pointer
movl r0,(%EP)          Overwrite top stack element
movl (r0),r1           Get tag
jmp *0_Unwind(r1)      Jump to Unwind code
```

The overwriting of the stack element 'shorts out' the indirection, so that it does not appear as a vertebra in the stack. The Eval code for an indirection cell, IND-EVAL, is similarly simple:

```
movl 4(r0),r0          Get the indirection pointer
movl r0,(%EP)          Overwrite top stack element
movl (r0),r1           Get tag
jmp *0_Eval(r1)        Continue Eval
```

The second thing we must do is alter the implementation of UPDATE. Recall that 'UPDATE k' updates the root of the redex, which is pointed to by the kth element of the stack, with the result, which is on top of the stack. The new implementation of 'UPDATE k' must therefore do three things:

(i) Overwrite the vertebra pointed to from the kth element of the stack with an indirection node, whose indirection pointer points to the result.
(ii) Overwrite the kth element of the stack to point directly to the result (not to the indirection node). This is really just an optimization, but ensures that the result of EVAL is never an indirection cell. This is helpful when, for example, the result of an EVAL is known to be an integer; in this case it is a nuisance to have to check for an indirection also.
(iii) Pop the result from the stack.

This gives the following code sequence for the 'UPDATE d' G-code instruction:

```
movl  4*d(%EP),r2           r2 points to root of redex
moval IND,(r2)+             IND tag
movl  (%EP),(r2)            Put result into indirection cell
movl  (%EP)+,4*d(%EP)       Overwrite vertebra and pop result
```

That's all! In addition, the garbage collection entry point(s) in the indirection cell entry table can perform the 'shorting out' of indirection nodes discussed in Chapter 17.

19.4.5 Boxed versus Unboxed Representations

The Chalmers G-machine uses boxed representations for all basic values. There are two reasons for this:

(i) A boxed representation of a basic value has a tag in just the same place as any other value, so that generic operations can be implemented uniformly. With unboxed representations generic operations would have to perform an initial test to separate pointers from non-pointers before doing case analysis as before.
(ii) An unboxed representation would need to carry around a pointer bit with each field. This is rather tiresome. On the VAX the pointer bit could either be packed into the same 32-bit word as the value, or kept in a separate byte (or word) which was moved around with the value. In the former case there has to be much stripping off and tacking on of pointer bits, and integers are restricted to only 31 bits. In the latter case there have to be two target code 'move' instructions instead of one whenever a value is moved around.

   Of course, this problem would go away in a target architecture more specifically suited to graph reduction.

19.4.6 Summary

We have seen that the technique of implementing generic operations by using cell tags as pointers to entry tables gives two main advantages:

(i) it is easy to add new node types (indirection nodes, for example);
(ii) it is fast, because generic operations are implemented uniformly using an indexed jump.

19.5 Getting it all Together

How does all the code we generate hold together? For a start, the G-code for each supercombinator begins with a GLOBSTART instruction. This instruction must generate the following segments of target code:

(i) UNWIND code, which checks the number of arguments and rearranges the stack;
(ii) GC code, which will depend on the garbage collector;
(iii) the entry table for the supercombinator (the EVAL, PRINT, etc. entries are the same for all supercombinators);
(iv) the function node itself, which can be allocated at the beginning of the function code, outside the main heap;
(v) overflow-checking code, which immediately precedes the target code for the function body, and checks for overflow of stack and heap.

Thus the target code for each function is preceded by some code fragments, the entry table and the function node. This completes the code generation for each function.

Finally we must consider what the BEGIN and END G-code instructions do. The BEGIN instruction is responsible for initializing the whole system. In particular it must generate target code to

(i) initialize the stack pointer EP;
(ii) initialize the heap (in particular, the heap pointer HP).

In any particular system there will certainly be other initialization tasks to perform, and the BEGIN instruction is the opportunity to perform them.

The END instruction simply terminates execution of the entire program.

19.6 Summary

In this chapter we have seen how an abstract machine model can provide a precise description for G-code and a secure basis for code generation.

We have also examined some techniques for generating good code. The details of good code generation are, however, beyond the scope of this book.

References

Aho, A.V., and Ullman, J.D. 1977. *Principles of Compiler Design*. Addison Wesley.

Bauer, F.L., and Eickel, J. 1976. *Compiler Construction*. Springer Verlag.

Landin, P.J. 1964. The mechanical evaluation of expressions. *Computer Journal*. Vol. 6, pp. 308–20.

Wulf, W., Johnsson, R.K., Weinstock, C.B., Hobbs, S.O., and Geschke, C.M. 1975. *The Design of an Optimising Compiler*. Elsevier.

Twenty

OPTIMIZATIONS TO THE G-MACHINE

We now give a long sequence of optimizations to the G-code compilation schemes. In the main they are independent of each other and any combination of them could be implemented. All of them are based on the idea of compiling special code to avoid building graphs.

One particular optimization, concerning spine allocation, is so important that we devote the next chapter to it.

20.1 On Not Building Graphs

The principal reason why implementations of functional languages have the reputation for being very slow is that they spend a lot of time allocating and garbage-collecting cells from the heap. A heap provides a very general storage allocation mechanism, but it is also very expensive. Each cell used costs us in four ways:

(i) it must be allocated;
(ii) it must be filled with data;
(iii) the data in it will normally subsequently be read;
(iv) the cell must be recovered when it becomes unreferenced.

A stack, by contrast, is a much less flexible allocation mechanism but store is recovered immediately it becomes unused, and this recovery is very cheap (decrementing the stack pointer). In addition, because stacks seldom grow large, it is often possible to implement the stack with faster technology, so that accessing stack elements is faster than going to the heap.

A primary objective of our optimizations, then, will be to use the stack rather than the heap wherever possible. In particular, the compilation scheme **C** (Section 18.5.3) builds graph structures in the heap, and many of our optimizations will be directly aimed at replacing uses of the **C** compilation scheme with alternative (and cheaper) schemes in particular cases.

20.2 Preserving Laziness

This optimization should be regarded as essential, since without it laziness may be lost.

As we mentioned when we introduced the first version of the **R** scheme (Section 18.5.2), it gives poor performance when the body of the supercombinator is a single variable. This problem was discussed at some length in Section 12.4, and we discovered that the solution was to evaluate the variable before updating the root of the redex with its value.

The same problem arises with a supercombinator definition such as

```
$G x = letrec v1 = ...v2...x...
              v2 = ...v1...
       in v2
```

where the body of the supercombinator is a letrec, whose body is a single variable.

What we must do is to redefine **R** to have a separate case for each kind of expression, just as we did for **C**. Figure 20.1 gives such an **R** scheme. The code for a body which is just a single variable loads the value onto the stack, uses EVAL to evaluate it, and only then updates the root of the redex with the result. Notice the way let and letrec are handled rather elegantly by recursively applying the **R** scheme, having first compiled the definitions.

At first it may seem that the EVAL in the rule for a global, f, is redundant,

R⟦ E ⟧ ρ d

generates code to apply a supercombinator to its arguments.
Note: there are d arguments.

R⟦ i ⟧ ρ d	= PUSHINT i; UPDATE (d+1); POP d; RETURN
R⟦ f ⟧ ρ d	= PUSHGLOBAL f; EVAL; UPDATE (d+1); POP d; UNWIND
R⟦ x ⟧ ρ d	= PUSH (d − ρ x); EVAL UPDATE (d+1); POP d; UNWIND
R⟦ E_1 E_2 ⟧ ρ d	= **C**⟦ E_1 E_2 ⟧ ρ d; UPDATE (d+1); POP d; UNWIND
R⟦ let x=E_x in E ⟧ ρ d	= **C**⟦ E_x ⟧ ρ d; **R**⟦ E ⟧ ρ[x=d+1] (d+1)
R⟦ letrec D in E ⟧ ρ d	= **CLetrec**⟦ D ⟧ ρ′ d′; **R**⟦ E ⟧ ρ′ d′ where (ρ′, d′) = **Xr**⟦ D ⟧ ρ d

Figure 20.1 Modifications to the **R** scheme to preserve laziness

since most globals (such as built-in functions, and supercombinators) plainly do not need to be evaluated. However, the global might be a CAF (a zero-argument supercombinator), in which case it may be reducible, so the EVAL is mandatory. There is scope for a simple optimization here, by omitting the EVAL in non-CAF cases, and it will have a large performance benefit. The optimization can, however, be carried out by a peephole optimizer (see Section 20.10), so we do not perform it here.

The other point of interest is that we have used RETURN instead of UNWIND for the integer case, because we know that the integer cannot be applied to anything (assuming that the program was type-checked), and hence the expression being evaluated must now be in WHNF.

20.3 Direct Execution of Built-in Functions

This is probably the next most important optimization we will study, and it concerns the compilation of expressions such as (P x_1 x_2) when

(i) P is a built-in function;
(ii) all its arguments are present.

In many such cases we will be able to compile far superior code by directly executing P.

20.3.1 Optimizations to the R Scheme

As our first example, consider compiling (CONS E_1 E_2) with the **R** scheme:

R[[CONS E_1 E_2]] ρ d
= **C**[[CONS E_1 E_2]] ρ d; UPDATE (d+1); POP d; UNWIND

With the present scheme we construct the graph of ($CONS E_1 E_2), and then promptly unwind it. When the unwind completes we will find $CONS at the tip of the spine, we will discover that it does indeed have enough arguments, and so we will enter the code for $CONS. This will form a CONS node from its two arguments and RETURN.

We can short-circuit this completely predictable process by executing the CONS directly, like this:

R[[CONS E_1 E_2]] ρ d
= **C**[[E_2]] ρ d; **C**[[E_1]] ρ (d+1); CONS;
UPDATE (d+1); POP d; RETURN

We construct the graphs for E_2 and E_1, execute the CONS G-code instruction to form a CONS cell, update the root of the redex and RETURN. This allocates fewer nodes in the heap, uses fewer G-code instructions, and avoids executing the code for the $CONS function we developed in Chapter 18. So we win all round. We can achieve this optimization simply by adding the above **R** rule to the **R** scheme.

As a second example, consider compiling the expression (IF E_c E_t E_f) with the **R** scheme:

```
R[[ IF Ec Et Ef ]] ρ d
= C[[ IF Ec Et Ef ]] ρ d; UPDATE (d+1); POP d; UNWIND
```

This code will construct the graph of ($IF E_c E_t E_f), unwind it, find $IF at the tip of the spine, discover that it does indeed have enough arguments, and enter the code for $IF. The code for $IF will evaluate its first argument, test it and conditionally jump on the result. We can again short-circuit this process by generating the following code:

```
R[[ IF Ec Et Ef ]] ρ d
= C[[ Ec ]] ρ d; EVAL; JFALSE L;
          R[[ Et ]] ρ d;
  LABEL L;
          R[[ Ef ]] ρ d
```

First of all we evaluate the condition, and conditionally jump based on its value. Then we can complete the code in each branch using a recursive application of the **R** scheme. Notice how this neatly allows all the optimizations we are developing to be applied in each branch. Notice also that, since the code generated by **R** ends by returning to the caller, no jump is necessary to 'join up the branches of the if'. The CASE-n function can be compiled in an analogous manner, except using a multi-way jump (CASEJUMP) instead of a two-way jump (JFALSE).

Precisely analogous remarks apply to expressions such as (+ E_1 E_2) and (HEAD E). Rather than construct their graph and then immediately unwind into them, we execute them directly:

```
R[[ + E1 E2 ]] ρ d
= C[[ E2 ]] ρ d; EVAL; C[[ E1 ]] ρ (d+1); EVAL; ADD;
  UPDATE (d+1); POP d; RETURN

R[[ HEAD E ]] ρ d
= C[[ E ]] ρ d; EVAL; HEAD; EVAL;
  UPDATE (d+1); POP d; RETURN
```

These optimizations can be achieved by simply adding the above **R** rules into the **R** scheme. They constitute an extremely worthwhile improvement to our compilation algorithm, but there is more to come!

20.3.2 The E Scheme

A cursory inspection of the extra **R** rules reveals the frequent occurrence of the sequence

```
C[[ E ]] ρ d; EVAL
```

Now suppose (as at the beginning of the last section) that E was of the form (CONS E_1 E_2). Then we would compile code to construct the graph of ($CONS E_1 E_2) and promptly EVALuate it. But this is precisely the kind of situation that the optimizations of the previous section succeeded in spotting. How can we perform the same optimization for the **C**-EVAL sequence?

The reason that the **C**-EVAL sequence performs badly is that the **C** scheme proceeds in ignorance of the fact that the result is going to be evaluated. What we need is a new scheme, **E**, which is a version of **C** that delivers an evaluated result. To be specific:

E⟦ E ⟧ ρ d

produces G-code which evaluates E to WHNF and leaves the result on top of the stack.

This is, of course, precisely what the **C**-EVAL sequence did. Figure 20.2 gives the **E** compilation scheme. In exactly the same way as the **R** scheme, **E** looks for a number of special cases, and produces good code for these cases. Notice how often it is possible to apply **E** recursively to compile subexpressions. For example, when the result of (+ E_1 E_2) is needed then we are sure the results of E_1 and E_2 will be needed, so they can be compiled with **E**. This achieves the desirable effect of propagating demand into the expression. In the same way as **R**, **E** propagates down inside lets and letrecs. If, however, none of the special cases applies, **E** takes the easy way out and uses **C** followed by EVAL.

```
        E[[ E ]] ρ d

Evaluates E, leaving the result on top of the stack.

E[[ i ]] ρ d                 = PUSHINT i
E[[ f ]] ρ d                 = PUSHGLOBAL f; EVAL
E[[ x ]] ρ d                 = PUSH (d − ρ x); EVAL
E[[ NEG E ]] ρ d             = E[[ E ]] ρ d; NEG
E[[ + E1 E2 ]] ρ d           = E[[ E2 ]] ρ d; E[[ E1 ]] ρ (d+1); ADD
E[[ CONS E1 E2 ]] ρ d        = C[[ E2 ]] ρ d; C[[ E1 ]] ρ (d+1); CONS
E[[ HEAD E ]] ρ d            = E[[ E ]] ρ d; HEAD; EVAL
E[[ IF Ec Et Ef ]] ρ d       = E[[ Ec ]] ρ d; JFALSE L1;
                                   E[[ Et ]] ρ d; JUMP L2;
                               LABEL L1;
                                   E[[ Ef ]] ρ d;
                               LABEL L2
E[[ let x=Ex in E ]] ρ d     = C[[ Ex ]] ρ d;
                               E[[ E ]] ρ[x=d+1] (d+1); SLIDE 1
E[[ letrec D in E ]] ρ d     = CLetrec[[ D ]] ρ' d'; E[[ E ]] ρ' d'; SLIDE (d'−d)
                               where
                               (ρ', d') = Xr[[ D ]] ρ d
E[[ E1 E2 ]] ρ d             = C[[ E1 E2 ]] ρ d; EVAL
```

Figure 20.2 The **E** compilation scheme

We can now use **E** by replacing all uses of the **C**-EVAL sequence in the **R** scheme with a call to **E** (see Figure 20.3). The **R**⟦ E_1 E_2 ⟧ rule is used if none of the special cases is applicable; it has not changed since Figure 20.1, and is only put in here as a reminder.

As well as allocating less store and using fewer G-code instructions, these optimizations have the effect of reducing the number of calls to EVAL. This means that there will be longer code sequences with no uses of EVAL, which may mean that an implementation is able to keep things in registers rather more effectively.

```
R[[ NEG E ]] ρ d          = E[[ E ]] ρ d; NEG;
                            UPDATE (d+1); POP d; RETURN
R[[ + E1 E2 ]] ρ d        = E[[ E2 ]] ρ d; E[[ E1 ]] ρ (d+1); ADD;
                            UPDATE (d+1); POP d; RETURN
R[[ CONS E1 E2 ]] ρ d     = C[[ E2 ]] ρ d; C[[ E1 ]] ρ (d+1); CONS;
                            UPDATE (d+1); POP d; RETURN
R[[ HEAD E ]] ρ d         = E[[ E ]] ρ d; HEAD;
                            UPDATE (d+1); POP d; RETURN
R[[ IF Ec Et Ef ]] ρ d    = E[[ Ec ]] ρ d; JFALSE L;
                                R[[ Et ]] ρ d;
                            LABEL L;
                                R[[ Ef ]] ρ d
R[[ E1 E2 ]] ρ d          = C[[ E1 E2 ]] ρ d;
                            UPDATE (d+1); POP d; UNWIND
```

The cases for i, j, x, let and letrec are unchanged.

Figure 20.3 Modifications to the **R** scheme to optimize known functions

20.3.3 The RS and ES Schemes

There is still one important hole in the new optimizations we have developed in this section. Consider the expression

(HEAD E_1 E_2)

We expect E_1 to evaluate to a CONS cell, whose head will be a function which is applied to E_2. Let us compile it with the **R** scheme:

```
R[[ HEAD E1 E2 ]] ρ d
= C[[ HEAD E1 E2 ]] ρ d; UPDATE (d+1); POP d; UNWIND
```

We have been unable to take advantage of the optimization of HEAD given in the preceding sections, because of the second argument E_2. This problem can occur with any built-in function which can deliver a function as its result;

in particular HEAD and IF, together with their analogs SEL-k-i and CASE. What we would like to generate for the above example is this:

```
R[[ HEAD E1 E2 ]] ρ d
= C[[ E2 ]] ρ d; E[[ E1 ]] ρ (d+1); HEAD; MKAP;
  UPDATE (d+1); POP d; UNWIND
```

Achieving this optimization requires us somehow to apply an **R**-like compilation scheme recursively to the (HEAD E_1) subexpression, rather than just giving up and using **C**. We call this new compilation scheme **RS**, and we want **RS** to have a rule something like

```
RS[[ E1 E2 ]] ρ d = C[[ E2 ]] ρ d; RS[[ E1 ]] ρ (d+1)
```

We could then use **RS** by replacing the **R**[[E_1 E_2]] rule with

```
R[[ E1 E2 ]] ρ d = RS[[ E1 E2 ]] ρ d
```

(*Warning*: these rules are not yet correct as they stand here.) With these modifications, the compilation of (HEAD E_1 E_2) would begin thus:

```
R[[ HEAD E1 E2 ]] ρ d
= RS[[ HEAD E1 E2 ]] ρ d
= C[[ E2 ]] ρ d; RS[[ HEAD E1 ]] ρ (d+1)
```

Now the (HEAD E_1) expression can be picked up with a special case in the **RS** scheme.

The **RS** rule given above causes **RS** to descend the spine of the expression, constructing its ribs using **C**, and putting them on the stack. The question arises, however, of what **RS** should do when it reaches the bottom. At this point, all the ribs of the expression are on the stack, so what **RS** should do is to generate an appropriate number of MKAPs to construct the spine of the expression, update the root of the redex, pop the arguments and UNWIND. This means that **RS** must know how many ribs are on the stack, so it needs an extra parameter, n. The real rule for **RS** now becomes

```
RS[[ E1 E2 ]] ρ d n = C[[ E2 ]] ρ d; RS[[ E1 ]] ρ (d+1) (n+1)
```

It is invoked from the **R** scheme like this:

```
R[[ E1 E2 ]] ρ d = RS[[ E1 E2 ]] ρ d 0
```

When it reaches the bottom, **RS** simply constructs the spine with n MKAPs, updates the root of the redex, pops the arguments and UNWINDs:

```
RS[[ f ]] ρ d n
= PUSHGLOBAL f; MKAP n; UPDATE (d−n+1); POP (d−n); UNWIND

RS[[ x ]] ρ d n
= PUSH (d − ρ x); MKAP n; UPDATE (d−n+1); POP (d−n); UNWIND
```

'MKAP n' is an extended version of MKAP, equivalent to n repetitions of MKAP. The offsets in the UPDATE and POP instructions take into account the

> **RS**⟦ E ⟧ ρ d n
>
> completes a supercombinator reduction, in which the top n ribs of the body have already been put on the stack.
>
> **RS** constructs instances of the ribs of E, putting them on the stack, and then completes the reduction in the same way as **R**.

```
RS[[ f ]] ρ d n             = PUSHGLOBAL f; MKAP n;
                              UPDATE (d-n+1); POP (d-n); UNWIND

RS[[ x ]] ρ d n             = PUSH (d - ρ x); MKAP n;
                              UPDATE (d-n+1); POP (d-n); UNWIND

RS[[ HEAD E ]] ρ d n        = E[[ E ]] ρ d; HEAD; MKAP n;
                              UPDATE (d-n+1); POP (d-n); UNWIND

RS[[ IF Ec Et Ef ]] ρ d n   = E[[ Ec ]] ρ d; JFALSE L1;
                                  RS[[ Et ]] ρ d n;
                              LABEL L1;
                                  RS[[ Ef ]] ρ d n

RS[[ E1 E2 ]] ρ d n         = C[[ E2 ]] ρ d;
                              RS[[ E1 ]] ρ (d+1) (n+1)
```

> Note: **RS** cannot encounter a let or letrec.

Figure 20.4 The **RS** compilation scheme

fact that the stack has gained one element as a result of the initial PUSH and lost n elements as a result of the 'MKAP n'. No case is needed for an integer, since the appearance of an integer at this point would mean that it was being used as a function.

Now we have done the hard work, and Figure 20.4 summarizes the **RS** scheme. The occurrence of a let or letrec would cause **RS** problems, since it assumes that the n ribs constructed so far occupy successive stack locations. Fortunately it is easy to ensure that **RS** can never encounter a let or letrec, by transforming any expression of the form

```
(letrec <definitions> in E1) E2
```

into

```
letrec <definitions> in (E1 E2)
```

This is precisely achieved by the algorithm described in Section 15.5.4.

Notice that we do not need special cases for functions such as NEG, + and CONS, because their result must be a data object, and hence will be caught by the **R** scheme.

It may seem that all this is a lot of work to cope with a few unusual cases. However, it has one other major benefit: it is readily generalized to optimize supercombinators as well as built-in functions, a subject we tackle in Chapter 21.

Just as optimizing the **R** scheme provoked us into developing the **E** scheme, so the **RS** scheme has a counterpart, the **ES** scheme, given in Figure 20.5. Notice that the structure of the **ES** scheme is exactly the same as that of the **RS** scheme; they differ only in the **ES**⟦ f ⟧ and **ES**⟦ x ⟧ cases. Figure 20.6 summarizes the modifications to the **R** and **E** schemes to use the new optimizations.

> **ES**⟦ E ⟧ ρ d n
>
> completes the evaluation of an expression, the top n ribs of which have already been put on the stack.
>
> **ES** constructs instances of the ribs of **E**, putting them on the stack, and then completes the evaluation in the same way as **E**.

```
ES[[ f ]] ρ d n            = PUSHGLOBAL f; MKAP n; EVAL

ES[[ x ]] ρ d n            = PUSH (d − ρ x); MKAP n; EVAL

ES[[ HEAD E ]] ρ d n       = E[[ E ]] ρ d; HEAD; MKAP n; EVAL

ES[[ IF Ec Et Ef ]] ρ d n  = E[[ Ec ]] ρ d; JFALSE L1;
                                 ES[[ Et ]] ρ d n; JUMP L2;
                             LABEL L1;
                                 ES[[ Ef ]] ρ d n
                             LABEL L2

ES[[ E1 E2 ]] ρ d n        = C[[ E2 ]] ρ d;
                             ES[[ E1 ]] ρ (d+1) (n+1)
```

> Note: **ES** cannot encounter a let or letrec.

Figure 20.5 The **ES** compilation scheme

```
R[[ E1 E2 ]] ρ d = RS[[ E1 E2 ]] ρ d 0
E[[ E1 E2 ]] ρ d = ES[[ E1 E2 ]] ρ d 0
```

Figure 20.6 Modifications to **R** and **E** to use **RS** and **ES**

20.3.4 η-reduction and Lambda-lifting

In Section 13.3.1 we showed how redundant supercombinator parameters could be eliminated by η-reduction. For a G-machine implementation, this is actually *undesirable*, unless it eliminates a supercombinator definition, which is always a good thing.

To see why it is undesirable, consider the definition

```
$F x y = IF E1 E2 y
```

where E_1 and E_2 do not use y. Now, it is true that

```
$F x = IF E1 E2
```

is an equivalent definition for $F, but it will generate *much less efficient* G-code. The reason is that the IF no longer has enough parameters, so **R** cannot use the efficient test-and-jump sequence it would have generated for the previous definition of $F.

This applies quite generally, and means that η-reduction should only be performed if it eliminates a whole definition. In fact, the opposite process, η-abstraction, may be desirable! However, η-abstraction risks losing full laziness, and we will not study it further.

A closely related point concerns the lambda-lifting algorithm. The optimizations described in this section apply to expressions such as (f E_1 E_2 . . .), *where we know what* f *is*. If we do not know what f is, it will generate less good code. The way in which this tends to occur is:

```
f x g y = g (+ x y)
```

that is, when a function is passed in as an argument and then applied. Unfortunately, fully lazy lambda-lifting results in many such expressions, and this is the main motivation for eliminating redundant full laziness (see Section 15.6).

20.4 Compiling FATBAR and FAIL

So far we have not made any mention of the built-in function FATBAR, and its companion value FAIL. In this section we will show a rather subtle optimization due to Augustsson [1985], which implements them extremely efficiently.

Suppose we have to compile

$$\mathbf{R}[\![\ \text{FATBAR}\ E_1\ E_2\ ]\!]\ \rho\ d$$

First, recall the semantic equations for FATBAR:

$$\begin{array}{lll} \text{FATBAR a} & \text{b} = \text{a} & \text{if a} \neq \bot \text{ and a} \neq \text{FAIL} \\ \text{FATBAR FAIL} & \text{b} = \text{b} & \\ \text{FATBAR} \bot & \text{b} = \bot & \end{array}$$

One way to proceed would be to compile E_1 with the **E** scheme, test the result for FAIL and return E_2 or E_1 accordingly:

$$\begin{array}{l} \mathbf{R}[\![\ \text{FATBAR}\ E_1\ E_2\ ]\!]\ \rho\ d \\ = \mathbf{E}[\![\ E_1\ ]\!]\ \rho\ d;\ \text{JFAIL L; UPDATE (d+1); POP d; UNWIND;} \\ \quad \text{LABEL L;}\ \mathbf{R}[\![\ E_2\ ]\!]\ \rho\ d; \end{array}$$

'JFAIL L' tests whether the value on top of the stack is FAIL; if so, it pops the stack and jumps to L; otherwise it does not pop the stack and does not jump.

A better way is to evaluate E_1 with the **R** scheme, but to *jump to the evaluation of* E_2 *if* FAIL *is encountered*. This entails adding two new parameters to the **R** scheme, j and s, where j is the label to jump to, and s is the depth of the current context expected by the code at j.

Now we can proceed as follows:

```
R[[ FATBAR E1 E2 ]] ρ d j s
= R[[ E1 ]] ρ d L d;
  LABEL L; R[[ E2 ]] ρ d j s
```

together with the rule

```
R[[ FAIL ]] ρ d j s
= POP (d−s); JUMP j
```

The effect is the same as before. The 'POP (d−s)' instruction sets the stack to the level expected by the code at j, while the 'JUMP j' instruction sets the program counter; together they put the G-machine into the same state as it would have had when executing the code at j in the first version.

The code is considerably more efficient, because the FAIL data value can no longer be generated, and hence it need never be tested for, nor do we need to provide a representation for it.

All other **R** scheme cases pass on j and s unchanged. Similar optimizations apply to the **E**, **RS** and **ES** schemes. To avoid complicating all the compilation schemes with the extra parameters j and s, we will not incorporate the modifications in subsequent figures. However, Figure 20.7 summarizes the modifications required.

The optimization is rather subtle, and its formal justification would be relatively more difficult than the others we are studying. At the very least it relies on the observation, made in Section 5.4.2, that FAIL can only be returned if it appears explicitly in the expression.

```
R[[ FATBAR E1 E2 ]] ρ d j s       = R[[ E1 ]] ρ d L d;
                                    LABEL L; R[[ E2 ]] ρ d j s

R[[ FAIL ]] ρ d j s               = POP (d−s); JUMP j

RS[[ FATBAR E1 E2 ]] ρ d n j s    = RS[[ E1 ]] ρ d n L d;
                                    LABEL L; RS[[ E2 ]] ρ d n j s

RS[[ FAIL ]] ρ d n j s            = POP (d−s); JUMP j

E[[ FATBAR E1 E2 ]] ρ d j s       = E[[ E1 ]] ρ d L d; JUMP L1;
                                    LABEL L; E[[ E2 ]] ρ d j s;
                                    LABEL L1

E[[ FAIL ]] ρ d j s               = POP (d−s); JUMP j

ES[[ FATBAR E1 E2 ]] ρ d n j s    = ES[[ E1 ]] ρ d n L d; JUMP L1;
                                    LABEL L; ES[[ E2 ]] ρ d n j s;
                                    LABEL L1

ES[[ FAIL ]] ρ d n j s            = POP (d−s); JUMP j
```

Figure 20.7 Modifications to **R**, **RS**, **E** and **ES** schemes for FATBAR

20.5 Evaluating Arguments

Suppose a supercombinator body consists of an expression of the form (f E_1 E_2), where we cannot execute f directly as described in the preceding section. Then we will compile the following code:

```
R[[ f E1 E2 ]] ρ d
= C[[ E2 ]] ρ d; C[[ E1 ]] ρ (d+1); PUSHGLOBAL f;
  MKAP 2; UPDATE (d+1); POP d; UNWIND
```

Notice that we have to construct the graph of E_1 and E_2. Suppose, however, that we knew that f would evaluate its first argument. Then we would be safe to compile E_1 with the **E** scheme (which will evaluate it), thus avoiding constructing the graph of E_1 before subsequently evaluating it.

If we know that f evaluates its first argument we say that f is *strict* in its first argument (see Section 2.5.4). The optimizations of this section try to avoid using **C** to compile E_1 and E_2 by using information about the strictness of functions.

20.5.1 Optimizing Partial Applications

Suppose we are compiling the supercombinator

```
f x = + (NEG x)
```

Here the result returned by f is a function which adds (NEG x) to its argument. With our present compilation schemes we will get

```
R[[ + (NEG x) ]] ρ d          (where ρ=[x=1], d=1)
= PUSH 0; PUSHGLOBAL $NEG; MKAP; PUSHGLOBAL $+; MKAP;
  UPDATE 2; POP 1; UNWIND
```

We cannot apply the **R**[[+ E_1 E_2]] optimization of the last section, because the + is only given one argument.

However, the reason we are evaluating (f x) must be to apply it to something, and when it is applied to something the first argument of the + will be evaluated. Hence we could evaluate the first argument straight away, giving:

```
R[[ + (NEG x) ]] ρ d          (where ρ=[x=1], d=1)
= PUSH 0; NEG; PUSHGLOBAL $+; MKAP;
  UPDATE 2; POP 1; UNWIND
```

This is better because it does not construct the graph for ($NEG x). The general rule is

```
R[[ + E ]] ρ d
= E[[ E ]] ρ d; PUSHGLOBAL $+; MKAP;
  UPDATE (d+1); POP d; UNWIND
```

This optimization applies to all built-in functions with more than one argument which evaluate their first argument. In particular, this means +, IF and their analogs −, ∗, etc., and CASE.

In fact, we can do rather better for IF. Consider the function (IF TRUE). It behaves as follows:

$$\text{(IF TRUE) } E_1\ E_2 \rightarrow E_1$$

that is, it behaves exactly like the K combinator. What does (IF FALSE) behave like? Suppose we generalize the K combinator to a family of combinators K-n-i (where i≤n), which have the semantic rule

$$\text{K-n-i } E_1 \ldots E_i \ldots E_n = E_i$$

Then K is the same as K-2-1, and (IF FALSE) behaves like K-2-2. Now we can use the following rule for IF:

```
R[[ IF E ]] ρ d
= E[[ E ]] ρ d; JFALSE L;
          PUSHGLOBAL $K-2-1; UPDATE( d+1); POP d; UNWIND
   LABEL L;
          PUSHGLOBAL $K-2-2; UPDATE( d+1); POP d; UNWIND
```

This is better than the previous rule, both because it does not construct the graph of (IF E), and because it does not subsequently need to inspect the graph of (IF E). A precisely similar optimization applies to CASE.

The only exception to the statement that the (f x) will eventually be applied to something is when the result of the whole program is the function (f x), which we ignore because most implementations insist that the result of the program is a data object.

The modifications required to the **R**, **RS**, **E** and **ES** schemes to achieve these optimizations are given in the next section. The rule for + is omitted, since it is subsumed by the optimization described in the next section. The rule for IF is put in the **RS** and **ES** schemes to maximize its effectiveness.

20.5.2 Using Global Strictness Information

The optimizations of the previous section rely on special information concerning the built-in functions. Consider, however, the supercombinators

```
$F x y = + y x
$G x = $F (∗ x x) (+ x x)
```

We can see at a glance that $F will certainly evaluate both its arguments (i.e. $F is strict in both arguments), so when compiling $G we could use **E** to compile the (∗ x x) and the (+ x x). Unfortunately, this information is not so obvious to the compiler.

Similar remarks apply to let-expressions; for example, when evaluating the expression

```
let x = E in (+ x 1)
```

it is clear that x will be evaluated, so we could compile E with the **E** scheme. Letrecs are more problematic, since there is a danger that we might try to evaluate a HOLE, so we will not attempt to optimize them.

We would therefore like to do two things:

(i) We would like to work out which functions are sure to need the values of their arguments. This process of inferring which functions are strict is called *strictness analysis* and is treated in detail in Chapter 22. We can then use such strictness information to *annotate* applications of strict functions. For example, we could annotate the body of $G thus:

```
$G x = $F ! (* x x) ! (+ x x)
```

where we use an infix '!' to indicate strict application. We can annotate let-expressions in a similar way. For example, we could use a ! after the variable name:

```
let x! = E in (+ x 1)
```

(ii) Secondly, we need to modify our compilation schemes to take advantage of this new information.

The latter task is rather easy. We need only to add a clause to the **ES** scheme to say

$$\mathbf{RS}[\![\ E_1\ !\ E_2\ ]\!]\ \rho\ d\ n = \mathbf{E}[\![\ E_2\ ]\!]\ \rho\ d;\ \mathbf{RS}[\![\ E_1\ ]\!]\ \rho\ (d+1)\ (n+1)$$

and make a similar modification to the **ES** scheme. This gives the effect of call-by-value, in which the argument E_2 is evaluated before the function E_1 is applied to it. A similar modification applies to the handling of let-expressions in **R** and **E**. All of these modifications are given in Figure 20.8, together with

$\mathbf{R}[\![$ let x! = E_x in E $]\!]\ \rho$ d	= $\mathbf{E}[\![\ E_x\ ]\!]\ \rho$ d; $\mathbf{R}[\![$ E $]\!]\ \rho$[x=d+1] (d+1)
$\mathbf{E}[\![$ let x! = E_x in E $]\!]\ \rho$ d	= $\mathbf{E}[\![\ E_x\ ]\!]\ \rho$ d; $\mathbf{E}[\![$ E $]\!]\ \rho$[x=d+1] (d+1); SLIDE 1
$\mathbf{RS}[\![$ IF E $]\!]\ \rho$ d n	= $\mathbf{E}[\![$ E $]\!]\ \rho$ d; JFALSE L; $\mathbf{RS}[\![$ \$K-2-1 $]\!]\ \rho$ d n; LABEL L; $\mathbf{RS}[\![$ \$K-2-2 $]\!]\ \rho$ d n
$\mathbf{RS}[\![\ E_1$! $E_2\ ]\!]\ \rho$ d n	= $\mathbf{E}[\![\ E_2\ ]\!]\ \rho$ d; $\mathbf{RS}[\![\ E_1\ ]\!]\ \rho$ (d+1) (n+1)
$\mathbf{ES}[\![$ IF E $]\!]\ \rho$ d	= $\mathbf{E}[\![$ E $]\!]\ \rho$ d; JFALSE L1; $\mathbf{ES}[\![$ \$K-2-1 $]\!]\ \rho$ d n; JUMP L2 LABEL L1; $\mathbf{ES}[\![$ \$K-2-2 $]\!]\ \rho$ d n; LABEL L2
$\mathbf{ES}[\![\ E_1$! $E_2\ ]\!]\ \rho$ d n	= $\mathbf{E}[\![\ E_2\ ]\!]\ \rho$ d; $\mathbf{ES}[\![\ E_1\ ]\!]\ \rho$ (d+1) (n+1)

Figure 20.8 Modifications to **R**, **RS**, **E** and **ES** to evaluate arguments

those from the previous section. Notice that partial applications of + (and its analogs) will be annotated with ! by the strictness analyzer, so this subsumes the explicit treatment of such partial applications given in the previous section.

20.6 Avoiding EVALs

EVAL is perhaps the most costly instruction in the G-machine instruction set, and optimizations that eliminate uses of EVAL are extremely worthwhile. We will discuss two ways of avoiding EVAL in this section.

20.6.1 Avoiding Re-evaluation in a Function Body

Consider compiling an expression such as (+ x x) with the **E** scheme. We will get

```
E⟦ + x x ⟧ ρ d
= PUSH (d − ρ x); EVAL; PUSH (d + 1 − ρ x); EVAL; ADD
```

This is wasteful, because the second EVAL is not necessary – x has already been evaluated once, so it will now be in WHNF. We would prefer to generate

```
PUSH (d − ρ x); EVAL; PUSH (d + 1 − ρ x); ADD
```

This can be achieved by keeping track of which variables have been evaluated, and checking for this when performing the **E**⟦ x ⟧ case. From a conceptual point of view this is very simple, but to write it into our compilation schemes rather destroys their simple structure, so we will content ourselves with a description of how to do it!

It turns out that it is convenient to keep track of which *stack locations* are evaluated, rather than which *variables* are evaluated. As far as this section goes there is no benefit from this generalization, but we will need it in the next section. All that is required is to add an extra parameter, σ, to each compilation scheme, which gives context information in a similar manner to ρ. σ is a function which, given an offset from the base of the current context, returns a flag indicating whether or not that stack location is evaluated.

Furthermore, each compilation scheme must now return two pieces of information, the code it generates (as before) and a new σ. The new σ returned by a scheme is the same as the σ which was passed to it, except that the flags on some of the stack locations have been set to indicate that they have been evaluated.

20.6.2 Using Global Strictness Information

Consider the supercombinator definition

```
$F x = IF (= x 0) 0 ($F (- x 1))
```

$F is clearly strict in x, and the strictness analyzer can spot this. So the definition as annotated by the strictness analyzer would look like this:

```
$F x = IF ! (= ! x ! 0) 0 ($F ! (- ! x ! 1))
```

Hence, when $F is called recursively, its argument is known to be already evaluated. However, $F does not know that this is always true, so it will go ahead and call EVAL on its parameter during the calculation of (= x 0).

What we would like is another supercombinator $F_NOEVAL which behaves just like $F except that it assumes that its argument is evaluated already. Then we could use $F_NOEVAL for the recursive call, and avoid the redundant evaluation of x.

$F_NOEVAL is so like $F that it can share much of its code. All that is needed is to move the EVAL of x to the beginning of the code for $F, and then $F_NOEVAL can be implemented as an entry point to $F just after this EVALuation. This suggests that

> the code for a supercombinator should begin with EVALs for each argument in which the supercombinator is strict.

This requires that:

(i) The strictness analyzer annotates supercombinator definitions as well as application nodes with strictness information. For example, $F might be annotated:

```
$F ! x = ...
```

to indicate that $F was strict in x.

(ii) The information that certain arguments had been evaluated is kept in the context (σ) using the mechanism outlined in the previous section. Having evaluated x at the beginning, we do not want to re-evaluate it!

(iii) The NOEVAL entry of a function is used when we know that all its strict arguments are evaluated. The appropriate version of the function can be selected by **RS** or **ES** (in the general case), depending on whether its arguments are known to be evaluated. On entry to the function, the arguments are held in the (anonymous) top few stack locations, which is why σ describes which stack locations are evaluated (rather than which variables are evaluated). Note: this optimization applies to built-in functions as well.

Experience with the Ponder compiler suggests that this optimization turns out to be extremely worthwhile in practice.

A further nice benefit is that, since many EVALs are moved to the beginning of the code for a function, the main body of code is less broken up with EVALs (which, remember, are tiresome – see Section 19.3.3).

20.7 Avoiding Repeated Unwinding

Sometimes an application node is known *not* to be the root of a redex, but because this information is not recorded we will unwind it every time we EVAL it, only to find that it is already in WHNF. If this information were present in the application node, EVAL would see this and return immediately (as it does for integers, for example) rather than beginning an unwind.

This optimization only becomes important when strictness analysis is being used, because then functions may be EVALuated when they are passed as strict arguments. Without strictness analysis, functions are only evaluated when they are applied.

We can incorporate the information that an application node is in WHNF rather easily. All that is required is an extra tag AP-WHNF, which replaces the AP tag on application nodes which are known to be in WHNF (i.e. irreducible at the top level). If case analysis is implemented as outlined in Section 19.4, then the EVAL entry of AP-WHNF's entry table will be the same as that for integers; that is, an immediate return to the caller. This is much faster than UNWINDing and then returning when the function at the tip of the spine is found to have too few arguments.

There are two ways in which an application node can be given an AP-WHNF tag:

(i) At compile-time, when the **C** scheme is compiling the application of a known function to too few arguments. The required modification is shown in Figure 20.9. The condition in curly braces means that the top application node of the graph is known to be in WHNF. The lower vertebrae will also be so identified by the recursive call to **C**.

$$\begin{aligned}&\mathbf{C}[\![\ \mathsf{f}\ \mathsf{E}_1\ \ldots\ \mathsf{E}_n\ ]\!]\ \rho\ \mathsf{d} \quad \{\text{where f is a global of arity} > \mathsf{n}\}\\ &= \mathbf{C}[\![\ \mathsf{E}_n\ ]\!]\ \rho\ \mathsf{d};\ \mathbf{C}[\![\ \mathsf{f}\ \mathsf{E}_1\ \ldots\ \mathsf{E}_{n-1}\ ]\!]\ \rho\ (\mathsf{d}+1);\ \mathsf{MKAP\text{-}WHNF}\end{aligned}$$

Figure 20.9 Modifications to the C scheme to use AP-WHNF

Similar optimizations apply to **RS** and **ES**, but we will see a more elegant way of describing them (and the **C** modification too) in the next chapter.

(ii) At run-time, when rearranging the stack before entering a function. Referring back to Section 18.5.1, all the vertebrae that are below the root of the redex at the completion of the UNWIND instruction are known to be in WHNF, since each represents the application of a function to too few arguments. For example, consider the graph

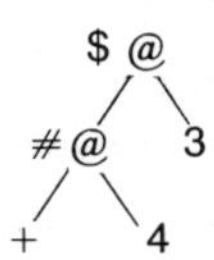

UNWIND will identify the node labelled $ as the root of the redex, and it follows that the node labelled # is in WHNF, because it represents the application of + to one argument only.

The tag on these vertebrae could therefore be changed to AP-WHNF as they are removed from the stack. We can formally describe this by modifying one of the clauses describing the UNWIND instruction:

$$\langle v_0{:}v_1{:}\ldots{:}v_k{:}S,\ G\begin{bmatrix} v_0=\text{FUN } k\ C \\ v_i=\text{AP } v_{i-1}\ n_i,\ (1\le i\le k)\end{bmatrix},\ \text{UNWIND}{:}[\,],\ D\rangle$$

$$\Rightarrow\ \langle n_1{:}n_2{:}\ldots{:}n_k{:}v_k{:}S,\ G[v_i=\text{AP-WHNF } v_{i-1}\ n_i,\ (1\le i\le k)],\ C,\ D\rangle$$

For a sequential implementation this modification would make the stack rearrangement take longer, since the tags of all the vertebrae have to be changed. Whether it is worth the extra effort depends on the balance between this cost and the benefits arising from faster EVALs.

20.8 Performing Some Eager Evaluation

Under certain circumstances we may wish to perform a reduction even though a completely lazy implementation would postpone it. Consider compiling the expression (CONS E_1 E_2) with the **C** scheme:

$$\mathbf{C}[\![\ \text{CONS } E_1\ E_2\ ]\!]\ \rho\ d$$
$$= \mathbf{C}[\![\ E_2\ ]\!]\ \rho\ d;\ \mathbf{C}[\![\ E_1\ ]\!]\ \rho\ (d+1);\ \text{PUSHGLOBAL \$CONS; MKAP; MKAP}$$

But it is clear that when (and if) evaluated, the expression (CONS E_1 E_2) will simply return a CONS cell, with $\mathbf{C}[\![\ E_1\ ]\!]$ in one branch and $\mathbf{C}[\![\ E_2\ ]\!]$ in the other. So it would be much better to construct it directly, with the code:

$$\mathbf{C}[\![\ \text{CONS } E_1\ E_2\ ]\!]\ \rho\ d$$
$$= \mathbf{C}[\![\ E_2\ ]\!]\ \rho\ d;\ \mathbf{C}[\![\ E_1\ ]\!]\ \rho\ (d+1);\ \text{CONS}$$

The code is shorter and fewer cells are allocated, so we win all round (despite being less lazy). We can achieve this optimization simply by adding the above rule to the **C** compilation scheme.

If we have the information described in the previous section, telling which variables have been evaluated, we can perform some further optimizations to **C**. **C** is used when we are not sure if an expression will be evaluated or not. However, consider compiling (+ x 3) with the **C** scheme in a context where x has already been evaluated. Our present scheme will produce

$$\mathbf{C}[\![\ +\ x\ 3\ ]\!]\ \rho\ d$$
$$= \text{PUSHINT 3; PUSH } (d - \rho\ x);\ \text{PUSHGLOBAL \$+; MKAP; MKAP}$$

It would be considerably cheaper to generate

$$\mathbf{C}[\![\ +\ x\ 3\ ]\!]\ \rho\ d \qquad \{\ x \text{ evaluated}\}$$
$$= \text{PUSHINT 3; PUSH } (d - \rho\ x);\ \text{ADD}$$

This risks performing an addition which turns out not to be necessary (because the graph constructed by **C** may be discarded), but on almost any conceivable machine it would be cheaper to perform the addition than to construct the graph. The reason we cannot do this in any old context is that the evaluation of x might not terminate; but we can safely perform this optimization in any context where we are sure that x is evaluated. Exactly the same optimization can be used for any other built-in function. For example,

```
C[[ HEAD y ]] ρ d        {y evaluated}
= PUSH (d – ρ y); HEAD
```

We would also like to propagate this information upwards. For example, we would like to arrange that

```
C[[ + (+ x 5) y ]] ρ d        {x and y evaluated}
= PUSH (d – ρ y); PUSHINT 5; PUSH (d – ρ x); ADD; ADD
```

To achieve this, we would simply need **C** to return an extra piece of information to say when its result was known to be evaluated. But this is already available to us in the form of σ, which records which stack locations are evaluated, so the optimization is easily incorporated.

The optimizations in this section depend on the relative costs of performing certain built-in operations (for example, addition versus heap cell allocation). As such, they need to be considered carefully with a particular machine in mind. However, the examples presented here would be worth doing on most machines. They would not be nearly so attractive if, for example, the + operator was an arbitrary precision addition function.

20.9 Manipulating Basic Values

Consider the following function definition

```
f x y = + x (+ y 1)
```

This will compile to

```
PUSHINT 1; PUSH 2; ADD; PUSH 1; ADD;
UPDATE 3; POP 2; RETURN
```

In an implementation which uses a boxed representation of integers (see Section 10.6) the first ADD will

(i) take two integers (y and 1) out of their boxes,
(ii) add them,
(iii) allocate a new box,
(iv) and put the result in the new box.

The second ADD will promptly take the result out of the box in order to add it to x. Hence, the allocation of the box and the act of putting the intermediate result in it were wasted.

Even in an implementation which uses an unboxed representation of integers some work may have to be done to strip off the pointer bits before adding, and to add the pointer bit afterwards. This is much less serious than in the boxed case, but we would like to avoid it even so. For the rest of this section we will assume a boxed implementation, but everything applies (though with less weight) to an unboxed implementation.

The inefficiency outlined above arises when we are manipulating *basic values* such as integers, characters, booleans and so on. A basic value with no box is called *naked*; those enclosed in a box are *clothed*. For efficiency reasons we would like to work with naked basic values wherever possible, only clothing them when unavoidable.

We begin by defining explicit instructions to get naked basic values out of their boxes and to clothe them again. Thus the instruction GET takes the top item on the stack out of its box, leaving the result on top of the stack as a naked basic value. The instruction MKINT wraps an integer box around the top item on the stack. (In an unboxed implementation, these instructions would strip off and stick on the pointer bit. A trick that may help is to use a zero pointer bit for atoms, so that often nothing need be done to stick on the pointer bit.)

We then redefine the instructions which operate on basic values, such as ADD, so that they operate on naked bit patterns. ADD will now take the top two words on the stack, treat them as 32-bit integers (or whatever), add them and put the result back on the stack. Clearly this is outside the hygienic world of graph reduction, but by the time such integers get back into the heap they will have been nicely boxed.

How, then, can we compile our programs to use such instructions? We begin by defining a new compilation scheme **B**, which is just like **E** except that it leaves the result as a naked basic value on the stack. It therefore assumes that the result is indeed a basic value (and not a function, or a CONS cell, for example). We can obtain the **B** scheme by a direct transliteration of the **E** scheme (see Figure 20.10, which was prepared by performing minor edits on Figure 20.2). This assumes that certain G-code instructions, such as JFALSE, are altered to expect their arguments as naked basic values on the stack; this is discussed in detail below.

The 'PUSHBASIC i' instruction pushes a naked basic value onto the stack, so one instruction suffices for basic values of all types. If **B** does not recognize the expression it is compiling, it evaluates it with **E** and then GETs the basic value out of its box.

All that remains is to modify **E** and **R** to use **B**. They will use **B** in all contexts where the result is known to be a basic value. Figures 20.11 and 20.12 show the modifications required to the **R** and **E** schemes. Notice the way both **R** and **E** use **B** to compute the condition of an IF. **E** uses **B** to compute the results of all arithmetic operations, following it with a MKINT to clothe it. Finally, **R** has an optimization when the result of the whole supercombinator reduction is known to be an integer. In this case **R** uses **B** to compute the naked integer, and then uses 'UPDINT d' to update the root of the redex with the clothed value.

```
B⟦ E ⟧ ρ d
```

Evaluates E, leaving the result on top of the stack as a naked basic value.

```
B⟦ i ⟧ ρ d                 = PUSHBASIC i
B⟦ NEG E ⟧ ρ d             = B⟦ E ⟧ ρ d; NEG
B⟦ + E1 E2 ⟧ ρ d           = B⟦ E2 ⟧ ρ d; B⟦ E1 ⟧ ρ (d+1); ADD
B⟦ IF Ec Et Ef ⟧ ρ d       = B⟦ Ec ⟧ ρ d; JFALSE L1;
                                B⟦ Et ⟧ ρ d; JUMP L2;
                             LABEL L1;
                                B⟦ Ef ⟧ ρ d;
                             LABEL L2
B⟦ let x=Ex in E ⟧ ρ d     = C⟦ Ex ⟧ ρ d;
                             B⟦ E ⟧ ρ[x=d+1] (d+1); SLIDE 1
B⟦ letrec D in E ⟧ ρ d     = CLetrec⟦ D ⟧ ρ' d'; B⟦ E ⟧ ρ' d'; SLIDE (d'−d)
                             where
                             (ρ', d') = Xr⟦ D ⟧ ρ d
B⟦ E ⟧ ρ d                 = E⟦ E ⟧ ρ d; GET      (otherwise)
```

Figure 20.10 The **B** compilation scheme

```
R⟦ i ⟧ ρ d              = B⟦ i ⟧ ρ d; UPDINT (d+1); POP d; RETURN
R⟦ NEG E ⟧ ρ d          = B⟦ NEG E ⟧ ρ d; UPDINT (d+1); POP d; RETURN
R⟦ + E1 E2 ⟧ ρ d        = B⟦ + E1 E2 ⟧ ρ d;
                          UPDINT (d+1); POP d; RETURN
R⟦ IF Ec Et Ef ⟧ ρ d    = B⟦ Ec ⟧ ρ d; JFALSE L;
                          R⟦ Et ⟧ ρ d;
                          LABEL L; R⟦ Ef ⟧ ρ d
```

Similar modifications apply to the **RS** scheme.

Figure 20.11 Modifications to the **R** scheme to use **B**

```
E⟦ NEG E ⟧ ρ d          = B⟦ NEG E ⟧ ρ d; MKINT
E⟦ + E1 E2 ⟧ ρ d        = B⟦ + E1 E2 ⟧ ρ d; MKINT
E⟦ IF Ec Et Ef ⟧ ρ d    = B⟦ Ec ⟧ ρ d; JFALSE L1;
                             E⟦ Et ⟧ ρ d; JUMP L2;
                          LABEL L1;
                             E⟦ Ef ⟧ ρ d;
                          LABEL L2
```

Similar modifications apply to the ES scheme.

Figure 20.12 Modifications to the **E** scheme to use **B**

The extra instructions required are given in Figure 20.13.

The only remaining problem with this optimization concerns garbage collection. When garbage collection is initiated, the garbage collector has to traverse all the accessible graph, including that only accessible from the stack.

```
Note: Redefined instructions are marked with *
GET       <n:S, G[n=INT i], GET:C, D>  ⇒  <i:S, G, C, D>
MKINT     <i:S, G, MKINT:C, D>  ⇒  <n:S, G[n=INT i], C, D>
NEG*      <i:S, G, NEG:C, D>  ⇒  <−i:S, G, C, D>
ADD*      <i1:i2:S, G, ADD:C, D>  ⇒  <i1+i2:S, G, C, D>
JFALSE*   <false:S, G, JFALSE L:...:LABEL L:C, D>  ⇒  <S, G, C, D>
          <true:S, G, JFALSE L:C, D>  ⇒  <S, G, C, D>
UPDINT    <i:n1:...:nk:S, G, UPDINT k:C, D>
          ⇒  <n1:...:nk:S, G[nk=INT i], C, D>
```

Figure 20.13 G-code instructions for basic values

This means that the garbage collector needs to know whether an item in the stack is a pointer or not. Unfortunately, the stack now contains both naked and clothed values, and a naked value may be indistinguishable from a pointer.

There are four possible solutions:

(i) Somehow mark naked values on the stack. This is tantamount to clothing them.

(ii) Let the garbage collector treat naked basic values as pointers and treat any structure accidentally accessible from them as in use. This risks the garbage collector not recovering some store. All 'pointers' should also be checked to see that they point into the heap, in order to avoid memory protection faults and reduce fruitless 'pointer' chasing. This method is successfully used in the SASL system.

(iii) Use two stacks instead of one, a stack V for naked values and the spine stack S for clothed values. It is easy to decide, for each instruction, which stack is referred to. The instructions GET and MKINT transfer values between stacks in either direction. The trouble with this is that we need yet another stack.

(iv) Stack naked values on the dump! This is a clever trick, used by the Chalmers G-machine. It is based on two premises:

  (a) The garbage collector does not need to follow pointers from the dump, since all accessible store can be marked from the spine stack (or rather all the spine stacks which are sitting on top of each other). Hence naked values on the dump pose no problem.

  (b) At the moments when we want to restore the old stack and code pointers from the dump, or refer to the old stack pointer to check whether the present supercombinator has enough arguments, there are no naked basic values on the dump.

It turns out, therefore, that we can safely combine the V and D stacks, and this seems altogether the nicest choice. If it is used then the let and letrec cases of the **B** scheme should conclude with POP instead of SLIDE, because the naked value is on the dump, not the S stack.

20.10 Peephole Optimizations to G-code

We now come to some optimizations which can most easily be regarded as *peephole optimizations* to the G-code. A peephole optimizer fits between the G-code compiler and the code generator. It looks at short consecutive sequences of G-code instructions, and replaces them by some shorter or more optimal sequence.

20.10.1 Combining Multiple SLIDEs and MKAPs

Imagine compiling this expression with the **C** scheme:

```
let x = Ex
in letrec y = Ey
          x = Ez
in E
```

The end of the code will be the sequence:

```
...SLIDE 2; SLIDE 1
```

Clearly these can be combined to the single instruction

```
...SLIDE 3
```

This sort of optimization is exactly what peephole optimizers are for. We may describe the optimization like this:

SLIDE k_1; SLIDE k_2 $\Longrightarrow$ (SLIDE k_1+k_2)

using $\Longrightarrow$ to denote the optimization. In a similar way, the **C** scheme generates multiple MKAP instructions:

C⟦ E_1 E_2 E_3 ⟧ ρ d
= **C**⟦ E_3 ⟧ ρ d; **C**⟦ E_2 ⟧ ρ (d+1); **C**⟦ E_1 ⟧ ρ (d+2); MKAP; MKAP

These MKAP sequences can be combined into an 'MKAP n' instruction by the optimization

MKAP k_1; MKAP k_2 $\Longrightarrow$ MKAP (k_1+k_2)

where we regard MKAP as equivalent to 'MKAP 1'.

20.10.2 Avoiding Redundant EVALs

As remarked in Section 20.2, we frequently generate redundant EVALs, in the sequence

```
PUSHGLOBAL f; EVAL
```

The EVAL is redundant if f is a built-in function, or a supercombinator of one or more arguments, but it is necessary if f is a CAF. The peephole optimizer can easily eliminate the EVAL if it is redundant:

PUSHGLOBAL f; EVAL $\Longrightarrow$ PUSHGLOBAL f (if f is not a CAF)

20.10.3 Avoiding Allocating the Root of the Result

Consider the supercombinator

```
$F x f = f x
```

At present we will generate the following G-code for it:

```
PUSH 0;       Push x
PUSH 2;       Push f
MKAP;         Make an application node
UPDATE 3;     Update the root of the redex
POP 2;        Pop parameters
UNWIND;       Continue
```

In an implementation which uses copying for UPDATE this code is rather wasteful, since it allocates an application cell with MKAP and then immediately copies it over the root of the redex, thus discarding the application cell just allocated. It would be better to construct the root of the result directly on top of the root of the redex, thus:

```
PUSH 0;       Push x
PUSH 2;       Push f
UPDAP 4;      Build application over root
POP 2;        Pop parameters
UNWIND;       Continue
```

The 'UPDAP 4' instruction takes the top two items on the stack and, using them, builds an application node on top of the root of the redex, whose position in the stack is four from the top. We could modify the **RS** scheme to incorporate this optimization by using the following rule:

RS⟦ f ⟧ ρ d n = PUSHGLOBAL f; MKAP (n−1);
UPDAP (d−n+2); POP (d−n); UNWIND

and a similar one for **RS**⟦ x ⟧. Just the same optimization can be made when the result of the function is a CONS cell (using yet another instruction

UPDCONS). Furthermore the optimization can also be applied to the updates performed by **CLetrec**.

We could describe the optimization by modifying the **RS** and **CLetrec** compilation schemes, in the manner indicated above, to generate UPDAP and UPDCONS instructions. This description has two disadvantages:

(i) It complicates the compilation schemes. In particular, we will have to introduce a brand new scheme to handle the top level of **CLetrec** (try it!).
(ii) It is quite a low-level optimization to be allowed to clutter up the compilation schemes.

Fortunately, we can describe it in quite a different way. All we are really doing is performing the optimization

```
MKAP n; UPDATE d  ==>  MKAP (n-1); UPDAP (d+1)
```

which is precisely the sort of thing that a peephole optimizer could spot. Accordingly, we choose to implement the optimization in the code generator. There is also the related optimization

```
CONS n; UPDATE d  ==>  CONS (n-1); UPDCONS (d+1)
```

Notice that this description automatically catches cases generated by **CLetrec** as well as **R**, and will also optimize the definition of the \$CONS built-in function (Section 18.8.2).

20.10.4 Unpacking Structured Objects

The compilation of case-expressions, using the optimization described in Section 6.3.3, resulted in the frequent occurrence of expressions such as

```
let   v1 = SEL-SUM-k-1 v
      ...
      vk = SEL-SUM-k-k v
in E
```

where v, v_1, . . ., v_k are variables. If this is compiled by the **R** scheme in a context in which v is evaluated, normally by an enclosing CASE function, we will get the following G-code:

```
PUSH (d - ρ v); SELSUM k,1;
...
PUSH (d+k-1 - ρ v); SELSUM k,k;
R[[ E ]] ρ' (d+k)
```

where $\rho' = \rho[v_1=d+1,\ldots,v_n=d+k]$. (We are assuming here that the optimization which avoids repeated EVALs described in Section 20.6 is implemented, so that no EVALs precede the SELSUM instructions; and that the optimization which performs eager evaluation of applications of SEL-SUM-k-i described in Section 20.8 is also implemented.)

This sequence of PUSH/SELSUM instructions simply unpacks v onto the stack, and hence is readily optimized to:

PUSH (d − ρ v); UNPACKSUM k;

where 'UNPACKSUM k' is a new G-code instruction, which unpacks the top element on the stack into its k components, placing them on top of the stack. As before, the optimization can be performed by a peephole optimizer.

Everything in this section applies analogously to product types, reading SEL-k-i and SELPRODUCT k,i instead of SEL-SUM-k-i and SELSUM k,i.

20.11 Pattern-matching Revisited

The UNPACK peephole optimization presented above puts the finishing touch to our strategy for compiling pattern-matching. A function which uses pattern-matching is now compiled to

(i) a code sequence to evaluate the argument;
(ii) a multi-way jump (CASEJUMP), based on the structure tag of the argument (see Section 18.8.4);
(iii) an unpack instruction, which takes the structure apart, and puts its components on the stack;
(iv) a code sequence to evaluate the appropriate right-hand side of the function, in the correct context (namely, free variables accessible in the stack, and the components of the structure on top of the stack).

It is hard to see how pattern-matching can be compiled more efficiently!

Notice how important the optimization of case-expressions presented in Section 6.3.3 has proved. There we showed how to transform a case-expression into a let-expression, without using a lambda abstraction. If the lambda abstraction had been present, it would have been lambda-lifted, and we would have generated a separate supercombinator for each right-hand side of a pattern-matching definition. As it is, we generate a single supercombinator with far more efficient code.

20.12 Summary

In this chapter we have developed a long sequence of optimizations to the basic G-machine. It is the possibility of making such optimizations that makes the G-machine strategy so attractive. What started as an optimization to improve the efficiency of template instantiation has turned out to offer many avenues for improved performance. Figures 20.14 and 20.15 give the final versions of the **R** and **RS** schemes, combining all our modifications, while Figures 20.16 and 20.17 give the final versions of the **E** and **ES** schemes.

R⟦ E ⟧ ρ d

generates code to apply a supercombinator to its d arguments.

R⟦ i ⟧ ρ d	= **B**⟦ i ⟧ ρ d; UPDINT (d+1); POP d; RETURN
R⟦ f ⟧ ρ d	= **E**⟦ f ⟧ ρ d; UPDATE (d+1); POP d; UNWIND
R⟦ x ⟧ ρ d	= **E**⟦ x ⟧ ρ d; UPDATE (d+1); POP d; UNWIND
R⟦ NEG E ⟧ ρ d	= **B**⟦ NEG E ⟧ ρ d; UPDINT (d+1); POP d; RETURN
R⟦ + E_1 E_2 ⟧ ρ d	= **B**⟦ + E_1 E_2 ⟧ ρ d; UPDINT (d+1); POP d; RETURN
R⟦ CONS E_1 E_2 ⟧ ρ d	= **E**⟦ CONS E_1 E_2 ⟧ ρ d; UPDATE (d+1); POP d; RETURN
R⟦ HEAD E ⟧ ρ d	= **E**⟦ HEAD E ⟧ ρ d; UPDATE (d+1); POP d; RETURN

R⟦ IF E_c E_t E_f ⟧ ρ d	= **B**⟦ E_c ⟧ ρ d; JFALSE L;
	    R⟦ E_t ⟧ ρ d;
	LABEL L;
	    R⟦ E_f ⟧ ρ d

R⟦ E_1 E_2 ⟧ ρ d	= **RS**⟦ E_1 E_2 ⟧ ρ d 0;
R⟦ let x=E_x in E ⟧ ρ d	= **C**⟦ E_x ⟧ ρ d; **R**⟦ E ⟧ ρ[x=d+1] (d+1)
R⟦ let x!=E_x in E ⟧ ρ d	= **E**⟦ E_x ⟧ ρ d; **R**⟦ E ⟧ ρ[x=d+1] (d+1)
R⟦ letrec D in E ⟧ ρ d	= **CLetrec**⟦ D ⟧ ρ' d′; **R**⟦ E ⟧ ρ' d′ where (ρ', d′) = **Xr**⟦ D ⟧ ρ d

Figure 20.14 The final **R** scheme

RS⟦ E ⟧ ρ d n

completes a supercombinator reduction, in which the top n ribs of the body have already been put on the stack.

RS constructs instances of the ribs of E, putting them on the stack, and then completes the reduction in the same way as **R**.

RS⟦ f ⟧ ρ d n	= PUSHGLOBAL f; MKAP n; UPDATE (d−n+1); POP (d−n); UNWIND
RS⟦ x ⟧ ρ d n	= PUSH (d − ρ x); MKAP n; UPDATE (d−n+1); POP (d−n); UNWIND
RS⟦ HEAD E ⟧ ρ d n	= **E**⟦ E ⟧ ρ d; HEAD; MKAP n; UPDATE (d−n+1); POP (d−n); UNWIND

RS⟦ IF E_c E_t E_f ⟧ ρ d n	= **B**⟦ E_c ⟧ ρ d; JFALSE L;
	    RS⟦ E_t ⟧ ρ d n;
	LABEL L;
	    RS⟦ E_f ⟧ ρ d n

RS⟦ IF E ⟧ ρ d n	= **B**⟦ E ⟧ ρ d; JFALSE L;
	    RS⟦ $K-2-1 ⟧ ρ d n;
	LABEL L;
	    RS⟦ $K-2-2 ⟧ ρ d n

RS⟦ E_1 E_2 ⟧ ρ d n	= **C**⟦ E_2 ⟧ ρ d; **RS**⟦ E_1 ⟧ ρ (d+1) (n+1)
RS⟦ E_1 ! E_2 ⟧ ρ d n	= **E**⟦ E_2 ⟧ ρ d; **RS**⟦ E_1 ⟧ ρ (d+1) (n+1)

Note: **RS** cannot encounter a let or letrec.

Figure 20.15 The final **RS** scheme

$\mathbf{E}[\![E]\!] \rho\ d$

evaluates E, leaving the result on top of the stack.

$\mathbf{E}[\![i]\!] \rho\ d$	= PUSHINT i
$\mathbf{E}[\![f]\!] \rho\ d$	= PUSHGLOBAL f; EVAL
$\mathbf{E}[\![x]\!] \rho\ d$	= PUSH $(d - \rho\ x)$; EVAL
$\mathbf{E}[\![\text{NEG } E]\!] \rho\ d$	= $\mathbf{B}[\![\text{NEG } E]\!] \rho\ d$; MKINT
$\mathbf{E}[\![+ E_1\ E_2]\!] \rho\ d$	= $\mathbf{B}[\![+ E_1\ E_2]\!] \rho\ d$; MKINT
$\mathbf{E}[\![\text{CONS } E_1\ E_2]\!] \rho\ d$	= $\mathbf{C}[\![E_2]\!] \rho\ d$; $\mathbf{C}[\![E_1]\!] \rho\ (d+1)$; CONS
$\mathbf{E}[\![\text{HEAD } E]\!] \rho\ d$	= $\mathbf{E}[\![E]\!] \rho\ d$; HEAD; EVAL

$\mathbf{E}[\![\text{IF } E_c\ E_t\ E_f]\!] \rho\ d$	= $\mathbf{B}[\![E_c]\!] \rho\ d$; JFALSE L1;
	    $\mathbf{E}[\![E_t]\!] \rho\ d$; JUMP L2;
	LABEL L1;
	    $\mathbf{E}[\![E_f]\!] \rho\ d$;
	LABEL L2

$\mathbf{E}[\![E_1\ E_2]\!] \rho\ d$	= $\mathbf{ES}[\![E_1\ E_2]\!] \rho\ d\ 0$
$\mathbf{E}[\![\text{let } x{=}E_x \text{ in } E]\!] \rho\ d$	= $\mathbf{C}[\![E_x]\!] \rho\ d$; $\mathbf{E}[\![E]\!] \rho[x{=}d{+}1]\ (d+1)$; SLIDE 1
$\mathbf{E}[\![\text{let } x!{=}E_x \text{ in } E]\!] \rho\ d$	= $\mathbf{E}[\![E_x]\!] \rho\ d$; $\mathbf{E}[\![E]\!] \rho[x{=}d{+}1]\ (d+1)$; SLIDE 1
$\mathbf{E}[\![\text{letrec } D \text{ in } E]\!] \rho\ d$	= $\mathbf{CLetrec}[\![D]\!] \rho'\ d'$; $\mathbf{E}[\![E]\!] \rho'\ d'$; SLIDE $(d'-d)$ where $(\rho', d') = \mathbf{Xr}[\![D]\!] \rho\ d$

Figure 20.16 The final **E** compilation scheme

$\mathbf{ES}[\![E]\!] \rho\ d\ n$

completes the evaluation of an expression, the top n ribs of which have already been put on the stack.

ES constructs instances of the ribs of E, putting them on the stack, and then completes the evaluation in the same way as **E**.

$\mathbf{ES}[\![f]\!] \rho\ d\ n$	= PUSHGLOBAL f; MKAP n; EVAL
$\mathbf{ES}[\![x]\!] \rho\ d\ n$	= PUSH $(d - \rho\ x)$; MKAP n; EVAL
$\mathbf{ES}[\![\text{HEAD } E]\!] \rho\ d\ n$	= $\mathbf{E}[\![E]\!] \rho\ d$; HEAD; MKAP n; EVAL

$\mathbf{ES}[\![\text{IF } E_c\ E_t\ E_f]\!] \rho\ d\ n$	= $\mathbf{B}[\![E_c]\!] \rho\ d$; JFALSE L1;
	    $\mathbf{ES}[\![E_t]\!] \rho\ d\ n$; JUMP L2;
	LABEL L1;
	    $\mathbf{ES}[\![E_f]\!] \rho\ d\ n$;
	LABEL L2

$\mathbf{ES}[\![\text{IF } E]\!] \rho\ d$	= $\mathbf{B}[\![E]\!] \rho\ d$; JFALSE L1;
	    $\mathbf{ES}[\![\$K\text{-}2\text{-}1]\!] \rho\ d\ n$; JUMP L2
	LABEL L1;
	    $\mathbf{ES}[\![\$K\text{-}2\text{-}2]\!] \rho\ d\ n$;
	LABEL L2

$\mathbf{ES}[\![E_1\ E_2]\!] \rho\ d\ n$	= $\mathbf{C}[\![E_2]\!] \rho\ d$; $\mathbf{ES}[\![E_1]\!] \rho\ (d+1)\ (n+1)$
$\mathbf{ES}[\![E_1\ !\ E_2]\!] \rho\ d\ n$	= $\mathbf{E}[\![E_2]\!] \rho\ d$; $\mathbf{ES}[\![E_1]\!] \rho\ (d+1)\ (n+1)$

Note: **ES** cannot encounter a let or letrec.

Figure 20.17 The final **ES** scheme

Reference

Augustsson, L. 1985. Compiling pattern matching. In *Conference on Functional Programming Languages and Computer Architecture, Nancy*. Jouannaud (editor). LNCS 201. Springer Verlag.

Twenty-one

OPTIMIZING GENERALIZED TAIL CALLS

Simon L. Peyton Jones and Thomas Johnsson

Suppose we are compiling the body of a supercombinator such as

```
$F x y = W E1 E2 E3
```

where W is either a supercombinator, or a built-in function, or a variable (only x or y would be possible in this case). We will produce G-code to build an instance of the body of $F. However, at the end of this code is an UNWIND instruction which will unwind the spine of the instance onto the stack. When we then perform the W-reduction, all the newly allocated vertebrae below the root of the W-redex will immediately become garbage (note: this is actually a slight overgeneralization).

This chapter is devoted to techniques designed to avoid allocating vertebrae that are going to become garbage straight away. During the chapter we will use the $F supercombinator above as a running example.

Suppose that W was a supercombinator or built-in function. Then the code for $F would begin as follows:

```
C[[ E3 ]] ρ d;
C[[ E2 ]] ρ (d+1);
C[[ E1 ]] ρ (d+2);
PUSHGLOBAL W;
```

(If W was a variable, the only difference is that the last instruction would be a PUSH instead of a PUSHGLOBAL.) This puts all the ribs on the stack, but does not construct any vertebrae (which is done subsequently with an 'MKAP 3' instruction). After this sequence has executed, the current context looks like Figure 21.1 (remember that in all our pictures the stack grows downwards). In this figure, all the graph of the \$F-redex has been omitted except the root, which is always an application node.

At this point there are now a number of cases to consider, depending on the nature of W. Before we follow the main thread of this section we will treat an important special case, that of a tail call. This special case will be subsumed by the subsequent more general treatment, but it is an easier introduction.

21.1 Tail Calls

A tail call is the case when the result of one function is given by a call to another function with exactly the right number of arguments supplied. In our example, the call to W is a tail call if W is a supercombinator which takes exactly three arguments.

Under these circumstances \$F's body (W E_1 E_2 E_3) is itself a redex – in fact it will be the next redex to be reduced. Furthermore, the node that will be updated by the result of the ensuing W-reduction is the same node that will be updated by the result of the \$F-reduction. On entry to the code for the supercombinator W the current context will look like Figure 21.2, where the 'Root of \$F-redex' is the same as in Figure 21.1 (it is now the root of the W-redex).

One way to move from Figure 21.1 to Figure 21.2 would be to complete construction of the graph of (W E_1 E_2 E_3) in the heap, update the root of the redex with the result, pop the parameters of \$F and execute UNWIND. This would unwind the spine onto the stack, find W at the tip, rearrange the stack to look like Figure 21.2 and finally enter the code for W. This is just what the compilation algorithm we have developed in Chapters 18–20 will do, but it is plain that this is a very stupid way to proceed.

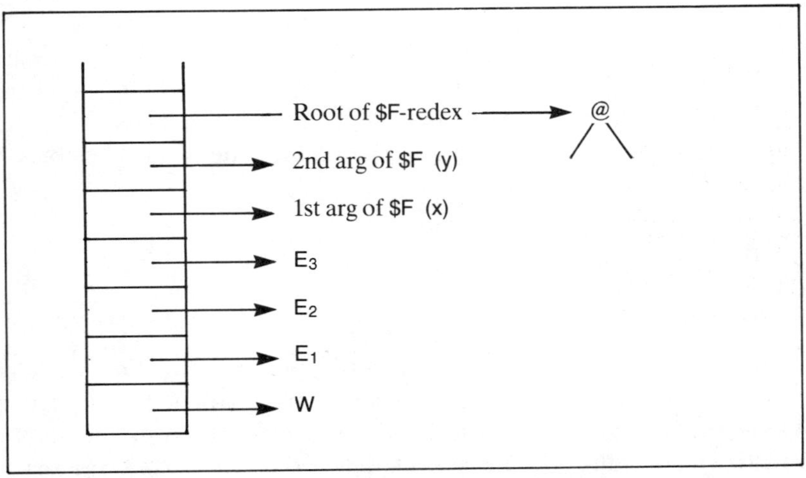

Figure 21.1 Current context of \$F after ribs have been built

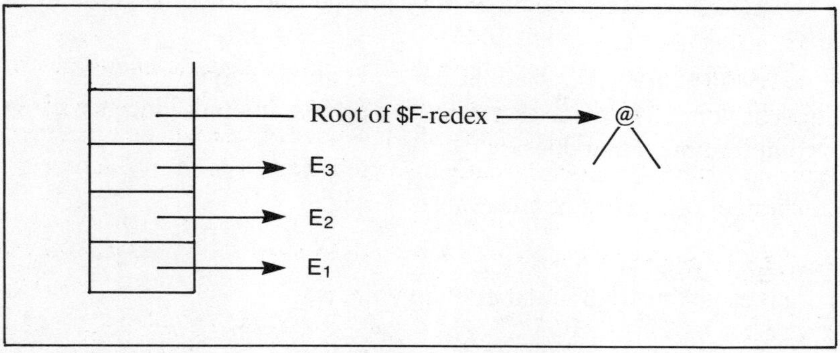

Figure 21.2 Current context on entry to three-argument supercombinator W

A much more efficient way to get from Figure 21.1 to Figure 21.2 is simply to slide the top four elements of the stack down, squeezing out the two arguments to $F. We write this instruction

```
SQUEEZE 4 2
```

meaning 'slide down the top four elements of the stack, squeezing out the two elements below them'. The rule for SQUEEZE is

$$\langle n_1 : \ldots : n_k : m_1 : \ldots : m_d : S,\ G,\ \text{SQUEEZE } k\ d : C,\ D \rangle$$
$$\Rightarrow \langle n_1 : \ldots : n_k : S,\ G,\ C,\ D \rangle$$

After doing this we want to enter the code for W, so we invent another new instruction

```
JFUN
```

which expects to find a function on top of the stack, pops it and enters its code (we omit a formal definition of JFUN as it will be subsumed by the next section). The complete code for $F would now read:

```
C[[ E3 ]] ρ d;
C[[ E2 ]] ρ (d+1);
C[[ E1 ]] ρ (d+2);
PUSHGLOBAL W;
SQUEEZE 4 2; JFUN
```

JFUN should, of course, enter the code after the arity check and stack rearrangement; that is, it should enter at the EXEC entry (see Section 19.4.3). This code makes a number of savings over our previous attempts:

(i) the vertebrae of the result of the $F-reduction are never allocated at all;
(ii) no update need take place at the end of the $F code because the code for W will update the same node;

(iii) the SQUEEZE takes the place of POP in getting rid of the parameters to $F;
(iv) no UNWIND need take place because it is already done;
(v) no check need be made that W has enough parameters, since we know at compile-time that it does.

These benefits only obtain, however, if

(i) we know what W is;
(ii) it takes just the right number of arguments.

In the ensuing section we will lift these restrictions.

Tail calls have been well studied in other contexts, and we now discuss briefly how our new implementation compares with others.

The optimizing of tail calls has been a standard feature in Lisp compilers for a long time (see Steele [1977], for example). Such compilers exploit the fact that a tail *call* to a function W can be replaced by a *jump* to W, thus saving the allocation of a new stack frame. A particular effect of this optimization is that tail recursion (which normally consumes a stack frame for each call) is transformed into iteration (which operates in constant space).

It is, however, a property of graph reduction that this optimization is performed automatically [Turner, 1979]! Even the first implementation of Chapter 18 performs tail recursion in constant stack space, and all our optimizations preserve this property. The reason for this is that at the end of a code sequence generated by the **R** scheme we used UNWIND to continue evaluation on the same stack, rather than using EVAL which creates a new stack. (Note: we differ here from the G-machine papers, which use EVAL at the end of **R**, at least to begin with.)

While even simple graph reduction implementations can do tail recursion in constant stack space, they still consume heap. Very many of the heap cells thus consumed are discarded very soon after they are allocated, and it is the purpose of the optimization we have described to avoid this turnover of heap cells.

We make one final observation before proceeding to a more general treatment of the spine. Consider the function

```
$H x = IF (= x 0) ($G 3 x) (+ 1 ($H (- x 1)))
```

where $G is a supercombinator which takes two arguments. The call to $G can properly be considered a tail call, since once the decision has been taken to take the 'then' branch of the IF, the result of the $H reduction is just ($G 3 x). Hence we would like our tail call optimizations to propagate into the branches of an IF.

Complete compilation schemes for tail calls are not given since they are an easy consequence of the next section.

21.2 Generalizing Tail Calls

The optimization of the previous section only applied when W was known at compile-time to be a supercombinator of three arguments. We generalize this idea for any W by simply replacing the JFUN instruction at the end of the code for $F given in the previous section with a new instruction

```
DISPATCH 3
```

The argument 3 to DISPATCH gives the number of ribs currently on the stack. The code for $F would then be

$\mathbf{C}[\![$ E_3 $]\!]$ ρ d;
$\mathbf{C}[\![$ E_2 $]\!]$ ρ (d+1);
$\mathbf{C}[\![$ E_1 $]\!]$ ρ (d+2);
PUSHGLOBAL W;
SQUEEZE 4 2; DISPATCH 3

regardless of what W is (except that the PUSHGLOBAL would be a PUSH if W was a variable). For the present we will not perform any compile-time analysis of W; instead, we will simply generate the above code for $F and leave it to the DISPATCH instruction to sort things out at run-time.

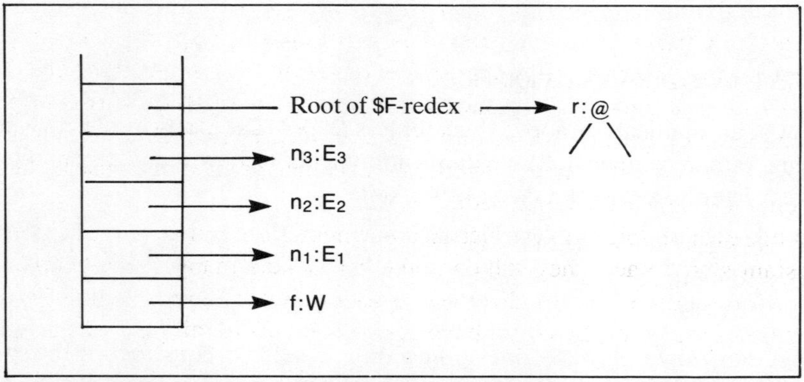

Figure 21.3 Current context on entry to the DISPATCH instruction

Figure 21.3 shows the current context at the moment the DISPATCH instruction is executed. We annotate the nodes with names using a colon to make it easier to follow the rules for DISPATCH. For example, the root of the $F-redex will be r in the rules for DISPATCH.

When the DISPATCH 3 instruction is executed it has to perform case analysis on the function which is on top of the stack. There are several possibilities:

(i) W is an application node;
(ii) W is a supercombinator of zero arguments;

(iii) W is a function (supercombinator or built-in) of exactly three arguments (this is the tail call case);
(iv) W is a function (supercombinator or built-in) of less than three arguments;
(v) W is a function (supercombinator or built-in) of more than three arguments.

We handle these cases separately in the succeeding sections. Since the built-in functions have G-code sequences just like supercombinators, we will not distinguish supercombinators from built-in functions in the following.

In discussing the execution of the DISPATCH instruction, the ground rules are:

(i) The current context looks like Figure 21.3 on entry to the DISPATCH instruction.
(ii) The execution of the DISPATCH instruction must be precisely equivalent to (though perhaps more efficient than) the following steps:

   (a) construct the spine in the heap from the ribs on the stack;
   (b) update the root of the redex (at the bottom of the current context) with the spine thus constructed;
   (c) UNWIND

21.2.1 W is an Application Node

If W is an application node, then (unless DISPATCH looks inside it, which seems rather complicated) we know nothing about how many arguments W takes. Therefore we take the easy way out:

(i) construct the spine of the body of $F;
(ii) update the root of the $F-redex;
(iii) UNWIND.

We can, however, make one optimization. Instead of constructing the spine in the heap and then unwinding it back onto the stack, we can perform the first part of the UNWIND as we construct the spine. When DISPATCH has done this, the context looks like:

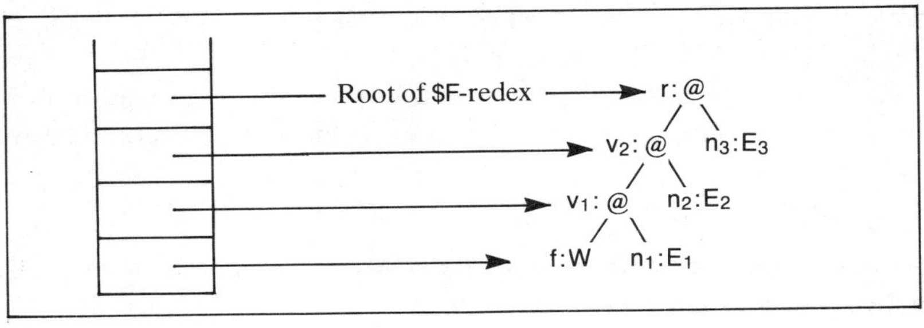

Now DISPATCH behaves just like UNWIND. We can formalize this transition with the rule

$$\text{<f:}n_1\text{:}n_2\text{:}\ldots\text{:}n_k\text{:r:S, G[f=AP } m_1\ m_2\text{], DISPATCH k:[], D>}$$

$$\Rightarrow \text{<f:}v_1\text{:}v_2\text{:}\ldots\text{:}v_{k-1}\text{:r:S, G}\begin{bmatrix} v_1\text{=AP f } n_1 \\ v_i\text{=AP } v_{i-1}\ n_i,\ (1<i<k) \\ r\text{ =AP } v_{k-1}\ n_k \end{bmatrix}\text{, UNWIND:[], D>}$$

Node r is the root of the current redex in this rule and the other DISPATCH rules, and nodes v_i are vertebrae nodes. This seems like quite a lot for one instruction to do, but the actual operations involved are quite simple.

Notice particularly that this would be a safe implementation of DISPATCH *regardless* of what W is, because it makes no assumptions about W. An implementation could therefore use this rule at first for all Ws and later be refined for efficiency. We have expressed the ule as specific to application nodes because we want to give other more efficient implementations of DISPATCH for special cases.

21.2.2 W is a Supercombinator of Zero Arguments

If W is a supercombinator of zero arguments we cannot improve on the previous case, so DISPATCH should behave in exactly the same way as if W was an application node.

21.2.3 W is a Function of Three Arguments

If W is a function of three arguments then we have the tail call case, and DISPATCH can simply enter the code for W. We can express this with the following rule:

$$\text{<f:S, G[f=FUN k C], DISPATCH k:[], D>}$$
$$\Rightarrow \text{<S, G, C, D>}$$

The justification for this was given in the section on tail calls. The code for the function should be entered *after the arity check*, since we know that it has enough arguments. This is the EXEC entry of the function (see Section 19.4.3).

21.2.4 W is a Function of Less Than Three Arguments

If W is a function of less than three arguments then *part* of the body of $F will be the next redex to be reduced.

Suppose W takes two arguments. Then we want to create a new current context in which W will execute, with its two arguments on top of the stack and a pointer to the root of the W-redex below them. We can achieve this by constructing only the top part of the spine of the body of $F. Here is what the stack looks like just before DISPATCH enters the code for W:

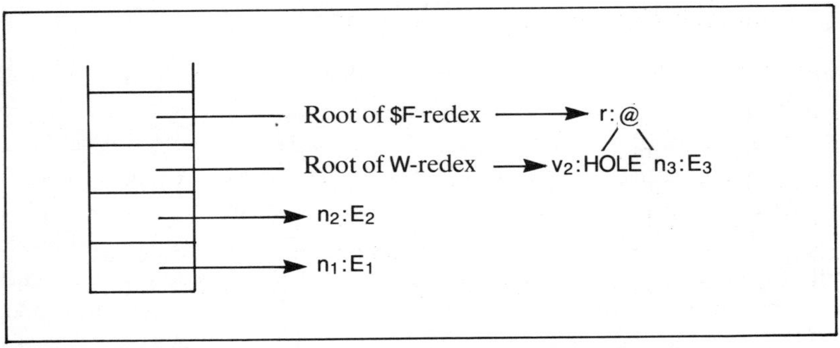

The context for the W-reduction consists of the top three elements on the stack. The HOLE must be allocated to receive the result of the W-reduction.

Here is the formal rule:

$$\langle f:n_1:n_2:\ldots:n_k:r:S,\ G[f=\text{FUN a C}],\ \text{DISPATCH}\ k:[],\ D\rangle$$

$$\{a<k\} \quad \Rightarrow \quad \langle n_1:\ldots:n_a:v_a:\ldots:v_{k-1}:r:S,\ G\begin{bmatrix} v_a=\text{HOLE} \\ v_i=\text{AP}\ v_{i-1}\ n_i,\ (a<i<k) \\ r=\text{AP}\ v_{k-1}\ n_k \end{bmatrix},\ C,\ D\rangle$$

21.2.5 W is a Function of More Than Three Arguments

If W is a function of more than three arguments, the body of $F is in WHNF, and we must update the root of the $F-redex to reflect this fact, since it may be shared. This involves constructing the spine in the heap as we did for the case when W was an application node.

However, the next thing that will happen is an attempt to reduce the application of W. Only if there are enough arguments in the stack will the reduction take place. This gives us the clue to what DISPATCH should do. Having constructed the spine and updated the root of the $F-redex, DISPATCH should test the depth of the stack. If there will not be enough arguments for W to reduce then evaluation is complete and DISPATCH can initiate a RETURN. If there are enough arguments then DISPATCH can rearrange the stack ready for W and enter W.

Suppose that W takes four arguments, and that at the beginning of the DISPATCH the stack looks like this:

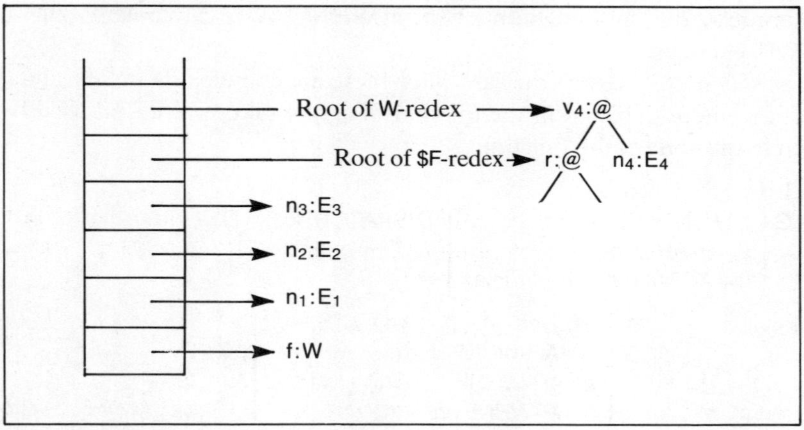

This is just an augmented version of Figure 21.3 showing a stack element below the context in which $F executes. In this case we want DISPATCH to rearrange the stack to:

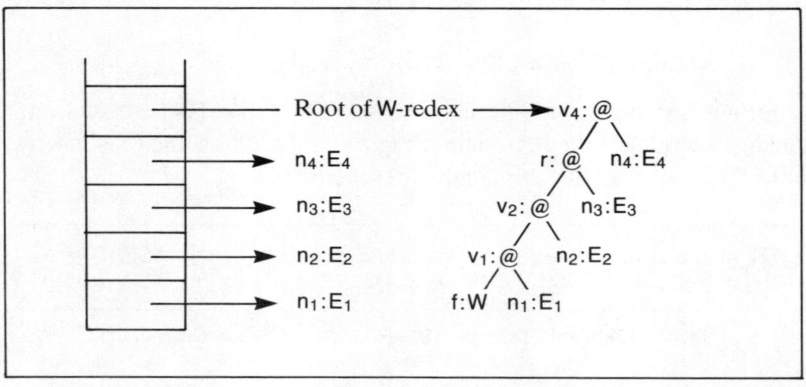

Now the root of the $F-redex has been correctly updated, and a new context has been set up ready to enter W. The occurrences of E_1–E_4 are shared, of course. Notice that E_1, E_2 and E_3 have remained unchanged in the same positions in the stack (which conveniently saves sliding them around).

Here, then, are the two rules for DISPATCH which cover this case. The first covers the case when there are not enough arguments for the function to reduce, so evaluation is complete and a return is made to the caller.

$$\langle f{:}n_1{:}n_2{:}\ldots{:}n_k{:}r{:}v_{k+1}{:}\ldots{:}v_d{:}[\,],\ G[f=\text{FUN a C}],\ \text{DISPATCH } k{:}[\,],\ (S,C'){:}D\rangle$$

$$\{k<d<a\} \;\Rightarrow\; \langle v_d{:}S,\ G\begin{bmatrix} v_1=\text{AP-WHNF } f\ n_1 \\ v_i=\text{AP-WHNF } v_{i-1}\ n_i,\ (1<i<k) \\ r\ =\text{AP-WHNF } v_{k-1}\ n_k \end{bmatrix},\ C',\ D\rangle$$

In this rule, k is the argument to DISPATCH, a is the arity of the function on top of the stack, and d is the number of arguments available. Notice that the vertebrae $v_1, \ldots, v_{k-1}$ are known to be in WHNF, so we can construct them as AP-WHNF nodes.

The second rule covers the case when there are enough arguments, and the rearrangement depicted in the previous diagram takes place, followed by a jump to the code of the function.

```
<f:n1:n2:. . .:nk:r:vk+1:. . .:va:S,
  G [ f=FUN a C                   ],DISPATCH k:[], D>
    [ vk+1=AP r nk+1              ]
    [ vi=AP vi-1 ni, (k+1<i≤a)    ]

{k<a}  =>  <n1:n2:. . .:nk:nk+1:. . .:na:va:S,
             G [ v1=AP-WHNF f n1                   ], C, D>
               [ vi=AP-WHNF vi-1 ni, (1<i<k)       ]
               [ r=AP-WHNF vk-1 nk                 ]
```

21.3 Compilation Using DISPATCH

In this section we discuss the compilation schemes and code generation necessary to use the DISPATCH instruction.

21.3.1 Compilation Schemes for DISPATCH

It is rather simple to compile code to use the DISPATCH instruction, by replacing two rules in the **RS** scheme (Figure 21.4). This is the reason why we went to the trouble of developing the **RS** scheme.

```
RS[[ x ]] ρ d n = PUSH (d − ρ x); SQUEEZE (n+1) (d−n); DISPATCH n
RS[[ f ]] ρ d n = PUSHGLOBAL f; SQUEEZE (n+1) (d−n); DISPATCH n
```

Figure 21.4 Modifications to the **RS** scheme to use DISPATCH

21.3.2 Compile-time Optimization of DISPATCH

So far we have assumed that DISPATCH will do all its work at run-time. This is potentially slow, and sometimes we know what W is at compile-time. We can easily make use of this information to improve the code we generate.

All that is needed is for the code generator to watch for the sequence

```
PUSHGLOBAL $H; SQUEEZE p q; DISPATCH k
```

Now the code generator can do much of the case analysis on $H that would be done at run-time. For example, it may observe that $H takes exactly k arguments, in which case we have a tail call and can generate code to jump directly to the code of $H. This would achieve precisely the effect we obtained in the section on tail calls. Such a jump should, of course, be to the EXEC entry of the function, after the arity check and stack rearrangement.

In particular cases we can do even better. For example,

```
PUSHGLOBAL $CONS; SQUEEZE 3 q; DISPATCH 2
```

can be optimized to

```
CONS; UPDATE (q+1); POP q; RETURN
```

This corresponds precisely to the CONS optimization in the **R** scheme, but moved to a peephole optimization in the code generator. All the special cases in **R** can be moved to the code generator in this way, but this loses opportunities to use **B**, so in practice we might wish to use both methods.

The difficult case is when we are confronted with

```
PUSH n; SQUEEZE p q; DISPATCH k
```

(that is, a PUSH of a variable). In this case the code generator can do no compile-time case analysis, so the case analysis must be done at run-time. Using the case analysis technique outlined in Chapter 19, we would then add a DISPATCH entry to each tag's entry table. The VAX target code for 'DISPATCH 3' might then be:

```
moval 3,r2               k is passed to DISPATCH code in r2
movl (%EP)+,r0           Pop function into r0
movl (r0),r1             Tag into r1
jmp *O_Dispatch(r1)      Case analysis jump
```

21.4 Optimizing the E Scheme

The optimizations we have applied to the **RS** scheme can equally be applied to the **ES** scheme. Like the **RS** scheme, the **ES** scheme constructs the spine of the expression and then unwinds into it, so we might hope to use the same technology to improve it.

Figure 21.5 gives the required modification. First we ALLOCate a HOLE to contain the result; for the **RS** scheme this is already present in the form of the root of the redex. Next we build the ribs using **ES**, pushing them on the stack. Finally we use a new G-code instruction, CALL, to finish the job. This CALL at the end, instead of the SQUEEZE–DISPATCH sequence, is the only difference between **RS** and **ES**.

CALL is very like DISPATCH, except that it first saves the stack and code pointers in the dump (just as EVAL is very like UNWIND except that it saves the

Modification to the **E** scheme

E⟦ E_1 E_2 ⟧ ρ d = ALLOC 1; **ES**⟦ E_1 E_2 ⟧ ρ d 0;

Modifications to the **ES** scheme

ES⟦ x ⟧ ρ d n = PUSH (d − ρ x); CALL n
ES⟦ f ⟧ ρ d n = PUSHGLOBAL f; CALL n

Figure 21.5 Modifications to the **E** and **ES** schemes to use CALL

stack and code pointers first). The rule for CALL is therefore rather straightforward:

$<f{:}n_1{:}n_2{:}\ldots{:}n_k{:}r{:}S,\ G,\ \text{CALL}\ k{:}C,\ D>$
$\Rightarrow\ <f{:}n_1{:}n_2{:}\ldots{:}n_k{:}r{:}[\,],\ G,\ \text{DISPATCH}\ k{:}[\,],\ (S,C){:}D>$

Uses of CALL can be optimized by a peephole optimizer in much the same way as DISPATCH, except that even more opportunities for optimization are available. For example, the sequence

```
PUSHGLOBAL $H; CALL k
```

where $H takes more than k arguments, can be optimized to

```
PUSHGLOBAL $H; MKAP k; SLIDE 1
```

Previously, an EVAL would have taken place at the end of the code sequence

$\mathcal{E}[\![\ \$H\ E_1\ \ldots\ E_k\ ]\!]\ \rho\ d$

(see Figure 20.17). Now, however, the peephole optimizer can spot that no EVAL is needed, which gives an important improvement to the optimizations of Section 20.6.

21.5 Comparison with Environment-based Implementations

We have concentrated in this chapter on avoiding allocating nodes on the spine wherever possible. To the extent to which we have been successful, the G-machine now shows a remarkable similarity to environment-based implementations.

In this section we will make a brief comparison of our final G-machine with Cardelli's Functional Abstract Machine (FAM) [Cardelli, 1983 and 1984].

The FAM is based on *delayed substitution* in which function application is carried out not by constructing an instance of the body of the function, but rather by evaluating the body of the function in an environment in which the formal parameters are bound to their actual values. The *environment* is a data structure which holds the values of all the variables currently in scope. If the result of evaluating the function is itself a function, then a *closure* is returned, which is a pair consisting of

(i) the code of the function;
(ii) the environment in which it should subsequently be executed.

This is the approach of the SECD machine, and the FAM can be considered as an optimized SECD machine:

(i) The SECD machine code is often implemented by direct interpretation of the abstract machine code. The FAM has a more powerful abstract machine code, and is compiled to a target machine code (VAX).

(ii) The SECD machine environment is often implemented as a linked list, and closures as a pair of pointers to the code and to the environment. The FAM constructs closures as an (N+1)-tuple, in which the first element points to the code of the function, and the other N elements are the values of only those variables that occur free in the function definition.

(iii) The SECD machine stack and dump are often implemented as a linked list. The FAM uses the target machine stacks, called AS (argument stack) and RS (return stack) respectively in Cardelli [1984].

Having said this, there is a close correspondence between the FAM and the G-machine:

(i) The G-machine equivalent to a FAM closure is a piece of graph consisting of a supercombinator applied to too few arguments. The arguments give the values of the variables used in the supercombinator body. It is an easy consequence of the lambda-lifting algorithm that all the extra arguments to a function produced by lambda-lifting are used somewhere in the supercombinator body. This corresponds to the fact that FAM closures only contain variables which may be required in the function.

(ii) Execution is stack-based for much of the time. Arguments to the current function are found on the stack. The difference here is that the FAM may also access free variables in the environment, whereas supercombinators have no free variables.

(iii) Arguments to be passed to a function are placed in the stack before calling the function. This is always the case in the FAM and the optimizations of this chapter mean that it will often be the case in the G-machine.

There are two major differences between the FAM and the G-machine:

(i) The FAM is not lazy. It is to preserve laziness that the G-machine often has to write the spine out into the heap, rather than always keeping it in the stack as the FAM does.

(ii) The G-machine is simply an efficient implementation of graph reduction. As we will see, graph reduction is a much more natural model to support parallel execution, so a parallel G-machine is probably much easier to build than a parallel FAM.

References

Cardelli, L. 1983. The functional abstract machine. *Polymorphism*. Vol. 1, no. 1.

Cardelli, L. 1984. Compiling a functional language. In *Proceedings of the ACM Symposium on Lisp and Functional Programming, Austin*, pp. 208–17. August.

Steele, G.L. 1977. Lambda – the ultimate goto. *AI Memo 443*. MIT Artificial Intelligence Lab. October.

Turner, D.A. 1979. A new implementation technique for applicative languages. *Software – Practice and Experience*. Vol. 9, pp. 31–49.

Twenty-two

STRICTNESS ANALYSIS

In Chapter 20 we saw the usefulness of being able to determine in advance whether a function would eventually evaluate its argument(s). As we will see later, in Chapter 24, this information is also useful to determine points at which parallel evaluation of the program can be begun. In this chapter we will discuss a method of compile-time analysis, called *strictness analysis*, which can determine which arguments a function is sure to evaluate.

The chapter is based on Clack and Peyton Jones [1985].

22.1 Abstract Interpretation

Strictness analysis is one of several compile-time optimizations that can be achieved through *abstract interpretation* of the program text.

We begin by giving an informal introduction to abstract interpretation, to set the framework for the rest of the chapter. In doing so, we try to give an intuitive grasp of the technique, and inevitably we gloss over several important theoretical issues. Fortunately, the intuitive approach leads us to a correct implementation. Unlike the rest of the book, this chapter makes use of some basic domain theory, including fixed points [Stoy, 1981].

22.1.1 An Archetypical Example: The Rule of Signs

Abstract interpretation is a technique for deducing information about a program from its text, by executing an abstract version of the program. An appropriate abstraction is chosen according to what information is wanted.

As an example, suppose we wanted to know the sign of

```
34 * (-5) * (-3993)
```

The hard way to find the sign of this number is to perform the two multiplications in full and look at the sign of the result, like this:

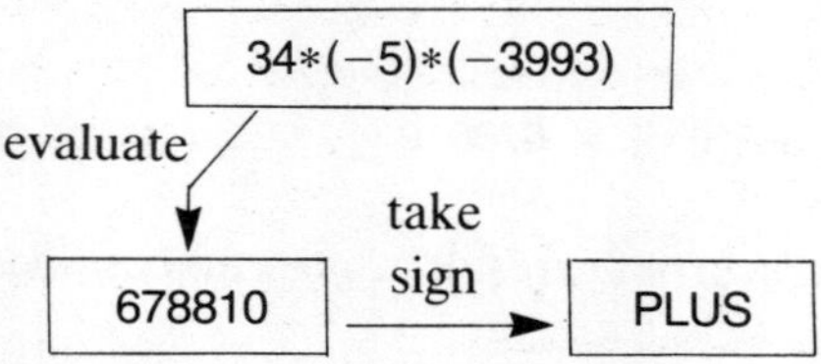

A simpler method is to perform a more abstract calculation:

PLUS ∗% MINUS ∗% MINUS = PLUS

We replace each number with an abstract representation (its sign), and replace the multiplication operator with an abstract operator ∗%, which implements the familiar 'rule of signs'.

```
PLUS  *% PLUS  = PLUS
MINUS *% PLUS  = MINUS
PLUS  *% MINUS = MINUS
MINUS *% MINUS = PLUS
```

Now it is easy to compute the answer 'PLUS', which tells us that the result of the original calculation would have been positive. We can think of this 'short-cut' in the following way:

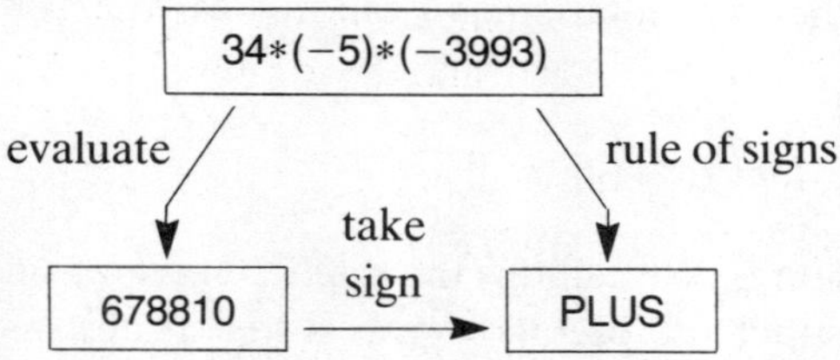

The rule of signs gives a short-cut from arithmetic expressions to the sign of their value, without going via a full evaluation. This is precisely what abstract interpretation is all about.

Let us now generalize the diagram, to show more clearly what is going on:

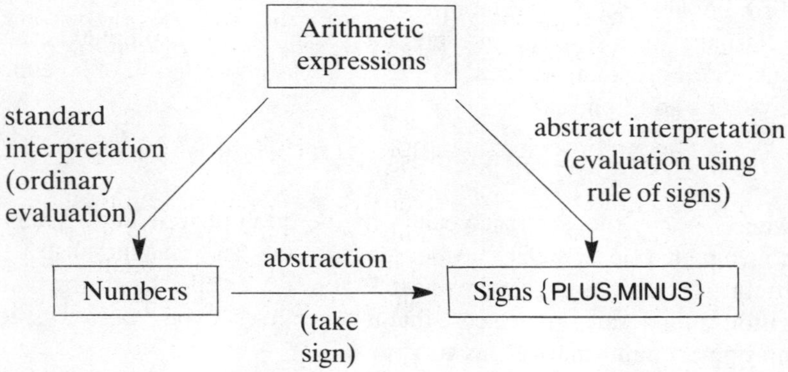

Beginning with an arithmetic expression (at the top), we may evaluate in the ordinary way, using **Eval** (see Section 2.5); we call this the *standard interpretation*.

Eval[[34∗(−5)∗(−3993)]] = 678810

Then we may take the sign of the result, using a function sgn::Number −> Sign, like this:

sgn 678810 = PLUS

The function sgn maps a number onto a two-point domain {PLUS,MINUS}. We call this operation *abstraction*, since it preserves certain information about its argument (in this case, its sign), while losing other information (for example, whether or not the argument is even).

Alternatively, we may evaluate the original expression using the rule of signs; we call this the *abstract interpretation*, and write it like this:

Eval%[[34∗(−5)∗(−3993)]] = PLUS ∗% MINUS ∗% MINUS
= PLUS

The crucial fact is that the short-cut gives the *same answer* as the long way round. Using the new notation, we can express this condition formally as follows:

sgn **Eval**[[E]] = **Eval**%[[E]]

for any expression E. We call this the *safety condition*, since it expresses the fact that the abstract interpretation gives correct (safe) answers.

Notice that the abstraction function is chosen to preserve exactly (and only) the information we need to answer the original question, which asked for the sign of the result. The abstract interpretation is then chosen to give a short-cut for that particular abstraction function. A different question, such as 'is the result even or odd?', would suggest a different abstraction function and a different abstract interpretation.

Usually the abstract interpretation cannot give completely accurate answers. For example, consider the abstract interpretation of an expression involving addition:

Eval%[[23 + (−45)]] = PLUS +% MINUS

where +% is the abstract version of the addition operator. There is no convenient rule of signs for addition, and the best that the abstract interpretation can do is to give the result 'PLUS or MINUS'. The abstract interpretation is then 'safe' in the sense that it never gives 'wrong' answers, though it may give 'uninformative' answers.

22.1.2 History and References

The pioneers in the field of abstract interpretation were Cousot and Cousot [1977]. Since then the theory has been extended by Mycroft [1981], whose doctoral thesis explained how the Cousots' theory could be applied to functional languages. In particular, he presented a formal explanation of strictness analysis, albeit limited to first-order functions and a poor treatment of data structures. His presentation is primarily theoretical, so we give a practical exposition of the approach in the following sections.

Since then substantial advances have been made, and the formal basis for abstract interpretation greatly clarified. Burn, Hankin and Abramsky give an excellent treatment of the topic, and their paper is strongly recommended [Burn *et al.*, 1985]. It addresses all the issues that are glossed over in this chapter.

22.2 Using Abstract Interpretation to do Strictness Analysis

Abstract interpretation is a general tool, and we choose the abstraction function and abstract interpretation to be appropriate for the questions we wish to answer. In this section we will develop an abstract domain and abstraction mapping which are suitable for strictness analysis.

22.2.1 Formulating the Question

First of all, we must pose the question we wish to answer in a formal way. Informally, the question is: 'does this function always need the value of its argument?' If we were given the answer to this question for all supercombinators, we could compile better code for the supercombinators (Chapter 20), or evaluate the argument in parallel (Chapter 24).

Recall from Section 2.5.4 that a function is *strict* if and only if it always needs the value of its argument. The formal definition was:

a function f is strict if and only if

$$\text{f}\ \bot = \bot \qquad (22.1)$$

That is, given a non-terminating argument, f will not terminate. Of course, f could be failing to terminate for reasons other than trying to evaluate its argument, but the net result is the same. Certainly if (22.1) holds then it is safe to evaluate the argument before the call of f (or in parallel with it).

The notion extends naturally to functions of several arguments. For instance, if g is a function of three arguments (x, y and z) we say that it is strict in y if

$$\text{g x}\ \bot\ \text{z} = \bot \qquad \textit{for any} \qquad \text{x and z}$$

We now have a formal way of posing the question, namely, 'given a function f, does (f ⊥) = ⊥?' We can depict the question using the now-familiar diagram:

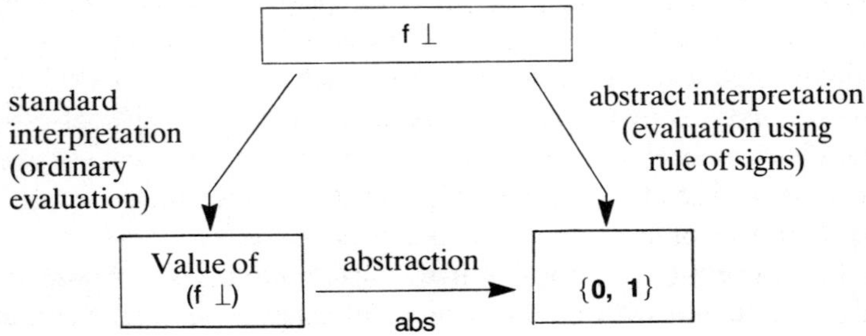

What should the abstraction map, and abstract domain, be? It is clear that we want the abstraction function abs to distinguish between ⊥ and all other elements, so that

abs ⊥ = **0**
abs x = **1** if x ≠ ⊥

The abstract domain needs only two elements, which we arbitrarily call **0** and **1**. Using the notation established earlier, f is strict if and only if

Eval⟦ f ⊥ ⟧ = ⊥

which is true if and only if

abs **Eval**⟦ f ⊥ ⟧ = **0**

All that remains is to pick a suitable abstract interpretation, which we call **Eval#**, to distinguish it from the abstract interpretation **Eval%** used for the rule of signs.

22.2.2 Choosing an Appropriate Abstract Interpretation

The abstract interpretation should have the following two properties:

(i) It *must* be 'safe'. By this we mean that it should never suggest that a function is strict, when in reality it is not.
(ii) It *should* be as 'informative' as possible, subject to (i). That is, the abstract interpretation should detect strict functions in as many cases as possible.

As in the case of the rule of signs, we can give formal expression to the safety requirement:

abs **Eval**⟦ E ⟧ ≤ **Eval#**⟦ E ⟧

for any expression E.

This equation says that, if **Eval**# errs from the 'right answer' (abs **Eval**[[E]]), then it must always err on the high side. If the right answer is **1**, then **Eval**# must produce the result **1**, since the only alternative is **0**, which is unsafe (this is property (i)). If the right answer is **0**, then **Eval**# can produce **0** or **1** but we hope that it will produce **0** most of the time, because that is more informative (this is property (ii)).

To put it another way, it must not be possible to use the short-cut abstract interpretation to conclude that a function is strict, when in reality it is not. Hence, the abstract interpretation must only produce the result **0** when the standard interpretation is guaranteed to produce $\perp$.

It follows that there is a range of possible abstract interpretations, all of which are safe, but which vary in their informativeness. In the rest of this section we will use informal arguments to develop a reasonably informative abstract interpretation **Eval**#.

For a start, the safety condition means that **Eval**# should have the following property:

Eval#[[E]] = **0**

only if the (ordinary) evaluation of E *definitely* fails to terminate.

Conversely,

Eval#[[E]] = **1**

if the (ordinary) evaluation of E *may* terminate.

Next, we recall, from the rule of signs example, that

Eval%[[34∗(−5)∗(−3993)]] = PLUS ∗% MINUS ∗% MINUS

Generalizing from this example, we might suggest the following rules for **Eval**%:

Eval%[[E_1 E_2]] = **Eval**%[[E_1]] **Eval**%[[E_2]]
Eval%[[∗]] = ∗%
Eval%[[−n]] = MINUS
Eval%[[n]] = PLUS

where E_1 and E_2 are expressions, ∗% is the abstract version of multiplication, and n is a number. The first two of these rules are quite general, while the last two are clearly specific to the rule of signs.

In the case of strictness analysis, we want to evaluate

Eval#[[f $\perp$]]

Using a similar rule to the first of those given for **Eval**%, we might proceed as follows:

Eval#[[f $\perp$]] = **Eval**#[[f]] **Eval**#[[$\perp$]]

Now, certainly **Eval**# ⟦ ⊥ ⟧ = **0** (since ⊥ certainly fails to terminate). Using this fact, together with a rule similar to the second **Eval**% rule, gives

```
Eval#⟦ f ⊥ ⟧ = Eval#⟦ f ⟧ Eval# ⟦ ⊥ ⟧
             = f# 0
```

Remember that we are free to invent whatever rules we like for **Eval**#, so long as we can prove that the safety condition holds. We will not do so here, but Burn *et al.* [1985] give the formal proofs.

To summarize our progress, for each function f we must first find its abstract version f#. Having done so, we compute (f# **0**), and if the result is **0** then f is certainly strict. The hope is that computing (f# **0**) is very much cheaper than computing (f ⊥). It would be hard to do worse, since the latter may fail to terminate!

22.2.3 Developing f# from f

We will now show how to produce the definition of f# from the definition of f, using the following example:

```
f p q r = IF (= p 0) (+ q r) (+ q p)
```

All we have to do is to take the abstract interpretation of the right-hand side:

```
f# p q r = Eval#⟦ IF (= p 0) (+ q r) (+ q p) ⟧
```

Using the rules of the previous section repeatedly gives

```
f# p q r = IF# (=# p 0#) (+# q r) (+# q p)
```

We have actually used one extra rule, namely

```
Eval#⟦ v ⟧ = v
```

where v is a variable. Now,

```
constant# = 1
```

(since the evaluation of constants always terminates) and hence

```
f# p q r = IF#(=# p 1) (+# q r) (+# q p)
```

The net effect is that, to obtain f# from f, we simply replace all constants and built-in functions in the body of f with their abstract (#) versions. To put this another way, **Eval**# gives a denotational semantics for the language, which differs from the standard semantics only in the interpretation of constants and built-in functions.

Finally, we must decide what the abstract versions of the built-in functions actually are. Beginning with the equality function =, we know that

(= E_1 E_2) *may* terminate if (E_1 *may* terminate)
and (E_2 *may* terminate)

and hence

```
=# x y  =  & x y
```

where we define & as the boolean AND operator (in the abstract domain). Similarly we define | as OR. The definition of +# is identical to that of =#. However, IF# is more interesting. We know that

(IF E_1 E_2 E_3) *may* terminate if (E_1 *may* terminate)
and ((E_2 *may* terminate)
or (E_3 *may* terminate))

Thus

```
IF# x y z = & x (| y z)
```

(All of these rules are proved in Burn *et al.*) We can now complete the definition of f#, thus:

```
f# p q r = IF# (=# p 1) (+# q r) (+# q p)
         = & (& p 1) (| (& q r) (& q p))
         = & p (& q (| p r))
```

At last, we are in a position to discover the strictness of f. For example, to find whether f is strict in its first parameter, p, we compute

```
f# 0 1 1 = & 0 (& 1 (| 0 1))
         = 0
```

This tells us that f fails to terminate if p fails to terminate, even if all the other arguments terminate; so f is strict in p. To discover strictness in q and r, we compute

```
f# 1 0 1 = 0   (so f is strict in q)
f# 1 1 0 = 1   (so f is not strict in r)
```

22.2.4 Fitting Strictness Analysis into the Compiler

Everything we have said so far assumes that the functions being analyzed have no free variables, and indeed it seems rather hard to analyze functions which do have free variables. Rather than address this problem directly, we can simply perform strictness analysis after lambda-lifting.

This makes sense in any case, because it is the supercombinator definitions that we want to annotate for subsequent passes of the compiler, not the original lambda abstractions.

22.3 Coping with Recursion

There is one fly in the ointment, which is that a user-defined function may be recursive. To see that we cannot simply execute the # version of the function normally, consider

```
f x y = IF (= x 0) y (f (- x 1) y)
```

The abstract version of f is therefore given by

```
f# x y = & x (| y (f# x y))
```

To find out whether f is strict in y we evaluate (f# **1 0**), but unfortunately this evaluation *will not terminate*. This would be a disaster, because this evaluation occurs at compile-time, so the compiler would loop. However, it is intuitively clear that f *is* strict in y, and we would like the compiler to be able to deduce this fact.

We will now examine algorithms for dealing with recursion, beginning with two attempts that turn out to be inadequate.

22.3.1 The First Wrong Way

At first it looks as if we could just assume that recursive calls to f# were strict in everything. Thus

```
f# 1 0 = & 1 (| 0 (f# 1 0))
       = & 1 (| 0 0)
       = 0
```

which is the correct answer. This simple method is, however, easily defeated. Consider the function

```
f x y z = if (= y 0) (f 0 1 x) x
```

The simple method says this function is strict in x and y, whereas it is, of course, only strict in y. In retrospect this seems obvious, but this mistake was actually made in two published implementations of Mycroft's work.

22.3.2 The Second Wrong Way

The reason the first method fails is that it uses a bad approximation to f#. To see this, observe that the definition of f# is a perfectly good recursive function definition. Domain theory tells us that the function thus defined is given by the least upper bound of an ascending sequence of approximations to f# – the *ascending Kleene chain* (AKC). For example,

if	f# x y z = ...f#...	(a recursive definition)
then	$f\#_0$ x y z = **0**	(zeroth approximation)
	$f\#_1$ x y z = ...$f\#_0$...	(first approximation)
	$f\#_2$ x y z = ...$f\#_1$...	(second approximation)

and so on.

Since we are in the abstract two-element domain, there are only a *finite number* of functions of three arguments. This sequence must therefore reach a limit in a finite number of steps. The first method failed because we used the first approximation only, which may not be the limit. So we must examine successive approximations until we reach a fixed point, and our problem boils down to deciding when this fixed point has been reached. Notice that the application of any $f\#_i$ to any arguments will always terminate.

The second bad method says 'we have reached a fixed point when the set of variables in which the approximations are strict remains unchanged from one approximation to the next'. This copes with the previous counterexample, because

$f\#_0$ is strict in { x, y, z }
$f\#_1$ is strict in { x, y }
$f\#_2$ is strict in { y }
$f\#_3$ is strict in { y }

and we conclude that f# itself is strict in y alone. This method is attractive because it is quite easy to compute the set of strict variables for a function from its boolean expression. Unfortunately, this is not a genuine check for a fixed point, as the following counterexample shows:

```
f x y z p = if (= p 0) (+ x z) (+ (f y 0 0 (- p 1)) (f z z 0 (- p 1)))
```

The test is better, so the counterexample is more contorted! Working out the details of this example is left as an exercise. The results are

$f\#_0$ is strict in { x, y, z, p }
$f\#_1$ is strict in { x, z, p }
$f\#_2$ is strict in { z, p }
$f\#_3$ is strict in { z, p }
$f\#_4$ is strict in { p }

The second and third approximations are the same, so we might conclude that the AKC has converged. However, the fourth approximation shows that this is false. We call such false convergence a *plateau*, and it is these plateaus that defeat the second bad method.

22.3.3 The Right Way

The only correct way to find a fixed point is to assure ourselves that

$f\#_n$ x y z = $f\#_{n+1}$ x y z *for any* x, y, z

This looks like an expensive test to perform, since there are 2^3 possible combinations of x, y and z, even in the first-order case. It turns out that in the worst case the cost of the test must be exponential in the number of arguments [Hudak and Young, 1986], but in practice it requires considerable contortion to invent examples with plateaus, so we expect rapid convergence in typical cases. A promising approach is therefore to develop representations and heuristics which will perform well in the common cases, and will still give correct answers (albeit more slowly) in the difficult cases.

This question is discussed at some length in Clack and Peyton Jones [1985].

22.3.4 Order of Analysis and Mutual Recursion

We have described how to find the fixed points of self-recursive definitions, and we now extend this to cover mutual recursion. Consider the definitions

```
f x = ...g...f...
g y = ...f...g...
```

Here we cannot fully analyze either function before the other; instead we must perform the fixed point iterations simultaneously, thus

```
f#₀ x = 0                    g#₀ y = 0
f#₁ x = ...g#₀...f#₀...      g#₁ y = ...f#₀...g#₀...
f#₂ x = ...g#₁...f#₁...      g#₂ y = ...f#₁...g#₁...
```

It is slightly more efficient (and gives the same result) to use $f\#_1$ in $g\#_1$, since $f\#_1$ is now available (assuming we perform each step of the f iteration before the corresponding g step).

Suppose the definition of a function f involves a function g but not vice versa, thus

```
f = ...g...f...
g = ...g...
```

Then we can safely first analyze g, find the fixed point of g#, and use this information in the subsequent analysis of f. This can prove very important when analyzing large systems of equations since finding the fixed point of f and g simultaneously is much more costly than analyzing g first, and using this information to analyze f. Unfortunately, functional programmers often write large collections of equations in a single letrec, so all the equations may potentially be mutually recursive. This is another reason for performing the dependency analysis described in Chapter 6, to separate definitions into minimal mutually recursive sets.

22.4 Extensions to Mycroft's Work, and Other Work

Mycroft's original work was restricted to first-order functions and flat domains (that is, domains without structured data types). Since higher-order functions and non-flat domains (providing structured data types, which may require lazy evaluation) are both important features of functional languages these restrictions were severe. Fortunately, recent work has extended the original ideas to cover these areas.

22.4.1 Higher-order Functions

Burn, Hankin and Abramsky [1985] have shown that the techniques developed to handle first-order functions have a natural extension to the higher-order case.

For example, consider

```
hof g x y = (g (hof (K 0) x (- y 1))) +
            (if (= y 0) x (hof I 3 (- y 1)))
```

where K x y = x

and I x = x

Performing abstraction in a straightforward way, we get

```
hof# g x y = & (g (hof# (K# 1) x y)) (& y (I x (hof# I# 1 y)))
```

We need to take some care when looking for a fixed point to ensure that successive approximations deliver the same result *for all values of* g. Since g is a function, it can take a whole lattice of values (three values in this case: (K **0**), I and (K **1**)), and this makes the finding of fixed points even more computationally expensive. This example is a particularly interesting one, since it turns out that we have to go to the fourth approximation to find a fixed point.

22.4.2 Non-flat Domains

Strictness analysis of non-flat domains tells us, for example, when a particular application of CONS is strict. Knowing this may enable us to generate better code.

Recent work by Hughes [1985] and Wadler [1985a] offers extensions of strictness analysis to cover this area.

22.4.3 Other Related Work

Wray [1986] describes a strictness analysis algorithm which, unusually, seems not to be based on abstract interpretation.

Another compile-time technique, designed to transform list-processing programs into a highly efficient form, is Wadler's *listless transformer* [Wadler, 1984 and 1985b]. The listless transformer is able to compile certain kinds of list-processing functions into a finite state machine, which runs without consuming any heap.

22.5 Annotating the Program

The purpose of strictness analysis is to annotate the program for the benefit of subsequent phases of the compiler. So far in this chapter we have shown how to derive the abstract version of each supercombinator from its definition. We now show how to use this information to add annotations to the program.

Suppose that we have produced the abstract versions of each of our supercombinators. There are two distinct ways in which we can use these abstract functions to annotate the original (lambda-lifted) program:

(i) We can annotate each supercombinator definition to indicate in which arguments it is strict. For example, the definition

```
$F ! x y ! z = . . .body of $F. . .
```

might indicate that $F is strict in x and z, but not in y. (The exclamation mark is, of course, just an arbitrary symbol chosen to allow us to write a concrete representation of an annotated definition.)

This kind of annotation was used in the optimizations of Section 20.6.2.

(ii) We can annotate individual application nodes in supercombinator bodies to indicate strict applications. For example, in the definition

```
$G p q = ...($F ! p 3 ! q)...
```

the application of $F to p is annotated with an infix exclamation mark to indicate a strict application. The application of ($F p 3) to q is similarly annotated.

This kind of annotation was used in the optimizations of Section 20.5.2.

At first it appears that the two sorts of annotation give duplicate information, and indeed they often do so. However, there are situations in which each is uniquely appropriate.

22.5.1 Annotating Function Definitions

Given a definition for the supercombinator $F, we want to annotate the definition to indicate the parameters in which it is strict. Using its abstract interpretation $F#, we can discover this information using the method described at the end of Section 22.2.3.

Suppose $F takes two arguments. Then in order to find whether $F is strict in its first argument we simply evaluate

```
$F# 0 1
```

If the answer is **0**, $F is certainly strict in its first argument. One slight complication is that the result of $F may be a function, so that the result of our abstract evaluation will also be a function. In this case we are interested in whether the result is the bottom element of the function domain, so we simply 'feed it **1**s' until it returns either **0** (in which case $F is strict) or **1** (in which case it is not). (The bottom element of a function domain is that function which returns the bottom element of its result domain regardless of its argument.)

For example, suppose $F was defined as

```
$F x y = + (+ x y)
```

Then $F# will be

```
$F# x y = & (& x y)
```

We evaluate

```
$F# 0 1  →  & (& 0 1)
         →  & 0
```

giving a function. To find out whether this function is bottom, we apply it to **1**, giving

```
& 0 1  →  0
```

so the function is indeed bottom (since it returns **0** no matter how well defined the argument is). Hence $F is strict in its first argument.

The other complication occurs if an argument to $F is a function. Then, instead of **0** and **1**, we must use the bottom and top of the appropriate function domain. All of this entails knowing the type of $F, which is perhaps another motivation for using a typed language.

22.5.2 Annotating Application Nodes

The reason for annotating application nodes is not as clear-cut as the reason for annotating supercombinator definitions. Consider the definition:

```
$G x y = y 3 x
```

and suppose that in the body of another supercombinator there occurred the expression

```
...($G E +)...
```

where E is some complicated expression. Clearly $G is not strict in x, because the function argument y may not be strict in its second parameter. However, *in this particular application of* $G the second argument is +, so E will certainly be evaluated subsequently. Hence E could be evaluated before the call of $G, and we could annotate the call thus:

```
...($G ! E ! +)...
```

Doing this is extremely worthwhile, because the optimizations of Section 20.5.2 will then apply, so that we can evaluate E rather than construct a graph for it.

Fortunately, it is also relatively simple to deduce this annotation. Given an expression ($G P Q), we can discover whether it is strict in P by evaluating

```
$G# 0 Q#
```

and in Q by evaluating

```
$G# P# 0
```

(To see that this is formally valid, consider the strictness of the functions $Dummy1 and $Dummy2, where

```
$Dummy1 e = $G e Q
$Dummy2 e = $G P e
```

$Dummy1 is strict in e if and only if the expression ($G P Q) is strict in P, and similarly for $Dummy2.)

One other point of interest occurs when analyzing a definition such as

```
$F x y = ...($G E y)...
```

where the formal parameters of the definition occur in the subexpression being analyzed. In order to compute strictness in E we evaluate ($G# 0 y#); but what value should we use for y#? The analysis we are performing should hold for *any* application of $F, so we should use 1 for y#, which reflects our lack of information about its value. If the type of the parameter is a function, then we replace occurrences of it with the top of the corresponding abstract function space.

22.5.3 Why Both Annotations Are Needed

It may now seem that the information provided by annotating application nodes is always superior to that provided by annotating function definitions, since the former is able to take advantage of contextual information. However, there are two reasons why it is important to annotate the function definition also.

The first is that the optimization of Section 20.6 requires annotations on the function definition, so that it can compile the best possible code for the function, which is nevertheless applicable in all possible contexts.

The second reason concerns parallel evaluation, and is explained in Section 24.4.1.

22.5.4 Summary

In summary, we should annotate both the formal parameters of a supercombinator definition and each application node of a supercombinator body. These two forms of annotation are complementary, and neither can be omitted without loss.

Annotation is carried out by performing evaluations in the abstract domain, using the abstract versions of the supercombinators.

It turns out that precisely the same annotations are needed for parallel machines (see Chapter 24).

References

Burn, G., Hankin, C.L., and Abramsky, S. 1985. Strictness analysis of higher order functions. *Science of Computer Programming* (to appear); also DoC 85/6, Dept Comp. Sci., Imperial College, London. April.

Clack, C.D., and Peyton Jones, S.L. 1985. Strictness analysis – a practical approach. In

Conference on Functional Programming and Computer Architecture, Nancy. pp. 35–49. Jouannaud (editor). LNCS 201. Springer Verlag.

Cousot, P., and Cousot, R. 1977. Abstract interpretation: a unified lattice model for static analysis of programs by construction or approximation of fixed points. In *Proceedings of the 4th ACM Symposium on Principles of Programming Languages, Los Angeles*, pp. 238–52.

Hudak, P., and Young, J. 1986. Higher order strictness analysis in untyped lambda calculus. In *Proceedings of the 12th ACM Symposium on Principles of Programming Languages*, pp. 97–109, January.

Hughes, R.J.M. 1985. *Strictness Detection in Non-flat Domains*. Programming Research Group, Oxford. August.

Mycroft, A. 1981. Abstract interpretation and optimising transformations for applicative programs. PhD thesis, Dept Computer Science, University of Edinburgh.

Stoy, J.E. 1981. *Denotational Semantics*. MIT Press.

Wadler, P. 1984. Listlessness is better than laziness: lazy evaluation and garbage collection at compile-time. In *Proceedings of the ACM Symposium on Lisp and Functional Programming, Austin, Texas*. August.

Wadler, P. 1985a. *Strictness Analysis on Non-flat Domains*. Programming Research Group, Oxford. November.

Wadler, P. 1985b. Listlessness is better than laziness II: composing listless functions. In *Programs as Data Objects*, Ganzinger, H., and Jones, N.D. (editors). LNCS 217. Springer Verlag.

Wray, S.C. 1986. Implementation and programming techniques for functional languages. PhD thesis, University of Cambridge. January.

Twenty-three

THE PRAGMATICS OF GRAPH REDUCTION

The goal of a programmer is to write programs that are

(i) (absolutely) correct, i.e. they should meet their specification;
(ii) (reasonably) efficient, i.e. they should consume as few machine resources as possible.

In order to achieve these goals the programmer has to reason about

(i) the meaning of his program, to assure himself that it has the same meaning as the specification;
(ii) the resource consumption of his program, to assure himself that it will consume only reasonable resources.

In conventional imperative languages it is relatively hard to reason about the meaning of a program, because the semantics of the programming language is generally rather complex. On the other hand, it is normally fairly straightforward to reason about the memory space and CPU cycles consumed by a program, because the programmer has an accurate mental model of how execution takes place.

A major strength of functional languages is their semantic simplicity, which makes it much easier to reason about the meaning of a program. This topic has been well discussed elsewhere (for example Backus [1978], Turner [1981]) and is outside the scope of this book. On the other hand, *a major weakness of functional languages is the difficulty of reasoning about their space and time behavior*, especially the former. In particular, a functional program may have much worse space–time behavior than the programmer might expect.

This chapter is mainly concerned with a discussion of the various forms in which this problem occurs, as a warning to the unwary implementor. No good solutions are yet known to most of these problems; they are very much research issues. Meira [1985] takes the efficiency of functional programs as the main subject of his thesis, and chapter 6 of Stoye's thesis [Stoye, 1985] gives a good summary of the area. Both served as major sources for this chapter.

23.1 The Time Behavior of Functional Programs

Normally we are only concerned with the result of a functional program, rather than the exact time at which the parts of the result are produced. In the case of an interactive program, however, we need more control over the order of evaluation.

We may write interactive functional programs by specifying the program as a function from a (finite or infinite) list of input characters to a (finite or infinite) list of output characters. Such finite or infinite lists of data items are often called *streams*. We may draw such a system like this:

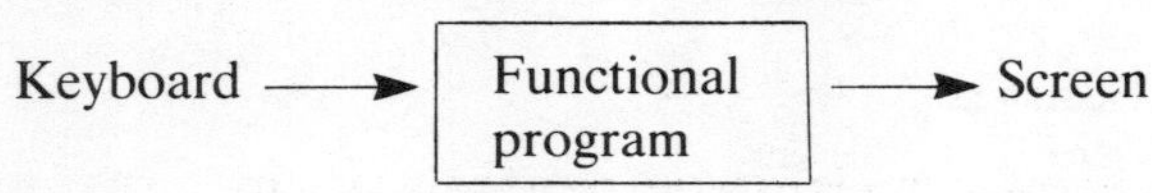

Suppose we wanted to write a program which repeatedly prompted the user with

```
Enter number:
```

then read a number (17, say) from the input stream, and then output

```
Result is: 34
```

where the result is double the input number. We could write the program using a function double, which takes the input stream as its argument and produces the output stream as its result:

```
double inputStream
= "Enter number: " ++
    "Result is: " ++
    numToChars (2*n) ++
    double restInput
    where
    (n, restInput) = charsToNum inputStream
```

numToChars is a function which takes a number and converts it to a list of characters. charsToNum takes a list of characters and converts an initial segment of the list to a number, returning the number and the rest of the list. The ++ operator is Miranda's infix list concatenator.

Unfortunately, when we run the program we will get the prompt

```
Enter number: Result is:
```

The system outputs the result message before reading the number. It does this because the result message does not depend on the value of the number; lazy evaluation has postponed the evaluation of (charsToNum inputStream) until after the result message has been output.

This is an example of a case when we want some control over the evaluation order in order to make the program behave correctly in time. In this case there is a straightforward solution. What is needed is a built-in function seq, with the behavior

```
seq ⊥ y = ⊥
seq x y = y
```

Pragmatically,

> seq evaluates its first argument, discards it,
> and then returns its second argument.

We can now rewrite double, thus:

```
double inputStream
= "Enter number: " ++
   seq n "Result is: " ++
   numToChars (2*n) ++
   double restInput
   where
   (n, restInput) = charToNum inputStream
```

Now the 'Result is:' message is made to depend on the value of n, so the message will not be output until n has been evaluated (and hence input).

This is the first example of a situation in which lazy evaluation gives slightly unexpected results. In this case, however, it is possible to reason about the order in which results appear in the output stream, so the problem is not nearly so serious as those which follow.

23.2 The Delicacy of Full Laziness

We have described what it means for an implementation to be lazy or fully lazy only in very operational terms, and they are difficult concepts to reason about. Programs that look lazy sometimes turn out not to be for subtle reasons, and we will see some examples in the following sections.

23.2.1 Ordering of Parameters

We recall the Miranda program from Chapter 15 which we used to develop the concept of full laziness:

```
f     = g 4
g x y = y + sqrt x
-------------------
(f 1) + (f 2)
```

Now consider a rather similar program in which g takes its parameters in a different order:

```
f y   = g y 4
g y x = y + sqrt x
--------------------
(f 1) + (f 2)
```

We might hope that the (sqrt 4) would only be computed once, as before, but it will in fact be computed twice. This is because (sqrt x) is no longer an MFE of any lambda expression (try it!). This, in turn, is a consequence of the ordering of the parameters of g.

We might take this as a clue to the compiler to put g's parameters in the other order and change all the calls of g appropriately. But suppose the definition of g was

```
g x y = sqrt x + sqrt y
```

Now no order is 'right', and its laziness depends on the way it is used. If g is used many times with its first parameter fixed then all is well, but if it is used many times with its second parameter fixed we will recompute (sqrt y) each time.

There is an asymmetry in the laziness of g with respect to different parameters. The onus is on the programmer to put the parameters to his functions in the 'best' order to maximize laziness.

23.2.2 Full Laziness and Recursion

Consider the following Miranda program (due to William Stoye):

```
f x 0 = 0
f x n = sqrt x + f x (n-1)
--------------------------
 f 4 1000
```

How many times does the (sqrt 4) get evaluated, once or 1000 times? The answer is 1000 times. Now consider another program, which is plainly equivalent:

```
f x = g where g 0 = 0
              g n = sqrt x + g (n-1)
------------------------------------
f 4 1000
```

Now how many times does the (sqrt 4) get evaluated? The answer is once. These are not obvious answers, and it takes a little while with the lambda-lifter to discover how lazy they are, yet a program transformation system might easily transform one into the other without expecting the serious degradation in performance that would result.

23.2.3 Summary

We conclude that it is by no means obvious how lazy a function is, and that we do not at present have any tools for reasoning about this. Laziness is a delicate property of a function, and seemingly innocuous program transformations may lose laziness.

23.3 The Space Behavior of Lazy Functional Programs

So far in this book we have largely taken for granted that lazy evaluation is a Good Thing, since it postpones evaluation until it is certain that the result of the evaluation is required.

However, this view is rather naive since it takes into account only the number of reductions performed, while discounting the memory consumption of the evaluation. It is actually rather difficult to work out what the space consumption of a lazy program will be, and we will examine a number of examples in this section.

23.3.1 Space Leaks

Consider the following Miranda program:

```
f = drop 1000
drop n xs = xs,          n=0
          = drop (n-1) (tl xs)
-----------------------------
(...f...f...f...)
```

(drop n xs) returns the list xs with the first n elements knocked off it. The function f is drop applied to one argument, 1000, and is used at various points in the program.

Now, the lambda expression for drop is

drop = λn.λxs.IF (= n 0) xs (drop (− n 1) (TAIL xs))

When fully lazy lambda-lifting is performed, the expressions (= n 0) and (drop (− n 1)) will be lifted out of the λxs abstraction, giving two supercombinators:

```
$drop n        = $L (= n 0) ($drop (− n 1))
$L NO DN1 xs = IF NO xs (DN1 (TAIL xs))
```

Consider now the value of f:

```
f = $drop 1000
   → $L (= 1000 0) ($drop (− 1000 1))
   → $L FALSE ($L (= 999 0) ($drop (− 999 1)))
   → $L FALSE ($L FALSE ($L (= 998 0) ($drop (− 998 1))))
     etc.
```

The second argument to $L can be reduced again and again. Of course, f *alone* will never be expanded with successive reductions like this. However, on the first occasion when f is applied to a list, the ($drop (− 1000 1)) expression will be reduced, and the result will *overwrite* the ($drop (− 1000 1)) redex. Also the (= 1000 0) redex will be evaluated, and the result will overwrite the (= 1000 0) redex. Therefore the graph representing f will grow in the manner indicated above, until it is 1000 levels deep.

Nothing has gone wrong. The system is simply preserving full laziness. The next time f is applied to a list, many fewer reductions will have to be done, because the recursion has been unrolled in advance. This is closely analogous to the optimization sometimes performed by conventional compilers of *loop unrolling*, in which the body of a loop is duplicated as many times as the loop was to iterate in order to avoid performing a test on each iteration. Sensible compilers only do this when the number of iterations is small, but our preoccupation with full laziness has led us to an implementation which unrolls loops regardless of the extra storage cost incurred.

Our campaign to save reduction steps by full laziness has succeeded, but at a substantial cost in terms of memory usage. Worse still, it is not at all obvious from the program that this will happen, nor is there any easy way to reason about the storage use of such functions.

This unpleasant phenomenon is called a *space leak* (because memory space leaks away invisibly) or *dragging* (because f drags around an unexpectedly large graph). This memory cost caused by space leaks means that the program may run out of memory and fail to complete evaluation, but, more insidiously, it will also mean that less memory is available for the rest of the computation, so garbage collection will be more frequent. Thus there is a time cost associated with memory usage which should ideally be set against the time saving from saving reduction steps.

No good automatic solutions are known to this problem. One trick that the programmer can use to avoid it is to define two new functions:

```
newDrop n xs = newDrop1 xs n
newDrop1 xs n = drop n xs
```

newDrop has just the same meaning as drop, but it turns out not to be as lazy, so that it does not have a space leak. This trick is based on the asymmetry in laziness caused by the order of arguments referred to above, but is hardly crystal clear! Furthermore, a clever compiler might 'optimize' newDrop to drop, which is certainly a correct transformation (and one that improves laziness), but will reintroduce the space leak.

23.3.2 Unevaluated Components of Data Structures

Consider the function addHead, where

```
addHead b (a:xs) = (add b a):xs
add b a = a+b
```

It just adds something to the first element of a list. Now suppose that addHead is applied to a list many times, thus:

```
demo = addHead 1 (addHead 2 (addHead 3 [10,11]))
```

If evaluated to WHNF, demo will reduce to

```
[add 1 (add 2 (add 3 10)), 11]
```

but it will *not* reduce to

```
[16, 11]
```

until the first element of the list is evaluated. Meanwhile the graph representing

```
add 1 (add 2 (add 3 10))
```

is taking up space in the heap. Laziness prohibits the evaluation of this graph until the value of the first element of the list is needed.

This is a specific instance of a general phenomenon. A less contrived instance is that of a dictionary or symbol table represented by a tree, which is updated as data are entered into the dictionary. These updates do not propagate immediately to the leaves of the tree. Instead an update will be performed one level at a time, probably in response to the need for a lookup function to search the tree. Parts of the tree which are not visited by the lookup function will not have the updates fully performed (quite rightly according to laziness, since they may never be visited). However, the half-performed updates take up space in the form of pieces of graph just as the half-performed addHead did above.

One way to fix this is to have a function which crawls over the tree visiting every node. In our addHead example we could use seq to give

```
demo = seq (hd xs) xs
       where xs = addHead 1 (addHead 2 (addHead 3 [10,11]))
```

The seq forces evaluation of the head of the list, before returning the list as before.

The same problems apply to this fix as to the others we have discussed. It is far from obvious when it is good to apply it, it is an extra onus on the programmer, and it contributes nothing to the meaning of the program.

It would be better if we could perform some kind of automatic analysis which would discover which components of the data structure will eventually be needed, and hence which could be evaluated straight away. This is just *strictness analysis* in another guise, except that it is a version of strictness analysis which can 'look inside lists'. It is very much a research issue at the moment. Furthermore, in the case of a dictionary, the parts of the tree that are visited are data-dependent, so even a clever strictness analyzer would not help.

23.3.3 Summary

This section has shown two contrasting ways in which a functional program may use more store than expected:

(i) By performing reductions and holding on to the result, which is bigger than the redex.

(ii) By not performing reduction but holding on to the unevaluated graph, which is bigger than the result.

Notice that one problem is caused by reducing too much and the other is caused by reducing too little.

23.4 Transient Store Usage

Some functions have a small amount of input data and a small amount of result data, but nevertheless consume a large amount of store while they compute their results. The *residency* of a program at a particular moment is the size of the graph at that moment, and this section is concerned with programs which have high transient residency.

Some functions allocate and discard transient store quite rapidly, but if the function was stopped at any moment there would not be a large amount of accessible store. Other functions allocate store and do not discard it until the very end. This behavior is even more undesirable, because just before the function completes it may be holding a large fraction of the heap. We will look at some examples of this latter behavior.

23.4.1 Recursion

Consider a function to add up the elements of a list:

```
sum []     = 0
sum (x:xs) = x + sum xs
```

This is a nice simple definition, but let us see it in practice:

```
     sum [1,2,3]
→    1 + sum [2,3]
→    1 + (2 + (sum [3]))
→    1 + (2 + (3 + sum []))
→    1 + (2 + (3 + 0))
→    1 + (2 + 3)
→    1 + 5
→    6
```

The evaluation consumes transient space linear in the length of the list. (Note: using an unboxed G-machine implementation this transient space would actually be on the stack; this is less bad than transient heap space, but still undesirable.)

This phenomenon is well known to the Lisp community, and any red-blooded Lisp programmer would never have written the above definition. Instead he would have used an accumulating parameter:

```
sum list = sum1 0 list
           where
              sum1 n [] = n
              sum1 n (x:xs) = sum1 (n+x) xs
```

The definition of sum1 is *tail recursive* (cf. Chapter 21), and on a Lisp system will execute in constant space. Unfortunately, many graph reduction implementations will not execute this in constant space:

```
     sum [1,2,3]
→    sum1 0 [1,2,3]
→    sum1 (0+1) [2,3]
→    sum1 ((0+1)+2) [3]
→    sum1 (((0+1)+2)+3) []
→    ((0+1)+2)+3
→    (1+2)+3
→    3+3
→    6
```

Here the first parameter to sum1 grows in size linearly with the length of the list. Stack usage is also linear in the length of the list.

In this case strictness analysis comes to the rescue, because it can infer that sum1 will eventually evaluate its first argument, so that its first argument can safely be evaluated before sum1 is applied. This will produce:

```
     sum [1,2,3]
→    sum1 0 [1,2,3]
→    sum1 (0+1) [2,3]
→    sum1 1 [2,3]
→    sum1 (1+2) [3]
→    sum1 3 [3]
etc.
```

Now the transient store is discarded as evaluation proceeds rather than being held until the end, and stack usage is constant too. In addition, the G-machine optimizations will work better, given the knowledge that the first parameter of sum1 will be evaluated. An unboxed G-machine implementation will compute sum1 without using any transient store at all.

23.4.2 Excessive Sharing

The goal of laziness is to avoid recomputing values by sharing them. Sometimes, however, the evaluation of an expression can cause it to grow in size so much that it would be cheaper to recompute it later than to hold on to its evaluated form until later.

Meira [1985] gives a nice example of this. Consider a function powerList, which takes a list as its argument and returns a list of all possible sublists of the original list (obtaining a sublist by omitting elements from the original list). Here is a possible definition of powerList:

```
powerList []     = [ [] ]
powerList (x:xs) = pxs ++ map (cons x) pxs
                   where
                      pxs = powerList xs
```

The second equation simply says that to get all possible sublists of (x:xs), return all sublists of xs together with x stuck on the front of all sublists of xs. This is fine, but suppose we wanted to count the number of sublists of a list of length 20:

```
length (powerList [1..20])
```

We might hope that length would eat up the list produced by powerList as it was produced. Unfortunately, after powerList has produced all the sublists of the list [2..20], and they have been consumed by length, powerList is still hanging on to all those sublists for use in the part after the ++. Hence all 19! of these sublists will exist in store at one time, and the machine will run out of store. The program has appalling $0(N!)$ transient residency. This residency happens because we share the use of pxs in powerList, rather than recomputing it.

A simple rephrasing of the program thus:

```
powerList []     = [ [] ]
powerList (x:xs) = powerList xs ++ map (cons x) (powerList xs)
```

will cause those sublists to be recomputed, and the function will now have constant residency. A very minor change to the program has produced a dramatic change in run-time behavior. Notice that a clever compiler might 'optimize' the second program into the first, by performing common subexpression analysis.

23.4.3 Transient Lists

One of the advantages of lazy evaluation is that data are only computed when needed. For example, in the Miranda program

```
square n = n*n
--------------------------
sum (map square [1..1000])
```

the list of integers between 1 and 1000 is squared and added up *as it is generated*. The system will not first produce the list of the first 1000 integers, then square them and then add them up. We may think of it like this:

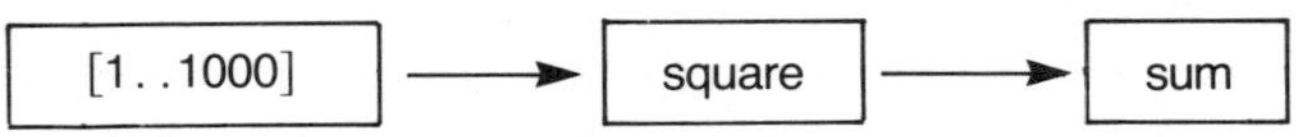

In a non-lazy system we would be tempted to write a special version of sum which squared the elements of the list before adding them, to avoid generating the intermediate list.

Unfortunately, this nice behavior does not always occur, as Hughes [1984] points out. Consider the program

```
average xs = (sum xs) / (length xs)
-----------------------------------
average (map square [1..1000])
```

If we wrote in Pascal, we could write a program which uses *bounded space* to compute the average of a list of integers, simply by maintaining a count of how many integers had been encountered so far and a running total of their values.

Unfortunately, a conventional functional language implementation will first evaluate one argument of the division operator and then evaluate the other. This means that the entire list of integers will reside in memory at once. It is clear that we would like to evaluate the arguments *in parallel* and *in a synchronized fashion* (notice that the former does not imply the latter).

In the particular example given, it is possible to write a more efficient version without resorting to parallelism, but the program is rather more obscure. More seriously, though, Hughes shows that there are simple and common programs which cannot run in bounded space on *any* sequential evaluator.

Another example of the seriousness of this problem is the space complexity of a straightforward coding of the quicksort algorithm. It turns out that this has a linear transient space usage on average, but a quadratic transient space usage in the worst case (the imperative algorithm uses linear space).

Hughes therefore suggests that even on a single processor implementation, some form of parallelism is desirable if functional programs are to run efficiently. His proposed solution is to introduce two new built-in functions, par and synch. The expression

```
par f x
```

is semantically equivalent to

```
f x
```

but evaluates x in parallel with applying f to x (note: this is slightly different from Hughes's definition, for uniformity with the rest of the book). The value of the expression

```
synch e
```

is

```
e:e
```

except that e will not be evaluated until *both* the head *and* the tail of (synch e) are required. If, for example, the head is required before the tail, then the (parallel) process trying to evaluate the head will be suspended until another process tries to evaluate the tail, at which point both processes continue in parallel again. In the example given above, two parallel processes to compute (sum xs) and (length xs) may be resynchronized whenever they consume a new element of xs.

The way in which these constructs can be used to alleviate the space usage problem is too complex to describe here, but suffice it to say that the technique *does not alter the program's structure*. Even so, putting in the par and synch constructs in the right place is a subtle business, and if done incorrectly can cause the program to work less efficiently or even to fail to terminate.

23.4.4 Summary

In this section, as in the preceding sections, we have seen examples of programs which are semantically identical, but which have very different pragmatic behavior.

These differences are not at all obvious to the programmer, and require him to make subtle changes to the way he writes his program to achieve a good performance. In addition, a proposed solution to the last problem involves major alterations to the implementation (synch and par).

23.5 Conclusions

The problems we have discussed in this chapter have a number of common features:

(i) Seemingly innocuous (and meaning-preserving) changes to a functional program may have dramatic effects on its run-time behavior.

(ii) We have no good means of reasoning about run-time behavior so as to understand how good or bad our programs are.

(iii) In order to reassure himself that his program does not have undesirable run-time behavior the programmer may have to know a lot about the particular implementation.

(iv) Even a clever programmer cannot solve all the problems without extensions to the implementation. Examples are strictness analysis (or the facility for the programmer to add annotations to indicate strictness) and parallel execution.

(v) There are as yet no automatic systems for alleviating these effects.

(vi) It is very difficult to tell when undesirable behavior is taking place, except that the program runs slower than expected. Even this relies on correct expectations, and gives no help in finding which part of the program is behaving badly. What is needed here is a good set of debugging tools which would assist the programmer in finding the 'hot spots' in the program. An example of such a tool in an imperative language is a profiling tool, which gives a breakdown of how much time is spent in each subroutine.

We should not get too downhearted! The fact is that most functional programs run quite satisfactorily. What this chapter has established is an urgent need for tools to help reason about the space and time behavior of functional programs. This seems a rather hard problem, and Stoye suggests that efforts might more profitably be directed to providing better debugging tools with which to identify the offending part of the program, leaving the programmer to fix the problem thus identified.

References

Backus, J. 1978. Can programming be liberated from the von Neumann style? A functional style and its algebra of programs. *Communications of the ACM*. Vol. 21, no. 8, pp. 613–41.

Hughes, R.J.M. 1984. *Parallel Functional Programs use Less Space*. Programming Research Group, Oxford.

Meira, S.R.L. 1985. On the efficiency of applicative algorithms. PhD thesis, Computer Laboratory, University of Kent, p. 36. March.

Stoye, W. 1985. The implementation of functional languages using custom hardware. PhD thesis, Computer Lab., University of Cambridge. May.

Turner, D.A. 1981. The semantic elegance of applicative languages. In *Proceedings of the ACM Conference on Functional Languages and Computer Architecture*, pp. 85–92. ACM.

Twenty-four

PARALLEL GRAPH REDUCTION

The possibility of parallel execution is often stated as an advantage of functional languages. In this chapter we will explore this exciting possibility in greater detail, and attempt to justify it.

Warning: this chapter describes current research work rather than a settled consensus of opinion. It therefore represents the author's personal view of the present state of affairs, and is not a definitive statement.

24.1 The Challenge of Parallelism

Cooperation is expensive, yet it is the only way to get large tasks done quickly.

This lesson is well illustrated by human organizations. Undoubtedly the most efficient way to get a task done is to assign a single individual to the task. There comes a time, however, when the sheer volume of work is more than a single individual can carry out in the required period of time, so he employs assistants to help him. Inevitably the assistants must be told what to do and how to do it, and a proportion of the time of all concerned is spent in communication rather than in doing profitable work.

As the company grows, the overheads of communication can become very burdensome. The amount of internally generated information grows with the company, but each individual's capacity to digest this information remains fixed. The solution is to partition the work of the company in such a way as to reduce the amount of interaction required between workers, so that they can spend more of their time on profitable work and less on communication. This may be easy if the company is engaged in a number of essentially independent activities, but it can be very difficult if the company's activities are highly interrelated.

A primary challenge facing computer architects is the effective exploitation of parallelism. Raw processing power is now cheap, through replication of silicon, but mechanisms for connecting processors together so that they cooperate to achieve a common goal are hard to build. Inextricably connected with this challenge is the challenge of programming a parallel machine, and partitioning the program in a way that minimizes communication.

In specific application areas it may be fairly easy to partition the problem so as to minimize communication. For example, in a multi-user Unix machine it is easy to assign a processor to each process awaiting execution. Less trivially, vector processors such as the Cray-1, or array processors such as the ICL DAP, have an arrangement of processing elements specifically adapted for the efficient execution of vector- or array-structured problems.

Programming vector or array processors is, however, a highly skilled and somewhat arcane art. In order to exploit the parallelism of the machine fully, the programmer needs an intimate understanding of its workings and of the workings of the compiler. The investment required to produce such programs is very large – an investment of 10 man-years' work or more in a single program is not unusual – and small program modifications risk destroying the program's finely balanced optimizations. Furthermore, such programs are often extremely complex, not because the task is complex, but in order to exploit the architecture most effectively.

An alternative approach is to have a number of processing elements connected together with some kind of network, each independently executing its own program (an MIMD machine). Such a machine is relatively easy to build, but gives no clues about how best to program it. The problem of dividing the task up into concurrent subtasks, programming these subtasks in a sequential language and arranging the intertask communication is left entirely to the programmer. Even when the program is written it is hard to be sure that it is correct, and concurrency gives much scope for transient and irreproducible bugs which only occur under particular circumstances.

The challenge, then, is to produce a parallel programming *system*, including both architecture and a programming methodology, which

(i) is feasible to program (this is the overriding consideration);
(ii) is highly concurrent (this allows us to buy speed with raw processing power);
(iii) minimizes communication.

24.2 Parallel Functional Programming

24.2.1 The Opportunity for Parallelism

One of the most attractive features of functional programming languages is that they are not inherently sequential, as conventional imperative languages are. At any moment there are a number of redexes in the program graph, and in principle they could *all* be reduced simultaneously. Thus the hope offered by functional languages is that

> parallel execution of functional programs, through concurrent graph reduction, may be possible without adding any new language constructs or detailed program tuning.

If taken without qualification this statement is rather misleading, since it seems to promise 'parallelism without tears', and as we remarked above, cooperation is always expensive. We can, however, take the statement as highlighting an opportunity, namely that functional programming offers a fruitful line of approach to the challenge of parallelism.

The idea of concurrent execution of programs without adding new language constructs is not new. The Fortran compiler for the Cray-1 vector processor is designed to spot vectorizable sections of programs written in (almost) ordinary Fortran. However, as we have remarked already, the effective use of the Cray relies on the programmer writing his program in such a way that

(i) it is vectorizable;
(ii) the compiler can spot that it is vectorizable.

We hope that in the case of functional languages the parallelism is more general, so that the programmer's task is made easier. First, therefore, we will discuss the task of writing parallel functional programs.

24.2.2 Writing Parallel Functional Programs

It is tempting to believe that an arbitrary functional program would run much faster on a parallel graph reduction machine. This comforting belief is quite erroneous [Clack and Peyton Jones, 1985]. Many functional programs are essentially sequential (that is, at any moment there are few redexes in the graph). For example, an insertion sort program cannot insert the next element into the result until the previous insertion has completed (or at least partly completed). It is simply unreasonable to expect any old functional program to run fast on a parallel machine.

In order to achieve good parallel performance the program must contain *algorithmic parallelism*. That is, the algorithm must contain gross inherent parallelism. The most obvious sort of algorithmic parallelism is given by *divide and conquer* algorithms, which divide the task at hand into two or more independent subtasks, solve these independently, and then combine the results to solve the original task. A standard example of such an algorithm is quicksort, which splits the set to be sorted into two subsets which can be sorted independently. Other examples include any kind of search algorithm (which covers many artificial intelligence applications) and large numerical computations. Experiments confirm that substantial parallelism is obtainable [Tighe, 1985; Clack and Peyton Jones, 1985].

It is therefore still the programmer's responsibility to create an algorithm which will partition the task at hand into reasonably independent subtasks. It is unreasonable to expect the machine to do this automatically, since it may involve major algorithmic changes (such as changing insertion sort to quicksort).

24.2.3 Writing Parallel Programs is Easier in a Functional Language

Why not program in a conventional language which supports multiple tasks, such as Ada? There are a number of ways in which writing a parallel program in a functional language is superior to this:

(i) In conventional languages the partition of the problem into separate tasks is static and fixed. A task is conceived as a relatively large unit, and tasks generally cannot be created and deleted dynamically. There will be relatively few tasks, and the programmer must clearly identify all of them in his design.

In a functional language the parallelism can be dynamic, and there is no static division of the problem into tasks. Instead, the programmer designs an algorithm whose inherent parallelism will enable concurrent reduction to take place at different places in the graph. The 'grain' of parallelism is therefore smaller and more dynamically adaptable as the computation proceeds.

(ii) In conventional languages the tasks communicate with each other by sending messages or making specially protected subroutine calls to each other. The programmer has to design synchronization and communication protocols between tasks so that they cooperate correctly and achieve mutual exclusion where necessary. It is up to the programmer to ensure that these communication protocols are correct, and failure to do so can result in a transient malfunction of the program.

In a functional program the synchronization between different reductions is mediated entirely by the shared graph. A reduction is made known to the graph by the indivisible operation of overwriting the root of the redex with the result of the reduction, and no other synchronization is necessary (though see the next section for efficiency considerations).

(iii) The tasking structure of conventional languages adds a layer of considerable complexity to the programmer's model of what is going on. It is difficult to reason about a multitasking program, because the programmer has to bear in mind all the possible time orderings in which execution might take place. The behavior of the program should be independent of the scheduling of the tasks, but the programmer must ensure that this is the case.

There are no extra language constructs required to write parallel functional programs. The result of the program is guaranteed to be independent of the way in which reductions are scheduled, though this scheduling may have a strong impact on efficiency. Thus it is no harder to reason about a parallel functional program than a sequential one.

To summarize, when using a functional language, the programmer does not have to design a static task partition, guarantee mutual exclusion and synchronization, or establish communication protocols between tasks. This allows the programmer to concentrate on the creative activity of designing a parallel algorithm.

24.3 Parallel Graph Reduction

We have seen that functional languages can form a basis for parallel programming. The benefits outlined above would in fact accrue to any parallel implementation of a functional language, but graph reduction is a particularly attractive execution model for a parallel implementation, for the following reasons:

(i) Graph reduction is an inherently *parallel* activity. At any moment the graph may contain a number of redexes and it is very natural to reduce them simultaneously.
(ii) Graph reduction is an inherently *distributed* activity. A reduction is a (topologically) local transformation of the graph, and no shared bottleneck (such as an environment) need be consulted to perform a reduction.
(iii) All communication is mediated through the graph. This gives a very simple model of the way in which concurrent activities cooperate, and it is a model in which we have considerable confidence (because it is the same as our sequential implementations!)
(iv) The entire state of the computation at any moment is well defined – it is the current state of the graph.

Graph reduction gives us a *rock-solid model of parallel computation* which can underpin the complexities of a parallel machine. As with the G-machine, we can think of ways to optimize the actual execution of graph reduction to get good performance, but as long as these are just short-cuts to achieve the same effect we can have confidence in the correctness of our implementation.

We now begin to consider how to perform parallel graph reduction.

24.3.1 A Model for Parallel Reduction

In a sequential implementation evaluation is performed by calling an *evaluator*, passing it (a pointer to) the root of the graph to be evaluated. The evaluator performs a sequence of reductions until the graph is in WHNF and then terminates.

Our model for parallel reduction is a simple generalization of this. We imagine a number of evaluator *tasks* simultaneously at work on the graph.

Each evaluator task is busy reducing some particular subgraph to WHNF; the task terminates when its subgraph reaches WHNF.

During its execution, a task may anticipate that it will require the value of a certain subgraph at some future time. In this case it may generate a new task to evaluate the subgraph in parallel by *sparking* the root node of the subgraph. (The term 'sparking' is intended to convey the idea of 'setting a match' to a subgraph, which ignites a processor evaluation which spreads through the subgraph autonomously.) The new (child) task will evaluate the graph rooted at the sparked node to WHNF, concurrently with the continued execution of the (parent) task that sparked it.

If the parent needs the value of the subgraph before the child has completed its evaluation, the parent becomes *blocked* until the child terminates. A task may also become blocked because a sibling task is evaluating a subgraph which the two tasks share. Mechanisms for implementing blocking are discussed below.

Synchronization between tasks is mediated entirely through the graph, so that the tasks do not communicate directly with each other at all. When performing a reduction a task overwrites the root of the redex with the result in a single indivisible operation, so that the reduction appears to all the other tasks to take place instantaneously. Thus the graph never appears in an intermediate state.

A task is executed by an *agent*. Typically an agent will be implemented by a physical processor. Agents are concrete pieces of hardware (we can point to one!), whereas a task is a virtual object (a piece of work to be done). An agent is *employed* if it is executing a task. An unemployed agent will look for a task to execute in the *task pool* which contains all the tasks awaiting execution.

Logically, the machine looks like Figure 24.1. This model raises a number of issues:

(i) Logical issues, concerning the management of parallelism. The particular issues we discuss are

  (a) When are nodes sparked to create new tasks?
  (b) What happens if two tasks start evaluating the same piece of graph?

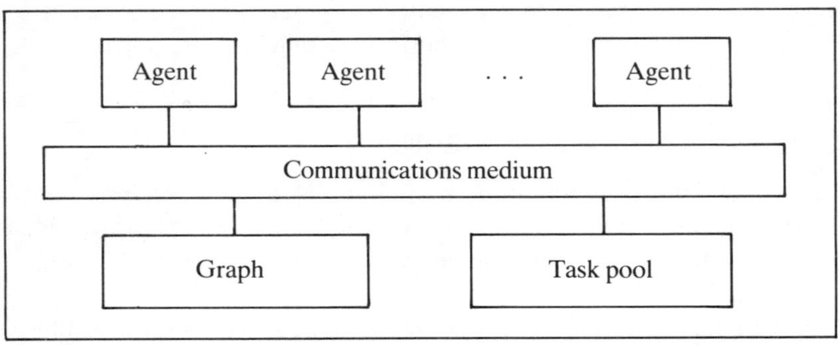

Figure 24.1 Logical structure of a parallel graph reduction machine

(ii) Representational issues, concerning how tasks can be represented inside the machine.
(iii) Locality issues, concerning how to deploy the resources of the machine to execute the concurrent tasks, while simultaneously minimizing communication.
(iv) Architectural issues, concerning the physical architecture of a machine for performing parallel graph reduction.

We will address these issues in decreasing levels of detail.

24.4 Sparking Tasks

When should a new task be sparked? There are two broad approaches:

(i) Spark a new task to evaluate a subgraph when it is *certain* that the subgraph will eventually be evaluated (*conservative* parallelism). This ensures that all tasks are doing useful work.
(ii) Spark a new task to evaluate a subgraph when it is *possible* that the subgraph will eventually be evaluated (*speculative* parallelism). This offers maximum opportunities for parallelism.

We will discuss these alternatives in turn.

24.4.1 Conservative Parallelism

If we insist that we will only spark a task when it is certain that its result will be needed, then we can initially start only one task, at the root of the whole graph. This is not very parallel! When can we spark new tasks?

The most obvious place to spark new tasks is to evaluate the arguments of a strict built-in function. For example, when evaluating

(+ E_1 E_2)

we could spark tasks to evaluate E_1 and E_2. It is certain that the values of E_1 and E_2 will be needed, so we can safely spark tasks to evaluate them. (Note: we might choose to spark only one new task, to evaluate E_1 say, and allow the task which is evaluating the whole (+ E_1 E_2) expression to evaluate E_2, since it has nothing better to do. This is a relatively minor technical consideration, however.)

Unfortunately, except for numerical analysis programs, this approach is so conservative that we will obtain little parallelism. Some programs contain no arithmetic! The idea is, however, easily generalized. Given the application of a function f to an argument, thus

f E

we are safe to begin parallel evaluation of E if we know that f will need the value of its argument, that is if f is *strict*. So here is another application of strictness analysis (Chapter 22), to identify points at which parallel evaluation can be started. We can perform strictness analysis, annotate the graph with information derived thereby, and use these annotations to control the sparking of new tasks.

24.4.1.1 Strictness annotations

In fact, two forms of annotation are desirable. Consider an application of a strict supercombinator $F to an argument E, which has a graph looking like this:

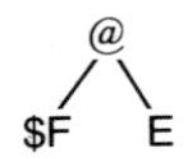

At first sight it looks as if we could annotate in one of two ways:

(i) Annotate the application node to indicate that the argument would be needed:

(ii) Annotate $F to indicate that it will need its argument:

Actually we should do both, because either one on its own sometimes fails to initiate parallelism. Suppose we decided to annotate application nodes only. Consider the expression

(IF E_c $F $G) E

where $F is strict but $G is not. Parallel evaluation of E cannot be started in case the result of the IF expression is $G, so the application of the IF expression to E cannot be annotated as strict. Hence E will not be evaluated in parallel. If, however, $F was annotated as strict, then after the IF had completed, $F would be applied to E, and parallel evaluation of E would begin as $F is applied to E.

On the other hand, suppose that we annotate supercombinators only, not application nodes, and suppose also that $G in the above example was strict. Then it would be safe to evaluate E in parallel with evaluating the IF expression, and it might be highly advantageous to do so (if E_c took a long time to evaluate, for example). But because we are only annotating supercombinators, the parallel evaluation of E will not be started until the IF has completed and either $F or $G is applied to E. A further example of the necessity of annotating application nodes is given by the following example. Suppose the supercombinator $T is defined thus:

```
$T x f = f x
```

Now consider the expression

```
$T E $F
```

where $F is strict. $T is not in general strict in its first argument, but in this context we would be safe to evaluate E in parallel, and we can achieve this by annotating the ($T E) application node.

We conclude that to maximize opportunities for parallelism we should annotate both functions and application nodes with strictness information. These issues are discussed by Hankin *et al.* [1986].

24.4.2 Speculative Parallelism

In this section we consider relaxing our constraint that a task should only be sparked if it is certain that its result will be needed, and consider what might happen if we are more speculative about sparking tasks. This has the advantage that it increases the opportunities for parallelism.

An extreme example of speculative parallelism is to spark a task for every node in the graph or, in other words, to regard any redex in the graph as a candidate for reduction. More conservative regimes are also possible, in which the arguments to some functions are sparked even though it is not certain that their result will be required.

24.4.2.1 The dangers of speculation

The danger of such speculative parallelism is that machine resources may be consumed, evaluating pieces of graph that will eventually be discarded. For example, consider the expression

$\mathsf{IF}\ E_c\ E_t\ E_e$

Only one of the 'then' (E_t) and 'else' (E_e) branches of the IF will be used, and the speculative evaluation of the other will consume machine resources uselessly. On the other hand, if the resources are available, we could begin evaluation of E_c, E_t and E_e simultaneously, and when the evaluation of E_c was completed we would have a head start on evaluating the selected branch.

The situation is not unlike a government job creation scheme. If agents are unemployed then we may as well find some work for them, but there is a danger that in our eagerness to find them jobs, the work they do may ultimately prove not to be useful.

This approach has hidden dangers. Suppose the evaluation of E_c would give the result TRUE after a few reductions, but the evaluation of E_e failed to terminate. Then after we begin concurrent evaluation of E_c, E_t and E_e there is a risk that the machine will squander all its resources evaluating E_e and never get around to evaluating E_c! In other words, we must also be careful that we do not employ so many agents on our job creation scheme that other work that is required is not done. The machine would not deliver incorrect answers, but it might take much longer to deliver the correct result.

This suggests that we would need to divide tasks into two classes, *vital tasks* and *speculative tasks*. The results of vital tasks are known to be needed, while the results of speculative tasks may or may not be needed. Vital tasks should have a higher priority than speculative tasks, so that only if the machine has spare resources will speculative tasks be executed. Seen in this light, conservative parallelism is simply a regime in which there are no speculative tasks.

24.4.2.2 Managing speculative tasks

At first, introducing a two-tier priority system seems quite innocuous, but in fact it poses some significant challenges:

(i) *A speculative task may become vital* when it is subsequently discovered that its result is needed. Thus its priority must be upgraded. This is easy enough, but in addition some (but not all) of the tasks which it has already sparked must also become vital. Identifying exactly which of these subtasks must become vital is not easy, especially as they are being created dynamically.

(ii) *A speculative task may be discarded* when it is subsequently discovered that its result is not needed after all. In this case the task must be killed, since it will otherwise continue to consume machine resources performing useless work. Furthermore, all the tasks it has sparked must also be killed, unless they are evaluating a piece of graph that is shared, and whose value is still required. Identifying this collection of subtasks is not easy either, especially as they might conceivably breed faster than they can be killed.

Speculative tasks therefore add a considerable resource-management problem. Nevertheless, some parallel machines are taking this approach [Hudak, 1984].

24.4.3 Too Little Parallelism

The potential problem with conservative parallelism is the danger that too little parallelism will be generated to use effectively the parallelism provided by the implementation.

However, as we remarked earlier, the major source of parallelism in any program is the algorithmic parallelism introduced by the programmer. This parallelism is normally of a conservative nature, in the sense that the results will be required of all the parallel computations which the programmer has in mind. Hence, sufficient conservative parallelism should be available.

In many functional programs, much of this parallelism is obtained by concurrent evaluation of components of data structures, so some sort of strictness analysis on non-flat domains is probably essential (see Section 22.4.2).

It is, of course, crucial that algorithmic parallelism is exploited by the system but, however clever the strictness analyzer is, the programmer will always fear that it may fail to spot the carefully introduced parallelism in particular cases. It seems desirable, therefore, that the programmer should be allowed to annotate the program with strictness information. As a safety feature the strictness analyzer could issue a warning message if the programmer annotates a function as strict when the analyzer fails to discover this.

24.4.4 Too Much Parallelism

The other side of the coin is that, even in a conservative regime, too much parallelism may be generated. This can raise serious resource-management problems, since during evaluation a graph often expands before it shrinks. There is a danger that the entire memory of the machine might become filled with half-finished computations, none of which could proceed for lack of space.

For example, consider a program in which a function f returns a list which is consumed by a function g, which examines the whole list. A clever strictness analyzer would spot that g used the whole list and, using this information, the implementation might set off a task to evaluate the whole list concurrently with its examination by g. Unfortunately, if f runs much faster than g, the memory of the machine might become filled with the intermediate list.

It seems likely that some kind of control over runaway parallelism of this kind will be necessary. This is very much a research area, and little experience has been accumulated so far.

24.4.5 Granularity, and the Problem of Tiny Tasks

In any parallel machine there is some administrative overhead associated with sparking, executing and completing a task. It is important that this overhead is small compared with the amount of work that the task does, otherwise the machine is in danger of spending a large fraction of its resources in task administration. Hence we must ensure that the tasks we spark are not too small.

The tasks generated by a divide and conquer program can be thought of as a tree, in which each node is a task and the descendants of a node are the subtasks which it sparks.

In a binary tree about half the nodes are leaves, so in a binary divide and conquer algorithm about half the tasks generated will be 'leaf tasks'; that is, tasks which the algorithm does not split into subtasks. For example, in the case of quicksort the 'leaf tasks' might be those which sort a set with only one element. There is a serious danger that

(i) these 'leaf tasks' will be uneconomically small;
(ii) there will be very many of them (e.g. half, or more, of the total).

If nothing is done about this problem the machine could well become swamped in a surfeit of tiny tasks. The solution must be to stop sparking subtasks when the 'size' of the problem is small enough. For example, when quicksort has to sort a set of 10 elements or less, it could avoid sparking subtasks and do the whole sort in a single task.

This is clearly not an easy decision to make, and is an important issue in designing parallel machines. At present there seems to be no alternative but to dump the problem back in the programmer's lap, but automatic techniques need to be developed to predict the approximate cost of execution of subtasks.

The issue of principle is one of *granularity*. The overheads of tasking begin to dominate when the 'grain' of parallelism has become too fine, which suggests that we should aim for coarse-grain parallelism even at the expense of some concurrency. On the other hand, if the grain becomes too coarse there will be too little concurrency and unemployed agents will be hanging around with nothing to do. This suggests that some sort of run-time adaptive system might be effective, in which a task is sparked only if there are fewer than a given number of tasks in the pool at that time. Ultimately, a combination of compile-time and run-time techniques will doubtless be used.

Goldberg and Hudak [1985] describe *serial combinators*, which give the coarsest grain of parallelism that does not lose concurrency, though, as we have said, a coarser grain still may be desirable.

24.4.6 Scheduling

In the light of the above discussion, the question of which task an unemployed agent should execute is rendered rather straightforward. It should execute a vital task if there is one, or a speculative task otherwise.

Any agent executing a speculative task should, however, keep an eye out for vital tasks joining the task pool. If this occurs the agent should return the speculative task to the task pool and begin executing the vital task instead.

In a conservative parallelism regime all tasks are vital, so an unemployed agent can execute any task in the pool. Furthermore, it can execute the task until it is complete or blocked, and there is no need to keep an eye on the task pool. This is another benefit of conservative parallelism.

The choice of exactly which task to execute next may, however, have a significant impact on the problems of controlling parallelism (Sections 24.4.3–24.4.5) and of locality (Section 24.7).

24.5 Blocking Tasks

What happens if two tasks start evaluating the same piece of graph? They might do this because the same node was sparked twice, or (more commonly) because the graphs being evaluated by the two tasks share a common subgraph.

As we will see in this section, for efficiency reasons we will need to introduce a mechanism whereby tasks can be *blocked* from evaluating a piece of graph which another task is already evaluating.

24.5.1 The Need for Blocking

The indivisibility of each reduction step assures us that nothing incorrect will happen if two tasks were to evaluate the same graph, but it would certainly be inefficient. They would execute in rough synchronization, and would either execute the same reduction at the same time or would 'leapfrog' each other. Their exact behavior would depend on the implementation but what is clear is that the *same result would be obtained by either of them alone*. For example, consider the program

```
let x = * 4 5
in + x x
```

We might spark two parallel tasks to evaluate the arguments to the +, both of which will try to evaluate the (* 4 5). They will both get the same result, so it is probably better to allow one to proceed and make the other wait for the result. Otherwise we risk tying up two agents to do the work of one.

For efficiency reasons, therefore, we would like it to be possible for one task to be *blocked* by another. Let us consider the blocking mechanism in more detail.

24.5.2 The Blocking Mechanism

A task proceeds by unwinding the spine until it finds a function at the tip, when it performs the appropriate reduction (if there are enough arguments). As the task unwinds the spine, it could mark the vertebrae nodes (by altering the tag), so that a marked node is a signal saying 'DANGER – task at work inside here'. (Note that this mark is, of course, entirely different from the mark used by a mark-scan garbage collector. It may be implemented by altering the tag on the node.)

Now, when another task comes across the marked node during its unwind, it would be blocked. As the first task rewinds the spine (i.e. pops vertebrae from its stack when a reduction is completed), it removes the mark from the vertebrae. Of course, the vertebra which is actually updated by the reduction must be overwritten before its mark is removed. Any tasks blocked by the marked nodes are now free to proceed.

Consider, for example, the following program:

```
let f     = g 6
    g x = + (- x)
in
    + (f 3) (f 1)
```

We might spark two tasks to evaluate the (f 3) and (f 1) subgraphs, which share a common subgraph f:

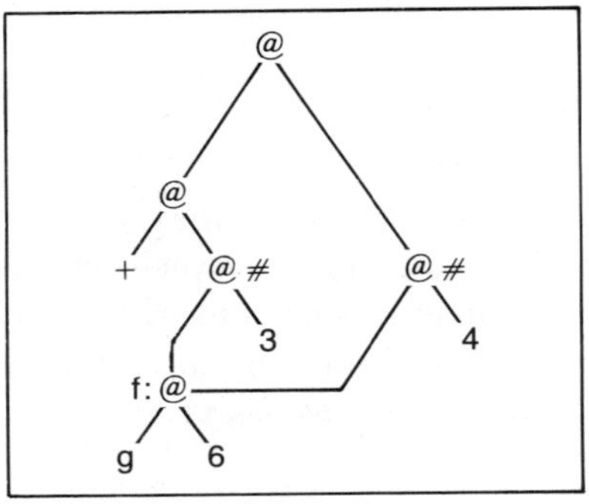

The + might spark the nodes marked #, thus creating two new tasks to evaluate the arguments to the +. The first of these tasks to unwind into the node labelled f will mark it (let us suppose it is the left-hand task in the picture). When the second task tries to unwind into this node it will be blocked. Meanwhile the first task will reduce the f node to WHNF by applying g to 6, and overwriting the node with the result (+ (−6)). Then, having evaluated the arguments (−6 and 3) it will add them, remove the mark from the f node as it pops the node from its stack, and overwrite the node marked # with the result (−3). Now the second task can proceed, so it will unwind into the f node, where it will see the (+ (−6)). It will never know that there was once a (g 6) redex there.

24.5.3 Reducing Mutual Exclusion

A disadvantage of the blocking scheme outlined above is that it risks unnecessary serialization. To take a common example, many books on functional programming point out the usefulness of higher-order functions. A typical example of this is the definition of sum, which sums the elements of a list, in terms of foldr, a higher-order function which combines the elements of a list using a given dyadic function:

```
foldr f b [] = b
foldr f b (x:xs) = f x (foldr b xs)

sum = foldr (+) 0
```

sum is thus defined as a partial application of foldr, and is represented by the graph

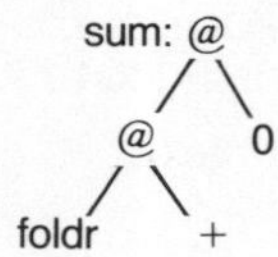

Now suppose we were evaluating an expression which used sum in many places. As a task unwinds into the sum graph it marks the top node, thus blocking any other tasks from unwinding into it. But the sum graph is *already in WHNF*, so there is no point in making other tasks block. It is perfectly safe to allow any number of tasks simultaneous access to the sum graph, and it is quite peculiar to insist on serial access to a commonly used function!

This is a specific instance of a general rule:

> Once a subgraph is in WHNF it will never be altered, so it is quite safe for many tasks to have (read only) access to it.

This suggests that we need another kind of application node, a WHNF application. A graph rooted at a WHNF application node is known already to be in WHNF, so the node is not marked when a task unwinds into it. Supercombinators, numbers, CONS cells and so on are, of course, already known to be in WHNF. This scheme will ensure that:

(i) if a graph may contain redexes, and hence may be altered, then only one task is allowed in it;
(ii) if a graph is known to be in WHNF, and hence cannot alter, then any number of tasks can have simultaneous access to it.

We must now consider when we can mark an application node as being in WHNF. Sometimes this will be possible at compile-time. Consider the supercombinator

```
$F x = IF (> x 0) x
```

The two application nodes in the body are known to be WHNF applications, since IF requires three arguments. Compile-time WHNF marking is not always possible, so that further improvements accrue from performing some run-time WHNF marking as well. Consider the expression ($G E_1 E_2 E_3), where $G is a supercombinator requiring three arguments. It has a graph like this:

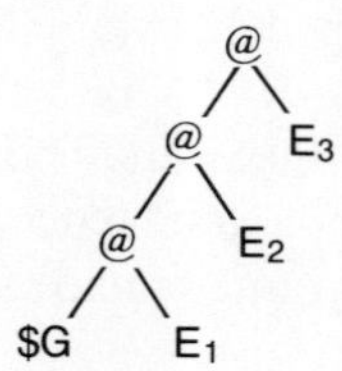

When it is reduced, the top node will be overwritten with the result. However, the lower two nodes are now known to be in WHNF, and can be marked as such before they are popped from the stack.

The observations are closely related to those of Section 20.7, but seen from a different perspective.

24.6 What is a Task?

When a task is not being executed by an agent it must be represented in some way in store. There are, of course, all sorts of ways of representing a task, but in this section we will explore some of them to reassure ourselves of the feasibility of our ideas so far.

The representation of a task must contain all the information required to continue executing the task from the point at which it was last suspended. In conventional multitasking operating systems this representation is often called a Task Control Block, and contains information such as

(i) the task's stack pointer;
(ii) the task's program counter;
(iii) the state of the task's registers.

By contrast, in our parallel reduction model a task can, in principle, be represented completely by a single pointer to the root of the graph it is evaluating. The *complete state* of a partially completed task is held in the graph, so that a pointer to the root of its graph suffices to represent a task *at any stage in its life* (not only when it is newly sparked). At any stage an agent can stop performing reductions on a task, put its root pointer back into the task pool, and begin executing another task.

24.6.1 Pointer-Reversal

The only trouble with the very simple representation of a task that we have described is that if a task is blocked and subsequently resumed, the agent has to unwind down the spine of the graph from the root. One way to avoid this is to use pointer-reversal.

In Chapter 11 we described how an evaluator could unwind the spine of an expression without using a stack by reversing pointers in the spine as it went. At first it appears that this is totally out of court in a parallel machine, since the pointer-reversed graph is in a 'peculiar state' which will be incomprehensible to other tasks.

However, pointer-reversal only reverses pointers in the vertebrae, and the *vertebrae are exactly the marked nodes*. Hence, no other task will look inside a pointer-reversed node, and it is quite safe to use this technique! The complete state of a task would now be represented by two pointers, the forward and backward pointers. Then when a suspended task is resumed, the forward and backward pointers are already pointing to the area of the graph which is of interest.

We have previously understood that pointer-reversal has a hidden cost, because the pointers have to be re-reversed when rewinding the spine (i.e. popping nodes from the stack). But even this is no longer necessarily true, since we have to mark vertebrae as being in WHNF as we pop them, and in a parallel machine there will probably be little extra cost to re-reverse the pointers as well. So pointer-reversal may save repeatedly unwinding the spine each time a task is blocked, and costs very little.

24.6.2 Using a Stack

During the development of the G-machine it became clear that the careful use of the stack was crucial to a fast implementation of graph reduction. Does the stack not then form part of the task state? Is it indeed possible to use a stack-based implementation like the G-machine for a parallel machine?

We recall that the entire G-machine development was simply a sequence of optimizations to ordinary graph reduction. In effect, part of the state of the computation is held in the stack for efficiency reasons, but we should be able to stop execution at any point, and (using information in the stack) fix up the graph to represent the current state of affairs. If this sounds like a lot of work, remember that straightforward graph reduction effectively involves flushing the current state out into the graph at every reduction step, while a parallel G-machine would, in effect, keep part of the state of the graph in the stack over a sequence of reduction steps.

There is no reason why this approach should not be combined with the pointer-reversing idea. They can be used either individually or together.

24.6.3 Reawakening Blocked Tasks

So far we have not discussed what happens to a task when it is blocked. There are two main alternatives:

(i) We could simply return it to the pool of tasks awaiting execution. In due course an unemployed agent looking for work will resume execution of the task. It will very soon encounter the node that blocked it before. If this node is still marked, the task is blocked again, and is returned to the pool of tasks, otherwise it can continue to execute normally.

(ii) We could somehow suspend the task, so that it is not considered for execution by unemployed agents, and reawaken it when the node which blocked has its mark removed. Reawakening it would consist of putting it in the pool of tasks awaiting execution.

The first method has the advantage of simplicity, but it is rather inefficient, since repeated attempts are made to execute a task which is still blocked for the same reason. Some care would have to be taken to ensure that the machine did not spend all its time trying to resume blocked tasks, while never getting around to executing the tasks which would remove the blockage.

In order to implement the second method we would somehow have to attach the blocked task to the marked node. Then when the mark is taken off the node, the blocked task can be put back in the task pool. We could achieve this by adding an extra field to every application node, which pointed to a list of tasks which should be reawakened when the mark on the node is removed. This is the approach taken by the ALICE machine (see below).

Attaching an extra field to every application node seems rather wasteful, since most of them will not have any tasks blocked on them, and an alternative would be to overwrite the head of the application node with a pointer to a list of blocked tasks, and to remember the old head in the tail of the list. Some mechanism would then be required to indicate that there were blocked tasks queued up on a marked node.

24.7 Locality

All the issues we have discussed so far have been logical issues, concerning the abstract model of agents reducing a graph. Having fixed the details of the model we then need to take decisions concerning its physical embodiment. For the most part we regard a discussion of these physical issues as beyond the scope of this book, since they are largely technological.

There is, however, one question which straddles the boundary between these two areas, and which has a pervasive effect on the architecture of the machine, namely the question of locality.

24.7.1 What is Locality?

Consider the communication within a commercial company. The organization of the company is intended to enable workers to perform their tasks by communicating mainly with fellow workers in the same office. Somewhat less often a worker may need to communicate with someone further away but in the same building, and less often still he may need to communicate with a colleague further away. Longer-distance communication costs more, however, both in time and money, and an excessive proportion of non-local communication generally indicates an inefficiently organized company. It is therefore important to achieve predominantly local communication, a property we call *locality of reference*.

The idea of locality is well established in conventional computer architecture. It is an observed property of most programs that they tend to reference data which have either been referenced in the recent past (temporal locality), or which are physically adjacent to recently referenced data (spatial locality) [Denning, 1972]. A conventional cache exploits locality of reference (both temporal and spatial) to hold actively used data in fast memory close to the processor [Smith, 1982].

Functional programs are not so well behaved, since the physical adjacency of two cells in the heap bears no relation to their logical adjacency, resulting in a loss of spatial locality. This is, as we now discuss, particularly serious for parallel machines.

Locality is a statistical property of programs, and the best we can hope to do is to develop effective heuristics for achieving predominantly local references. This is at present an area more of speculation than experiment, though some simulations have been performed [Keller and Lin, 1984; Hudak and Goldberg, 1985a].

24.7.2 Shared Memory and Distributed Memory

Broadly speaking, a parallel graph reduction machine can be organized in one of two ways:

(i) In a *shared memory* machine the graph resides in a large shared memory system, probably consisting of a number of distinct memory units. The processors are connected to the memory system by some kind of communications system and, as the number of processors increases, so does the transit time of processor–memory transactions through the communications system.

Hence, adding more processors causes the existing processors to run more slowly.

(ii) In a *distributed memory* machine each processor has a local memory unit attached to it, forming a composite processor/memory unit. The graph is distributed among these local memory units. Processors access graph nodes in remote memory units using a communications system which interconnects all the processor/memory units.

Accessing a local graph node is therefore very much cheaper than accessing a remote one. If local accesses predominate, then more processors can be added without slowing down existing processors, a very desirable property.

There is no reason in principle why accessing a remote graph node in a distributed memory machine should take any longer than in a shared memory machine (the communication system needs to be used in either case), and this is one of the insights of the Rediflow architecture (see below).

We see, therefore, that to be able to add more processors to a machine without slowing down the existing processors we must

(i) use a distributed memory scheme,
(ii) achieve locality.

It is for this reason that locality plays such a key role in parallel reduction machine architecture.

24.7.3 Locality versus Concurrency

There is one easy way to achieve perfect locality: execute all tasks and allocate all cells on a single processor/memory unit! This shows up the tension between locality and concurrency. When is it best to export a task to another processor (to maximize concurrency), and when is it best to perform it locally (to maximize locality)?

We cannot expect any general answers to this question. For particular programs a good task distribution may suggest itself, and one approach is to allow the programmer to annotate his program to indicate this [Hudak and Smith, 1985]. The alternative is to develop effective heuristics for distributing the tasks through the machine. It seems intuitively plausible that a heavily loaded processor should export tasks to a lightly loaded neighbor, and this leads to the idea of *load balancing* [Keller and Lin, 1984] (also called *diffusion scheduling* [Hudak and Goldberg, 1985a]). The idea is that tasks are 'pushed away' from busy processors; in addition it would improve locality if tasks were 'drawn towards' memory units to which they have global references.

The granularity of the task is also important, since it is more worthwhile to export a large computation than a small one.

Much more experience will need to be gained before we can make any confident assertions about achieving locality in a parallel machine.

24.8 Parallel Reduction Machine Projects

A number of research teams are in the process of building parallel graph reduction machines. The details of their architecture are beyond the scope of this book, but we mention some current projects here to serve as a starting-point for further reading.

The Rediflow project at the University of Utah is a substantial research program aimed at unifying the ideas of reduction and dataflow in a single parallel architecture (hence the name) [Keller, 1985]. Rediflow is the successor to the AMPS (Applicative Multiprocessor System) project [Keller *et al.*, 1979]. The reduction model is considerably more general (and complex) than that described in this chapter. The architecture consists of a collection of processor/memory/switch units, called Xputers, where the switching portion of the Xputers collectively forms a multistage communications network, over which the processors communicate using message-passing. Each Xputer is directly connected to a fixed number of neighboring Xputers, regardless of the total number of Xputers in the network, so the machine is readily extensible. The graph is distributed over the memories of the Xputers, so locality and granularity are major issues.

ALICE (Applicative Language Idealized Computing Engine) is a parallel reduction machine based at Imperial College, London [Darlington and Reeve, 1981]. The reduction model is a slight variant of supercombinator reduction, but the architecture permits generalizations of the model to be explored. It is constructed using Inmos Transputers which access grobally addressable memory using a multistage network switch [Cripps and Field, 1983]. Locality is not a major issue, since the graph is held in globally addressable memory. ALICE became operational in February 1986.

As part of the DAPS project (Distributed Applicative Parallel Systems), a group at Yale University is implementing a parallel graph reduction engine called Alfalfa [Hudak, 1985]. The parallel reduction model is based on *serial combinators* [Hudak and Goldberg, 1985b], a variant of fully lazy supercombinators. The hardware base is a 128-node Intel Hypercube [Intel, 1985], a distributed multiprocessor without shared memory, in which processors communicate using messages. From an abstract point of view, this is not unlike the Rediflow architecture, but the research is more closely focused on purely functional languages. As with Rediflow, the absence of shared memory means that locality and granularity are major issues.

GRIP (Graph Reduction In Parallel) is a parallel supercombinator graph reduction machine under construction at University College London [Peyton Jones *et al.*, 1985; Clack and Peyton Jones, 1986], funded by the UK Alvey Directorate. In contrast with the other projects described, GRIP is based on a bus architecture, which places an inherent limit on the achievable parallelism [Peyton Jones, 1986]. The intention is to deliver significantly better performance for a given cost than more ambitious designs.

24.9 Summary

We have seen that functional languages are a good medium in which to write parallel programs, and that graph reduction provides a secure basis for exploiting the concurrency of a multiprocessor to execute them.

Parallel implementations of functional languages are now beginning to appear, and the next few years should see the testing in practice of some of the assertions made in this chapter. It is an exciting field.

References

Clack, C.D., and Peyton Jones, S.L. 1985. *Generating Parallelism from Strictness Analysis*. Internal Note 1679, Dept Comp. Sci., University College London. February.

Clack, C.D., and Peyton Jones, S.L. 1986. The four-stroke reduction engine. In *ACM Conference on Lisp and Functional Programming, Boston*. pp. 220–32, August.

Cripps, M.D., and Field, A.J. 1983. *An Asynchronous Structure-independent*

Switching System with System-level Fault Tolerance. Dept Comp. Sci., Imperial College, London.

Darlington, J., and Reeve, M. 1981. ALICE – a multiprocessor reduction machine for the parallel evaluation of applicative languages. In *Proceedings of the ACM Symposium on Functional Languages and Computer Architecture, Portsmouth*. pp. 65–76, October.

Denning, P.J. 1972. On modeling program behavior. In *Proceedings of the Spring Joint Computer Conference, 40*, pp. 937–44. AFIPS Press.

Goldberg, B., and Hudak, P. 1985. Serial combinators – optimal grains of parallelism. In *Functional Programming Languages and Computer Architecture*. pp. 382–99. LNCS 201. Springer Verlag.

Hankin, C.L., Burn, G.L., and Peyton Jones, S.L. 1986. An approach to safe parallel combinator reduction. *European Symposium on Programming*. Robinet, B., and Wilhelm, R. (editors), pp. 99–110. LNCS 213. Springer Verlag. March.

Hudak, P. 1984. *Distributed Applicative Processing Systems*. YALEU/DCS/TR-317. Dept Comp. Sci., Yale. May.

Hudak, P. 1985. *Functional Programming on Multiprocessor Architectures – Research in Progress*, Dept Comp. Sci., Yale University. November.

Hudak, P., and Goldberg, B. 1985a. Distributed execution of functional programs using serial combinators. *IEEE Transactions on Computers*. Vol. C-34, no. 10.

Hudak, P., and Goldberg, B. 1985b. Serial combinators. In *Conference on Functional Programming and Computer Architecture, Nancy*. Jouannaud (editor). LNCS 201. Springer Verlag.

Hudak, P., and Smith, L. 1985. *Para-functional Programming – a Paradigm for Programming Multiprocessor Systems*. YALEU/DCS/RR-390. Dept Comp. Sci., Yale University. June.

Intel 1985. *iPSC User's Guide*. Intel Corporation, Order Number 175455-003. October.

Keller, R.M. 1985. *Rediflow Architecture Prospectus*. UUCS-85-105. Dept Comp. Sci., University of Utah. August.

Keller, R.M., and Lin, F.C.H. 1984. Simulated performance of a reduction based multiprocessor. *IEEE Computer*. Vol. 17, no. 7, pp. 70–82.

Keller, R.M., Lindstrom, G., and Patil, S. 1979. A loosely-coupled applicative multiprocessing system. In *AFIPS Conference Proceedings*, pp. 613–22, June.

Peyton Jones, S.L. 1986. Using Futurebus in a fifth generation computer. *Microprocessors and Microsystems*. Vol. 10, no. 2.

Peyton Jones, S.L., Clack, C.D., and Salkild, J. 1985. *GRIP – a Parallel Graph Reduction Machine*. Dept Comp. Sci., University College London. November.

Smith, A.J. 1982. Cache memories. *ACM Computing Surveys*. Vol. 14, no. 3, pp. 473–530.

Tighe, S. 1985. *A Study of the Parallelism Inherent in Combinator Reduction*. Parallel processing program, MCC, Austin, Texas. August.

Appendix

AN INTRODUCTION TO MIRANDA

David Turner

Miranda is a strongly typed functional language based on higher-order recursion equations. The basic ideas of Miranda are taken from the earlier languages SASL [Turner, 1976; Richards, 1984] and KRC [Turner, 1982], with the addition of a type discipline essentially the same as that of ML [Gordon *et al.*, 1979]. The Miranda system is a product of Research Software Limited, and is implemented on a variety of computers, running under the Unix operating system.† A full description of the language and its programming environment is in preparation. We give here a very brief introduction to the language, concentrating on those features which are needed to follow the use of Miranda notation in this book. We omit discussion of a number of features of the language which are not relevant to the material covered in the book.

Basic Ideas

The Miranda programming language is purely functional – there are no side-effects or imperative features of any kind. A program (actually we don't call it a program, we call it a 'script') is a collection of equations defining various functions and data structures which we are interested in computing. Here is a very simple example of a Miranda script:

```
z = sq x / sq y
sq n = n * n
x = a + b
y = a - b
a = 10
b = 5
```

The Miranda system is interactive, and its basic action is to evaluate expressions in the environment of the current script. So typing z to the system after the above script had been entered would produce the response 9.

Notice that Miranda scripts have very little by way of excess syntactic baggage –

† Unix is a trademark of AT&T Bell Laboratories; Miranda is a trademark of Research Software Ltd.

Miranda is, by design, rather terse. There are no mandatory type declarations, although (see later) the language is strongly typed. There are no semicolons at the end of definitions – the parsing algorithm makes intelligent use of layout. Note that the notation for function application is simply juxtaposition, as in sq x. In the definition of the sq function, n is a formal parameter – its scope is limited to the equation in which it occurs (whereas the other names introduced above have the whole script for their scope).

Certain basic data types are built into the language; these are numbers, characters and truth values. There are two kinds of built-in data structure, called lists and tuples.

The most commonly used data structure is the list, which in Miranda is written with square brackets and commas, e.g.:

```
week_days = ["Mon","Tue","Wed","Thur","Fri"]
days = week_days ++ ["Sat","Sun"]
```

In fact a string is just a list of characters, so writing e.g. "Mon" is equivalent to writing the list ['M','o','n']. Lists may be appended by the ++ operator.

Other useful operations on lists include infix : which prefixes an element to the front of a list, # which takes the length of a list, and infix ! which does subscripting. So, for example, 0:[1,2,3] has the value [0,1,2,3], #days is 7, and days!0 is "Mon".

There is also an operator -- which does list subtraction. For example [1,2,3,4,5] -- [2,4] is [1,3,5].

There is a shorthand notation using .. for lists whose elements form an arithmetic series. Here, for example, are definitions of the factorial function, and of a number result which is the sum of the squares of the odd numbers between 1 and 100 (sum and product are library functions, which add together and multiply, respectively, the elements of a list):

```
fac n = product [1..n]
result = sum [1,3..100]
```

The elements of a list must all be of the same type. A sequence of elements of mixed type is called a tuple, and is written using parentheses instead of square brackets. For example:

```
employee = ("Jones",True,False, 39)
```

Tuples are analogous to records in Pascal (whereas lists are analogous to arrays). Tuples cannot be subscripted – their elements are extracted by pattern-matching (see below).

Guarded Equations and Block Structure

An equation can have several alternative right-hand sides distinguished by 'guards' (a guard is a boolean expression written following a comma). So, for example, the greatest common divisor function can be written:

```
gcd a b = gcd (a-b) b, a>b
        = gcd a (b-a), a<b
        = a, a=b
```

The semantics specifies that the guards are tested in order, from top to bottom, but it is probably bad style to write code which takes advantage of this. It is best to have a set of guards which are mutually exclusive, as above, so that the order in which the cases are written is not relevant. The keyword otherwise may be used as the last guard, indicating that this is the case which applies if all the other tests fail. Thus,

```
f  args = rhs1, test1
        = rhs2, test2
        ...
        = rhsN, otherwise
```

(N.B. Earlier versions of the Miranda compiler permitted the guard to be left off in the last case – the programs in the main part of this book are written in this older form.)

It is also permitted to introduce local definitions on the right-hand side of a definition, by means of a where clause. Consider for example the following definition of a function for solving quadratic equations (it either fails or returns a list of one or two real roots):

```
quadsolve a b c = error "complex roots", delta<0
                = [-b/(2*a)], delta=0
                = [-b/(2*a) + radix/(2*a),-b/(2*a) - radix/(2*a)], delta>0
                  where
                  delta = b*b - 4*a*c
                  radix = sqrt delta
```

Note that the scope of the where clause, if present, is all the right-hand sides associated with a given left-hand side. Where clauses may occur nested, to arbitrary depth, allowing Miranda programs to be organized with a nested block structure. Indentation of inner blocks is compulsory, as layout information is required by the compiler to determine the correct parse. This is done using Landin's 'offside rule' [Landin, 1966].

Pattern-matching

It is permitted to define a function by giving several alternative equations, distinguished by the use of different patterns in the formal parameters. This provides another method of case analysis which is often more elegant than the use of guards. Here are some simple examples of pattern-matching on lists:

```
sum [] = 0
sum (a:x) = a + sum x

reverse [] = []
reverse (a:x) = reverse x ++ [a]
```

The range of possibilities permitted by Miranda in pattern-matching is quite rich – for example, patterns can be nested, and repeated identifiers can be used to imply equality of subcomponents. Pattern matching can also be combined with the use of guards. As an example which shows this, here is a definition of a function for removing adjacent duplicate elements from a list

```
no_dups x = x, #x<2
no_dups (a:a:x) = no_dups (a:x)
no_dups (a:b:x) = a : no_dups (b:x), a ~= b
```

Notice the way in which guards are here used to fully separate the cases, so that the meaning of the script is not sensitive to the order in which the equations are written. In fact the semantics of the language specifies that cases are tested in the order written, but as a general rule it is better to avoid writing code which depends on this (although this is not always possible without clumsiness).

Accessing the elements of a tuple is also done by pattern-matching. For example, the selection functions on 2-tuples can be defined thus

```
fst (a,b) = a
snd (a,b) = b
```

Currying and Higher-order Functions

Miranda is a higher-order language – functions are first class citizens and can be both passed as parameters and returned as results. Function application is left-associative, so when we write f x y it is parsed as (f x) y, meaning that the result of applying f to x is a function, which is then applied to y. So for example if we define the function plus by:

```
plus x y = x + y
```

then plus 3 is a function in its own right – it is the function that adds 3 to its argument. This device, whereby any function of two or more arguments is treated as a higher-order function, is known as 'currying' (after the logician H.B. Curry).

The use of higher-order functions is an important feature of the programming style made possible by functional languages, and often lends itself to very concise forms of expression. As a simple example of higher-order programming consider the function foldr, defined by:

```
foldr op k [] = k
foldr op k (a:x) = op a (foldr op k x)
```

All the standard list processing functions can be obtained by partially parameterizing foldr. Examples:

```
sum = foldr (+) 0
product = foldr (*) 1
reverse = foldr postfix []
          where postfix a x = x ++ [a]
```

Note that in Miranda an operator can be passed as a parameter, by enclosing it in parentheses.

Lazy Evaluation

Miranda's evaluation mechanism is 'lazy', in the sense that no subexpression is evaluated until its value is known to be required. One consequence of this is that it is possible to define functions which are non-strict (meaning that they are capable of returning an answer even if one of their arguments is undefined). For example, we can define a conditional function as follows:

```
if True x y = x
if False x y = y
```

and then use it in such situations as if (x=0) 0 (1/x).

The other main consequence of lazy evaluation is that it makes it possible to write down definitions of infinite data structures. Here are some examples of Miranda definitions of infinite lists (note that there is a modified form of the .. notation for endless arithmetic progressions)

```
ones = 1 : ones
 nats = [0..]
odds = [1,3..]
  fibs = f 0 1
         where f a b =  a : f b (a+b)
```

The last example is the list of all Fibonacci numbers – 0,1,1,2,3,5,8,13 . . . (each number from the third onwards is the sum of its two predecessors).

The presence of infinite data structures in a programming language is far from being a mere curiosity – as with higher-order functions it has a strong effect on programming style and gives the functional programmer access to a range of programming possibilities not available to his imperative counterpart.

Infinite lists also provide the means for handling problems of interactive input/output and communicating processes within a functional framework.

ZF Expressions

ZF expressions (also called list comprehensions) give a concise syntax for a rather general class of iterations over lists. The notation is adapted from Zermelo Frankel set theory (whence the name ZF). A simple example of a ZF expression is:

```
[ n*n | n <- [1..100] ]
```

This is a list containing (in order) the squares of all the numbers from 1 to 100. The above expression would be read aloud as 'list of all n*n such that n drawn from [1..100]'. Note that n is a local variable of the above expression. The variable-binding construct to the right of the bar is called a 'generator' – the '<–' sign denotes that the variable introduced on its left ranges over all the elements of the list on its right. The general form of a ZF expression in Miranda is:

```
[ body | qualifiers ]
```

where each qualifier is either a generator, of the form var<–exp, or else a filter, which is a boolean expression used to restrict the ranges of the variables introduced by the generators. When two or more qualifiers are present they are separated by semicolons. An example of a ZF expression with two generators is given by the following definition of a function for returning a list of all the permutations of a given list:

```
perms [] = [[]]
perms x = [ a:y  | a <- x; y <- perms (x--[a]) ]
```

The use of a filter is shown by the following definition of a function which takes a number and returns a list of all its factors,

```
factors n = [ i | i <- [1..n div 2]; n mod i = 0 ]
```

ZF notation often allows remarkable conciseness of expression. We give two examples. Here is a Miranda statement of Hoare's 'Quicksort' algorithm, as a method of sorting a list:

```
sort [] = []
sort (a:x) = sort [ b | b <- x; b<=a ] ++ [a] ++ sort [  b | b <- x; b>a ]
```

Here is a Miranda solution to the eight queens problem. We have to place eight queens on chess boards so that no queen gives check to any other. Since any solution must have exactly one queen in each column, a suitable representation for a board is a list of integers giving the row number of the queen in each successive column. In the following script the function queens n returns all safe ways to place queens on the first n columns. A list of all solutions to the eight queens problem is therefore obtained by printing the value of (queens 8). This example is taken from Turner [1982].

```
queens 0 = [c] ]
queens n = [ q:b | q <- [0..7];b <- queens(n-1); safe q b ], n>0
safe q b = and [ ~checks q b i | i <- [0..#b-1] ]
checks q b i = q=b!i \/ abs(q - b!i)=i+1
```

It is interesting to note that this is a problem whose solution would have involved backtracking if it had been programmed in an imperative language. Lazy evaluation enables us to avoid backtracking, by programming explicitly in terms of a list of all solutions, without necessarily incurring the penalty of actually constructing all the solutions. In fact if we only want the first solution we can print hd (queens 8) and the remainder of the solution list will not be instantiated. (Note: in the definition of checks, the infix operator \/ means logical 'or'.)

Polymorphic Strong Typing

Miranda is strongly typed. That is, every expression and every subexpression has a type, which can be deduced at compile-time, and any inconsistency in the type structure of a script results in a compile-time error message. We here briefly summarize Miranda's notation for its types.

The three primitive types are called num, bool and char. The type num comprises integer and floating point numbers (the distinction between integers and floating point numbers is handled at run-time – this is not regarded as being a type distinction).

If T is type, then [T] is the type of lists whose elements are of type T. For example, [[1,2],[2,3],[4,5]] is of type [[num]], that is it is a list of lists of numbers.

If T1 to Tn are types, then (T1,. . .,Tn) is the type of tuples with objects of these types as components. For example, (True,"hello",36) is of type (bool,[char],num).

If T1 and T2 are types, then T1->T2 is the type of a function with arguments in T1 and results in T2. For example the function sum is of type [num]->num. The function quadsolve, given earlier, is of type num->num->num->[num]. Note that -> is right-associative.

Miranda scripts can include type declarations. These are written using :: to mean 'is of type'. For example:

```
sq :: num -> num
sq n = n * n
```

The type declaration is not necessary, however. The compiler is able to deduce the type of sq from its defining equation. Miranda scripts often contain type declarations even though they are not really necessary, since these are useful for documentation (and they provide an extra check, since the type-checker will complain if the declared type is inconsistent with the inferred one).

Types can be polymorphic, in the sense of Milner [1978]. This is indicated by using the symbols * ** *** etc. as an alphabet of generic type variables. For example, the identity function, defined in the Miranda library as

```
id x = x
```

has the following type

```
id :: * -> *
```

This means that the identity function has many types, namely all those which can be obtained by substituting an arbitrary type for the generic type variable, e.g. num->num, bool->bool, (*->**) -> (*->**) and so on.

We illustrate the Miranda type system by giving types for some of the functions so far defined in this appendix

```
fac :: num -> num
sum :: [num] -> num
reverse :: [*] -> [*]
fst :: (*,**) -> *
snd :: (*,**) -> **
foldr :: (*->**->**) -> ** -> [*] -> **
perms :: [*] -> [[*]]
queens :: num -> [[num]]
```

User-defined Types

The user may introduce new types. This is done by an equation using ::=. For example a type of labelled binary trees (with numeric labels) would be introduced as follows,

```
tree ::= Nilt | Node num tree tree
```

This introduces three new identifiers – tree which is the name of the type, and Nilt and Node which are the constructors for trees. Nilt is an atomic constructor, while Node takes three arguments, of the types shown. Here is an example of a tree built using these constructors:

```
t1 = Node 7 (Node 3 Nilt Nilt) (Node 4 Nilt Nilt)
```

Notice that constructors always begin with an upper-case letter (and any identifier beginning with an upper-case letter is assumed by the compiler to be a constructor).

To analyze an object of user-defined type, we use pattern-matching. For example here is a definition of a function for taking the mirror image of a tree:

```
mirror Nilt = Nilt
mirror (Node a x y) = Node a (mirror y) (mirror x)
```

User-defined types can be polymorphic – this is shown by introducing one or more generic type variables as parameters of the ::= equation. For example, we can generalize the definition of tree to allow arbitrary labels, thus:

```
tree * ::= Nilt | Node * (tree *) (tree *)
```

this introduces a family of tree types, including tree num, tree bool, tree(char->char) etc.

The types introduced by ::= definitions are called 'algebraic types'. Algebraic types are a very general idea. They include scalar enumeration types, e.g.

```
color ::= Red | Orange | Yellow | Green | Blue | Indigo | Violet
```

and also give us a way to do union types, for example:

```
bool_or_num ::= Left bool | Right num
```

It is interesting to note that all the basic data types of Miranda could be defined from first principles, using ::= equations. For example here are type definitions for bool, (natural) numbers and lists,

```
bool ::= True | False
nat ::= Zero | Suc nat
list * ::= Nil | Cons * (list *)
```

Having types such as num built in is done for reasons of convenience and efficiency – it isn't logically necessary.

It is also possible to associate 'laws' with the constructors of an algebraic type, which are applied whenever an object of the type is built. For example we can associate laws with the Node constructor of the tree type above, so that trees are always balanced. We omit discussion of this feature of Miranda here – interested readers will find more details in the references [Thompson, 1986; Turner, 1985].

In addition to algebraic types as sketched above, there are two other ways in which the Miranda programmer can introduce new types (these are not discussed in the main part of this book, but we mention them for completeness). These are:

(i) Type synonyms

The Miranda programmer can introduce a new name for an already existing type. We use == for these definitions, to distinguish them from ordinary value definitions. For example:

```
string == [char]
matrix == [[num]]
```

Type synonyms are entirely transparent to the type-checker – it is best to think of them as macros. It is also possible to introduce synonyms for families of types. This is done by using generic type symbols as formal parameters, as in

```
array * == [[*]]
```

so now, e.g., array num is the same type as matrix.

(ii) Abstract data types
In addition to concrete types, introduced by ::= or == equations, Miranda permits the definition of abstract types, whose implementation details are 'hidden' from the rest of the program. Abstract data types (and the related idea of free types) become important in constructing larger pieces of software, which may evolve over time. The way in which abstract data types are declared in Miranda is one of the innovatory features of the language – for a partial discussion of this see Turner [1985].

(Note: further information about the Miranda system and its availability for various computers may be obtained from Research Software Limited, 23 St Augustines Road, Canterbury, Kent CT1 1XP, UK, or from the following electronic mail address: mira-request @uk.ac.ukc.)

References

Gordon, M.J., Milner, A.J., and Wadsworth, C.P. 1979. Edinburgh LCF. *Springer Lecture Notes in Computer Science*. Vol. 78.

Landin, P.J. 1966. The next 700 programming languages. *Communications of the ACM*. Vol. 9, no. 3.

Milner, A.J. 1978. A theory of type polymorphism in programming. *Journal of Computer and System Sciences*. Vol. 17.

Richards, H. 1984. An overview of ARC SASL. *SIGPLAN Notices*. October.

Thompson, S.J. 1986. Laws in Miranda. *Proceedings of the 4th ACM International Conference on LISP and Functional Programming, Boston, Mass.* August.

Turner, D.A. 1976. SASL language manual. *St Andrews University Technical Report*. December.

Turner, D.A. 1982. Recursion equations as a programming language. In *Functional Programming and its Applications*, Darlington *et al.* (editors). Cambridge University Press.

Turner, D.A. 1985. Miranda: a non-strict functional language with polymorphic types. In *Proceedings of the IFIP International Conference on Functional Programming Languages and Computer Architecture, Nancy*. Springer Lecture Notes in Computer Science. LNCS 201.

INDEX

⊥, **31**–33, 69, 71, 73, 105–109, 125, 383–6
[], 40, 51, 57, 61, 76, 94, 96, 125
α-conversion, **18,** 21, 226, 263
β-abstraction, **18**, 226
β-conversion, 15, **18**
β-reduction, **15**, 41, 226
η-conversion, **19**, 20, 269
η-reduction, **19**, 122, 228, 230, 248, 253, 256, 276
  effect on lambda-lifting, 346

A compilation scheme (*see* compilation scheme, A)
abstract data type, 438
abstract domain, 383
abstract interpretation, 259, 380, **382**
abstracting a free variable, 226
abstraction, **382**
acyclic graph (*see* graph, acyclic)
ADD, 323
agent, **414**, 424
algebraic type, 437
Algol68, 146
ALICE, 426, 429
ALLOC, 309, 323
allocation (*see* storage allocation)
alternative, 58, 432
AND, 12
annotation, director string, 275
annotation, strictness (*see* strictness annotation)
append, 432
applicative order, 195
AP-WHNF, 354, 376, 423
argument evaluation (*see* evaluating arguments)
arity, 52, **223**
arity check, 333, 373
array, 189
array processor, 410
association list, 173

B combinator, **268**
B′ combinator, **272**
B compilation scheme (*see* compilation scheme, B)
basic block, 329
basic value, **357**
block move, 231
block-structured language, 221
blocking a task, **414**, 421
body
  of definition, 41
  of function, 12
bottom, **31**, 99
bound, by let(rec)-expression, 41
bound variable (*see* variable, bound)
boxed representation, **190**, 320, 326, 332, 335, 356
brackets, 11, 40
built-in function, 11, 31, 17, 46, 200, 212, 313
built-in type, 53

C combinator, **269**
C′ combinator, **272**
C compilation scheme (*see* compilation scheme, C)
CLetrec compilation scheme (*see* compilation scheme, CLetrec)
cache, 427
CAF (*see* constant applicative form)
CALL, 377
call-by-need, **193**
call-by-value, **193**
case analysis, 52
case-expression, 3, 40, 50, 51, 75, 79, 81, 121
CASEJUMP, 317, 341, 363
CASE-n, 300, 317, 341, 344, 362
CASE-T, **123**, 125
cdr-coding, 284
cell, **187**, 320, 325
  fixed-size, **187**, 188, 192
  variable-size, **187**, 189, 192, 215
cell lifetime, 287
character, 432

character constant, 12
Church-Rosser Theorem I, **24**
Church-Rosser Theorem II, **25**
closure, 378
clothed value, **357**
coalesced graph, 120
code generation, 294, 327
combinator, **224**
common sub-expression, 241, 405
communication, between tasks, 412, 426
compaction, 281
compilation, 221
compilation scheme
  A, 264
  B, **357**, 358
  C, 264, 305, **306**, 339
  CLetrec, 309
  E, 342, 365, 377
  ES, 343, 365, 377
  F, **302**, 304
  R, **304**, 339, 364
  RS, 343, 364, 376
  Xr, 309
compile-time reduction, 240
complexity, 5
conditional equations, 58, **63**
conformality check, 110, 115
conformality transformation, 117
CONS, 12, 17, 53, 298, 300, 316, 323, 340
constant applicative form, **224**, 227, 248, 253, 311, 312, 321, 361
constant sub-expression, 243
constrained variable (*see* type variable, constrained)
constructor rule, **84**
constructors, 12, **52**, 187, 195
  lazy, 52, 197
context, 303
conversion rules, **14**, 21, 23, 34
convertibility, 19, 34
coordinate, 140
copying garbage collection, 282
copying root of result, 214, 217, 334
correctness, 2, 138, 293, 396
Cray-1, 410
current context, 303, 367
currying, **10**, 16, 185, 30, 434
cycle (*see* graph, cyclic)
cyclic graph (*see* graph, cyclic)
cyclic structure (*see* graph, cyclic)
cyclic Y, 219

DAP, 410
DAPS, 429
dataflow analysis, 119
de Bruijn number, 230
debugging, 190, 408
definition (*see* let(rec)-expression)
delayed substitution, 378
delta conversion, **22**
delta rules, **22**
denotation, 29
denotational semantics, 28, 37, 386
  of lambda calculus (*see* lambda calculus)
dependency analysis, 118, **119**, 150, 254, 390
dependency graph, 120
Deutsch-Schorr-Waite algorithm, 203, 283
diagonalization, 129
diffusion scheduling, **428**
directed edge, 186
director, **275**
director string, **274**
discriminated union, **55**
DISPATCH, 371, 376
distributed memory, 427
divide and conquer, 411
domain, 30
domain theory, 28, 31, 162
dragging, **401**
dump, 203, 315, 320, 359
dump
  G-machine, 320
  G-machine representation, 326

ES compilation scheme (*see* compilation scheme, E)
eager evaluation, **194**, 355
efficiency, 73, 80, 113, 115, 119, 133, 221, 396
embarrassing pause, 282
empty rule, **87**
enriched lambda calculus (*see* lambda calculus, enriched)
entry table, 288
enumeration type (*see* type, enumeration)
environment, 29, 31, 221, 378
equality, 34
equation, 26
equations
  conditional, 97
  overlapping, 99
  sequential, 101
  solving, 166
  strongly left-sequential, 101
ERROR, **61**
Eval, 29, 382
EVAL, 314, 321, 323, 329, 331, 343, 352, 370, 377
EVAL, avoiding, 361
evaluating arguments, 200, 203, 349
evaluator, **193**, 200, 202, 212, 413
EXEC entry, 369, 373, 376
extension, of substitution, 168
extensional equality, 35, 262, 269

F compilation scheme (*see* compilation scheme, F)
FAIL, **61**, 69, 94, 96, 125, 347

failure
  of pattern-matching, 61
  of type-checker, 165
FALSE, 12
FAM (*see* Functional Abstract Machine)
FATBAR, **125**, 300, 347
field, **52**, **187**, 325
filter, **128**, 435
fixed point, **26**, 28, 388
  of substitution, 167
fixed-size cells (*see* cell, fixed size)
fixpoint (*see* fixed point)
floating let(rec)s outwards (*see* let(rec)s, floating)
formal methods, 136
formal parameter, 12
FP/M, 296
frame pointer, 298
free occurrence, 17
freer, **230**
free variable (*see* variable, free)
free variable set, 250
from-space, 282
full laziness, 5, 210, 220, 245, 267, 401
  delicacy of, 398
  effect of recursion, 399
  redundant, 256
Functional Abstract Machine, 378
functional programming, parallel, 410

G-code, 294, **319**
G-machine, 5, 231, **293**
  parallel, 424
garbage, 367
garbage collection, 5, 281, 312, 326, 328, 330, 335, 358, 401
garbage collector, 192, 209, 213, 217
generator, **128**, 435
generic operation, 330
generic variable (*see* type variable, generic)
GET, 357
global, 314
GLOBSTART, 304
grain of execution (*see* granularity)
granularity, 279, 419, 428
graph, **186**, 233, 320
  acyclic, 120, **187**
  concrete representation of, 187
  cyclic, 218, 233, 282, 285, 308
  G-machine, 320
  G-machine representation, 325, 330
graph reduction, 208
  lazy, 1, 112
  parallel, 5, 413
  supercombinator, 221
graphical body, 234, 236
GRIP, 429
ground type, 140
guard, 58, 63, 432

HEAD, 12, 17, 300, 316, 323, 344
head normal form, 199
heap, 192, 325, 338
  persistent, 282
higher-order function, 390
HNF (*see* head normal form)
hole, **308**, 351, 374
Hope, 2, 56, 80, 194

I combinator, **260**
I-transformation, **262**
IF, 12, 105, 300, 317, 344
indirection cell, 214
indirection node, 213, 217, 287, 334
infinite data structure, **194**, 434
infinite list, 195
infinite types, 155
innermost spine reduction, 199
input, 196, 197, 435
instance, 15, 157
  of lambda body, 207, 220
instantiate function, 210, 220, 231
instantiation, 210
  lazy, 265
intermediate code, 294
intermediate language, 2
irrefutable pattern (*see* pattern, irrefutable)
Iswim, 56

J combinator, **277**
J′ combinator, **277**
JFAIL, 347
JFALSE, 317, 323, 341
JFUN, 369
JUMP, 317, 323, 329

K combinator, **260**
K optimization, 267
K-n-i, 350
K-transformation, **262**
KRC, 2, 127, 194

lambda abstraction, **12**, 13, 43
  native, 252
  pattern-matching, 40, 50, 57, **60**, **76**, 104
lambda calculus, 3, **9**, 150
  denotational semantics, 28
  enriched, 3, **39**, 50, 104, 133
  operational semantics, 14, 28
  ordinary, **39**, 50, 104, 111
  syntax, **9**
lambda expression, **13**
  representation of, 185
lambda-lifting, 150, 220, 221, 228, 379, 387
  context-dependent, 258
  effect of η-reduction, 346
  fully lazy, **248**

laws, 437
laziness, **33**, 215, 347, 355, 379
lazy constructors (*see* constructors, lazy)
lazy evaluation, 131, **194**, 243, 398, 406, 434
lazy graph reduction, 212
lazy product-matching, **71**, 72, 113, 115, 116
least upper bound, 388
left-to-right rule, 63, 65, 101
let (*see* let-expression)
let-expression, **40**, 42
  compilation of, 307, 345
  irrefutable, 112
  pattern-matching, **67**
  redundant, 241
  simple, 40, 112
  top-level, 155
let(rec)-expression, 109, 234
  definitions of, **41**, 42
  floating outwards, **249**, 250, 254
  general, **111**
  irrefutable, **111**
  simple, 43, **111**
letrec (*see* letrec-expression)
letrec-expression, 40, **42**
  compilation of, 308, 345
  general, 115
  irrefutable, 113, 114
  pattern-matching, **67**
  simple, 42
  top-level, 157
level number (*see* lexical level-number)
lexical level-number, **230**, 235, 252, 255
lifetime, of cell, 287
linearization, 284
Lisp, 370
list, 53, 108, 141, 432
list comprehension, 127, 435
  pattern-matching, 136
listless transformer, 288, 391
LML, 2, 80, 194, 294
load balancing, **428**
locality, 284, 415, 426
loop unrolling, 401

mark-scan garbage collection, 282
match, 57
match, 81
maximal free expression, **245**, 246, 247
  size of, 254
maximally general unifier, 168
memo function, 217
MFE (*see* maximal free expression)
MIMD machine, 410
Miranda, 2, **37**, 56, 102, 127, 194, 197, 265, 431
mixture rule, **88**
MKAP, 298, 307, 323, 360
MKINT, 357
ML, 2, 56, 139, 148, 194
monomorphic, 145
mutual exclusion, 422
mutual recursion, 157, 232, 390

named value, **357**
name-capture, **21**, 173, 199, 256
native lambda abstraction, 252
NEG, 300, 314, 323
nested pattern (*see* pattern, nested)
NIL, 12, 53
node, **186**, 320
non-flat domain, 391
non-generic type variable, 172
non-strict, 33, 434
non-strict semantics, 2
NORMA, 191, 205, 265
normal form, 23, 197
normal order, 25, 195
NOT, 12
NPL, 56, 127
number, 432

occupancy, of heap, 284
occurs bound, **14**
occurs free, **14**
offside rule, 433
operational semantics, **14**
OR, 12
ordinary lambda calculus (*see* lambda calculus, ordinary)
Orwell, 2, 56, 127, 194
otherwise, 58, 432
output, 196, 322, 435
overloading, 147
overwriting root of redex (*see* updating root of redex)

PACKPRODUCT, 316
PACK-PRODUCT-r, **108**, 300, 316
PACKSUM, 316
PACK-SUM-d-r, **107**, 300, 316
PAIR, 54
par, 407
parallel evaluation, 406
parallel functional programming, 410
parallel graph reduction, 413
parallel reduction machine, 206, 209, 282, 284, 394
parallelism, 409
  algorithmic, 411
  conservative, **415**
  dynamic, 412
  speculative, **417**
parameter order, 229, 253, 398
parentheses, 11
partial application, 258, 349
partial function, 143
partial object, 161

Pascal, 146
pattern matching, 3, 50, **51**, 52, 57, 15, 150, 433
pattern-matching, compilation, **78**, 137, 362
pattern-matching compiler, 50, 78
pattern-matching lambda abstraction (*see* lambda abstraction, pattern-matching)
patterns, 43, 57, **59**, 129
  constant, **69**, 105
  irrefutable, **110**
  multiple, 80
  nested, 58, **60**, 70, 80, 110
  on left-hand side of definition, 67
  overlapping, 57
  product, 59, 69, 105
  product-constructor, **59**
  refutable, **110**, 129
  simple, **60**
  sum, **59**, 69, 106
  sum-constructor, **59**
  variable, 83
peephole optimization, 340, 360, 377, 378
persistent heap, 282
plateau, **389**
pointer, tagged, 191
pointer-bit, 191, 357
pointer-reversal, 203, 283
  in parallel machine, 424
polymorphic typing (*see* type-checking, polymorphic)
polymorphism, 139, 143
  ad hoc, 147
  parametric, 147
Ponder, 2, 194, 295, 353
POP, 298, 305, 323
prefix form, 9, 40
PRINT, 322
printing mechanism, 196, 322
priority of task, **418**
product type (*see* type, product)
product
  lifted, **73**
  ordinary, **73**
program, **44**
program transformation, 56, 221, 400
projection function, 216
proper subexpression, **246**
PUSH, 298, 306, 323
PUSHBASIC, 357
PUSHGLOBAL, 298, 306, 323
PUSHINT, 306, 320, 323

qualifier, 128, **128**, 435

R compilation scheme (*see* compilation scheme, R)
rearranging top of stack (*see* stack, rearranging top of)
RS compilation scheme (*see* compilation scheme, RS)
reawakening a task, 425
recursion, 42, 43, 66, 150, 162, 238, 263, 387
  effect on full laziness, 399
  effect on residency, 403
recursive functions, 25
redex, **10**
  supercombinator, **223**
  top-level, **198**
reduction, 4
  compile-time, 240
reduction order, 4, 23, 193, 397
  optimal, 25
reduction rule, 129
redundant let-expression, 241
reference count
  one bit, 286
  shared, 285
reference counting, 219, 282, 285
refutable pattern (*see* patterns, refutable)
region, 287
repeated variables, **65**
residency, **403**, 405
RETURN, 315, 323, 340
rewrite rules, 225
rib, 202
rule of signs, **380**, 385
run-time checks, 139
run-time library, 301, 319
run-time type-checking (*see* type-checking, run-time)

S combinator, **260**
S′ combinator, **270**
S-transformation, **261**
safety condition, **382**, 386
SASL, 2, 56, 102, 127, 194, 197, 265, 358
scheduling, **420**
schematic generality, 144
schematic variable (*see* type variable, schematic)
Scheme, 295
script, 431
SECD machine, 221, 324, 378
SELPRODUCT, 317
SEL-r-i, **108**, 300, 317, 344
SELSUM, 317
SEL-SUM-r-i, 125, 300, 317, 362
SEL-SUM-s-i, **124**, 125
SEL-t-i, **71**, 76, 108
semi-decidable, 158
sequential evaluation, 406
serial combinator, 420, 429
serialization, 422
set abstraction, 127
set comprehension, 128
shared memory, 427
sharing, 187, 208, 233
  excessive, 405

shorting out indirections, 287, 334
simulated stack, 328
SK combinators, 5, **260**
SK compilation algorithm, **263**
SKIM, 191, 265, 278, 286, 295
SLIDE, 308, 323, 360
space leak, **400**
sparking a task, **414**
spine, 202
spine stack, 202
SQUEEZE, 369
stack, 194, 205, 302, 319, 325, 338
  G-machine, 319
  G-machine representation, 325
  in parallel machine, 424
  rearranging top of, 296, 302, 322, 334, 355, 368, 374
  simulated, 328
  spine, 202
stack frame, 203, 221, 370
standard interpretation, **382**
state transition, 320
state of task, 424
storage allocation, 192, 338
storage fragmentation, 281
storage management (*see also* garbage collection), 192, 281
stream, **194**, 397
strict, **33**, 200, 383
strict product-matching, 71
strictness analysis, 5, 74, 351, 353, **380**, 403, 404, 416, 419
strictness annotation, 391, 416
string, 432
string reduction, 208
strongly connected component, 120, 285
structural induction, 56
structure tag, **107**, **187**, 189
structured data, 362
structured type (*see* type, structured)
subscripting, of lists, 432
substitution, 17, 41, 130, 166
substitution instance, 144
substitution
  delta, 167
  extending, 169
  fixed point, 167
  idempotent, 167
  identity, 167
  notation, **22**
substitutions, composition of, 166
sum type (*see* type, sum)
sum-of-products, **56**
supercombinator, 5, 150, 220, **223**
  recursive, 238
supercombinator graph reduction (*see* graph reduction, supercombinator)
supercombinator redex, **223**
supercombinators, fixed set of, 260
synch, 407
synchronization of tasks, **414**, 421
syntax tree, 185, 275
system tag, **189**

T, 295
TD translation scheme (*see* translation scheme, TD)
TE translation scheme (*see* translation scheme, TE)
tag, **185**, 187, 325
TAIL, 12, 17, 300, 317
tail call, **368**, 373
  generalized, 367, **371**
tail recursion, 370, 404
target machine, 324
task, **413**
  speculative, **418**, 420
  tiny, 419
  vital, **418**, 420
task control block, 424
task pool, **414**
template, 210
template instantiation, **231**, 256, 363
term rewrite system, 225
tip of spine, 202
to-space, 282
topological sort, 120
TQ translation scheme (*see* translation scheme, TQ)
TR translation scheme (*see* translation scheme, TR)
transformation, **39**, 56
translation, **38**
translation scheme, **45**
  TD, 45, 68, 81, 82
  TE, 44, 68, 81, 132
  TQ, 134
  TR, 64, 66
tree, 185, 186
TRUE, 12
truth value, 432
tuple, **54**, 140, 432
type
  algebraic, 437
  boolean, **55**
  enumeration, **55**, 437
  ground, 140
  of function, 142
  product, **56**, 122
  structured, 51, 141
  sum, **56**, 122
  union, 437
  user-defined, 437
type checker, **176**, 202
type checking, 3, 50, 163, 109, 110, 139
  polymorphic, 28, 436
  run-time, 109
type declaration, 52, 436
type environment, **173**

type expressions, 164
type-forming operator, 53, 54, 142, 164
type inference, 149
type labels, 151
type scheme, **171**
type synonym, 437
type template, 171
type variable, 53
  constrained, 160, 171
  generic, 53, 144, **172**
  non-generic, 172
  schematic, 53, 144, 171
  unknown, **172**
types, infinite, 155
typing, compile-time, 190
typing, run-time, 190, 191

unboxed representation, **190**, 214, 335, 404
unification, 168
unification algorithm, 170
unifier, 168
uniform definitions, 98, **100**
union type, 437
unknowns (*see* type variable)
unmoved variable, 167
UNPACK-PRODUCT-r, **108**
UNPACK-PRODUCT-t, **106**, 122, 125
UNPACK-SUM-d-r, **107**
UNPACK-SUM-s, **106**, 123, 125
unwind, 202
UNWIND, 298, 305, 315, 322, 323, 332, 370, 377
UPDAP, 361
UPDATE, 298, 305, 323
updating root of redex, 203, 208, 209, 214, 217, 298, 339, 414
UPDCONS, 362
user-defined type, 437

variable pattern (*see* pattern, variable)
variable rule, **83**
variable
  bound, **14**, 154, 159
  free, **14**, 171, 222, 226
variable-sized cells (*see* cell, variable-size)
VAX, 324
VAX assembler, 324
vector processor, 410
vertebra, of spine, 202
virtual memory, 283, 284

weak head normal form, **198**, 422
well-typed, 151
where clause, **66**, 118, 433
WHNF (*see* weak head normal form)

Xr compilation scheme (*see* compilation scheme, Xr)

Y combinator, **27**, 42, 43, 114, 126, 150, 155, 218, 232, 263

ZF expression, 3, 50, 127, 435